The Gospel of Mark and the Roman-Jewish War of 66–70 CE

The Gospel of Mark and the Roman-Jewish War of 66–70 CE

Jesus' Story as a Contrast to the Events of the War

Stephen Simon Kimondo

FOREWORDS BY
Jonathan Draper
AND
David Rhoads

☙PICKWICK *Publications* · Eugene, Oregon

THE GOSPEL OF MARK AND THE ROMAN-JEWISH WAR OF 66–70 CE
Jesus' Story as a Contrast to the Events of the War

Copyright © 2018 Stephen Simon Kimondo. All rights reserved. Except for brief quotations in critical publications or reviews, no part of this book may be reproduced in any manner without prior written permission from the publisher. Write: Permissions, Wipf and Stock Publishers, 199 W. 8th Ave., Suite 3, Eugene, OR 97401.

Pickwick Publications
An Imprint of Wipf and Stock Publishers
199 W. 8th Ave., Suite 3
Eugene, OR 97401

www.wipfandstock.com

PAPERBACK ISBN: 978-1-5326-5302-5
HARDCOVER ISBN: 978-1-5326-5303-2
EBOOK ISBN: 978-1-5326-5304-9

Cataloguing-in-Publication data:

Names: Kimondo, Stephen Simon, author. | Draper, Jonathan, foreword. | Rhoads, David, foreword.

Title: The Gospel of Mark and the Roman-Jewish War of 66–70 CE : Jesus' story as a contrast to the events of the war / Stephen Simon Kimondo ; forewords by Jonathan Draper and David Rhoads.

Description: Eugene, OR: Pickwick Publications, 2018. | Includes bibliographical references.

Identifiers: ISBN 978-1-5326-5302-5 (paperback). | ISBN 978-1-5326-5303-2 (hardcover). | ISBN 978-1-5326-5304-9 (ebook).

Subjects: LCSH: Bible. Mark—Criticism, interpretation, etc. | Jews—History—Rebellion, 66–73.

Classification: BS2585.52 K57 2018 (print). | BS2585.52 (ebook).

Manufactured in the U.S.A.   07/16/18

Scripture quotations are taken from the New Revised Standard Version Bible, copyright © 1989 National Council of the Churches of Christ in the United States of America. Used by permission. All rights reserved worldwide.

To my mother, the late Enisala Njaala, for raising me up

To my beloved wife, Mbumi, and our daughters,
Nuru, Bahati, and Neema,
for their enduring love, prayers, and moral support

Contents

Foreword by Jonathan Draper | ix
Foreword by David Rhoads | xi
Acknowledgments | xv
Abbreviations | xvii

1. Introduction | 1
2. The Date and Origin of Mark's Gospel | 38
3. The Use and Bias of Josephus | 71
4. The Onset of Empires | 114
5. Campaigns in Galilee: Vespasian and Jesus | 140
6. Contrast of Values: Wealth, Status, and Power | 187
7. Conclusion | 229

Bibliography | 233

Foreword
by Jonathan Draper

WHILE THE IMPORTANCE OF Josephus's historical writings for New Testament studies as a contemporary source has long been recognized, their value has also been a source of controversy. So, for example, while Theodore J. Weeden has argued that Josephus provides a literary source for Mark's Gospel, scholars such as Richard A. Horsley and David M. Rhoads have seen Josephus as providing historical evidence mostly for the background to particular events and circumstances. Scholars have been reluctant to trust Josephus as a historian because of his role as a 'traitor' to the Jewish forces and his surrender to Rome. The works written after the Fall of Jerusalem are replete with obvious personal apologetics for his conduct and certainly need to be read with caution as to their facticity. Stephen S. Kimondo, in this fresh study of Mark's Gospel, here takes a different approach. His book presents a systematic reading of Mark against the background of Josephus's account of the war and its aftermath, not only with respect to individual pericopes, but to the shape of the narrative itself.

Kimondo places the date of the composition of Mark in Galilee after the destruction of Jerusalem and the temple, and subsequent to the acclamation of Vespasian as the emperor. However, unlike Weeden, he does not view the relationship between Mark and Josephus as one of literary dependence. Rather, he mines Josephus for the social and historical context of Mark as it would have shaped the reception of Mark's narrative in Galilee by those who had lived through the war, who would have known the important events that Josephus describes, however accurately or inaccurately he presents them. In particular, Kimondo views the Gospel as providing an anti-imperial counternarrative based on the career of Vespasian and his conduct of the war, together with incidents factual or perceived, which would have been widely known in Galilee. Read in this light, the acclamation of Jesus as Son of God and messianic king of the kingdom of God specifically in Caesarea Philippi provides a contrast to and rejection of the acclamation of Vespasian as the divine Roman emperor over the world (over land and sea) in Alexandria CE. The final journey of Jesus from Galilee to Jerusalem following his acclamation as the Christ, and his prophecy of that city's destruction provides a deliberate contrast to and subversion of the brutal military strategy of Vespasian in his progress from Galilee to Jerusalem. A detailed inter-textual and intra-textual reading builds up a case for the value of Josephus as a source for understanding the context of Mark's narrative. Historical reconstructions of this kind will always be partial and depend on their persuasive power as a whole. In this book, Kimondo's reading of Josephus and Mark's Gospel side by side has provided a plausible new scenario for Markan studies—a scenario that does not depend on individual pericopes but on a cumulative account.

While Kimondo does not explicitly describe his interpretation as an "Imperial Reading" of Mark, this is in effect what is provided here. It finds Mark's Gospel a consistent critique of the cruelty, rapacity, and corruption of the imperial system, the complicity and duplicity of the local elite in the face of imperial power, and its impact of the poor and marginalized people of Galilee. The perspective is that of the colonized and exploited peoples of an imperial system. Again, while it is nowhere explicitly stated, the experience and perspective of post–imperial Africa provides the unwritten context of Kimondo's reading. His concern for the economic consequences of systems of imperial domination on the poor, to which Mark's Jesus is opposed, is aptly captured in the Tanzanian proverb used in the title of his master's thesis: "to milk a starving cow."

Jonathan Draper
Professor of New Testament,
University of KwaZulu–Natal, South Africa

Foreword
by David Rhoads

THIS IMPORTANT STUDY INTERPRETS the Gospel of Mark squarely in the historical context of the Roman-Jewish War 66–70 CE. Stephen Kimondo shows how audiences in Palestine shortly after the war likely experienced Mark's Gospel, not only as the good news about Jesus, but also through direction, indirection, contrast, and irony, as commentary on their own tragic time and circumstance.

We might say about the Gospel of Mark that we have fallen short in the quest to interpret Mark in context, partly because we have not seen Mark as a document fully rooted in the history of its time. The Gospel of Mark was likely composed and recounted in and around Palestine just after the Roman-Jewish War, which resulted in the tragic defeat and devastating destruction of Israel, Jerusalem, and the Temple. While a few studies have dealt with various aspects of Mark's historical context in relation to the war, this is the first comprehensive analysis to situate Mark's audience solidly in the immediate aftermath of the war.

Imagine briefly a hypothetical biographer of Gandhi (1889–1948), writing just after the Indian-Pakistani War of 1965, not having the account of Gandhi profoundly colored by the violent deaths and massive displacement of both Hindus and Muslims as a result of the war, a tragedy that flew in the face of everything Gandhi believed and did and taught. In like manner, it is difficult to imagine the composer of Mark proclaiming the Jesus story in and around Galilee shortly after the Roman-Jewish War without the composing and hearing of the story being profoundly shaped by the war and its devastation, which flew in the face of everything Jesus believed and did and taught. Kimondo lays out what such an approach might look like.

The Roman-Jewish War was crushing: multiple Roman Legions of over 5000 troops each swept down into Israel; cities and villages throughout Galilee and Judea were decimated; the slash-and-burn tactics of the Roman army destroyed the crops that peasants needed for survival; countless Jewish men, women, and children were killed; the walls of the holy city of Jerusalem were torn down; the Temple was reduced to rubble; thousands were crucified both during and after the war; and many more were sold into slavery. Israel was now directly occupied by Roman troops. And the war still continued, likely as Mark wrote, with an entire Roman legion actively fighting to the south and west of Jerusalem to destroy the holdout fortresses of Machaerus, Herodium, and Masada, a military campaign that continued through 74 CE.

Not a family in Israel was untouched by the cruelty and death wreaked upon the Jewish people. The losses of kin, land, villages, cities, pilgrimages to Jerusalem, and the rituals of the Temple were devastating. Given the hunger for news of the war and the oral culture network spreading information from village to village, everyone in Israel would have known the stories of the war, including the leading Jewish and Roman military figures, the battles, the outcome of the war, and the current state of affairs in Israel after the war. How could it be otherwise? It is in the immediate wake of this national tragedy that Mark composes and audiences hear this remarkable story about Jesus.

Stephen Kimondo takes this historical context with utmost seriousness. His work seeks to address this question: How could the communal audiences hearing Mark's good news in village marketplaces and homes and open spaces not have experienced the story of Jesus without relating what they heard to this war, the events leading up to it, and the impact that those events had upon them? For the most part, scholars have treated Mark as a response to the *fact* of the war and the absence of the Temple, often taking a scattershot approach to Markan correlations and sometimes proof-texting the historical writings of Josephus. By contrast, Kimondo offers a thoroughgoing analysis of the way in which Mark's composition would have been heard in relation to the war as a whole—its prelude, causes, events, dynamics, figures, and impacts.

Kimondo is cautious not to project the connections that he sees onto the intention of the author. He is not trying to read the mind of the composer of Mark. Rather, his focus is on reception by the audiences. Even then, he does not assume that the hearers would necessarily have made all the connections and correlations that he suggests. Nevertheless, he rightly imagines what audiences of Mark may well have experienced when hearing this story in association with all of their fresh memories and experiences of the Roman-Jewish War. He gets at the purpose indirectly by focusing on the implied reception.

Also, Kimondo is circumspect regarding his use of Josephus. He does not think that either Mark or his hearers knew Josephus or his account of the war. Nevertheless, like Mark, Josephus wrote his *Jewish War* shortly after the end of the war, likely in the late 70s. He wrote in great detail about the history of Israel in the first century, including the war. Kimondo is aware of the difficulties of taking Josephus at face value. Nevertheless, despite exaggerations, embellishments, and distortions, as well as outright lies, Josephus tells us a great deal. After all, he fought as a Jewish general against the Romans in Galilee and then as Titus' prisoner he witnessed the rest of the war, including the siege of Jerusalem. He could not stray too far from the truth and still have a credible account. So we know a lot from Josephus about events leading up to and encompassing the war. Events that Josephus recounts comprise the primary historical context of the Gospel. It is these events that the hearers of Mark know all too well in very visceral ways. It is these events that form the immediate context for the hearers to experience Mark primarily as a story of Jesus but also as a commentary on their situation and circumstances.

Kimondo understands that Mark's Gospel is a counter-narrative to imperialism. Mark was providing an alternative on three fronts. First was the imperialism of the Roman Empire, which occupied Israel during the time of Jesus and the time of Mark after the war. They are instruments of death and destruction. Second were the Jewish authorities in Israel who, in Mark's portrayal, reflected the imperial values, tactics, and mentality of the Romans they represented. Third were the Jewish revolutionaries and other peasants who supported the revolt. They sought to gain imperial power by force. Mark's narrative counters all three groups, sometimes in direct but mostly in indirect ways. The key to the distinctiveness of Mark's counter narrative is that it does not seek to replace one dominating empire with another. Quite the contrary. His story seeks to persuade hearers to abandon imperialism as such by "not lording over" and by becoming servants and slaves of all.

As Kimondo makes clear, the beginning of the Gospel teaches hearers how to listen to the rest of the story as an alternative reality to the imperial realities they live with. The opening of Mark shows that the relationships and dynamics of the kingdom of God are a thorough contrast to and rejection of the kingdom of Caesar: the good news (an imperial term) of Jesus, Jesus as anointed one, Jesus as the son of God (a title for Caesar), leveling the road, the preparation of an arrival, the ambassador John, the declaration of God, and Jesus' announcement of the arrival of the reign ("empire") of God. The rest of the story of Jesus then displays the realities of the reign of *God* in contrast to the imperialistic reign of Caesar—a restorative realm of sacrifice for others, service to the least, and a slave's use of power. Along the way, there are relevant places, healings, exorcisms (including "Legion"), conflicts, feedings (in military formation!), sayings, prophecies, warnings, and a "royal" entrance (on a donkey rather than a horse)—with allusions, associations, analogues, contrasts, indirections, and parallels to the war that would lead hearers to embrace a new and different option—follow Jesus to announce and bring God's life-giving good news.

Kimondo suggests numerous implied correlations—parallels and contrasts—between (Vespasian as) the emperor and Jesus as the messiah. Then in an illuminating analysis, Kimondo contrasts the three-part pattern of Vespasian's campaign with that of Jesus. First, with an overwhelming force of Roman soldiers, Vespasian swept through Galilee, pillaging and destroying everything in his wake. Then came a pause in the fighting as troops rested at Caesarea (named for an earlier emperor) Philippi before the next phase of the campaign, around the time that Vespasian became emperor. After this, Vespasian's son Titus marched to Jerusalem and led the siege and destruction of city and the temple. In parallel and contrasting fashion, Mark's Jesus begins with a Galilean campaign of life-giving activity, healing and forgiving and welcoming everyone in his wake. This was followed by an out-of-the-way stop at Caesarea Philippi where Jesus was recognized by his disciples as the anointed one. Then came Jesus' determined march to Jerusalem during which he taught the disciples the values of God's rule in contrast to human imperial rule. This journey culminated in the events in Jerusalem where Jesus confronted the authorities and was rejected, tormented, and crucified by them. The most startling contrast is that, despite the adulation and clamor of the crowds, Jesus refused to be the military son of David they were hoping for.

Kimondo shows how Mark challenges imperial values and reverses them: lose life, be least, use power as a slave. It had to be a bitter pill, in light of the countless crucifixions in this tragic war, for audiences to hear an invitation to "take up your cross and follow me" (with a refusal to use force) and to experience so graphically the crucifixion of Jesus. It must have been difficult in the face of the humiliating defeat of Israel to hear that greatness lies in being least. It must have been horrendous in light of their kinsmen sent into slavery to be told to become a slave voluntarily in service to others, service rather than servitude. Yet Mark's story turns slavery and humility into a high calling to love your neighbor as yourself. And he transforms the cross as a sign of defeat into a sign of faith in the ultimate victory of God's non-violent, life-giving realm.

In light of this historical context, we are able to see Mark's Gospel as a virtual echo chamber of the people and events and dynamics of the Roman-Jewish War. While some may disagree with specific associations made by Kimondo, others will be persuaded by the great number of correlations and see this approach as a potential new chapter in the study of Mark's Gospel. I am grateful for the courage and imagination of Stephen Kimondo in more fully exploring and charting this new territory. Read and be challenged.

David Rhoads
Professor of New Testament Emeritus,
Lutheran School of Theology at Chicago

Acknowledgments

THIS BOOK IS A revised version of my doctoral dissertation completed in May 2011 at the Lutheran School of Theology at Chicago, USA. Like any project of this nature, this work is a result of contributions received from many individuals and the labor of many people. I therefore would like to express my sincere and deep gratitude and appreciations to all individuals who contributed to the completion of this work.

I am especially thankful to Prof. David M. Rhoads, who supervised this work when it was being prepared as a dissertation. His vast knowledge and scholarly expertise in both Mark's Gospel and Josephus's works have indeed benefited and enriched this work. I am forever thankful for his guidance, encouragement, constructive criticisms, and useful comments.

Moreover, I extend my heartfelt appreciations to members of my dissertation committee, Prof. Barbara Rossing and Prof. Raymond Pickett, for their invaluable and useful criticism that led to a much improved manuscript. My thanks are also due to Prof. Esther Menn for her refreshing sense of humor expressed in her encouragement and generous moral support during the period of my writing the dissertation.

Furthermore, my deep gratitude and appreciation are also due to my colleagues in the Faculty of Theology at the University of Iringa for their persistent encouragement that I revise my dissertation for publication. Rev. Dr. Elia Mligo deserves special appreciation for his critical reading of the manuscript and useful comments that shaped its final form, and hence the publication of this book.

The strength to accomplish this project largely came from my family's faithful love manifested in prayers and encouragement they gave me. They have given me more than I could ever repay, and to them I am forever grateful.

Since the completion of the dissertation and the preparation of the manuscript for this book, several pertinent works have appeared that I was not able to bring into the discussion. Some of these are:

Bedenbender, Andreas. *Frohe Botschaft am Abgrund: Das Markusevangelium und der Jüdische Krieg*. Arbeiten zur Bibel und ihrer Umwelt 2. Leipzig: Evangelische Verlagsanstalt, 2013.

Dewey, Joanna. *The Oral Ethos of the Early Church*. Biblical Performance Criticism Series 8. Eugene, OR: Cascade Books, 2013.

Gelardini, Gabriella. *Christus Militans: Studien zur politisch-militarischen Semantik im Markusevangelium vor dem Hintergrund des ersten judisch-romischen Krieges*. NovTSup 165. Leiden: Brill, 2016.

Mason, Steve. *A History of the Jewish War, A.D. 66–74*. Cambridge: Cambridge University Press, 2016.

———. *Orientation to the History of Roman Judaea*. Eugene, OR: Cascade Books, 2017.

Rhoads, David M., et al. *Mark as Story: An Introduction to the Narrative of a Gospel*. 3rd ed. Minneapolis: Fortress, 2012.

Wire, Antoinette Clark. *The Case for Mark Composed in Performance*. Biblical Performance Criticism Series 3. Eugene, OR: Cascade Books, 2011.

Abbreviations

Ancient

Aen.	*Aeneid* (Virgil)
Agric.	*Agricola* (Tacitus)
Ann.	*Annals* (Tacitus)
Ant.	*Antiquities* (Josephus)
Apol.	*Apolocyntosis* (Seneca the Younger)
b.	Babylonian Talmud
2 Bar.	2 Baruch (Syriac Apocalypse)
Clem.	*De Clementia* (Seneca the Younger)
Decl.	*Declamationes* (Pseudo-Quintilian)
Embassy	*On the Embassy to Gaul* (Philo)
1 En.	1 Enoch
Ep.	*Moral Epistles* (Seneca)
Flacc.	*Against Flaccus* (Philo)
Geogr.	*Geography* (Strabo)
Georg.	*Georgics* (Virgil)
Git.	*Gittin*
Hist.	*Histories* (Tacitus, Polybius)
J.W.	*Jewish War* (Josephus)
Legat.	*Legatio ad Gaium* (Philo)
Life	*The Life* (Josephus)
LXX	Septuagint
Mek.	*Mekilta*
Mor.	*Moralia* (Plutarch)
Nat. Hist.	*Natural History* (Pliny the Elder)

Pol.	*Politics* (Aristotle)
Pomp.	*Pompey* (Plutarch)
P.Mich.	University of Michigan papyri
P.Oslo	*Papyri Osloënses.* 2–3 vols. Edited by S. Eitrem and L. Amundesen. Oslo, 1931–1936
P.Oxy.	Oxyrhynchus papyri
Pss. Sol.	Psalms of Solomon
P.Teb.	Tebtunis papyri
1QapGen	Genesis Apocryphon
1QSa	*Rule of the Congregation* (1Q28a, Qumran document)
4Q521	*Messianic Apocalypse* (Qumran document)
Rab.	Rabbah (+ biblical book)
Rab. Perd.	*Pro Rabirio Perduellionis Reo* (Cicero)
Rom. Hist.	*Roman History* (Dio Cassius)
Sanh.	Sanhedrin
Sat.	*Satires* (Juvenal)
Sat.	*Satyricon* (Petronius)
Sir	Sirach/Ecclesiasticus
T. Levi	Testament of Levi
Vesp.	*Vespasian* (Suetonius)
Vit. pud.	*De vitioso pudore* (Plutarch)
Wis	Wisdom of Solomon

Modern

AB	Anchor Bible
ADB	*Anchor Bible Dictionary*
ABRL	Anchor Bible Reference Library
AnBib	Analecta biblica
ANRW	*Aufstien und Niedergang der römischen Welt: Geschiche und Kultur Rons in Spiegel derneueren Forschung.* Edited by H. Temporini and Haase. Berlin, 1972–
BAR	*Biblical Archaeology Review*
BASOR	*Bulletin of American School of Oriental Research*
BBR	*Bulletin for Biblical Research*

BDAG	Walter Bauer, Frederick W. Danker, William F. Arndt, and F. Wilbur Gingrich. *Greek-English Lexicon of the New Testament and Other Early Christian Literature.* 3rd ed.Chicago: University of Chicago Press, 2000.
BETL	Bibliotheca ephemeridum theologicarum lovaniensium
Bib	*Biblica*
BibIntSer	Biblical Interpretation Series
BJS	Brown Judaic Studies
BNTC	Black's New Testament Commentaries
BR	*Biblical Research*
BSac	*Bibliotheca Sacra*
BT	*The Bible Translator*
BTB	*Biblical Theology Bulletin*
BZ	*Biblische Zeitschrift*
CBQ	*Catholic Biblical Quarterly*
CCARJ	*Central Conference of American Rabbis Journal*
CGTC	Cambridge Greek Testament Commentary
CPL	*Clavis partum latinorum.* Edited by E. Dekkers. 2nd ed. Steenbrugis, 1961.
CurBR	*Currents in Biblical Research*
CurTM	*Currents in Theology and Mission*
EBib	*Etudes Bibliques*
EvQ	*Evangelical Quarterly*
ExpTim	*Expository Times*
GBS	Guides to Biblical Scholarship
GOA	*Griechische Ostraka aus Ägyten und Nubien.* Vol. 2. Edited by U. Wilcken. Leipzig, 1899.
GRBS	*Greek, Roman, and Byzantine Studies*
HT	*History Today*
HTR	*Harvard Theological Review*
HUCA	*Hebrew Union College Annual*
IEJ	*Israel Exploration Journal*
IGR	*Inscriptiones Graecae ad res romanas pertinentes.* Edited by R. Cagnat et al. 4 vols. (vol. 2 unpublished). Paris: Leroux, 1911–1927. Reprint, Rome: L'Erma, 1964

IM	*Die Inschriften von Magnesia am Mäander.* Edited by O. Kern. Berlin, 1900
Imm	*Immanuel*
Int	*Interpretation*
JAAR	*Journal of American Academy of Religion*
JBL	*Journal of Biblical Literature*
JBR	*Journal of Bible and Religion*
JGRCJ	*Journal of Greco-Roman Christianity and Judaism*
JJS	*Journal for Jewish Studies*
JQR	*Jewish Quarterly Review*
JRH	*Journal of Religious History*
JSJ	*Journal for the Study of Judaism in the Persian, Hellenistic, and Roman Periods*
JSNT	*Journal for the Study of the New Testament*
JSNTSup	*Journal for the Study of the New Testament: Supplement Series*
JSOT	*Journal for the Study of the Old Testament*
JSS	*Journal of Semitic Studies*
JTS	*Journal of Theological Studies*
LCL	Loeb Classical Library
LNTS	Library of New Testament Studies
NICNT	The New International Commentary on the New Testament
NIGTC	The New International Greek Testament Commentary
NovT	*Novum Testamentum*
NovTSup	Novum Testamentum Supplements
NRSV	New Revised Standard Version
NTL	New Testament Library
NTOA	Novum Testamentum et Orbis Antiquues
NTS	*New Testament Studies*
OBT	Overtures to Biblical Theology
OGIS	*Orientis Graecea Inscriptiones Selectae.* Edited by W. Dittenberger. 2 vols. Leipzig: Hirzel, 1903–1905. Reprint, Hildesheim: Olms, 1960
PEQ	*Palestine Exploration Quarterly*

PRSt	*Perspectives in Religious Studies*
PSI	*Publicazion della Socitǎ italiana per la Recerca dei Papiri greci e latini en Egitto: Papiri greci e latini.* Edited by G. Vitelli et al. 15 vols. Florence: Felice le Monnier [and other publishers], 1912–1979
SB	*Sammelbuch griechischer Urkunden aus Aegypten.* Edited by F. Preisigke 5 vols. Strassburg: Teubner, 1915–1955
SBL	Society of Biblical Literature
SBLTT	Society of Biblical Literature Texts and Translations
SBT	Studies in Biblical Theology
SEG	*Supplimentum epigraphicum graecum.* Leiden and Amsterdam: Gieben, 1923–
SIG	*Sylloge inscriptionum graecarum.* Edited by W. Dittenberger, 4 vols. 3rd ed. Leipzig, 1915–1924
SJ	Studies in Judaism
SJT	*Scottish Journal of Theology*
SNT	Studien zum Neuen Testament
SNTSMS	Society for New Testament Studies Monograph Series
SP	Sacra Pagina
TBT	*The Bible Today*
TDNT	*Theological Dictionary of the New Testament.* Edited by Gerhard Kittel and Gerhard Friedrich. Translated by Geoffrey W. Bromiley. 10 vols. Grand Rapids: Eerdmans, 1964–1976
TST	Toronto Studies in Theology
UBS	United Bible Societies
UPA	University Press of America
WBC	Word Biblical Commentary
WUNT	Wissenschaftliche Untersuchungen zun Neuen Testament
WW	*Word and World*
ZNW	*Zeitschrift für die neutestamentliche Wissenschaft und die Kunde der Kirche*
ZSCHI	Zalman Shezer Center for History of Israel

1

Introduction

Purpose and Thesis

THE ROMAN-JEWISH WAR OF 66–70 CE brought serious and devastating results on the Jewish people. In addition to the loss of so many lives among the Jews, the city of Jerusalem and its temple were destroyed such that future visitors would not believe that the place had ever been inhabited. Josephus painfully describes this horrific consequence of that horrible war:

> The army now having no victims either for slaughter or plunder, through lack of all objects on which to vent their rage . . . Caesar ordered the whole city and the temple to be razed to the ground . . . All the rest of the wall encompassing the city was completely leveled to the ground as to leave the future visitors to the spot no ground for believing that it had ever been inhabited. Such was the end to which the frenzy of the revolutionaries brought to Jerusalem, that splendid city of the worldwide renown. (*J.W.* 7:1–4)

That bloody war started as a Jewish revolt against Rome. Rome responded very harshly with all its military might, destroying Jerusalem and its temple as Josephus's account indicates. The reference to the destruction of the temple in Mark 13:2 suggests that Mark had knowledge of the fall of the holy place.[1] In this respect, I consider the events of the Roman-Jewish War of 66–70 CE to have been the background of Mark's Gospel and that Mark's hearers had fresh memories of that war and its devastating consequences.

This book explores the reading of Mark's Gospel in the light of the Roman-Jewish War of 66–70 CE. In doing so, I seek to explore how Mark's hearers, people who had fresh memories of the war, which they either witnessed or had heard stories about from those who had firsthand knowledge of the events of that war, might have heard and evaluated Mark's story of

---

1. For further links between Mark and the events of the war, see the section on Method, Sources, and Justification below (pp. 2–13).

Jesus. Put differently, the question I ask is, how might hearers have related Mark's story of Jesus to the events of the war that they had experienced or had heard about? The focus is therefore primarily on how hearers might have evaluated Mark's story of Jesus, rather than on Mark's possible intentions.

In this book I wish to argue that Mark's hearers, living in rural Galilee, southern Syria, or both, heard the Gospel shortly after the end of the Roman-Jewish War of 66–70 CE not only as a proclamation of Jesus but also as a commentary on the war (not just on the fact of the war but on the events, dynamics, and purposes of that war). I further argue that Mark's hearers who had experienced the war and its consequences would have interpreted (a) God's empire proclaimed by Jesus as a contrast to the Roman Empire under Vespasian, (b) Jesus' life-giving campaign in Galilee as a contrast to Vespasian's military campaign in the area, and (c) the values of God's empire embodied in Jesus' teachings while on his way to Jerusalem as contrasts to the values of the Roman Empire embodied in the actions of both Roman and Jewish authorities. Generally, this thesis suggests that Mark's hearers viewed Mark's story of Jesus as a contrast to the events of the war.

Method, Sources, and Justification

This book employs a combination of two methodologies: literary criticism and the historical reconstruction of the background of the Gospel. According to Mark Allan Powell, literary criticism deals with the text in its final form; treats the unity of the text as a whole (i.e. individual passages are interpreted in terms of their contribution to the entire story); focuses on the understanding of the narrative as its goal (the text as an end in itself); and is based on a communication model that focuses on the composer, text, and hearer or reader.[2]

Since literary criticism is of many types, I primarily use a reader-response approach.[3] The significance of this approach is that the reader or hearer plays an active role in the creation of meaning of the text or story. Resseguie expresses this idea thus: "The reader is active, not passive, and contributes to the production of textual meaning. The reader of a literary text must apply the portions which are not written but are implied—the

---

2. Powell, *What Is Narrative Criticism?*, 7–8.
3. For detailed discussions concerning this approach, see Fowler, *Let the Reader Understand*; Fowler, "Reader-Response Criticism," 59–93; Rhoads, "Narrative Criticism," 272–73; Resseguie, "Reader-Response Criticism," 307–24; Barton, "Think about Reader-Response Criticism," 147–51; Iser, *Implied Reader*; Iser, *Act of Reading*.

areas of 'indeterminacy' or 'gaps.'"[4] It is also worth noting that among other things reader-response criticism is concerned with "what the text *does* to and how it *affects* its reader, that is, what actions the text calls forth, what mental moves, emotional feelings, anticipations, attitudes, persuasions, realizations, convictions, etc. the text causes its reader to experience in order to produce the meaning latent in the text and thus to bring its act of communication to completion."[5]

In order for the communication process to be effective and fruitful, there must be some presuppositions the "implied author" and the "implied" reader" have in common.[6] In the case of Mark's Gospel, the shared knowledge between Mark and his hearers include the events, dynamics, and purposes of the Roman-Jewish War of 60–70 CE. Thus, when Mark's hearers experience Mark's story of Jesus, they evaluate that story in terms of what they already know about the war. Because of their presupposed knowledge, Mark's hearers would be able to fill in the gaps in the story.[7] The major strength of reader-response approach is that it considers the meaning of the text as dynamic, an ever-changing creation of the reader in the act of reading. It recognizes the role of the reader in creating meaning of the text

---

4. Resseguie, "Reader-Response, Criticism," 308. See also Iser, *Implied Reader*, 38–40; Horsley, *Hearing the Whole Story*, 8, who argues that "In reader-response the meaning is not something buried in the text waiting to be discovered and extracted but is established by the actively engaged reader in the act of reading. While most other approaches assume the spatial orientation of print culture, reader-response emphasizes the temporal experience of reading a narrative."

5. Heil, *Gospel of Mark as Model for Action*, 2. Cf. Rhoads, "Narrative Criticism," 272–73.

6. Fowler, *Let the Reader Understand*, 31–32. He shows that the "implied author" and "implied reader/hearer" respectively represent the image of the implied author and the reader/hearer in the act of reading or hearing the text of the narrative. The terms are used in the place of the *narrator* and *narratee*—the persons who are supposed to be telling and listening to the story. The terms are also used in contrast to the "real author" and the "real reader," which respectively represent the "living, flesh-and-blood persons who actually produce the text and read it." See also Anderson and Moore, *Mark & Method*, 237; Resseguie, "Reader-Response Criticism," 308, who argues that an "implied reader is an individual who comes to a text with certain social and cultural norms . . . [and] is able to take the clues or guidelines transmitted in the text, and can concretize the meaning . . . The reader can interact with the text only to the extent that conventions are shared by both text and reader"; Iser, *Act of Reading*, 69, who states that the reader's interaction with the text takes place "in the form of references to earlier works, or to social and historical norms, or to the whole culture from which the text has emerged."

7. Cf. Fowler, *Let the Reader Understand*, 134–38; Fowler, "Reader-Response Criticism," 70–74; Resseguie, "Reader-Response Criticism," 308–9, who states that "each reader selects and organizes the parts of a text and fills in the gaps in his or her own way."

in the act reading,[8] and emphasizes the temporal experience of reading a story rather than the spatial orientation of print culture.[9]

In addition to literary criticism, I also employ the historical approach to construct the context of Mark's Gospel. I do this because I believe that a historical context helps to clarify Mark's Gospel and the hearers' possible response. As Horsley has correctly noted, the meaning of a story depends on the historical context in which the story was told. He points out that knowing the historical situation of the story deepens and enhances our understanding of that story.[10] A historical approach investigates the world behind the text in order to gain some knowledge useful for understanding the text. Therefore, in order to understand Mark's story of Jesus, it is crucial that we understand the context to which it was responding and in which it was told. Since I consider the Roman-Jewish War of 66–70 CE the immediate context of Mark and his hearers, I use Josephus's report on the events of the war. My point here is not that I claim that Josephus's report was Mark's source, for Mark and his hearers did not know about that report. But both Mark and his audience had experienced the events that Josephus describes.[11] Josephus's report on the war is not only a useful source for understanding Mark's story of Jesus, but also an important aid for interpreting the Gospel.

In using the stated approaches, I must make it clear that no attempt is made to identify Mark's source material. While I agree that the final form of Mark's Gospel is a product of a redactional process, I doubt the interpreter's ability to fully reconstruct the layers of tradition of the final form of the Gospel narrative. My doubt is based on the fact that, given its literary priority, Mark's Gospel "provides no sources against which to check the distinction between traditional and redactional material."[12] Accordingly, I read Mark's Gospel in its final form focusing on how hearers heard and evaluated it. In this regard, I make several assumptions. First, Mark's story of Jesus is a sufficiently unified and coherent narrative that has to be heard as a whole and not in fragments.[13] Second, the priority of Mark is assumed. That is, Mark's Gospel came into being before the other Synoptic Gospels, and hence, to be ready independently from them.[14]

---

8. Fowler, "Reader-Response Criticism," 51–52.
9. Horsley, *Politics of Plot*, 8.
10. Ibid., 24.
11. The question of the reliability of Josephus is dealt with in chapter 3.
12. Peterson, *Origins of Mark*, 9.
13. Rhoads et al., *Mark as Story*, 3–4.
14. Ibid., 5.

Third, I assume that Mark's historical context is important for understanding the Gospel. I therefore take seriously the historical situation from which the Gospel arose[15] and the context to which Mark was responding and in which the story was told.[16] Since I consider Mark's Gospel to be a postwar document, I take the war situation as the primary context of the Gospel. Finally, I assume that Mark's hearers were people who had experienced the crisis and traumatic results of the war living in rural Galilee, southern Syria, or both.[17] The primary sources used are therefore Mark's Gospel and Josephus's works. Unless otherwise stated, all the biblical references given refer to Mark's Gospel. The references to Josephus's works, namely, the *Jewish War*, *Jewish Antiquities*, *Life*, and *Against Apion*, are abbreviated as *J.W.*, *Ant.*, *Life*, and *Ag. Ap.*, respectively.

One of the striking features of Mark's Gospel is its pervasive associations to the events of the Roman-Jewish War of 66–70 CE. Throughout the entire narrative, Mark persistently links Jesus' story to the events of the war which Josephus, an ancient Jewish historian who writes about the history of the war, reports.[18] The point I make here is not that Mark or his hearers knew or had read Josephus's works about the war. Rather, the events of the war that Josephus describes were also known to Mark and his hearers, for they were widespread through personal experience and word of mouth. So the events are the focus, not Mark's literary dependence on Josephus or the hearers' knowledge of Josephus.

A number of associations that Mark's hearers may have made with the events of the war can be highlighted here. However, before I proceed, I first introduce what I believe to have been the most significant and impressive item related to the war that Mark's audience may have associated with when they heard Mark's story of Jesus. This item relates to Mark's reference to Caesarea Philippi. Mark's Jesus visited the villages of Caesarea Philippi during his Galilean campaign. There his life-giving Galilean campaign culminates, his messiahship is declared, and his journey to Jerusalem starts (8:27–30). The Roman generals Vespasian and Titus also visited Caesarea Philippi. Vespasian rested at Caesarea Philippi with his troops being hosted by King Agrippa II and gave thanksgiving to a god there for his Galilean military achievements (*J.W.* 3:443–444). Titus, too, rested at Caesarea Philippi shortly after the war. While there, Titus entertained himself with games in which

---

15. Horsley, *Hearing the Whole Story*, 24.

16. Ibid., 25.

17. See a diversity of opinions concerning the place of Mark offered in Marcus, "Jewish War," 441.

18. Josephus, *J.W.*, books 1–7.

the Jewish prisoners of war perished while fighting either with wild beasts or with one another (*J.W.* 7:23-24); celebrated his brother's birthday with great splendor (*J.W.* 7:37); and heard about the capture of Simon bar Gioras (*J.W.* 7:32). Thus Mark's audience may not have avoided associating Mark's story of Jesus, especially Jesus' visit in the villages of Caesarea Philippi, his messiahship, and his journey to Jerusalem, with the war events related to Vespasian and Titus, including their rest at Caesarea Philippi.[19]

The beginning of Jesus' life-giving campaign in Galilee is one of the events that Mark's audience may have associated with the war events when they heard the Gospel story. Jesus began his campaign in Galilee before he advanced to Jerusalem where he met his own death. Hearers may have associated this with Vespasian's military campaign, which also started in Galilee before it ended with the destruction of Jerusalem and its temple. Jesus went from Nazareth of Galilee to be baptized by John in the Jordan River (1:9). Shortly after his test in the wilderness that followed immediately after his baptism, Jesus began his redemptive campaign in Galilee (1:14—8:26). Coming from Rome, the center of the empire, Vespasian, too, began his military campaign in Galilee to stop the Jewish revolt in Judea. Since the campaigns of both Jesus and Vespasian began in Galilee, they provide a close link between Mark's story of Jesus and the events of the war.

Next, Mark's language about "the good news" and the reference to Jesus as the "Messiah, Son of God" (1:1) respectively can be associated with "the good news" related to Vespasian's military victory, his rise to power, and the claim that he had divine status.[20] In the ancient world, military victory, political success, and entrances of a king or an emperor into a city were celebrated as good news. When Vespasian was proclaimed emperor based on his military achievement in Judea, the cities in the east received the report as "good news" (*J.W.* 4:618). Upon his arrival in Alexandria, the new emperor "was greeted by the good news from Rome" of Mucianus's victory against Vitellius, who also fought to gain the imperial throne (*J.W.* 4:656-657). The people in Rome celebrated twofold good news: the good news of victory and the good news related to Vespasian's rise to imperial power; both pieces of good news were marked during a single festival (*J.W.* 4:654-55). In regard to divine status, Vespasian was hailed in divine terms as "saviour and benefactor" (*J.W.* 3:459-460), "master . . . of land and sea

---

19. Further details regarding the association of Mark's story of Jesus with the war events related to Caesarea Philippi are presented in the next pages.

20. Cf. Evans, *Mark*, lxxxii–iii, who provides a list of divine titles for the Roma emperors. Elsewhere, he shows that Nero, under whose reign the Jewish revolt occurred, bore the titles "god" and "son of god." Although Vespasian lacks the title "son of god," he bears the title "god."

and the whole human race" (*J. W.* 3:402), and so on. Mark's hearers may have associated these expressions with Jesus in Mark's story.

Further, Mark's proclamation of Jesus' entrance, "Prepare the way of the Lord, make his paths straight" (1:3), also links the Gospel to the war. The announcement to prepare the way and to make it straight parallels Vespasian's entrances during the war. According to Josephus, before the Romans entered Jotapata to destroy the city and the Jews who took refuge there, Vespasian ordered his troops to level the road for easy passage to the city. Josephus relates:

> Vespasian was impatient to make an end of Jotapata, having heard that it was the refuge to which most of the enemy had retired, and that it was, moreover, their strong base; he accordingly sent a body of infantry and cavalry in advance to *level the road* leading to it, a stony mountain track, difficult for infantry and quite impracticable for mounted troops. In four days their task was completed and a broad highway opened for the army. (*J. W.* 3:141)[21]

Leveling roads for easy passage into a city during a war was a common task for Roman soldiers. The proof of this is in the fact that within the Roman military were pioneers whose role was "to strengthen sinuosities on the route, to level the rough places and to cut down obstructing woods, in order to spare the army the fatigues of a toilsome march" (*J. W.* 3:118).

Furthermore, Mark's mention of Caesarea Philippi may have reminded his audience of the Roman-Jewish War of 66–70 CE. Located at the foot of Mount Hermon, the place was originally called Paneas after the Greek god Pan who was worshiped there. Herod the Great built a temple there for emperor worship (*J. W.* 1:404–406; *Ant.* 15:363–364). Herod Philip renamed the place Caesarea Philippi and used it as his capital (*J. W.* 2:168; *Ant.* 18:28). In Mark, Jesus visits the villages of Caesarea Philippi after his successful campaign in Galilee, and there he is proclaimed Messiah and starts his journey to Jerusalem (8:27–33). During the war, Vespasian rested there for twenty days with his troops after his destruction of Galilee. While there, he fêted himself and "gave thank offering to God for the successes which he had gained" (*J. W.* 3:443). His son Titus also rested at Caesarea Philippi shortly after the end of the war, and there he caused many Jewish prisoners to perish in games with wild beasts (*J. W.* 7:23–25). Hence, Mark's portrayal of Jesus being proclaimed the Messiah in the village of Caesarea Philippi makes an intriguing connection with the war.

21. Italics are added.

This view is strongly supported by Josephus's report concerning Vespasian's messianic status. When Mark's Gospel was being composed, Vespasian had just become emperor. His rise to imperial power was associated with both his divine status and messianic claims for him. First, after the fall of Jotapata, Josephus prophesied that Vespasian would become emperor:

> You imagine, Vespasian, that in the person of Josephus you have taken a mere captive; but I come to you as a messenger of greater destinies . . . You will be Caesar, Vespasian, you will be emperor, you and your son here. Bind me then yet more securely in chains and keep me for yourself; for you, Caesar, are Master not of me only, but of land and sea and the whole human race. For myself, I ask to be punished by stricter custody, if I have dared trifle with the words of God. (*J.W.* 3:400–402; cf. 4:622–429)

Next, in a passage about an ambiguous oracle, Josephus affirms that Vespasian was the fulfillment of that Jewish oracle. He writes:

> But what more that all else incited them [the Jewish revolutionaries] to the war was an ambiguous oracle, likewise found in their sacred scriptures, to the effect that at that time one from their country would become ruler of the world. This they understood to mean someone of their own race, and many of their wise men went astray in their interpretation of it. The oracle, however, in reality signified the sovereignty of Vespasian, who was proclaimed Emperor on Jewish soil. (*J.W.* 6:312–314)

These accounts support a link between Peter's proclamation of Jesus as the Messiah and messianic claims for Vespasian as the fulfillment of the ambiguous Jewish oracle. Most likely Mark's audience evaluated Peter's proclamation of Jesus as the Messiah at Caesarea Philippi in terms of Vespasian, who had become emperor thanks to both messianic and divine claims made about him at just the time when Mark's Gospel was composed and first heard.

Jesus' entry into Jerusalem riding on a donkey (11:1–11), too, links the Gospel with the war. Mark's episode has commonly been viewed as "a messianic journey"[22] that expresses Jesus' "lowly messiahship in contrast to the more nationalistic expectations of the day."[23] In this way, Jesus' march to Jerusalem reflects some messianic pretensions made by some Jewish revolutionary leaders during the war. For example, at the outbreak

---

22. LaVerdiere, "Jesus' Entry into Jerusalem," 271.

23. Tatum, "Jesus' So-Called Triumphal Entry," 129–43. Cf. Kelber, *Mark's Story of Jesus*, 57–59. Similarly, Myers, *Binding the Strong Man*, 294, who notes that the episode provides ironic or contrasting messianic signals.

of the war, Menachem broke into King Herod's armory at Masada, took arms, marched to Jerusalem "like a veritable king" (*J.W.* 2:433–444), and appeared in the temple "in royal robes" (*J.W.* 2:444).[24] Simon bar Gioras, another revolutionary leader, also made messianic pretensions during the war. First, he made a royal-like proclamation of "liberty for slaves and rewards for the free" (*J.W.* 4:508).[25] Next, his followers were obedient "to his command as to a king" (*J.W.* 4:510). Finally, shortly after the fall of Jerusalem and its temple, he emerged from the ground at the place where the temple formerly stood while dressed "in white tunics and buckling over them a purple mantle" (*J.W.* 7:29). The actions of both Menachem and Simon bar Gioras suggest the two made messianic pretensions. Hence, Jesus' messianic entry into Jerusalem links the Gospel story with these messianic acts performed during the war.

Jesus' saying about the temple being turned into a den of robbers instead of being a house for international prayer (11:17) also links Mark's Gospel to the war. Mark presents Jesus as speaking to his audience in the temple: "Is it not written, 'My house shall be a house of prayer for the nations? But you have made it a den of robbers" (11:17). This saying recalls the brigands who during the war occupied the temple and made it their fortress. Josephus frequently uses the term *lēston* (plural for *lēstēs*) to refer to the Jewish revolutionaries and the Zealots (e.g., *J.W.* 2:434, 441, 593; 4:135).[26] Hence, Mark's use of the term *lēstēs*[27] is suggestive of the link between the Gospel and the war. More significantly, Josephus shows that during the war the Zealots "invaded the sanctuary" (*J.W.* 4:150) and made it their stronghold. They "converted the temple of God into their fortress and refuge from any outbreak of popular violence, and made the Holy Place the headquarters of their tyranny" (*J.W.* 4:151; cf. *J.W.* 4:172, 261–262).

Moreover, Mark's saying also reflects the revolutionaries' cessation of sacrifice offered by Gentiles on behalf of Caesar, an action that provoked war with Rome. According to Josephus, Eleazar ben Ananias the high priest, then captain of the temple, persuaded the temple officials responsible for

---

24. Cf. Duff, "March of a Divine Warrior," 62n31.

25. Perhaps this was done as fulfillment of Isaiah's prophecy: "to bring good news to the oppressed . . . to proclaim liberty to the captives, and release to prisoners; to proclaim the year of the LORD's favor, and the day of vengeance of our God" (Isa 61:1–2).

26. For detailed list of Josephus's use of the term *lēstēs* and its cognates, see Rhoads, *Israel in Revolution*, 182.

27. Mark uses the word *lēstēs* or its cognates elsewhere in his Gospel. The agents of the chief priests, the scribes, and the elders go with swords and clubs to arrest Jesus as if Jesus was a "bandit" or "brigand" (14:48). When Jesus was crucified, two brigands were crucified with him (15:27).

Temple services not to accept gifts or sacrifices from foreigners, an action which laid the foundation of the war with the Romans because such sacrifices were offered on behalf of both the nation of Israel and the emperor in Rome (*J.W.* 2:409; cf. 2:404). The rejection of gifts and sacrifices from foreigners was, in other words, a refusal to collect tribute for Rome, an action that the Romans considered a rebellion against the emperor, hence an action not to be tolerated. Moreover, the rejection of sacrifices from foreigners was also an act excluding Gentiles from worship in the temple. Such an act implied denying the sanctuary its role as a house of prayer for all nations. Jesus' temple saying was therefore recalling the events of the war.

The war situation in Mark 13, too, links the Gospel with the Roman-Jewish War of 66–70 CE. The warnings and prophecies in Mark 13 reflect the realities of the Roman-Jewish War of 66–70 CE—from the warning not to be led astray by those who come in Jesus' name (13:5) to the references to "wars and rumors of war"; from nations rising up against one another to persecution and to betrayals within families (13:9–13); from "the desolation of sacrilege" in Jerusalem to false messiahs, false prophets (13:21–22) and omens followed by suffering. For example, the warnings not to be led astray and against false messiahs and false prophets may have reflected the messianic or prophetic pretenders active during and shortly after the war.[28] The reference to famines reflects the terrible famine that occurred during the siege of Jerusalem. Josephus underscores the horror of famine when Jerusalem was under siege:

> The victims of famine were dropping in countless numbers . . . a shadow of food was a sign of war, and the dearest of relatives fell to blows, snatching from each other the pitiful supports of life . . . Necessity drove the victims to gnaw anything, and

---

28. Cf. *J.W.* 6:286–287, where Josephus reports of the existence of many false prophets during the siege of Jerusalem. He writes: "Numerous prophets, indeed, were at this period suborned by the tyrants to delude people, by bidding them await help from God, in order that desertions might be checked and that those who were above fear and precaution might be encouraged by hope. In diversity man is quickly persuaded; but when the deceiver actually pictures release from prevailing horrors, then the sufferer wholly abandoned himself to expectation." In connection to this, Josephus puts blame on one false prophet for six thousand Jews who perished in the temple as a result of his false prophecy. Referring to the Jews who perished, Josephus states that "they owed their destruction to a false prophet, who had on that day proclaimed to the people in the city that God had commanded them to go up to the temple court, to receive there the tokens of their deliverance" (*J.W.* 6:285). Josephus also mentions Jonathan the Weaver, who made a messianic or prophetic pretension, when after the war he had led people "into the desert, promising them a display of signs and apparitions" (*J.W.* 7:438). These false prophets are over and above the Jewish revolutionary leaders who also made messianic pretensions such as Menachem and Simon bar Gioras.

> objects which even the filthiest of brute beasts would reject they condescended to collect and eat: thus in the end they abstained not from belts and shoes and stripped off and chewed the very leather of their bucklers. (*J.W.* 6:193-197)[29]

Elsewhere Josephus reports that because of the famine, a woman named Mary was forced to eat the flesh of her own son. He writes of Mary thus: "Seizing her child, an infant at the breast . . . she slew her son . . . roasted the body and devoured half of it" (*J.W.* 6:205-208).[30] Concerning Mark's mention of omens, this may have recalled the omens that appeared in the Jewish land before the war started. Josephus testifies that numerous omens or portents appeared in Judea to foretell of the coming catastrophe among the Jews.[31]

The references to persecutions and betrayals among family members (13:9-13) reflect the sufferings during and after the war. As David Rhoads has stated, "The time of the war was difficult for followers of Jesus. On the one hand, they were the target of persecution from other Jews, because they opposed the war. On the other hand, they were suspected by the Romans, because their leader had been executed as a revolutionary. They faced ridicule, rejection, ostracism from family and community, betrayal, arrests, trials, floggings, and death (13:5-23)."[32]

There is evidence showing that even after the war, persecutions of Jews continued in Egypt. Josephus states that shortly after the war, Jews who had

---

29. See also *J.W.* 5:429-435, where Josephus gives another account of the horrors of the famine during the war. "Pitiful was the fare and lamentable the spectacle, the stronger taking more than their share, the weak whimpering. Famine, indeed, overpowers all the emotions, but of nothing is it so destructive as of shame . . . wives would snatch the food from husbands, children from fathers, and—most pitiable sight of all—mothers from the very mouths of their infants, and while their dearest ones were pining in their arms they scrupled not to rob them of the life-giving drops . . . Horrible were the methods of torture which they [the Jewish rebels] devised in their search for food, blocking with pulse the passages in their poor victims' frames and driving sharp stakes up their bodies; and one would shudder at the mere recital of pangs to which they were subjected to make them confess to the possession of a single loaf or to reveal the hiding-place of a handful of barley-meal."

30. For the entire account about this horrific incident, see *J.W.* 6:201-213.

31. Josephus includes the following omens or portents in his list: a star like a sword that stood over Jerusalem, and a comet that existed for a year; the brilliant light that shone around the altar, and the sanctuary at midnight; a cow that gave birth to a lamb in the midst of the temple court; the self-opening of the iron gate at night; the appearance of celestial armies before sunset; the voice in the temple that cried, "We are departing" (*J.W.* 6:300), and the portent related to Jesus, son of Ananias. See *J.W.* 6:288-309.

32. Rhoads, *Reading Mark*, 61.

taken refuge in Egypt were persecuted because of their refusal to acknowledge the lordship of Caesar. Josephus writes:

> For under every form of torture and laceration of body, devised for the sole object of making them acknowledge Caesar as lord, no one submitted nor was brought to the verge of utterance; but all kept their resolve, triumphant over constraint, meeting the tortures and the fire with bodies that seemed insensible of pain and souls that well-nigh exulted in it. But most of all were the spectators struck by the children of tender age, not one of whom could be prevailed upon to call Caesar lord. So far did the strength of courage rise superior to the weakness of their frames. (*J.W.* 7:418–419)

This passage does not specifically refer to Christian persecution. However, given the fact that the persecution was associated with a denial to acknowledge Caesar as lord, it is possible that Christians were also involved.

Mark's mention of "the desolating sacrilege" and the suffering that follow thereafter (13:14–23) reflects the entrance of Titus and his troops in the temple court. Josephus reports that when the temple was in flames, the Roman troops "carried their standards into the temple court and, setting them up opposite the eastern gate, there sacrificed to them, and with rousing acclamations hailed Titus as imperator" (*J.W.* 6:316). Shortly after this "desolating sacrilege," Titus ordered the execution of the priests who were still in the temple (*J.W.* 6:322), thereafter destroyed the temple and then the entire city of Jerusalem.[33] All these observations testify that Mark 13 expresses the realities of the recent war that Mark's audience must have been aware of.

Finally, the consensus among scholars that the composition of the Gospel was influenced by the events of the Roman-Jewish War of 66–70 CE also demonstrates the link between the Gospel and the war. The consensus is based on the dating of Mark shortly before or after the fall of Jerusalem and its temple in 70 CE.[34] This agreement is strong evidence that scholars

---

33. Cf. Winn, *Purpose of Mark's Gospel*, 69, who underscores that 13:14–23 has to be "understood in light of Jerusalem's destruction and, more specifically, the destruction of the temple itself. Though the exact referent for the 'abomination of desolation' is debated, it is generally equated with an event closely related to the Jerusalem temple. The immense suffering that followed the abomination is equated with the suffering experienced in Jerusalem during its capture."

34. Although scholars generally agree that Mark's Gospel was composed just before or after the fall of Jerusalem in 70 CE they are divided as to whether the Gospel came into being before or after the temple was razed by fire to the ground by Titus at the end of the Roman-Jewish War in 70 CE. Scholars who date Mark before the destruction of the temple include Myers, *Binding the Strong Man*, 418; van Iersel, *Mark*, 47; Brown,

recognize the link between the Gospel and the war. Joel Marcus and David Rhoads, for example, have independently argued that the writing of Mark's Gospel was influenced by the first Jewish revolt against the Romans. Marcus writes, "Mark's Gospel reflects the influence on his community of the first Jewish Revolt."[35] Similarly, Rhoads states that "the Roman-Jewish War of 66–70 C.E. affected the writing of Mark's Gospel."[36]

In spite of the consensus about the link between the Gospel and the war, not many scholars have treated the serious connection between Mark and the events of that war. Those who have attempted to read Mark in the light of the war have either acknowledged the fact that the Gospel is linked to the situation of the war without dealing with the dynamics of that war, or they have treated Mark in relation to one aspect of the war. This book, which focuses on the reading of Mark's Gospel in the light of the Roman-Jewish War of 66–70 CE, is important because it takes seriously the events, dynamics, and purposes of that war as the background and context for the first audience of Mark's Gospel.

Criteria of Correlation

In this section I identify some criteria and names used to determine the correlation between the episodes in Mark and the events of the war that a Jewish audience would have resonated with. Such criteria are based on what would lead us to think that Mark's audience in Galilee and southern Syria may have experienced and understood the Gospel against the backdrop of the events related to the war. In this respect, six criteria have been considered: (1) the criterion of names of places, (2) the criterion of geographical proximity, (3) the criterion of formation, (4) the criterion of people and empire, (5) the criterion of verbal parallels, and (6) the criterion of events. These criteria are the basis for the conclusion that the Gospel might have evoked memories of recent events and experiences of the war. In the following paragraphs I present a brief explanation of each criterion.

Introduction to the New Testament, 163; Hengel, *Studies*, 22, 28. The following represent scholars who date Mark after the fall of the temple: Kelber, *Mark's Story of Jesus*, 14; Such, *Abomination of Desolation*, 3, 171; Radcliffe, "Coming of the Son of Man," 176.

35. Marcus, "Jewish War," 442.

36. Rhoads, "Social Criticism," 138. Similarly, Kelber, *Mark's Story of Jesus*, 14, notes that the "Roman-Jewish War and the destruction of the temple provide the broad historical backdrop for the Gospel of Mark, and the reader may keep these events in mind in reading the Gospel."

Names of Places

The criterion of names of places considers places where the first phase of Vespasian's and Jesus' campaigns started and culminated. Both Vespasian and Jesus began their campaigns in Galilee and visited Caesarea Philippi after their operations. Thus, this criterion involves these two places: Galilee and Caesarea Philippi. Josephus describes Jewish Galilee of his day by defining its boundaries in terms of the surrounding territories. Having shown that the country with its two parts, Upper and Lower Galilee, was enclosed by Phoenicia and Syria, he lists the borders of Galilee. According to him, the region of Ptolemais, Mount Carmel (formerly in Galilee, now under Tyre), and Gaba (the city of cavalry) lay on the western side; Samaria and Scythopolis on the south; Gadara, Hippos, and Gaulanitis on the east; and Tyre on the north (J.W. 3:35–40). The importance of Galilee in this work is that both Jesus and Vespasian began their campaigns there before they proceeded to Jerusalem.

Jesus' liberative campaigns were primarily based in Galilee, Capernaum being the headquarters of his campaigns (1:21; 2:1; 3:19c; 6:1). In the villages and countryside of Galilee and its neighboring regions, Jesus healed, drove out demons, taught, fed the hungry, and performed other redemptive works. Beyond Galilee and its neighboring regions (after Mark 8), Jesus did not perform life-giving acts apart from the exorcism of a demon that had oppressed a boy from his childhood (9:14–29) and the restoration of Bartimaeus's sight in Jericho (10:46–52). Vespasian also began his military campaigns in Galilee before he advanced to besiege Jerusalem.[37] Coming from Rome via Antioch and Ptolemais in Syria, Vespasian entered Galilee with his mighty army of sixty thousand soldiers (J.W. 3:29, 69, 127), though likely Josephus's significant exaggeration. While Jesus' campaign was focused in villages and the countryside and sought to bring life to people, Vespasian's campaign was focused on fortified cities[38] seeking to destroy life. Given the

---

37. Vespasian began his campaign in Galilee as a military strategy to make sure that there would be no attacks from behind as he proceeded with his troops to besiege Jerusalem. This view is suggested in a passage where Josephus relates Vespasian's decision to establish a Roman garrison in Sepphoris. According to Josephus, following the Sepphorians' request for protection Vespasian provided a large force "sufficient to repel invasions in the event of the Jews causing trouble; indeed, it appeared to him that the loss of Sepphoris would be a hazard gravely affecting the impending campaign, as it was the largest city of Galilee, a fortress in an exceptionally strong position in the enemy's territory, and adapted to keep guard over the entire province" (J.W. 3:33–34).

38. This is not only in Josephus's remark when he states that before Vespasian began his devastation of Galilee he first "made reparations for besieging the strongholds" (J.W. 3:128), it is also evident in the actual campaign of the war. Vespasian went and destroyed fortified Galilean cities and town one after another. Beginning with the city

parallels and contrasts between the two Galilean campaigns, Mark's audience may certainly have heard and interpreted Jesus' campaigns in light of Vespasian's campaigns.

Regarding Caesarea Philippi, this was a city built by Herod Philip at the base of Mount Hermon at the sources of the river Jordan in the district of Paneas. Named in honor of Caesar Tiberius, it served as Philip's capital (*J.W.* 2:168). In modern times the place is known as Banias. During the time of the war, the city was within the territory of Herod Agrippa II (*J.W.* 3:443). Both Vespasian and Jesus visited this area after their campaigns in Galilee. Vespasian along with his troops was hosted at Caesarea Philippi by Herod Agrippa II, and there he gave a thankoffering to a god for his military successes (*J.W.* 3:443-444).[39] Vespasian visited Caesarea Philippi in the summer of 67 CE shortly after Josephus's prophecy about him that he would be emperor, master of land and sea, and of the entire human race (*J.W.* 3:401-402),[40] which was realized in 69 CE (*J.W.* 4:601, 655).

According to Josephus, the proclamation of Vespasian as the emperor was a fulfillment of the Jewish oracle that expected a world ruler to come from Jewish soil (*J.W.* 6:312-314). It is interesting that Jesus also passed in the villages of Caesarea Philippi and was proclaimed there as the Messiah (8:27). Titus was also there celebrating at the time just after the war when Mark's Gospel was being composed (*J.W.* 7:23-24). Hence, Mark's mention of Caesarea Philippi as the place where Jesus was proclaimed the Messiah may indeed have reminded Mark's audience of the recent war, especially with respect to the messianic claims associated with Vespasian.

Mark's location for the proclamation of Jesus as the Messiah in the village of Caesarea Philippi is a critical correlation with Josephus's description of Vespasian because scholars generally cannot otherwise explain why any events would have happened in a remote place like Caesarea

---

of Gabara (*J.W.* 3:132), Vespasian and his troops continued his destructive campaign to other cities in this order: Jotapata (*J.W.* 3:141, 316); Japha (*J.W.* 3:289); Joppa (*J.W.* 3:414); Tiberias (*J.W.* 3:446); Scythopolis, the capital of Decapolis and about twenty miles from Tiberias (*J.W.* 3:446); Tarichaeae, a city south of Tiberias near the Sea of Galilee (*J.W.* 3:462-463); Gamala, a city near and east of the Sea of Galilee, opposite Tiberias (*J.W.* 4:2, 9); and finally, Gischala (*J.W.* 4:84, 91). The cities of Tiberias and Sepphoris were spared from destruction because they were primarily pro-Roman (see *J.W.* 3:30-31, 457, 459-461).

39. Note that at Caesarea Philippi was a temple built by Herod the Great, who dedicated it to Caesar. The temple served the purposes of emperor worship (*J.W.* 1:404-406; *Ant.* 15:363-364).

40. Note that Josephus made the prophecy at Jotapata after his submission to the Romans between June and July, 67 CE (see *J.W.* 3:142 and 3:282), and that Vespasian rested at Caesarea Philippi shortly before he conquered Tarichaea in September 67 CE (*J.W.* 3:542).

Philippi. The correlations with Vespasian and Titus in Caesarea Philippi during and after the war adequately explain why Mark chose to have Jesus end his Galilean campaign, begin his journey to Jerusalem, and be acclaimed the Messiah there.

Geographical Proximity

The criterion of geographical proximity considers the places that were close enough for Mark's audience in rural Galilee and southern Syria to be able to know the events of the war in those places. Even though such places may not necessarily be mentioned in Mark's Gospel, they must have been places where significant events of the war occurred. The cities of Sepphoris, Tiberias, and Tyre fit this criterion.

Sepphoris was the largest city of Galilee located about four miles northwest of Nazareth.[41] Josephus refers to Sepphoris as "the strongest city in Galilee" (*J.W.* 2:511) and "the ornament of all Galilee" (*Ant.* 18:27). The Roman governor of Syria, Varus, once destroyed the city and sent its residents into slavery (*J.W.* 2:68). But Herod Antipas rebuilt and called it Autocratoris (*Ant.* 18:27).[42] During the war, Sepphoris, though a Jewish city, was primarily pro-Roman (*Life* 61, 394–396). Its residents pledged loyalty to Vespasian before he arrived in the city; sent delegates to receive him in Ptolemais, a Syrian city located on the cost of the Mediterranean Sea; and promised Vespasian "their active support against their countrymen." In turn, Vespasian supplied their city with a garrison of "a thousand cavalry and six thousand infantry under the command of the tribune Placidus" to ensure security of both the city and the entire region (*J.W.* 3:59; cf. *J.W.* 3:29–34). This garrison brought calamity to the neighboring villages and countryside such that "Galilee from end to end became a scene of fire and blood; from no misery, no calamity was it exempt" (*J.W.* 3:62–63).

Tiberias was also a Galilean city. It was founded in 20 CE by Herod Antipas as his new capital to replace Sepphoris. The city was located on the

---

41. Strange, "Sepphoris," 1090. Cf. Meyers, "Roman Sepphoris," 321, who states that Sepphoris is "located approximately 5 km. northwest of Nazareth and 30 km. east of the Mediterranean, and exactly the same distance from the Sea of Galilee and Tiberias."

42. The term *Autocratoris* probably was used to refer to Sepphoris as an "imperial city" or a "capital city." Since the Greek form of the term, *autokratōr* is equivalent to "Imperator," one of Emperor Augustus's titles, it is probable that Herod Antipas gave this name to the city in honor of Augustus. But it is highly probable that the word was used to refer to Sepphoris as the capital city of Galilee. See *Ant.* 18:27, note b. Similarly, Strange, "Sepphoris," 109, states that "Antipas probably granted Sepphoris the rank of capital of Galilee."

western coast of the Sea of Galilee, just a few miles south of Capernaum.[43] The name Tiberias indicates that it was given in honor of Emperor Tiberius. Since this city was built on the site of tombs, it was primarily populated by Gentiles (*Ant.* 18:36-38). In 61 CE, Emperor Nero gave the city to Herod Agrippa II, son of Agrippa I (*J.W.* 2:252; *Ant.* 20:159). At the beginning most Tiberians supported the Jewish revolt against Rome. Jesus ben Sapphias, the chief magistrate of the city was the ringleader of the rebels (*J.W.* 2:599; 3:449; *Life* 66; 134). When the war started, Josephus made Tiberias the capital of his Galilean command and established there a council of seventy elders to decide on capital cases (*J.W.* 2:570-571). When Vespasian entered Tiberias with his troops, the residents showed no resistance. As a result, Vespasian spared the city (though he breached part of the south wall), and returned it to Agrippa II (*J.W.* 3:445-461). In the stadium of Tiberias twelve thousand war prisoners from Tarichaea were executed at Vespasian's order, while 36,400 others were sent into slavery (*J.W.* 3:539-542).[44]

Neither Sepphoris nor Tiberias feature at all in Mark's story of Jesus.[45] This serves as evidence that Jesus never entered them during his Galilean campaign. Mark's silence is, however, not an indicator that his audiences were not aware of the events of the war in these places. Nazareth of Galilee, Jesus' hometown was a satellite of Sepphoris, just five miles south of the city. Capernaum, the center of Jesus' Galilean campaigns, too, was about 6.33 miles or 10.19 kilometers north of Tiberias.[46] The places are close enough and relate enough that people in Galilee and southern Syria would know what was happening in all these places nearby.

Concerning Tyre, this was one of the cities in southern Syria, thus in the geographical proximity of Mark's audience. Mark's Jesus' visited the area during his healing campaign and healed there a Syrophoenician woman's daughter (7:24-30). Also the people from "the region of Tyre and Sidon" were among the multitudes that came to Jesus on the shore of the Sea of Galilee where he cured many who had various diseases (3:7-10). In relation to the war, Josephus reports that at the initial stages of the war, Tyrians killed many Jews in the city of Tyre and in the villages under their control, while

---

43. Strange, "Tiberias," 548.

44. Cf. ibid., 547-49.

45. Even in the entire Bible, the city of Tiberias is mentioned only once and in passing when John reports of people who search for Jesus: "some boats from Tiberias came near the place where they had eaten bread after the Lord had given thanks" (John 6:23; cf. 6:1; 21:1 where the name appears as a name of a Sea, i.e. "Sea of Tiberias"). As for Sepphoris, it is associated with the biblical Kitron (Judg 1:30) or Rakkath (Josh 19:35). In the New Testament, the city is never mentioned. See Strange, "Sepphoris," 1091.

46. "Distance between Tiberias and Capernaum," para 1.

they put other Jews in chains (*J. W.* 2:478). Hence, Mark's portrayal of Jesus dealing with a Syrophoenician woman may have evoked among his audience memories of their volatile relations with the Tyrians, which was part of the Jewish and Gentile hostility that triggered the war with Rome.[47]

Geographical Formation

The criterion of geographical formation concerns bodies of water where some very dramatic events of the war took place. The best candidates for this criterion are the Sea of Galilee and the Mediterranean Sea. Josephus refers to the Sea of Galilee as "Lake Genesar(eth)" (*J. W.* 2:573; 3:463, 515–516),[48] or "Lake Tiberias" (*J. W.* 3:57; 4:456). Pliny calls it the Lake of Gennesareth and Lake Tarichaea (*Nat. Hist.* 5:71).[49] In Mark, Jesus frequently crosses and performs his redemptive activities on or beside this Sea. From the Sea of Galilee he calls his first disciples (1:16–20); on its shore he teaches a large crowd in parables (4:1–34) and crosses to go to Gennesaret, a place where he liberates many people from various illnesses (6:53–56). More importantly, Jesus liberates his disciples from the threat of death due to a severe storm on the Sea of Galilee (4:35–41; 6:45–52).

During the war, the Romans massacred numerous Jews who had taken refuge on the Sea of Galilee. Josephus reports on a horrific naval engagement:

> When any [Jew] who had sunk rose to the surface, an arrow quickly reached or a raft overtook them; if in their despair they sought to board the enemy's fleet, the Romans cut off their heads or their hands. Thus perished these wretches on all sides in countless numbers and countless manners, until the survivors were routed and forced to the shore, their vessels surrounded by the enemy. As they streamed forth from them many were speared in the water; many sprang on land, where they were slain by the Romans. One could see the whole lake red with blood and covered with corpses, for not a man escaped. During the following days the district reeked with a dreadful stench and presented a spectacle equally horrible. The beaches were strewn with wrecks and swollen carcasses: these corpses, scorched and clammy in decay, so polluted the atmosphere that the catastrophe which plunged the Jews in mourning inspired

---

47. Cf. Rhoads, *Reading Mark*, 93–94.
48. See also *Ant.* 5:84; 13:158; 18:28, 36. Cf. Luke 5:1; John 6:1.
49. Cf. Freyne, "Galilee, Sea of," 900. On the various names of the Sea of Galilee, see also Notley, "Sea of Galilee, 183–88.

even its authors with disgust. Such was the issue of this naval engagement. The dead, including those who fell in the previous defense of the town [of Tarichaeae], numbered six thousand seven hundred. (J.W. 3:527–531)

Mark's audience may have contrasted Jesus' liberative activities on the Sea of Galilee with Vespasian's horrific and catastrophic war events just cited above.

In regard to the Mediterranean Sea, the Romans crossed this sea in their move to crush the revolt in Judea. Before they entered Galilee, they encamped at Ptolemais on the Mediterranean coast west of Galilee. From there they advanced to Galilee. It was also on the Mediterranean Sea that a very dramatic and catastrophic war event occurred. The Jews who had taken refuge at Joppa perished either because of the strong storm on the Mediterranean Sea or by the sword of the Romans as they tried to escape the sea storm. Describing this horrendous and catastrophic event, Josephus writes that because of the furious north wind,

> Some of the ships [in which the Jews took refuge] were dashed to pieces against each other on the spot, others were shattered upon the rocks. Many from dread of this rock-strewn coast and the enemy that occupied it, strove to gain the open sea in the teeth of gale, and foundered among the towering billows. There was neither means of flight, nor hope of safety if they remained where they were: the fury of the wind repelled them from the sea, that of the Romans from the town. Piercing were the shrinks as the vessels collided, terrific the crash as they broke up. Of the [Jewish] crews who perished, some were engulfed in the waves, many crushed by the wreckage from which they could not extricate themselves; others, regarding the sword as a lighter evil than the sea, anticipated drowning by suicide. The majority, however, were swept to shore by the waves and their bodies hurled and mangled against the cliffs. A wide area was red with blood, and the coast was covered with corpses; for the Romans, lining the beach, massacred those who were cast up. The number of bodies washed up amounted to four thousand two hundred. The Romans took the town without opposition and razed it to the ground. (J.W. 3:423–427)

Jesus' rescue of his disciples from the deadly sea storm may well have evoked memories of this event of the war on the Mediterranean Sea. In general, Mark's narrative about Jesus' calming of the sea storm and thereby saving his disciples from the threat of death in the Sea of Galilee may have reminded his hearers of these horrible war events on the Sea of Galilee and the Mediterranean Sea.

People and Empire

This criterion concerns people who played an active role during the war in Judea in the service of the Roman Empire, and who at the time Mark's Gospel was composed assumed the title emperor, lord, or king. Vespasian, Titus, and Herod Agrippa II, are the best candidates for this criterion. While Vespasian and Titus assumed the titles emperor and lord, Herod Agrippa II served as a puppet king of the Romans in Judea. Each of them played an active role in the war, serving the interests of the Roman Empire. In the following paragraphs, I describe each one of them, showing each one's role in relation to the war and the Roman Empire.

Vespasian was a low-born Roman general. "He was born into the plebeian class of the Roman society—the Roman working class ranking below the patrician class of Roman nobility."[50] In 66 CE he was appointed by Emperor Nero to stop the Jewish revolt (*J.W.* 3:1–4). His campaign in Galilee was very destructive. Many Jews lost their lives while others were either sent into slavery or displaced (e.g., *J.W.* 3:539–541). While he was still on the battlefield, on Jewish soil, Vespasian was proclaimed emperor. Josephus and other ancient writers claim that Vespasian's rise to this position was a fulfillment of a Jewish prophecy that expected a world ruler to come from Judea (*J.W.* 6:312–313).[51] Vespasian's rise to the imperial throne is also credited to several things, including his military successes, some omens,[52] and his ability to work miracles.

---

50. Winn, *Mark*, 154.
51. Cf. Suetonius, *Vesp.* 4.5 and Tacitus, *Hist.* 5.13.1–2.
52. Omens associated with Vespasian are numerous. Here I show only a few of them as examples. First, at his birth, a sacred oak tree produced a branch with a image of a tree, which was a Roman imperial symbol. His father used this omen to claim that Vespasian would become emperor. Second, one day a dog brought a human hand to Vespasian's dining table, an omen which was associated with power. Another omen relates to an ox that entered Vespasian's dining room and bowed its head at Vespasian's feet, suggesting that he was the person before whom sacrifice was to be offered. Next, when Vespasian was on a battlefield in Judea, Nero had a dream in which he instructed Vespasian to move a sacred chariot of Jupiter to the general's house and then to the Circus. Also a statue of Julius Caesar in Rome turned from west to east, suggesting the origin of the next emperor. Moreover, two eagles fought at Betriacum, the field where witnessed Vitellius's victory over Otto. After one won, a third eagle appeared from the east and defeated the formerly victorious eagle. The parallels with the Roman civil war of 69 CE are undeniable. There were also Josephus's prophecy that indicated Vespasian

Vespasian's ability to perform miracles is evident in the restoration of the sight of a blind man and the healing of a man's withered hand. While Vespasian used spittle to heal the blind man, he restored the man's withered hand by stepping on it. His power to heal was granted by the god Serapis (Tacitus, *Hist.* 4:81; Suetonius, *Vesp.* 7.2). Since he originated from a lower class, and people thought it was impossible for one from that class to rise to the position of emperor, it has been argued that Vespasian used these omens, prophecies, and supernatural powers as propaganda tools to legitimize his imperial power.[53]

When he became emperor, Vespasian confiscated land in Judea and imposed a poll tax among the Jews. Josephus shows that after 70 CE, Vespasian owned land in Judea. Elsewhere, Josephus relates that "Caesar [Vespasian] sent instructions to Bassus and Laberius Maximus, the procurator, to farm out all Jewish territory. For he founded no city there, reserving the country as his private property, except that he did assign to eight hundred veterans discharged from the army a place for habitation called Emmaus, distant thirty furlongs from Jerusalem" (*J.W.* 7:216–217). It is evident from this account that Vespasian leased part of the land while he gave another part to his veterans. Vespasian also gave some land as a gift to his friends as he did to Josephus (*Life* 425). In regard to taxes, Vespasian imposed a poll tax to be paid annually by every Jew. Josephus confirms this: "On all Jews, wheresoever resident, he imposed a poll-tax of two drachmas, to be paid annually into the Capitol as formerly contributed by them to the temple at Jerusalem" (*J.W.* 7:218). Beside this poll tax, it is likely that Vespasian also imposed a property tax in Judea. With respect to Domitian, who became emperor after the death of his brother Titus, Josephus says, "He also exempted my [Josephus's] property in Judea from taxation" (*Life* 429). This statement, especially the word "also" suggests that Domitian did what Titus and Vespasian had previously done for Josephus. Based on this assumption, it can be concluded that Vespasian collected property taxes from the Jews in Judea. Vespasian's roles as a general in the war and also as the emperor represent the values of the Roman Empire that serve as the backdrop for Jesus' teaching about the values of God's empire.

Titus was Vespasian's son born in 39 CE. He was emperor of Rome between 79 and 81 CE.[54] During the war, Titus fought hand in hand with his father to crush the Jewish revolt in Judea. During the Galilean campaign, he

---

would be emperor (*J.W.* 3:399–408; cf. 6:313–314) and an oracle on Mount Carmel (probably in 68 CE) that promised success to Vespasian in whatever he would attempt to do (Suetonius, *Vesp.* 8.5). See also Winn, *Mark*, 158–59.

53. Winn, *Mark*, 154–64.
54. Jones, "Titus," 580–81.

was prominent in the sieges of Jotapata, Japha, Tarichaea, and Gamala (*J. W.* 3:142—4:11). He also led the attack upon and conquest of Gischala (*J. W.* 3:84–120). When Vespasian left for Rome to officially occupy the imperial throne, Titus became the chief commander of the Roman armies in Judea and led the siege of Jerusalem that climaxed in the fall of the holy city and its temple in 70 CE (*J. W.* 6:354–55, 228; 7:1–4). In order to ensure that Jews would not attempt any other revolt, Titus left in Jerusalem "the tenth legion, along with some squadrons of cavalry and companies of infantry" (*J. W.* 7:5). In June 71 CE, he celebrated a joint triumph with his father in Rome (*J. W.* 7:123–57) and served as a "deputy-emperor."[55] It is therefore not surprising that Josephus frequently refers to him as Caesar (e.g., *J. W.* 5:67, 94, 97; 6:182, 215, 256, 266; 7:96), "imperator" (*J. W.* 6:316), or "lord" (*J. W.* 5:88).[56] Titus died in 81 CE and thereafter was deified.

Titus's military campaign in Jerusalem was catastrophic among the Jews. So many Jews lost their lives. He punished the Jewish captives either by crucifixions or by forcing them to fight with wild beasts. He ordered the crucifixions of masses of Jewish captives such that it was hard to find space for the crosses or the crosses for the bodies. Josephus writes painfully that at Titus's order, the Jews upon their capture:

> were accordingly scourged and subjected to torture of every description, before being killed, and then crucified opposite the walls. Titus indeed commiserated their fate, five hundred or sometimes more being captured daily ... [Titus's] main reason for not stopping the crucifixions was the hope that spectacle might perhaps induce the Jews to surrender, for fear that continued resistance would involve them in similar fate. The [Roman] soldiers out of rage and hatred amused themselves by nailing their prisoners in different postures; and so great was their number, that space could not be found for crosses nor crosses for the bodies. (*J. W.* 5:449–451)

---

55. Milns, "Vespasian," 852. Similarly, Jones, "Titus," 581, states that "Vespasian granted him power so extensive that he was almost co-ruler." See also Dio Cassius, *Rom. Hist.* 65.1, who writes that when "Vespasian was declared emperor by the senate ... [his sons] Titus and Domitian were given the Title of Caesar."

56. Josephus's full account about the reference to Titus as "lord" reads this way: "The friends who out of regard for the commander-in-chief stood their ground indifferent to danger, all earnestly entreated him to retire before these Jews who courted death, and not to risk his life for men who ought to have remained to protect him; he should consider what he owed to fortune, and not act the part of a common soldier, lord as he was alike of the war and of the world; he on whom all depended ought not to face so imminent a risk."

It is evident from this citation that Titus's motive for crucifying such a huge number of Jews was to terrorize, so that the rest of the Jews would be forced to capitulate. Josephus reports on games with wild beasts as another form of torture that Titus inflicted upon his Jewish prisoners. First, he reports that Titus presented multitudes of the captives "to various provinces, to be destroyed in theatres by sword or by wild beasts" (*J.W.* 6:418). Then, he relates that these prisoners died in violent celebratory games, either with wild beasts or with one another in Caesarea Philippi, Caesarea Maritima, Berytus, and in the Syrian cities that Titus visited after his conquest of Judea (*J.W.* 7:23-24, 37-39, 96).

Titus also sent prisoners into slavery and kept others for his triumph in Rome. Elsewhere, Josephus shows that Titus authorized the selection of "the tallest and most handsome youths" among the prisoners to be reserved for the triumph in Rome and those above seventeen years old to be sent into slavery in Egypt (*J.W.* 6:417). Josephus adds that at Caesarea Maritima, Titus ordered that Simon bar Gioras be kept for the triumph soon to be celebrated in Rome (*J.W.* 7:36). In other cases, Titus punished the Jewish captives by cutting off their hands—both to distinguish them from the citizens who submitted to the Romans and to force other Jews to capitulate. About this matter Josephus writes that Titus "gave orders to cut off the hands of several of the prisoners, that they might not be mistaken for deserters and that their calamity might add credit to their statement" (*J.W.* 4:455). All these dealings with the prisoners of war are expressive of Titus's tyrannical behavior and brutality.

Titus was not only tyrannical and brutal, but he was also extravagant. He displayed lavish behavior in the cities he visited after his successful victory over the Jews. At Caesarea Philippi Titus displayed "all kinds of spectacles" (*J.W.* 7:23) and at Caesarea, a city on the coast of the Mediterranean Sea, "he celebrated his brother's birthday with great splendor" (*J.W.* 7:37). At Berytus (modern Beirut), Titus displayed "still greater magnificence on the occasion of his father's birthday, both in the costliness of the spectacles and in the ingenuity of various other items of expenditure" (*J.W.* 7:39). This event was followed by many other "costly spectacles" in the Syrian cities (*J.W.* 7:96) and in Zeugma, on the Euphrates where he provided a banquet to the delegates of Bologeses, king of Parthia who received him there (*J.W.* 7:100-106). This extravagant behavior is expressive of how Titus used his wealth to maintain his status and honor.

Titus's wealth is also expressed in terms of his land ownership in Judea. Elsewhere Josephus relates that Titus reserved land for the Roman garrison that was quartered there and that he gave a gift of land to Josephus (*Life* 422). The fact that Josephus says specifically that Titus gave him land and that he reserved some for his troops (probably the legion, *J. W.* 7:5) is strong evidence that Titus had land in Judea. He either confiscated it after the conquest of Jerusalem or inherited it from his father. Titus, perhaps like his father, farmed out his land to others. There is also evidence that when he became emperor, he collected property taxes from Judea. Josephus's remark that he was exempted from paying a tax for his property in Judea (*Life* 429) strongly suggests that the tax was farmed from other Jews. While Josephus was exempted, other Jews paid it.

As for Herod Agrippa II, he was the son of Herod Agrippa I and king of Judea the entire period of the war. He became king in 48 CE, following the death of Herod, king of Chalcis. At first, Emperor Claudius appointed him to rule Chalcis (*J. W.* 2:223). Although he began as ruler of a small kingdom, he was later assigned a larger kingdom encompassing what previously under Herod Philip were called "Trachonitis, Baranaea, and Gaaulanitis; [and] the kingdom of Lysania and the old tetrarchy of Varus" (*J. W.* 2:247). During the time of Nero, Herod Agrippa II's kingdom expanded to include cities of "Abila and Julias and Perea, and Tarichaea and Tiberias in Galilee" (*J. W.* 2:252). Gamala, near the Sea of Galilee and opposite Tiberias (*J. W.* 3:56; cf. 4:2) also became part of his realm. Titus's roles in the war, too, serve as a foil for Jesus' teaching concerning values in the empire of God.

In relation to the war, Agrippa II was pro-Rome. Josephus expresses the king's pro-Roman attitude in various ways. For example, shortly before the war, when the populace protested against Florus's abuses: plunder of funds from the Temple treasury, his tyranny involving crucifixions, and corrupt behavior (*J. W.* 2:293-308), Agrippa II treated the Jews repressively. He may have been truly indignant at Florus's brutality as Josephus narrates, "but diplomatically turned his resentment upon the Jews who at heart he pitied, wishing to humiliate their pride . . . to divert them from revenge" (*J. W.* 2:337). Although the chief priests, the leading citizens and the council, "being men of position, and as owners of property desirous of peace, understood the benevolent intention of the king's reprimand" (*J. W.* 2:336, 338), the ordinary people, however, pressed for appeal to Nero (*J. W.* 2:342).

For his part, the king maintained that the Jews should keep loyalty to Caesar. In his long speech stating that he intended to avoid the war with Rome, Agrippa II urged the Jews to pay tribute to Caesar: "you have not paid your tribute to Caesar . . . pay the tax" (*J. W.* 2:404). Although the arrears of the tribute amounting to forty talents was collected, not all agreed with the king. The people "heaped abuse upon the king and formally proclaimed his banishment from the city" (*J. W.* 2:405-407). This incident was immediately followed by the abandonment of the sacrifices for Caesar. Eleazar ben Ananias, the captain of the temple persuaded those who served in the Temple not to accept sacrifices from foreigners. The act "laid the foundation of the war with the Romans" (*J.W.* 2:409; cf. 2:403, 414).

King Agrippa II expressed his pro-Roman attitude throughout the war. During the revolt in Jerusalem, he provided the authorities with two thousand troops in order to suppress the revolt (*J.W.* 2:421). At the outbreak of the war he not only supplied Cestius, governor of Syria with troops (two thousand foot soldiers and less than two thousand horses) that fought against the Jews in Alexandria (*J.W.* 2:500), but he also "personally accompanied Cestius, to guard and provide for the interest of the army" (*J.W.* 2:503). At the coming of Vespasian to stop the revolt, king Agrippa II and his troops received the Roman general at Antioch, Syria (*J.W.* 3:29). He also gave Vespasian "two thousand bowmen and a thousand cavalry" (*J.W.* 3:68) and at Caesarea Philippi entertained the Roman general with a lavish feast. According to Josephus, King Agrippa II entertained "the general and his troops with all the wealth of his royal household" (*J.W.* 3:443). During Titus's campaign at Gamala, the king was also there with his troops fighting on the Roman side. He also received 30,400 war prisoners from Taricharea that Vespasian gave, but he sold them into slavery (*J.W.* 3:541). Agrippa's role in the war shows how Jewish leadership was supportive or acquiescing Roman oppression, which may help to explain Mark's altitude towards some Jewish leaders.

The criterion of people and Empire manifests the values of the Roman Empire exemplified in Vespasian's and Titus's behavior and actions. The two commanders used military power, not only to dominate others, but also to acquire the "whole world" and wealth in the form of land for themselves. They also crucified others in order to terrorize them. Moreover, they lorded over others by imposing taxes on them or by enslaving them. Further, they displayed their wealth in lavish feasts while they starved others. Mark's reference to Jesus' teachings on the values of God's empire—carrying the cross, losing and saving life, gaining the whole world (8:34–38); being a slave and servant of all, and not lording over as the Gentiles do (10:42–45; cf. 9:35)—may have reminded Mark's audience, though by contrast, of the actions and values of Vespasian and Titus, the representatives of Gentile rulers. Mark's reference "to paying taxes to the emperor" (12:14) may have evoked Jewish memories of the cessation of sacrifices on behalf of Caesar by the revolutionaries that marked the beginning of the war (*J.W.* 2:409; cf. 2:197, 404, 413) as well as the current taxes imposed by Vespasian after the war.

As a puppet of the Romans, King Herod Agrippa II not only served the interests of the Roman Empire, but also imitated the Roman values. He fought against and killed his own people to protect his own position of power, status, and honor. Mark's reference to Herod (6:17–29), for example, may have evoked among Mark's hearers memories about the role of Herod Agrippa II in the war. In relation to Jesus' teaching about the values of God's empire, Mark's audience may have viewed Herod Agrippa II as a negative example of Jesus' teaching about not using power and authority in a manner of the Gentile authorities (10:42–45).

Verbal Parallels

The criterion of verbal parallels concerns the events of the war that Mark depicts in the Gospel. The verbal parallels that Mark makes in relation to war events include the military terms and expressions evident in the story of the Gerasene demoniac (5:1–20) and in the feeding story (6:30–44). In the story of the Gerasene demoniac there are many military terms, but the most important one is the term *legion*.[57] This term is expressive of the Roman military forces. Such a term may have reminded Mark's audience of the Romans' fifth, tenth, fifteenth, or twelfth legions and other forces (*J. W.* 3:65–69; 5:41) that had just destroyed their fellow citizens, that had plundered their property, and put their nation under continual Roman domination. It may also have reminded them of the presence in Jerusalem of the "tenth legion, along with some squadrons of cavalry and companies of infantry" that Titus left there after his conquest of the city and its temple (*J. W.* 7:5).

The military expression in Mark's feeding story (6:30–44) relates to the arrangement of people in groups. Mark shows that the people who were fed by Jesus were ordered to sit in companies group by group (6:39–40). Sitting in companies group by group is a military expression linking Mark's story of Jesus and events of the war. Mark's audience may have seen the Roman troops sit in such formation during times of rest and eating. Hence, Mark's feeding story may also have evoked among Mark's audience memories of the events of the recent war.

Events

The criterion of events involves the imperial entrances and the march to Jerusalem. The first event compares Mark's portrayal of Jesus' entrance (1:1–13) and Vespasian's entrances in cities and his establishment of his imperial rule. In regard to the imperial entrances, Mark opens the Gospel by indicating that the advent of Jesus was formerly announced in order to let people prepare for his coming. Mark has God's messenger proclaim:

---

57. A Roman legion consisted of about 6,120 men. See *J. W.* 3:69, note c.

"Prepare the way of the Lord, make his paths straight" (1:3). The Lord here refers to Jesus, whom John identifies as "the one who is more powerful (1:7). When the *kairos* of the coming was ready, "Jesus came from Nazareth of Galilee and was baptized by John in the Jordan" (1:9). Shortly thereafter, Jesus inaugurated his liberative campaigns in Galilee, which he termed the "good news of God" concerning the arrival of God's empire (1:14-15). For Mark, this "good news of God" was inseparable from "the good news of Jesus Messiah, Son of God" (1:1).

Mark's reference to the preparation and making of the Lord's way straight may have been associated with the leveling of the roads for easy passage by the Roman armies. For example, as noted above, before Vespasian entered Jotapata to deal with the Jewish revolutionaries, he first "sent a body of infantry and cavalry in advance to level the road leading to it, a stony mountain track, difficult for infantry and quite impracticable for mounted troops. In four days their task was completed and a broad highway was opened for the army" (*J.W.* 3:141-142). Mark's Jewish audience may have associated the call to "prepare the way of the Lord" (1:3) with the leveling of the road in order to provide easy access for Vespasian's military troops to Jotapata. Reporting about Vespasian's entrances in various cities, Josephus says that Vespasian was received and hailed in divine terms. Upon his arrival at Tiberias, Vespasian was hailed as "savior and benefactor" (*J.W.* 3:459; cf. Titus's entrance at Gischala, *J.W.* 4:112-113).

Moreover, following the proclamation of Vespasian as the emperor, residents of cities received the news of the new emperor as good news. People in all cities in the east celebrated "the good news and offered sacrifices on his behalf" (*J.W.* 4:618). The governors of Alexandria, Moesia, Pannonia, and Berytus, including the legions and people under their authority, all pledged allegiance to Vespasian (*J.W.* 4:619, 621). In Rome, the people waited for Vespasian's arrival with "heartfelt-joy and satisfaction . . . and were paying respect to him in their hearts as if he were already come, mistaking, in their keen desire, their expectation of him for his actual arrival" (*J.W.* 7:63-64). The people, the Senate, and the army, all were confident that Vespasian alone would "bring them salvation," "security," and "prosperity" (*J.W.* 7:66-67). Thus when Vespasian arrived in Rome, they hailed him as their "'benefactor,' 'savior,' and 'only worthy emperor of Rome'" (*J.W.* 7:71). Mark's hears may have linked the narrative about Jesus' entrance, the good news, his status as Son of God, and the announcement of God's empire to these events of the war associated with Vespasian's entrances, military victory, and the establishment of his imperial rule—all of which were celebrated as good news, and his divine status.

Furthermore, Jesus' entry into Jerusalem on a donkey (11:1–11) and the reference to the temple being turned into "a den of robbers" instead of being a house for international prayer (11:17) also link the Gospel with the war. Jesus' triumphal entry alludes to Menachem's and Simon bar Gioras's messianic claims[58] and their respective "entries" to Jerusalem, as well as to the triumph in Rome that marked Vespasian's enthronement and Titus's victory against the Jews (J.W. 7:70–71, 122–162). The status of the temple being changed into "a den of robbers" instead of being "a house of prayer for all the nations" (11:17) reflects the Zealots' occupation of the temple and making it the center of their tyranny (J.W. 4:155–157, 196–207; 5:5)[59] and the revolutionaries' refusal to accept sacrifices from the Gentiles, an action that meant a declaration of war with Rome (J.W. 2:209–415, 404). Therefore, Jesus' entry into Jerusalem may have evoked memories among Mark's audience of the messianic pretenders who were active during the war.

In sum, I do not intend to apply those criteria to each item I discuss in this book. They have guided me. Naming them may assist others in further developing a methodology for correlations between Mark's Gospel and the war.

Literature Review

In his PhD dissertation, "A Social Description of the Community Reflected in the Gospel of Mark" (1974), James A. Wilde reads Mark using a twofold methodology: redaction criticism and constructive typology from sociological theory. His primary goal is to give "a social description of the religious community or communities reflected in the Gospel of Mark."[60] Wilde argues that Mark wrote to respond to his community's eschatological expectations, Roman imperial domination (primarily the advance of

---

58. The messianic claims of these revolutionaries are expressed either through their own actions or the actions of people toward them. At the beginning of the revolt, Menachem marched from Masada to Jerusalem "like a veritable king" (J.W. 2:433–434) and entered the temple while dressed "in royal robes" (J.W. 2:44). Simon bar Gioras proclaimed release of slaves and reward to the liberated (J.W. 4:508), people expressed loyalty to him "as to a king" (J.W. 4:510), they praised him as "their savior" (J.W. 4:575–576), and after the temple was destroyed he appeared in "white tunics" and "purple mantle" (J.W. 7:26–36). If Jesus' entry into Jerusalem is viewed in terms of the Davidic messianic hopes, then Jesus' procession can also be seen as reflecting Menachem's and Simon bar Gioras's messianic pretentions, hence Mark's false messiahs (13:21–22).

59. Cf. Mason, *Josephus and the New Testament*, 93, who notes that Mark 11:17 "corresponds to Josephus' most typical description of the rebel leaders as bandits, who have perversely made the temple their fortress."

60. Wilde, "Social Description," 1.

the Roman troops into Judea), legalistic Judaism, and the zealot military movement.[61] He contends that a revolutionist response is key for understanding Mark's community.[62]

Wilde views Mark 13 as crucial for dating and interpreting the whole Gospel. He argues that the contents of this chapter reflect the situation of 66–70 CE hence presenting not only the immediate local situation that occasioned the writing of the Gospel, but also the dimensions of the broader world as Mark sees it.[63] Although Wilde insists that the Gospel was written primarily to respond to the situation of 69–70 CE,[64] he dates it prior to the fall of the temple, either in 67 CE when Cestus Gallius threatened to destroy it or in the spring of 70 CE when Titus gathered his Roman forces before the walls of Jerusalem.[65]

Wilde's analysis of Mark 13 provides useful insights about Mark's Gospel. For example, that the "many" who will come in Jesus' name (13:5–6) and "the false messiahs and false prophets" (13:21–22) are the revolutionaries who incited others to take up arms to join the war;[66] councils and synagogues (13:9) relate to Jewish courts during the war representing the Romans and Jewish authorities";[67] "the desolating sacrilege" (13:14) signifies Titus and his troops in Judea when they brought their standards in the temple court in late 69 or early 70 CE.[68] Wilde notes that in the context of impending war against the Roman imperial domination, "Mark looked forward to transformation of

---

61. Ibid., 284–85. Wilde argues that the Zealot messianists who resisted Titus's advancing troops by military means provided the immediate occasion for the writing of the gospel. They campaigned and recruited other Jews to make up arms and confront the Roman troops: "Mark's more immediate opponents, providing a proximate occasion for writing the Gospel, were the Zealot messianists who resisted Titus' advancing troops with extreme militancy . . . Their proposal was to enlist the help of anyone around (including members of Mark's community and their friends in Judea) to confront the Roman army. This recruiting effort took advantage of revolutionalist religious rhetoric from messianic traditions which pointed to the necessity of war to usher the final time. They transported a revolutionalist response into a revolutionary one to serve their highly charged military interest."

62. Ibid., 61.
63. Ibid., 69.
64. Ibid., 288.
65. Ibid., 85.
66. Ibid., 100–105, 256–58.
67. Ibid., 79.
68. Ibid., 83, 183. The desolating sacrilege here is the presence of the Roman troops in the holy land. Since Wilde dates the gospel prior to the fall of the temple, the sacrilegious desolation does not include Titus's entrance into the temple with his troops and their action therein.

the whole social world by divine agency in the imminent arrival of the Son of Man on clouds with power and glory (13:26)."[69]

Although Wilde's work offers a great contribution to the scholarship of Mark's Gospel, it is however, not without weaknesses. For example, even though Wilde admits that the Jewish revolt occasioned the writing of the Gospel, he fails to include in his dissertation some very important events of that war. Nowhere does he show how Jesus' triumphal entry into Jerusalem might have been linked to Menachem's march from Masada to Jerusalem at the early stages of the war (J.W. 2:433–434). When he makes reference to the act of turning the temple into being a "hideout for thieves" or "robbers' hideout,"[70] Wilde makes no effort to link this with the zealots' occupation of the temple at the beginning of the war (J.W. 4:155–157; 196–207; 5:5). Neither does he discuss the revolutionaries' exclusion of Gentiles from accessing God in the temple as expressed by their denial of Gentiles' sacrifices, an action that provoked the Romans to take up arms (J.W. 2:409–410, 414–415). Elsewhere, Wilde shows that Mark's Jesus is "truly the promised Davidic Messiah (14:61; 15:32), though clearly not of this world,"[71] but he gives no details as to how this understanding differs from that of other Davidic messianic expression depicted in the Gospel (e.g., 10:46–52; 11:10–11; 12:35–37).

In *Mark's Story of Jesus* (1979), Werner Kelber uses a literary approach in his attempt to interpret the story of Jesus in Mark's Gospel. He views Mark's Gospel as a document from the northern Galilean-Syrian region composed in the aftermath of the Roman-Jewish War.[72] Since he believes that the crisis of the war and the fall of the temple provide the broad historical context of Mark's Gospel, Kelber insists that the reading of the Gospel must consider the events of the war.[73] He himself does so by reading the whole Gospel of Mark in the light of the war and draws his conclusion about the purpose and significance of the Gospel on the basis of the destruction of the Holy City. Kelber writes, "Viewed in light of the destruction of Jerusalem the Gospel does not pronounce judgment on the mother church as much as it seeks an explanation for its extinction. Mark is . . . a prophetic type of writer who searches for an answer to a terrible crisis. It is from this perspective also that the religious significance of

---

69. Wilde, "Social Description," 279.
70. Ibid., 218, 241.
71. Ibid., 239.
72. Kelber, *Mark's Story of Jesus*, 13.
73. Ibid., 14.

Mark's Gospel will come into full view."[74] Kelber's work is a successful attempt to read Mark in the light of the war. A major setback, however, is his failure to show how the Gospel narrative relates to the events of the war. His whole book (96 pages) contains no single reference to the writings of Josephus, who has written the history of the war, not to mention the lack of any reference from any other source.

Ched Myers (1988) reads Mark's Gospel in relation to the Roman-Jewish War of 66–70 CE. He considers the Gospel as a Galilean document composed in 69 CE, and argues that it responds to the whole dynamics of the war. Myers reads Mark from a political perspective using a multidisciplinary approach involving literary criticism, social historical, and political hermeneutics. Considering the Roman-Jewish War as the most immediate background of the Gospel, Myers reads Mark in the light of the events of the war when the temple was still standing.[75] He sees a number of links between the Gospel and the war. For example, he relates Jesus' entry into Jerusalem with Menachem's procession at the early stage of the revolt and notes that Mark's portrayal of Jesus riding on a donkey contrasts the military aspect of Davidic messianic hopes that Menachem expressed.[76] He argues that the words "wars and rumors of war" (13:7) were rebels' ideology used to recruit supporters to join their messianic final battle. Myers contends that Mark used the words to critique the rebel recruiters. He insists that "Mark is counter-recruiting, challenging the grounds upon which Jews are being conscripted into the 'final battle.'"[77]

In addition, Myers understands the "devastating sacrilege" (13:14) as referring not only to a single sacrilegious act in the temple, but also to the destruction of all of Jerusalem. He, however, insists that the Roman troops are the first referent as the desolating sacrilege.[78] He relates Mark's "false messiahs" with Menachem and Simon bar Gioras, the Jewish rebels who acted as popular kings in the tradition of David[79] and states that Mark critiqued the revolutionaries' view of a messiah that involves military campaigns. Mark contrasts the military messiah with Jesus whose messiahship is associated with crucifixion. Myers insists that "Mark was convinced that only the way of the cross, not the sword, could truly overthrow the historical

---

74. Ibid., 91.

75. Myers, *Binding the Strong Man*, 41. Elsewhere, he notes that the events in Mark 13:5–25 make "perfect sense when interpreted against the backdrop of the late years of the war, just before or during the siege of Jerusalem" (ibid., 418).

76. Ibid., 294–95, 319.

77. Ibid., 332.

78. Ibid., 335.

79. Ibid., 337.

reign of the powers."[80] Myers's study is insightful and intriguing. His treatment of the whole Gospel as a coherent narrative in the light of the war events is compelling. My reading of Mark draws insights from his work, but I differ from him in that I date Mark after the fall of the temple involving events and dynamics of the war after 69 CE.

In 1990, Paula Fredriksen wrote an article concerning Jesus and the temple in Mark.[81] In her article she examines the traditions about Jesus and the temple in the light of the Roman-Jewish War of 66–70 CE. She argues that the first Jewish revolt influenced the writing of the Gospel.[82] Although she makes this claim, Fredricksen does not show in her article how exactly Mark links the Gospel to the events of the war. There is no consideration at all of Jesus' reference to the temple as "a house of prayer for all nations" (11:17). It would have been more helpful if Fredricksen would have considered Mark's expression about the temple in relation to the events of the war, especially the Jewish revolutionaries' exclusion of Gentiles from participating in the temple, an action signified by their refusal to accept Gentile sacrifices (J.W. 2:409–410, 412–415).

Joel Marcus has made a serious attempt to read Mark's Gospel in light of the events of the first Jewish revolt against the Romans. Using a redaction critical approach in his insightful article, "The Jewish War and the *Sitz in Leben* of Mark" (1992), Marcus argues that Mark's Gospel manifests a massive influence from the Roman-Jewish War (66–74 CE), an event to which the community of Mark stood in both geographical and temporal proximity.[83] He views the prophecies in Mark 13, the description of the temple as "a den of brigands" (11:17), and Mark's treatment of the Davidic messianic hopes (10:46–52; 11:10–11; 12:35–37) as evidence for the setting of the Gospel. He considers Mark's Gospel as a post-war document written shortly after the fall of the temple in 70 CE in one of the Hellenistic cities of Palestine. Because of the explanations of the Jewish customs (7:3–4), Marcus believes that the community of Mark was "predominantly Gentile."[84] I agree with most of Marcus's arguments and this work builds on insights from his work. However, Marcus's argument that Mark's community was primarily Gentile is questionable because Mark's Gospel is full of references from Jewish Scriptures. Why would Mark write to Gentiles from such a strong Jewish perspective? It is my opinion that Mark's community was a faith community

---

80. Ibid., 430.
81. Fredriksen, "Jesus and the Temple," 293–310.
82. Ibid., 306–7.
83. Marcus, "Jewish War," 442.
84. Ibid., 460–61.

of people who had experienced the crisis and effects of the war living in rural Galilee and/or southern Syria.

Craig A. Evans has made a study on a similar text used by Fredricksen, but with a different emphasis. Evans examines the meaning of Jesus' action in the temple court (11:17) using redaction critical approach.[85] He argues that the phrase "cave of robbers" originates from Jesus himself who spoke alluding to Jeremiah 7:11, thus rejecting the view that the words were later Christian insertion. Evans argues that Jesus' utterance agrees with the action in the temple and the pre-70 CE social and religious setting.[86] Then he concludes by stating that the allusion to "Jeremiah's 'cave of robbers' constitutes an important link between Jesus' action in the temple and his execution."[87] What I see is lacking in Evans's article is the connection between the phrase "den of robbers" with the Zealots, who, at the beginning of the war, occupied the temple and made it their stronghold. The consideration of this aspect would have shown a useful link between Mark's Gospel and the events of the war.

In his book, *The Abomination of Desolation in the Gospel of Mark* (1999), William A. Such links Mark's Gospel with the Roman-Jewish War of 66–70 CE.[88] Such regards Mark as a post-70 CE document whose readers were located "in Syria" or in one of the "Hellenistic cities."[89] His primary goal is to understand the meaning of the phrase "the abomination of desolation" (13:14). Employing a syntactical analysis of the text and historical events that produced the text,[90] he argues in favor of Titus as the candidate in 13:14. His conclusion is based on Titus's order of his troops to perform sacrilegious activities in the temple court (*J. W.* 6:316).[91] My reading of Mark does not question Such's conclusion, but supplements it by including the referent in 13:14, the Zealots who, during the war occupied the temple and fought from there.

William R. Telford has studied Mark's Gospel from a theological point of view.[92] He dates the Gospel just after the fall of Jerusalem,[93] i.e. in the

---

85. Evans, "Jesus and the 'Cave of Robbers,'" 93–110.
86. Ibid., 108.
87. Ibid., 110.
88. Such, *Abomination*.
89. Ibid., 6.
90. Ibid., 6–8.
91. Ibid., 102, 206.
92. Telford, *Theology*.
93. Ibid., 13.

early 70s and places its origin in a Gentile location other than Rome.[94] In his study, Telford examines the theology of Mark focusing on "Christology, soteriology and eschatology,"[95] using traditional critical methods, form and redaction criticism, as well as literary critical insights.[96] On Christology, Telford argues that Mark's concern was to correct a false Christology current in the church. He claims that Mark attacks the Christology based only on glory held by the Jerusalem church in favor of the Christology based on the suffering and death of Jesus on the cross. He argues that for Mark, any attempt to see Jesus from the viewpoint of the Jewish messianic hopes is a false Christology[97] that Mark rejects.[98] Telford's study does not relate Jesus' Christological titles to actions of some Jewish revolutionary leaders who made pretentions during the war and Vespasian's imperial propaganda. In this regard, Telford does not take the events and dynamics of the war very seriously.

In his article, "Tyranny, Boundary and Might: Colonial Mimicry in Mark's Gospel" (1999),[99] Tar-siong Benny Liew writes about Jesus power and authority in Mark. Using a propaganda approach, Liew argues that Mark's Jesus imitates the Roman imperial power in at least three ways. First, he sees that Mark "attributes absolute authority to Jesus."[100] Using the example where Jesus as lord of the house authorizes his servants to keep watch (13:32–37), Liew argues that "Jesus is at the pinnacle of the hierarchy of his household, just as the Gentile or Roman rulers are at the pinnacle of their hierarchy of power, 'lording over' and 'exercising authority over' (10:42b) those who rank below them."[101] Second, Liew argues that since Mark maintains the binary opposites, of insider/outsider and portrays Jesus as an eschatological judge who will authoritatively annihilate all of his opponents, then Mark's Jesus mimics the imperial ideology of "serve-or-be-destroyed."[102]

Third, based on Jesus' authority associated with the events of the parousia, Liew argues that God's ultimate authority entrusted to Jesus "will right all wrongs with the annihilation of the 'wicked'" (12:1–12; 13:24–25). He accordingly states that Jesus authoritatively demands everyone to submit,

94. Ibid., 151–52.
95. Ibid., 8.
96. Ibid., 152.
97. Ibid., 13.
98. Ibid., 51.
99. Liew, "Tyranny, Boundary, and Might," 7–31.
100. Ibid., 13.
101. Ibid., 18.
102. Ibid., 23.

to annihilate anyone who refuses to do so, and defeats "power with power." Again Liew claims that Jesus mimics the ideology of Rome that led to imperial suffering and oppression. He says, "Mark's Jesus may have replaced the 'wicked' Jewish-Roman power, but the tyrannical, exclusionary and coercive politics goes on."[103] Liew's main point is that Mark's Jesus exercises power and authority in the model of the Roman imperial power. However, a careful and close reading of Mark's Gospel reveals that Liew's argument is misleading. Although Mark's Jesus has extraordinary power, he does not use that power to tyrannize or to lord over people. Instead, Mark's Jesus exercises his authority and power to serve to an extent that he is willing even to risk his life for others. Even where annihilation is associated with Jesus, it is not to the innocent in the present world, but it serves as punishment to the wrong doers, that will take place in the world to come.

Most recently Adam Winn has published a commendable book on Mark using historical-critical and comparative-historical approaches. His goal is to discover the purpose of Mark's Gospel based on the social-political realities of Mark and his hearers.[104] He dates the Gospel shortly after the fall of the temple[105] and considers Rome as its origin.[106] Winn argues that Mark's primary purpose was to respond to a Christological crisis within his community in Rome provoked by Vespasian's propaganda that he was the fulfillment of the Jewish messianic hopes. He believes that Mark wrote to tell his hearers that Jesus, not Vespasian, was the true God's Messiah and ruler of the world, and to encourage them to pay royalty to him.[107]

Moreover, Winn suggests two secondary purposes for the composition of Mark. Such goals were "to encourage his community to remain faithful to their Messiah in the face of (imminent) persecution" and "to alleviate his community's eschatological anxiety and confusion by providing eschatological instruction."[108] While the need for encouragement to remain faithful to Jesus was necessitated by the eschatological excitement created by the fall of Jerusalem,[109] the need for the alleviation of fear was provoked by

103. Ibid., 24–26.
104. Winn, *Mark*, 42.
105. Ibid., 76, 153.
106. Ibid., 92.
107. Ibid., 201, 203.
108. Ibid., 203–4.
109. Ibid., 203. According to Winn, the belief among Mark's hearers that the destruction of Jerusalem and the temple were signs of an imminent end of time provoked fear and confusion in the community. Mark responded by telling his community that those events were not eschatological signs of the imminent end, for the actual sign of the eschaton, which was "the abomination of desolation," had not yet come. Mark urged

the post-70 CE ant-Jewish expressions.[110] Winn's major contribution toward Mark's scholarship is his examination of the Christology of Jesus in light of Vespasian's reign in Rome after the Roman-Jewish War. This book differs from Winn's work in that apart from locating Mark's origin in rural Galilee and or southern Syria, it focuses on the hearers' response to the Gospel rather than on Mark's purpose as he does.

In sum, from the reviewed literature it is evident that most scholars of Mark recognize the fact that the Roman-Jewish War of 66–70 CE influenced the writing of Mark's Gospel. It is also true that not all scholars of Mark read the Gospel in the light of the events of the war. Even those who acknowledge that Mark was influenced by the war make no links to the events and dynamics of that war. These are issues clearly covered in this book. Since Mark was written shortly after the war, hearers with fresh memories of the war might have evaluated the Gospel in terms of the events, dynamics, and purposes of the war.

Outline and Synopsis

I indicated earlier that the goal of this book is to read Mark's Gospel in the light of the Roman-Jewish War of 66–70 CE in order to explore how Mark's hearers may have heard and evaluated Mark's story in relation to the events of the war. To reach this goal, I have divided this book into seven chapters. Chapter 1 has dealt with introductory issues: purpose and thesis, methodology, sources, and justification of the book, criteria of correlation, and literature review.

Chapter 2 addresses the issues of Mark's date and origin based on both the external and internal evidence. In this chapter I investigate different views given by scholars about the date and place of Mark's Gospel. Based on both the external and internal evidence from the Gospel, I argue that the Gospel was composed shortly after the Roman-Jewish War of 66–70 CE in rural Galilee and/or southern Syria. This chapter is important in that it highlights the arguments favoring a post war date for the Gospel and the first hearers of the Gospel as the people who had direct experience and effects of the war, hence a close link to the entire argument of the book.

Chapter 3 examines Josephus as a source. This chapter is set to give an account about Josephus as a person, his career, his credibility in using him as a source, and the cause and course of the Roman-Jewish War of 66–70 CE. The significance of this chapter is that it provides a reconstruction of

---

his hearers to be alert and watchful.

110. Ibid., 204.

Mark's Gospel that helps to clarify the hearers' possible response to Mark's story of Jesus.

The next three chapters are the heart of this book. Chapter 4 examines the contrasts between the onset of God's empire and that of the Roman Empire under Vespasian with respect to the use of the word *euangelion*, divine titles, and entrances in both Mark and in the Roman imperial activity. The primary argument in this chapter is that Jesus, not Vespasian, is the true agent of God. I also argue that the true good news is not that which results from military conquests or victory as the Romans understood it, but the coming of Jesus, God's true agent who, being empowered by the Holy Spirit, announced the arrival of God's empire.

Chapter 5 focuses on the contrasts between Jesus' Galilean life-giving campaign and Vespasian's destructive military campaign in Galilee. In this chapter, the events relating to Jesus' public ministry in Galilee are examined in light of Vespasian's military campaign in Galilee. Events of Jesus' public ministry to which attention is paid include the choosing of the twelve, movement from one village to another proclaiming the good news of the empire of God that involves works of power, and Peter's declaration of Jesus as the Messiah. All these events are evaluated in light of Vespasian's crossing of the sea from Rome to Judea, gathering and sending of troops to fight in the war, movement in Galilee, his goal to conquer on behalf of the Roman Empire, and the claim that he was the fulfiller of the Jewish oracle that anticipated a ruler of the world who is "lord of land and sea."

Chapter 6 is concerned with the contrasts of values based on the teachings of Jesus provided while on the way to Jerusalem with his disciples. The chapter highlights the contrasts between the values of God's empire illustrated by Jesus through his word and deed and those of the Roman imperial power exemplified by the Gentile and Jewish authorities as well as the disciples. Focus is primarily paid to issues related to wealth, status, and power. Chapter 7 concludes this book with a summary that highlights key contrasts between Mark's story of Jesus and the events of the Roman-Jewish War of 66–70 CE.

2

The Date and Origin of Mark's Gospel

Introduction

THE DATE AND ORIGIN of Mark's Gospel are still contested. The traditional view holds that the Gospel was composed in Rome in the 60s CE. This view is based primarily on Papias's testimony that Mark's Gospel was authored by Mark, who was an interpreter of the apostle Peter. Papias's testimony as preserved in Eusebius of Caesarea (ca. 260–339 CE), reads:

> Mark, became Peter's interpreter and wrote accurately all that he remembered, not, indeed, in order, of the things said or done by the Lord, nor had he followed him, but later on . . . followed Peter, who used to give teaching as necessity demanded but not making, as it were, an arrangement of the Lord's oracles, so that Mark did nothing in thus writing down single points as he remembered them. For to one thing he gave attention, to leave out nothing of what he had heard and to make no false statement in them.[1]

This testimony says nothing about the date and place of origin of Mark's Gospel. However, the early church fathers such as Irenaeus and Clement of Alexandria used it to argue for the composition of the Gospel in Rome when Peter was still alive.[2] Irenaeus shows that after the departure (*exodos*) of Peter and Paul from Rome, Mark "handed down to us things which were preached by Peter."[3] Clement of Alexandria is more explicit on this matter.

---

1. Eusebius, *Ecclesiastical History* 3.39.15.

2. The combination of Papias's statement that Mark was a companion of Peter and the reference to the same in 1 Peter 5:13 where "Babylon" is thought to be Rome and as a place from which "Peter" composed 1 Peter, forms the tradition that Mark's Gospel originates from Rome. See Donahue, "Quest for the Community of Mark's Gospel," 819.

3. Irenaeus, *Against Heresies* 3.1.2. The Greek word for "exodus" in Irenaeus's comment on Mark has to be translated to carry the sense of "departure" and not "death," as other scholars suggest. For further discussion on this view, see, e.g., Ellis, "Date and

His account preserved in Eusebius's work reads, "When Peter had publicly preached the word at Rome . . . those present . . . exhorted Mark, as one who had followed him for a long time and remembered what had been spoken, to make a record of what was said; and . . . [Mark] did this, and distributed the Gospel among those that asked him . . . when the matter came to Peter's knowledge he neither strongly forbade it nor urged it forward."[4] This view was also followed by Jerome[5] and Origen,[6] and finally, it became a common tradition in the early church.

The reliability on Papias's witness has not gone unchallenged. Kurt Niederwimmer questioned Papias's testimony and the tradition which identified John Mark (Acts 12:12) as the author of Mark's Gospel. Niederwimmer argued that the link between Mark and Peter in 1 Peter 5:13 is a creation of the author of 1 Peter and that Papias was inspired by this text and used it to give the Gospel an apostolic authority in order to defend it against the Gnostics. Niederwimmer, therefore, believes that Mark's Gospel was not authored by Mark, the interpreter of Peter.[7]

While Niederwimmer has challenged Papias's testimony on Mark, Martin Hengel has defended it as credible for dating Mark's Gospel.[8] In his defense of the plausibility of Papias's tradition, Hengel puts forward two claims. First, he appeals to the link between Mark and Peter, which he claims is independently attested in 1 Peter 5:13, and second, he argues that the Gospel itself was from the beginning "bound up with the authority of the name Peter."[9] Then he concludes claiming that Mark's Gospel "was written in a time of severe affliction in Rome after the persecution of Nero and before the destruction of Jerusalem, probably during AD 69, the 'year of revolution.'"[10] Despite Hengel's defense of the patristic tradition about the authorship of Mark's Gospel, "a direct and uniform Petrine connection has not in practice been a basic premise of most of the studies appearing in the 1960s onwards."[11] Lack of interest in historical questions has led to a shift

---

Provenance of Mark's Gospel," 801–16.

4. Clement, *Hypotypōseis (Outlines)* 6. The tradition is also cited in Theron, *Evidence of Tradition*, 45; and in Black, *Mark*, 137–38.

5. Jerome, *Famous Lives*, 8, cited in Black, *Mark*, 166. In his comment on Mark and his Gospel, Jerome acknowledges indebtedness to Clement and Papias.

6. Origen, *Gospel according to Matthew*, cited in Eusebius, *Ecclesiastical History*, 6.25.5.

7. See Matera, *What Are They Saying about Mark?*, 5. Cf. Black, *Mark*, 256–57.

8. Hengel, *Studies*, 47.

9. Ibid., 52.

10. Ibid., 30.

11. Telford, "Introduction," 2.

away from this traditional view.[12] Currently, a majority of scholars date Mark's Gospel around 70 CE and, besides Rome they locate the Gospel's origin in Palestine or Syria.

Since external evidence based on Papias's tradition has failed to provide plausible answers to the questions of date and place of origin of Mark's Gospel, in this chapter I attempt to establish the date and place of origin of the Gospel using internal evidence available from within the Gospel itself and archaeological finds where possible. I propose that the Gospel was written shortly after the end of the Roman-Jewish War of 66–70 CE and that the Gospel originated from an area directly affected by the crisis and events of that war in a rural location in northern Galilee or southern Syria. I will begin with a discussion on the date, and thereafter consider the place of origin of the Gospel.

Date of the Gospel

Most of the recent scholars of Mark link the Gospel to the events of the Roman-Jewish War of 66–70 CE.[13] However, it is debated whether the Gospel was composed before or after the fall of Jerusalem and the temple in 70 CE.[14] The solution is primarily dependent on how one interprets Mark 13. In this section I attempt to argue in favor of the date being shortly after the destruction of the temple based on internal evidence from the Gospel. But

---

12. Ibid., 2.

13. Marcus, "Jewish War," 442. He notes that "Mark's Gospel reflects the pervasive influence on the community of the first Jewish Revolt." Similarly Rhoads, "Social Criticism," 138, says, "the Roman-Jewish War of 66–70 C.E. affected the writing of Mark's Gospel"; Kelber, *Kingdom in Mark*, 1; Kelber, *Mark's Story of Jesus*, 14, notes that the "Roman-Jewish War and the destruction of the temple provide the broad historical backdrop for the Gospel of Mark, and the reader may keep these events in mind in reading the Gospel"; and Theissen, *Gospels in Context*, 258, assets that "There is a consensus that Mark's Gospel is strongly affected by its proximity to the Jewish war of 66–74 C.E."

14. Scholars who prefer a date before the destruction of Jerusalem and the temple include the following: Hengel, *Studies*, 16, 22, 28; Myers, *Strong Man*, 41, 418; Collins, "Apocalyptic Rhetoric," 15; van Iersel, *Mark*, 47–48; Wilde, "Social Description," 72, 82; Horsley, *Hearing the Whole Story*, 131. The following are scholars who date Mark after the fall of Jerusalem and the temple: Marcus, "Jewish War," 460; Kelber, *Mark's Story of Jesus*, 14; Such, *Abomination*, 3, 171; Radcliffe, "Son of Man," 176; Incigneri, *Gospel to the Romans*, 2, 116; Boring, *Mark*, 15; Brandon, *Fall of Jerusalem*, 185–205; Roskam, *Purpose of the Gospel of Mark*, 94; Theissen, *Gospels in Context*, 262; Moloney, *Gospel of Mark* 8; Telford, *Theology*, 13. The question is left undecided in Brown, *Introduction*, 163, who states that "the failure of New Testament works to make specific and detailed mention of the destruction of Jerusalem and the Temple is very hard to explain."

before I do this I first present the arguments that scholars use to argue for the date prior to the fall of the temple.

Pre–70 CE Date

Scholars who date Mark's Gospel prior to the fall of the temple raise a number of arguments to support their positions. The most important argument they make relates to Mark's description of the destruction of the temple (13:2). Adela Y. Collins, for example, argues that the prophecy in Mark does not correspond to Josephus's account about the destruction of the temple. She points out that while Josephus mentions that the Romans razed the whole city and the temple to the ground leaving only a few towers and portions of the western wall for protection of the garrison that was to be kept there (*J.W.* 6:413; 7:1–2), Mark lacks these details apart from the statement that says: "Not one stone will be left here upon another; all will be thrown down" (13:2). This leads her to conclude that "the prophecy of 13:2 was not fulfilled precisely," and that the "lack of correlation (with Josephus' account) raises doubt about its being a prophecy after the fact."[15] In her view, 13:2 does not represent "a prophecy after the fact" but a prediction of the event that will occur in the future[16] indicating that Mark wrote the Gospel before the temple was destroyed.

Bas M. F. van Iersel holds a similar view to that of Collins. He points out that Mark lacks even the faintest allusion to the destruction of the temple or the siege and conquest of Jerusalem. He argues that contrary to Josephus's details about the temple's destruction by fire (*J.W.* 5 and 6), Mark shows no hint of fire as the means by which the temple was destroyed. Van Iersel says, "While fires of imposing, historic buildings tend to make a great

---

15. Collins, *Mark*, 11; Cf. Hengel, *Studies*, 14, 16, who states that "the announcement of the complete destruction of the temple in Mark 13:2 in no way presupposes the catastrophe of 70. Mark may have formulated this simply in view of the threatening situation in Judea from the time of the sixties by using early tradition stemming from Jesus himself" (ibid., 16).

16. Collins, *Mark*, 11. She bases her argument on Josephus's description of the destruction of the temple in his *J.W.* 7:1–2 and 6:413. Cf. Horsley, *Hearing the Whole Story*, 131, who notes that Mark's story was "composed prior to the destruction of the Temple"; Hengel, *Studies*, 14–16; Sanders and Davies, *Studying the Synoptic Gospels*, 18, who argue that Mark's prediction is technically inaccurate and thus cannot be an action after the event: "The temple was destroyed by fire, and many of the stones remained standing—some can be seen to this day. Here probably have a genuine prediction, not a fake one written after the fact, since it did not come true in a precise sense." Contra Incigneri, *Gospel to the Romans*, 117–22; Harter, "Causes and Course of the Jewish Revolt," 138.

impression there is not a single trace of the burning of the Temple."[17] He emphasizes that 13:2 "cannot be accepted as an indication that Mark was written after the Temple's destruction in 70 C.E."[18] As a result, he proposes that the Gospel was written when the temple was still standing.[19]

Hengel also proposes that Mark's Gospel came into being while the temple was still standing. Mark's lack of details in his description about the siege of Jerusalem and destruction of the temple[20] has compelled him to conclude that "The announcement of the complete destruction of the temple in Mark 13:2 in no way presupposes the catastrophe of 70. Mark may have formulated this sentence simply in view of the threatening situation in Judea from the time of the sixties by using traditions stemming from Jesus."[21] In his view, Mark 13:2 is not a prediction after the event, but a prophecy for the future which, originating from Jesus, anticipated the destruction of the temple that would occur soon as the result of the war.[22]

The case for a pre-70 CE dating of Mark's Gospel also relates to Mark 13:14. The text reads, "But when you see the desolating sacrilege standing where it ought not to be (let the reader understand), then let those who are in Judea flee to the mountains." Our focus is placed on the reference to

---

17. Van Iersel, *Mark*, 46.

18. Ibid., 47; cf. Brown, *Introduction*, 163, shows that Mark has failed "to show any knowledge of the details of the first Jewish Revolt against Rome in AD 66–70 and to mention the fall of Jerusalem." Similarly, Ellis, "Date and Provenance of Mark's Gospel," 812, notes that Mark shows no knowledge of the fall of the temple. Other scholars with similar view include Guelich, *Mark*, xxxi; Gundry, *Mark*, 1042.

19. Van Iersel, *Mark*, 48. See also Lagrange, *Saint Marc*, xxxi, who states that "it is utterly impossible to date the Gospel of Mark after the destruction of the Temple of Jerusalem."

20. Hengel, *Studies*, 20, asserts that "it is extremely improbable that Mark should have written after the destruction of Jerusalem by Titus without clearly referring to it. The content does not suggest in any way that it was written after this catastrophic year (70 CE)."

21. Ibid., 16.

22. Contra Radcliffe, "Son of Man," 180. Objecting to dating Mark prior to the fall of the temple, Radcliffe lists references to the fate of the temple: Jesus overturns the tables of the money changers in the temple (11:15–17) and curses the fig tree that symbolizes the temple (11:20–21); the parable against the tenants of the vineyard is told in the temple (12:1–12), and Jesus utters a prophecy about the destruction of the temple (13:2); the charge against Jesus is that he said he would destroy the temple and build another (14:58); Jesus is mocked on the cross: "Aha! You who would destroy the temple and build it in three days, save yourself, come down the cross!" (15:29-30); and the temple curtain is ripped apart when Jesus dies (15:38). Finally, Radcliffe correctly concludes, "This obsession with the doomed sanctuary would have no sense if it was still standing when Mark wrote, especially as Josephus tells us that Romans had never intended to destroy it when they captured Jerusalem."

"the desolating sacrilege" and the call to flee from Judea to the mountains. Proponents of the theory that Mark's Gospel was written before the fall of the temple use these references as evidence in support of their view. Hengel, for example, believes that the references reflect the political situation in Rome shortly after Nero's death but before Titus destroyed the temple in 70 CE. Referring to Mark's Gospel, he states that: "It presumably came into being in the politically turbulent time after the murder of Nero and Galba and before the renewal of the Jewish War under Titus . . . between winter of 68/69 and the winter of 69/70. The destruction of the temple is not yet presupposed; rather, the author expects the appearance of Antichrist (as *Nero redivivus*) in the sanctuary and the dawn of the last, severest stage of the messianic woes before the parousia."[23]

Similarly, Collins sees that the reference to "the desolating sacrilege" and to the flight to the mountains as evidence for the dating of Mark's Gospel prior to 70 CE. She states that the narrator's comment: "let the reader understand" (13:14b) suggests that both "the abomination and command to flee were of immediate relevance to the audience at the time of writing,"[24] hence representing the events of the future from Mark's perspective.[25]

Collins, however, differs from Hengel regarding the interpretation of the abomination. While Hengel links the abomination to an appearance of an antichrist figure in the image of Nero, she considers the abominator as a statue. Collins links Mark's use of the term "abomination" to Caligula's failed attempt to erect a statue in the Jerusalem temple about 40 CE. She nevertheless argues that in the context of the Jewish revolt, "Mark may have expected the Romans to try again to set up a statue of the emperor as Zeus and to succeed this time."[26] She finally concludes, "it is highly unlikely that the Gospel was written after 70 C.E."[27]

Collins's argument that "the desolating sacrilege" stands for a statue is reinforced by the usage of the Greek word for "sacrilege" in the LXX, where it refers to the image of a god.[28] Collins believes that her interpretation of the word as a statue of a god is credible because, as she claims, in 13:14 the term carries the sense of both the image and the god that it represents. She argues further that this interpretation explains the change from the neuter

23. Hengel, *Studies*, 28. In this regard, Hengel views the appearance of *Nero* as the reverent for the "desolating sacrilege" as well as the false Christ.

24. Collins, *Mark*, 610.

25. Ibid., 13–14.

26. Ibid.

27. Ibid., 14.

28. Ibid., 610, based on Deut 7:25–26;27:14–15; 29:15–16 (vv. 16–17 in English); Isa 2:8, 20; 44:19; Cf. Jer 7:30; Ezek 8:10; 20:30.

noun for "sacrilege" to the masculine participle for "standing." According to her, the masculine participle represents the divine emperor or the god he represents or claims to be.[29] With this interpretation, Collins rejects the theories that "the desolating sacrilege" reflects the Zealots' occupation of the temple or Titus's entrance into "the holy place of the sanctuary" when the temple was in flames (J.W. 6:260).[30] She maintains that the events in Mark 13 reflect the situation in summer 66 CE after Menachem emerged as a messianic leader, and the situation prior to the destruction of the temple in August/September of 70 CE.[31] Collins therefore sets the date of Mark's Gospel before the fall of the temple.

In the case of the call to flee to the mountains (13:14c), advocates of the date prior to the destruction of the temple cite this as evidence for their argument. They argue that after the siege and destruction of Jerusalem and its temple, the call to flight would be irrelevant. Therefore they consider the call to flight as evidence for Mark's lack of knowledge of the last days of Jerusalem.[32] Collins, for example, contends that the agency of the flight would not make any sense if the Gospel was written after the temple had been destroyed. She rejects the idea that there were flights during the siege of Jerusalem and when the fire was consuming the temple. She asks: "what sense would it make to encourage those in Judea to flee at that stage of the war? And what would they be fleeing from?"[33] These questions intensify her rejection of Mark's date after the fall of Jerusalem and the temple.

Hengel shares Collins's view. He argues that once Judea was under the control of Vespasian after the death of Nero in 68 CE, the ability to flee to the mountains must have seemed nonsensical and even fatal for the fugitives. Those who would attempt to escape would risk falling into the hands of either the Romans or the Sicarii. Hengel maintains that even when fleeing was possible during the period before the siege, the flight was not from the city to the mountains, but rather from the countryside into the city.[34] His conclusion is that the flight from Judea to the mountains "does not fit at all into the situation at or after the destruction of the temple and the city or in

---

29. Ibid., 610, including n129.
30. Ibid., 608–10. See also Collins, "Apocalyptic Rhetoric," 25.
31. Collins, "Apocalyptic Rhetoric," 7.
32. Incigneri, *Gospel to the Romans*, 122.
33. Collins, *Mark*, 608–9; cf. Wilde, "Social Description," 86; Horsley, *Hearing the Whole Story*, 131, also argues that if Mark's Gospel was written after the fall of the temple, then it would be pointless "to include the warning against false messiahs and false prophets (13:22), since the outcome of events would have been unmistakably clear."
34. Hengel, *Studies*, 16–18.

the time of the siege, from July to September 70."³⁵ Thus both Collins and Hengel see Mark's Gospel as a document written before the destruction of Jerusalem and its temple. Hengel in particular says explicitly that 13:14 "has nothing to do with the siege or capture of the temple by Titus in 70."³⁶

In my view, the explanations given in favor of the dating of Mark's Gospel prior to the destruction of the temple are less compelling. It is not that the arguments are invalid on their own terms; rather, I find that there are better explanations for the Gospel's postwar date. Mark's internal evidence in support of the date after the fall of the temple is overwhelming. In the following paragraphs I argue that the events in Mark 13 and many other texts within the Gospel support a postwar date for the Gospel.

Post–70 CE Date

Mark 13 contains many references that support the situation of the recent Jewish revolt. The predictions therein are *ex eventu* prophecies that feature the recent Jewish revolt against the Romans, which had a profound effect on Mark's first hearers.³⁷ I contend that Mark 13:2 as a prediction after the event presents a more credible description of the temple than Josephus's account. The lack of precise agreement with Josephus's account on the nature of the temple's destruction is not a decisive argument against Mark's description. Mark's account may have been based on a testimony of witnesses who saw the temple when it was in the process of being torn down stone by stone. Both Matthew 24:2 and Luke 21:6 speak of stones to have been "thrown down" as the way the temple was destroyed. If pulling down of the stones was not the accurate way of talking about the destruction of the temple, these evangelists would not have preserved Mark's language on this matter. Since they speak of the temple's destruction in the sense that stones were "thrown down" supports the idea that Mark's account about the fate of the temple is accurate and that he wrote after the war.

Meanwhile, despite the fact that Josephus was an eyewitness to the events he describes, his account that the temple was razed to the ground by fire (*J.W.* 7:1–4) has been proved to be not only inaccurate but also an exaggeration. According to an Israeli archaeologist Meir Ben-Dov,

> the Temple Mount for which the Romans were responsible was not as grave as Josephus would have had us believe ... Although

---

35. Ibid., 16.
36. Ibid., 18.
37. Marcus, "Jewish War," 446.

> the Romans destroyed the Temple and severely damaged the compound surrounding it, the Temple Mount proper continued to stand as impressive structure; in fact, its walls rose to an appreciable height for centuries thereafter . . . [This leads] us to conclude that the walls from the Second Temple period were still standing up to the height of their decorations during the Byzantine period.[38]

In the light of this archaeological find, one recognizes Josephus's exaggerations on his account about the destruction of the temple. Josephus writes that except for the towers of Phasael, Hippicus, Mariamme, and the western walls, the rest of Jerusalem and the temple were razed to the ground by the Romans. He further reports that "all the rest of the wall encompassing the city was so completely leveled to the ground as to leave visitors to the spot no ground for believing that it had ever been inhabited (*J.W.* 7:1–4). But the archaeological evidence cited above testifies to the contrary. It reveals that Josephus's account is flawed, even though he was an eyewitness of the event.[39]

Josephus's report that the temple was destroyed by fire to the ground is also questionable. Ben-Dov's archaeological dig has revealed the presence of extraordinary huge stones that are thought to have been part of the wall excavated close to the Temple Mount. Those huge stones are present to the present day in the streets of the ancient city.[40] To burn the line stone of such huge sizes and heavy weight would require not only sizable timber but also a large number of them. Josephus, however, shows no indication that the Romans collected timbers for that purpose. His silence suggests that probably the temple was not really burnt to the ground. Hillel Geva's proposal that the temple was deliberately pulled down is very suggestive. Geva states that "Jewish prisoners of war had probably been forced by the Romans to undertake the long, tiring process of destroying the Temple and its surroundings."[41] It is therefore possible that the temple was pulled down, and not burnt down as Josephus claims.

It is possible that Mark was well informed of the initial process of pulling down of the temple, stone by stone. Hence, even if he did not witness the process to its completion, at the time he wrote the Gospel, he assumed that the whole temple was destroyed by having its walls pulled down. The

---

38. Ben-Dov, *In the Shadow*, 186. See also Cline, *Jerusalem Besieged*, 130.

39. Cf. Botha, "Historical Setting of Mark's Gospel," 34; Marcus, *Mark*, 38.

40. Ben-Dov, *In the Shadow*, 88, 185. See also Geva, "Searching," 36–37. Ben-Dov's archaeological find has unearthed remains of huge stones weighing two to five, ten, and fifty tons or more.

41. Geva, "Searching," 36.

idea that the temple was destroyed by pulling the stones down is reinforced by hints from Josephus himself. Elsewhere, Josephus mentions that when the temple was already in flames, Titus's troops "plundered everything that fell on their way" (*J.W.* 6:271) and that they rescued treasures from the temple (*J.W.* 6:387–391). He further relates that curtains or tapestries from the temple were part of the spoils that were displayed during the triumphal procession in Rome (*J.W.* 7:162). This implies that the fire was not severe enough to melt the huge lime stones that made up the temple walls. Otherwise the soldiers would not be able to withstand its heat.

Further, Josephus reports that after the temple had been destroyed Simon bar Gioras appeared at the very place where it formerly stood (*J.W.* 7:29–31). The question is, if the temple was really destroyed by fire, how would this be possible? If the temple had been destroyed by fire as Josephus suggests, one would expect the underground passage to the place where the temple formerly stood to have been blocked by hot rubbles and ashes. Even the spectator who rushed to fetch Simon bar Gioras would not be able to do so if the temple was really razed to the ground by fire. It is therefore likely that the temple was not burnt down as Josephus claims, but that it was pulled down as Mark 13:2 suggests.

If the temple was pulled down as Mark seems to suggest, how then can we explain the fact that Josephus mentions repeatedly that the temple was destroyed by fire? There are two possible ways to explain this. First, probably Josephus was not interested in the destruction of the entire building of the temple, but his focus rather was on the burning of furniture, temple tapestries (the wall-hanging or textiles), and other contents of the temple that could easily burn. The second possibility is to assume that Josephus used the term "fire" in the sense of "heavenly fire" to suggest that the destruction of the temple was ordained by God for the purpose of purifying it. Repeatedly Josephus speaks of the destruction of the temple as divinely ordained. He writes: "God, indeed long since, had sentenced [the temple] to the flames" (*J.W.* 6:250); "God it is then, God Himself, who with the Romans is bringing the fire to purge His temple and exterminating a city so laden with pollutions" (*J.W.* 6:110).[42] So it is possible that Josephus used the term fire to refer to divine punishment of the Jews.

Given the evidence provided, Mark's description about the destruction of the temple is more reliable and compelling than that of Josephus. The archaeological evidence favors Mark's account and stands against Josephus's description. Mark's account suggests that the temple was pulled down stone by stone rather than by fire. Although fire may have destroyed the furniture

---

42. Incigneri, *Gospel for the Romans*, 121.

and some temple tapestries, the total destruction of the temple (*J. W.* 7:1) cannot be credited to it. On the question of details, it is true that Mark does not give details of the events of the war as Josephus does. But there are two possible explanations for this. First, Mark and Josephus had different purposes for their writings. While Josephus's goal was to write a detailed account of the war, Mark's purpose was to proclaim the good news of Jesus and to comment on the events of the war using the story of Jesus. Second, probably Mark had heard of the destruction of the temple but knew nothing of the details. I contend that even without the details, Mark's first hearers would be able to understand the message of the Gospel. Certainly Mark 13:2 supports the dating of Mark's Gospel after the fall of the temple.[43]

There are still many other hints from Mark's Gospel which reinforce the postwar date. The phrase "the end is not yet" which is linked to warnings about "wars and rumors of the war" (13:7) has been considered by Adela Y. Collins as reflecting to the situation of the initial stages of the war, and not after the end of the war. She states that if the war had already been finalized, it would not be necessary for Mark to say that "the end had not yet come."[44] Contrary to Collins's view, I think that the words in question would make no sense at the beginning or at the middle of the war. If Mark wrote the Gospel while the war was still in progress he would not say "the end is not yet," but that the end was about to happen. The words "the end is not yet," would make sense only if Mark wrote the Gospel after the war. This view is supported by the words about the Lord having "shortened the days for the sake of the elect" (13:20). The war of 66–70 CE was the beginning of birth-pangs (13:8), but Mark's Gospel is giving thanks to the Lord that he cut short the days of the war for the sake of the chosen ones. Since Mark was aware that the war was over and that the end did not arrive, he insisted to his hearers that "the end is not yet." Probably Mark made this emphasis in order to correct the notion that the war between the Jews and the Romans constituted the end which then did not happen.[45] Mark did not doubt about the coming of the end, for he noted that "this must take place." However, before this happens "the good news must first be proclaimed to all nations (13:10).

---

43. Cf. Kloppenborg, "*Evocatio Deorum*," 432, who cites Schmithals's argument on Mark's date based on Mark 13:2: "Does the narrator anticipate the destruction of the Temple, or does he look back on it? The latter is more probable; for the *total* destruction of the Temple of which verse 2 speaks corresponds more naturally to the reaction of the Romans after the capture of Jerusalem *that could not be foreseen* . . . Accordingly the narrator is writing in or shortly after 70 C.E." Italics are original.

44. Collins, *Beginning of the Gospel*, 82.

45. Harter, "Causes and Course of the Jewish Revolt," 140.

The reference to "the desolating sacrilege set up where it ought not to be" and the call to "flee to the mountains" from Judea (13:14) also support Mark's date after the fall of the temple. The "desolating sacrilege" has received a variety of interpretations. As van Iersel has noted, "the occupation of the Temple by the Zealots (in 67–68 CE), the profanation of the Temple, the destruction of the Temple (by Titus), the erection of a Roman sacrificial altar or statue in the Temple, setting up of the Roman standards in the Temple, an inspection of the sanctuary by Titus, the manifestation of the antichrist (perhaps in the figure of a Nero *redivivus*), or a combination of two of these events."[46]

As I have noted elsewhere, Hengel and Collins respectively consider that the "desolating sacrilege" refers to an antichrist in the person of Nero *redivivus* and the installation of a statue of a foreign god or the Roman emperor. However, the best candidates for "the desolating sacrilege" seem to be the Zealots' occupation of the temple and Titus's entry into the temple's holy place. Josephus reports that during the war in 67/68 CE, the Zealots not only entered and occupied the temple, but also turned the sanctuary into a centre of their tyranny (*J.W.* 4:155–157, 196–207; 5:5). He says of Titus that when the temple was in flames, he entered and inspected "the holy place of the sanctuary" (*J.W.* 6:260; 4:182–183). Since the Greek term for the abominator is expressed in a neuter noun qualified with a masculine participle "standing" (13:14a), the referent is not a thing such as a statue, but a male person.[47] This understanding favors Titus and the Zealots as the candidates for "the desolating sacrilege" rather than the image of Nero *redivivus*, a statue or standards carried by the Roman troops into the temple's outer court (*J.W.* 7:316, cf. 220, 226).[48] However, in my view, the Zealots might have been tolerable by the Jews because they were also Jews. Titus fits

---

46. Van Iersel, *Mark*, 47–48. Cf. Incigneri, *Gospel to the Romans*, 126–27, who provides a longer list of the various meanings of "the desolating sacrilege," which include the following: "a personal, satanic, Antichrist expected to rule Jerusalem, imperial standards in the Temple in 19 CE, the expectancy of an idol in the Temple based on memories of Caligula's abortive attempt in 40, the expectance of a new Antiochus-like figure, the Roman army before Jerusalem, Jesus' own prophecy, the occupation of the Temple by Eleazar in 67/68, the installation of Phanias as High Priest in 67, and the expectation that Titus would enter the Temple."

47. Roskam, *Purpose of Mark*, 90; Such, *Abomination*, 102, identifies Titus as the candidate in 13:14. Contra Collins, *Mark*, 13–14, who considers Emperor Caligula's statue as the referent.

48. Juel, *Mark*, 179, views the abomination of 13:14 as Titus's standing in the temple. For the view that links the "desolating sacrilege in 13:14" with the Zealots, see Marcus, "Jewish War," 451–52; and Witherington, *Mark*, 345.

better to be the candidate for "the desolating sacrilege." This therefore serves as evidence for the postwar date for Mark's Gospel.

The call to flee to the hills (13:14b), too, is evidence for dating Mark after the war. Repeatedly Josephus indicates that during the war people were forced to flee the city when Titus and his troops entered Jerusalem in April 70 CE. Immediately, after he entered Jerusalem, "Titus dismissed the majority into the country, withersoever they could" (*J.W.* 5:422) and in order to force Jews to surrender rather than escape, he blocked the city (*J.W.* 5:499–508). The fact that he opted for blockage of the city implies that there were chances for the Jews to flee. Sometimes fleeing could mean escaping away from the control of the advocates of the war. For example, when Josephus made a speech before the Jews on behalf of Titus, some of the Jews under the control of the revolutionaries were "watching their opportunity for escaping in safety, off to the Romans." The priests and other aristocrats who managed to escape from Simon bar Gioras were sent to Gophna by the Romans (*J.W.* 6:113–116). Later, Josephus reports that many of those who planned to escape Simon bar Gioras's tyranny were put to death. Then he adds saying that "although multitudes were slain, a far larger number escaped" (*J.W.* 6:382). Given these expressions, I concur with Incigneri who argues that the flight was possible as soon as Titus and his troops laid siege to the city and the temple.[49] Mark's call to flee echoes a situation of the war in which Jews urged one another to escape from the enemies' hands if they could.

Another evidence for Mark's postwar date is found at 13:19. This verse reflects the time after the war rather than the time of Jesus. Mark uses Jesus' prediction to speak in his own time. Mark states thus, "*in those days* there will be suffering, such as has not been from the beginning of the creation that God created until *now*, and never will be." The word *now*, at the end of this verse is of special significance, thus requiring a close attention. The word is within the context of Jesus' prediction of the things which will take place in future, "*in those days*." We would thus expect to hear Mark's Jesus saying, "until *then*" instead of "until *now*." The verse shows a change from Jesus' perspective to that of Mark's perspective. From Jesus' point of view, the phrase "*in those days*" refers to future events. But the word "*now*," though it refers to the same events, represents Mark's perspective. Since the term now concerns the time of Mark, the tribulation expressed in 13:14–23 reflects the actual situation when Mark composed the Gospel.

Still further, the story of the withered fig tree (11:12–14, 20–25) reinforces a postwar date for Mark's Gospel. Mark tells that at Bethany, when Jesus was on his way to Jerusalem with his disciples, he found a fig tree

---

49. Incigneri, *Gospel to the Romans*, 122–26.

without fruits, and cursed it (11:12–14) causing it to wither away to its roots (11:20).[50] With amazement, Peter remarks, "Rabbis, look! The fig tree which you cursed has withered" (11:21). Jesus responds, "Have faith in God" (11:22), and continues to show the significance of putting faith in God, and the importance of prayer and forgiveness. Jesus shows that faith in God can move a mountain into a sea; can make a prayer be answered; and that forgiveness can result in God's forgiveness (11:23–25). In terms of the Hebrew Bible, the fig tree symbolizes Israel and its temple (e.g., Hos 9:10, 16–17; Mic 4:4; Jer 8:13; 24:1–10, etc.). In this regard, the tree's withering to its roots is symbolic of the destruction of the temple. As Warren Carter states: "The curse has taken effect and the tree is dead. In the context of Mark's framing design, the fig tree stands for the temple, and the disaster which befell the tree illustrates what occurred to the temple. Far from being 'cleansed' in order to serve in a new and purified fashion, the temple is condemned and ruined beyond all hope of recovery."[51]

The Torah shows that the temple in Jerusalem was God's dwelling place,[52] which served as a house of prayer and as a place of sacrifices for sin (Isa 56:7; cf. Mark 11:17). Marcus J. Borg comments: "As a place of God's presence, a sign of Israel's election, and the sole locus of sacrifice where atonement was made for sins and impurity it was an institution substantive to the definition and existence of Israel."[53] Its destruction by the Romans sealed God's abandonment of the temple (*J.W.* 6:300). After its destruction, the temple was no longer the point of contact with God. The living faith was now the means of contact between God and humanity (11:22). Mark assures his hearers that God is everywhere[54] and that this God can hear and respond to their prayers whenever and wherever they pray in faith (11:22–25).

50. Cf. Carter, *Roman Empire and the New Testament*, 51, who states that the absence of fruits on the fig tree "signifies the absence of God's life-giving blessing" and a "withered fig tree depicts God's judgment" on the Jewish ruling system (Jer 8:13; 29:17).

51. Kelber, *Kingdom in Mark*, 102; cf. Duff, "March of the Divine Warrior," 68, who notes that "the cursing of a fig tree actually indicates a curse of the Temple." Similarly, Telford, *Barren Temple*, 196, links the withering of the fig tree with the destruction of the temple. He states: "By placing the [fig tree] story . . . in the context of Jesus' visit to the temple, Mark has dramatically indicated that the expected fruitfulness associated with institution is not to be. Its destiny is rather to be withered—*ek rizōn*." The Greek transliteration is mine.

52. Borg, *Jesus: A New Vision*, 161. Cf. "For the LORD has chosen Zion; he has desired it for his habitation: 'This is my resting place forever; here I will reside, for I have desired it'" (Ps 132:13–14); when he completed building the house of God, Solomon said: "I have built you an exalted house, a place for you to dwell in forever" (1 Kgs 8:13).

53. Borg, *Conflict*, 174.

54. Cf. *J.W.* 5:458, where Josephus seems to give a similar impression that the temple in Jerusalem is not the only place for God's dwelling, for God can dwell and be available

Mark believes that forgiveness can be administered even away from Jerusalem. Traditionally forgiveness was exclusively reserved for God to offer through the priests based in the Jerusalem temple (Exod 34:6-7; Isa 43:25 and 44:22; cf. Mark 2:7). But Mark shows that now, forgiveness can be administered unconditionally among members of his community. Those who have faith in God can forgive not only among themselves but also everyone (11:25). In a community where its members experienced betrayal and hate due to the conditions of the war (13:9-13), the need for mutual forgiveness and reconciliation was necessary. With the demise of the temple, forgiveness could be administered everywhere and without the need of priests.

Mark's emphasis on forgiveness fits the situation of the war. Members of his community were to forget the past and instead practice mutual forgiveness. That forgiveness had to be free from any demand of sacrifices, just as Jesus had set an example in his dealing with a paralytic whereby forgiveness takes place far away from the Jerusalem temple and without a demand for sacrifices (2:5). Mark's emphasis on forgiveness in the absence of the temple implies that what is important is no longer the "burnt offerings and sacrifices" but love of God and the neighbor (12:33).

In addition to the teaching on forgiveness, Mark speaks of the faith that can move a "mountain . . . and cast it into the sea" (11:23). The reference to such faith that moves mountains suggests that the temple no longer exists. Although the temple was not literally "cast into the sea," its destruction symbolized its complete elimination.[55] The mention of "this mountain" would evoke in the minds of the readers the connection between the temple that once stood on a mountain, and the prayer and forgiveness administered therein. Mark's readers would recognize that "this mountain" stands for the temple which by its destruction had now been "removed into the sea." They would see that Mark's emphasis on prayer and forgiveness demonstrates that the absence of the temple was not meant to be a hindrance to prayer and forgiveness. They would understand that both prayer and forgiveness are no longer dependent on the temple, but on loyalty to God. Moreover, Mark's hearers would recognize that even in the absence of the temple, God would respond to their prayers no matter

---

to people everywhere, including outside the temple or even in its absence: "the world was a better temple for God than this one." The phrase, "this one" refers to the temple in Jerusalem. Josephus gives this statement with the knowledge of God's abandonment of that temple (J.W. 6:300).

55. Telford, *Barren Temple*, 118-19. He contends that the moving and tree-uprooting images were common among Jews and had different expressions, including not only mountain removal to another place, but also its complete elimination. He further points out that in Mark, the mountain in question is the "Temple Mount" for the Jews understood the temple as "'the mountain of the house' or 'this mountain.'"

when and where they pray, and that God would also forgive them so long as they also forgive others. Thus the teaching based on the withered fig tree that symbolizes the destruction of the temple fits the situation of Mark's community living shortly after the war.

Furthermore, the postwar date of Mark's Gospel is supported by the parable of the vineyard (12:1–12), especially the words referring to the owner of vineyard destroying the tenants and giving the vineyard to others (12:9). In the Old Testament, the one who plants the vineyard is God (Isa 5:2) and the vineyard itself is Israel (Isa 5:7; Ps 80:8–9). Therefore, in Mark's parable God is the owner of the vineyard; the Jewish people are the vineyard; and the tenants are the Jewish authorities: the chief priests, the scribes, and the elders, who have been entrusted by God to care for the Jewish people (12:1, 12). But the Jewish leaders abuse their authority. They beat and kill God's agents. They do not spare even the "beloved Son of God" (12:3–8).[56] Consequently, God, "the owner of the vineyard . . . will come and destroy the tenants, and give the vineyard to others" (12:9). The destruction of Jerusalem and the temple in 70 CE marked the end of the Jewish authority over the Jews. Since then the vineyard (Israel) was given to "others." Collins and Horsley have independently argued that the "others" in the parable refer to the Christians, the followers of Jesus.[57] It is likely they think that the "others" are the twelve, the representatives and projected leaders of Israel. But their view is not compelling because historically Christians have never been leaders of the whole of Israel.

In my view, the "others" are the Romans. After the fall of Jerusalem and its temple the Romans took over leadership of Israel from the hands of the local Jewish authorities, thus leaving the Sanhedrin without any authority. Emil Schürer states that following "the destruction of Jerusalem this Jewish council was immediately brought to an end; the Roman provincial

---

56. Elsewhere in Mark's Gospel, the Pharisees conspire with the Herodians wanting to destroy Jesus (3:6); "the chief priests and the whole council" seek "testimony against Jesus [in order] to put him to death" (14:55); and later they condemn him to death (14:64). Furthermore, Mark shows that the chief priests, the elders and scribes, and the whole council agree to bind Jesus and hand him over to Pilate, the Roman governor (15:1), who then orders his crucifixion (15:15, 24–27, 38).

57. Collins, *Mark*, 547, argues that the parable speaks of "the removal from power of the leaders who oppose Jesus" but like Horsley, refers to "the others" as "among those who accept Jesus as the messiah." Similarly Horsley, *Hearing the Whole Story*, 46, says that the "others" in the parable refer to "Israelite and other villagers represented by the Jesus movement." This proposal is based on his assumption that the parable does not pronounce a condemnation on all Jews, but on "the high priests, scribes, and elders." See also Sabin, *Reopening the Word*, 88, who also regards the "others" as the Christians.

constitution was enforced in a stricter form."[58] Josephus's remark that during the Jewish revolt against the Romans, God's fortune worked in favor of the latter (*J.W.* 3:354, 370), seems to support this view. The parable, therefore, fits the situation of Palestine after the fall of the temple when the Romans replaced the Sanhedrin's authority by their own. Hence, 12:9 is another plausible evidence for Mark's Gospel being a postwar document.[59]

Finally, 15:38 also suggests that Mark's Gospel is a postwar document. The text is part of Mark's description about the death of Jesus (15:33–39). Earlier, Mark had stated that Jesus, shortly before his spirit expired, cried with a loud voice: "My God, my God, why have you forsaken me?" (15:14). But after Jesus had "breathed his last" (15:38), "the curtain of the temple was torn in two from top to bottom" (15:39) indicating not only that "God has not forsaken Jesus,"[60] but also to foreshadow the destruction of the temple.[61] The fact that the incident is also a retrospection of the tearing of the heavens at Jesus' baptism (1:11) reinforces the idea that God did not forsake Jesus.

The tearing of the temple curtain symbolized God's withdrawal from the temple. The absence of God in the temple would therefore imply that the sanctuary was left without divine holiness and security.[62] That the event anticipated the destruction of Jerusalem temple itself, implies that for Mark the demise of the temple was declared by God at the moment Jesus' spirit expired as a consequence for the murder of his "beloved Son." This view agrees with Mark's idea that after the murder of God's beloved Son, the owner of the vineyard destroys the murderous tenants and entrusts his vineyard to others (12:9). The expression suggests that for Mark the victory of the Romans over the Jews and the destruction of the temple were an outcome of the Jews' rejection and killing of Jesus.[63] Mark spoke of these things with the knowledge of the fall of the temple. It is inconceivable that Mark would have described the destruction of the temple as a consequence for the murder of God's Son if the temple was still standing. Mark 15:38 suggests the date after the fall of the temple.

---

58. See Schürer, *History of the Jewish People*, 272; Cf. Lawrence, *IVP Atlas of Bible History*, 169; Rhoads, "Zealots," 1050.

59. Cf. Roskam, *Purpose of Mark*, 82–84.

60. Ibid., 92.

61. Hooker, *Mark*, 377–78.

62. Rhoads, *Reading Mark*, 168; Roskam, *Purpose of Mark*, 93.

63. Contra Roskam, *Purpose of Mark*, 93, who argues that the defeat of the Jews and the destruction of the temple by the Romans were God's vengeance, a view that seems to agree with Josephus's account that the destruction of Jerusalem and the temple by the Romans was ordained by God (*J.W.* 6:250, 110).

To conclude, the internal evidence I have investigated suggest that Mark's Gospel was composed after the fall of the temple in 70 CE. Mark's description of the destruction of the temple (13:2), the reference to "desolating sacrilege" and the call to "flee" (13:14), the "tribulation" that has never happened since creation "until now" (13:19), the story of the withered fig tree (11:12–14, 20–25), the parable of the vineyard (12:1–12), and the ripping apart of the temple curtain at the death of Jesus (15:38), all support the view that Mark wrote the Gospel with the knowledge of the fall of the temple in his mind. In view of the evidence given, I conclude that Mark's Gospel was written shortly after the fall of the Holy City and its temple.

Origin of the Gospel

From the Capital of the Empire?

In regard to the origin of Mark's Gospel, three major locations have been proposed including Rome, Syria, and/or Galilee. The traditional view locates Mark's origin in Rome.[64] This view is primarily based on the early church tradition and some arguments based on evidence from within the Gospel. The early church traditions are dependent on witnesses of Papias, Irenaeus, Anti-Marcionites, and Clement of Alexandria which link Peter with Mark, and the persecutions of the early Christians under Nero as evidence for Rome as the origin of Mark's Gospel.[65] But as we have noted earlier, the early church traditions are not credible because they are based on Pipias's unreliable tradition.

Advocates of Rome as the origin of Mark's Gospel also appeal to various issues within the Gospel to support their position. They argue that such factors as Mark's translations of Aramaic words,[66] the geographical errors (5:1; 7:31), explanations of Jewish customs (7:3–4), the use of the term "Syrophoenician" (7:26), the explanation of *lepton* (the two *lepta*) as *quadrans* (12:42), and the pervasive use of Latin words favor Rome as the origin of the Gospel.[67] Other internal factors used in favor of Rome relate to Mark's

---

64. Hengel, *Studies*, 1–30; Incigneri, *Gospel to the Romans*, 96–115; Moloney, *Mark*, 12; Williams, "Mission in Mark," 138; Guelich, *Mark*, xxix–xxxi; Donahue, "Windows and Mirrors," 1–26; Senior, "'With Swords and Clubs," 10–20.

65. Incigneri, *Gospel to the Romans*, 103–8; Hengel, *Studies*, 1–30; Moloney, *Mark* 12; cf. Irenaeus, *Against Heresies* 3.1.1.

66. Cf. e.g., 3:17; 5:41; 7:11, 34; 9:43; 14:36; 15:22, 34.

67. Incigneri, *Gospel to the Romans*, 101. See a list of Latin words from Mark's Gospel: "*dēnarion* (6:37; 12:15; 14:5), *modios* (4:21), a measure of grain, *xetēs* (7:4), a *Roman* liquid measure (a *sextrarius*), *spekoulator* (6:27: "executioner"), *legiōn* (5:9,

allusion to persecutions (13:9–13)[68] and the reference to divorce initiated by a wife (10:12).[69] Regarding the reference to divorce in 10:12, Incigneri argues that this favors Rome as the origin of the Gospel. He writes: "The Markan text on divorce gives a woman the right to initiate divorce, which accords with Roman law (10:12), but not Jewish law. This could, however, place the context anywhere that Roman law was regarded as the norm, and so it certainly suits Rome."[70]

Donald Senior adds the factor of power as evidence in support of Rome as the origin of Mark's Gospel. He argues that both the Jewish and Roman authorities used their power abusively,[71] and mentions the Pharisees (3:2, 6; 12:13), the scribes (12:38–40), Herod Antipas (6:16), Pilate under whose administration Jesus was condemned and crucified (15:1, 15), and other Roman authorities who "lord it over" and tyrannize people (10:42; cf. 13:9–11; 12:17), as examples of those who abuse their power.[72] Accordingly, Senior notes that Mark contrasts the authorities' abusive use of power with the life-giving power of Jesus (10:43–45). He then concludes claiming that no "place has better internal and external attestation for locating the origin of Mark's Gospel than Rome" and that this is the only place that offers a "more realistic setting for understanding of the difference between the power of those who wield 'swords and clubs' and those whose power rested on the hidden triumph of the Son of Man."[73]

The arguments given above in favor of Rome as the place of composition of Mark's Gospel can be challenged at different levels. First, Mark's translation of Aramaic words and the explanation of Jewish traditions do not necessarily indicate that the community of Mark was primarily Gentile or located in Rome. It rather could be due to the nature of Mark's community

---

15), *kenturiōn* (15:39, 44, 45), *praitōrion* (15:16), *phragellō* (15:15: "flog"), *kēnsos* 12:14: "tax"), and *kodrantēs* (12:42: "quadrans"). Incigneri stresses that "the administrative center of the empire where military language was common, Rome is the place where all these Latin terms came together most commonly." Elsewhere, he concludes, "Latin was certainly used throughout the Empire, but it was in Rome most of all that ordinary person was forced to deal with both [Latin and Greek] languages in daily life. The influence of Latin on the text [of Mark] does add weight to the argument for Rome" (102–3).

68. Ibid., 100; Van Iersel, *Mark*, 40–41.

69. Spivey and Smith, *Anatomy of the New Testament*, 68, argue that "divorce by women was not possible in Jewish Palestine."

70. Incigneri, *Gospel to the Romans*, 98–99; Jeffers, *Greco-Roman World*, 147, who states that the fact that Mark refers to the possibility of a woman initiating divorce supports the belief that the "Gospel was written for a Roman audience."

71. Senior, "Swords and Clubs," 10.

72. Ibid., 15, 16–17.

73. Ibid., 19.

consisting of both Jewish and Gentile Christians, a mix that could be found even in Palestine or Syria.[74] The fact that Mark is dominated by references to Jewish scriptures suggests a place where Jews were the majority. Second, the argument based on Latinism is also unsatisfactory because the language was not limited to Rome. Its influence spread all over the Roman world.[75] In addition, most of the Latin words used in Mark are primarily military, administrative, or commercial terms which could easily have spread throughout the Roman Empire.[76] Moreover, Latin expressions appear in other Gospels as well, and do so independently of Mark. Benjamin Bacon, though himself a proponent of Rome as the origin of Mark, rightly admits that "All these (Latin) expression had passed over into the current speech of Jews throughout the empire, so that their mere occurrence in Mark cannot prove anything as to its origin in the Latin-speaking region."[77]

The term "Syrophoenician" as well does not necessarily favor Rome as the origin of Mark's Gospel. The term either denotes a descent of Phoenician intermarried with Syrians (note the way Mark refers to her as a "Syrophoenician by *race*") or a native of the Phoenician part of Syria. In either case, the word distinguishes the woman from other types of Syrians, and it could be applied even in the East.[78] Concerning Mark's explanation of the "two *lepta* as equivalent to a *quadrans*" (12:42), Collins has indicated that in "Syria and Judea, Roman and local coin denominations coexisted, and local coins were understood in terms of Roman denomination."[79]

Concerning the error in describing some geographical locations, Roskam has convincingly argued for the credibility of Mark's description of places related to Galilee. He notes that the geographical error in Mark's Gospel do not disqualify the author from being familiar with the geography of Galilee, but that they indicate the author's unfamiliarity with the geography to Transjordan (5:1–20), Jerusalem and Judea (11:1, and of the improbable route to Jerusalem, Bethphage and Bethany).[80] As for

---

74. Roskam, *Purpose of Mark*, 110–12.

75. Boring, *Mark*, 18, rejects Rome as the origin of Mark's Gospel on other grounds. He points out that Mark's Gospel does not reflect Paul's letter to the Romans: key Pauline words and phrases (e.g., "law," "righteousness of God") are missing in the Gospel and that Mark's christological point of view is different from that of Paul. While Mark focuses on the historical Jesus, Paul is interested in the death and resurrection of Jesus.

76. Marcus, "Jewish War," 443–45.

77. Bacon, *Is Mark a Roman Gospel?*, 53–54.

78. Marcus, "Jewish War," 445–46. Cf. Collins, *Mark*, 9.

79. Collins, *Mark*, 589; Contra Incigneri, *Gospel to the Romans*, 98, who argues that a Roman copper (the *quadrans*) did not circulate in the East.

80. Roskam, *Purpose of Mark*, 97–100. Bethphage was closer to Jerusalem than

Jesus' strange route from Tyre to Decapolis via the Galilean Sea and Sidon (7:31), this was not impossible. The error here does not express the author's lack of knowledge of Galilee, but of the location of Sidon in relation to Tyre and the Galilean Sea.[81]

In addition, especially for the case of 5:1–20 and 7:31, it is possible that Mark mentioned these locations the way he did as a purposeful narrative strategy to highlight Jesus' ministry in Gentile settings.[82] In 5:1–20, Jesus enters a foreign land and heals a demoniac. Jesus' journey to the Sea of Galilee via Sidon and the region of Decapolis (7:31) appears immediately after his dealing with a Syrophoenician woman in the region of Tyre, another Gentile land (7:24–30). Although Jesus' journey at this point seems to us as confusing, for Mark and his readers that might not pose any problem at all. Since Mark knows that Jesus has already inaugurated his ministry in Gentile areas, he can easily portray him as passing through Gentile regions. For Mark, there is nothing that could hinder Jesus going from Tyre to the Sea of Galilee via the region of Decapolis. Myers observes that F. Lang had noted "a route from Sidon to Damascus to the eastern shore of the Sea of Galilee, one that may have been travelled by early Christian missionaries."[83] Thus the argument that Mark's Gospel was written in Rome on the basis of geographical errors is just not convincing.

The argument for Rome as the origin of Mark's Gospel can also be challenged based on the warnings against false messiahs and prophets expressed in Mark.[84] The severe warnings against messiahs and prophets who "lead many astray" (13:5–6, 21–22) reflect more clearly the situation in Palestine. The false messiahs who come in the name of Jesus and lead people astray reflect the Jewish messianic and prophetic claimants who appeared before and during the Jewish revolt of 66–70 CE. Josephus mentions several false messiahs and prophets who appeared before the war began. They include a certain Samaritan who led people to Mount Gerizim to unearth sacred temple vessels buried there by Moses but was blocked by Pilate's troops (*Ant.* 18:85–87); and Theudas who claimed to be a prophet and "deceived many" whom he persuaded "to take up their possessions and to follow him

---

Bethany.

81. Ibid., 108.

82. Cf. Theissen, *Gospels in Context*, 244–45.

83. Myers, *Binding the Strong Man*, 205.

84. Moloney, *Mark*, 15. He doubts the need for Christians in Rome to be warned against false messiahs and prophets (13:5–6, 21–22), the necessity for them would be to be told the Son of Man would not come until the gospel was proclaimed to all the nations (13:10), and the reality of councils and beatings in synagogues (13:11) before governors (13:9) in Rome.

to the Jordan River" where he had said "at his command the river would be parted and would provide them an easy passage" (*Ant.* 20:97-98; cf. Exod 14:21-22; Josh 3:14-17). While Theudas himself was put to death by procurator Cuspius Fadus, many of his followers were imprisoned.

Josephus also reports of "impostors and deceivers" who appeared when Felix was procurator of Judea. These "impostors and deceivers" called people to follow them into the desert with a promise that they would reveal to them "unmistakable marvels and signs that would be wrought in harmony with God's design." Josephus also tells of a certain Egyptian who appeared in Jerusalem before the war began and "declared that he was a prophet and advised the masses of the common people to go with him to . . . the Mount of Olives," where he would demonstrate that at his command the walls of the city would collapse and thus give them access to enter the city (*Ant.* 20:169-170; cf. *J.W.* 2:261-263; Josh 6:20; Acts 21:38). Although the "prophet" escaped Felix's punishment, many of his followers were killed and others put in prison. Another unnamed messianic prophet who appeared in Judea about 61 CE is said to have called people to follow him in the wilderness with the promise of offering them "salvation and rest from troubles." Josephus reports that both the false prophet and his followers perished at the order of the procurator Festus (*Ant.* 20:188).

Although Mark might have been aware of these messianic and prophetic pretenders before the war, it is likely that he was more interested in the Jewish messianic claimants who appeared during and shortly after the war. According to Josephus, there were several Jewish revolutionaries who made messianic pretensions during the war. At the initial stages of the war, Menachem seized arms from Masada and marched to Jerusalem as a messianic king (*J.W.* 2:433-434) and entered the temple while dressed "in royal robes" (*J.W.* 2:44). Simon bar Gioras, too, made messianic claims by proclaiming release of slaves and reward to the liberated (*J.W.* 4:508). His followers submitted to him "as to a king" (*J.W.* 4:510) and acclaimed him as "their savior and protector" (*J.W.* 4:575-576). After the temple was destroyed, Simon bar Gioras emerged dressed in "white tunics" and "purple mantle" at the very place where "the temple formerly stood" (*J.W.* 7:26-36), another expression of his messianic pretension. It is very likely that when Mark makes references to false messiahs he has these figures in mind, and his hearers would associate his message with these Jewish revolutionaries who incited people to join the war against the Romans. As Collins has pointed out, in any case Mark "defined Jesus' messiahship in contrast to the claims of these messianic pretenders."[85]

---

85. Collins, *Mark*, 605.

Further, Josephus indicates that false prophets also appeared in Jerusalem during the final stages of the war. One of these false prophets deceived people by proclaiming that God had commanded them to go to the temple's portico to receive rewards of their deliverance. As a result, six thousand Jews perished when the portico was set in flames by the Romans (*J.W.* 6:284–285). In the following passages, Josephus clearly shows that numerous "false prophets" (*J.W.* 6:286) and false "messengers of the deity" (*J.W.* 6:288) appeared during the final days of the war period. He claims that these false prophets were induced by the revolutionaries to mislead the people to wait help from God in order to control desertions and to give hope to the loyal.[86] In his own words, Josephus states: "Numerous prophets, indeed, were at this period suborned by the tyrants to delude the people, by bidding them to await help from God, in order that desertions might be checked and that those who were above fear and persecution might be encouraged by hope" (*J.W.* 6:286). Moreover, Josephus mentions Jonathan the weaver who also after the war made messianic pretension. Jonathan led some Jews from cities of Cyrene into a desert "promising them a display of signs and apparitions" (*J.W.* 7:437–438). Given the evidence shown in these paragraphs, I conclude that the references to "false messiahs" and "false prophets" who "lead many astray" in Mark's Gospel favor the situation of the war in Palestine, and not Rome.

In regard to the threats of persecution in Mark 13:9–11, these also do not necessarily point to Rome as the place of origin of Mark's Gospel. The text warns hearers of suffering they would face for the sake of the good news. Christians would be handed over to councils and be beaten in synagogues, face trials before governors and kings (13:9, 11); they would be hated, and even be put to death on account of the name of the messiah (13:12–13). Hengel[87] and Incigneri[88] have independently linked these threats with the execution of Christians that occurred in Rome by Nero's order which involved the execution of Paul (ca. 62–64 CE). On that basis they have used the text as evidence for Rome as the place of origin of Mark's Gospel. The possibility of Mark linking these threats to what took place during Nero's reign is undeniable. However, it is more likely that Mark would have associated these threats with the more recent crisis in Palestine.

---

86. Cf. Rhoads, *Israel in Revolution*, 163–64.

87. Hengel, *Studies*, 22–23. Elsewhere he concludes saying that Mark's Gospel "was written in a time of severe affliction in Rome after the persecution of Nero" (ibid., 30).

88. Incigneri, *Gospel to the Romans*, 108, writes that when Mark was writing the Gospel "only a few years after Nero's precedent-setting act, Rome was the only place where there was likely to be officially sanctioned executions, and the only place where they would already have had a severe effect on the readers of this Gospel."

The fact that Mark does not seem to have much interest in the capital city of the empire makes Rome less likely the origin of the Gospel of Mark. Mark's Gospel shows no impression that its readers had special interests in the city or the Roman people. The Roman characters in the Gospel are very minimal and kept to the margin even in the passion narrative. Generally, issues concerning Rome as a place in Mark's story appear to be negligible,[89] suggesting that the Gospel is not from the capital of the Roman Empire.

The argument that Mark's Gospel originates from Rome based on divorce account in 10:2–12 is also unsatisfactory. The motif of marriage and divorce appears elsewhere in Mark's Gospel. Mark has given a story about John the Baptizer who is executed because he challenged an illegal marriage between Herod Antipas and Herodias (6:17–29, especially vv. 17–19 and 27–28). The marriage was illegal because Herodias was formerly a wife of Philip, Herod Antipas's brother (6:17). Josephus gives a more elaborate account of this couple but with disapproval when he states that: "Herodias was married to Herod (Philip), the son of Herod the Great by Mariamme, daughter of Simon the high priest. They had a daughter Salome, after whose birth Herodias, taking it into her head to flout the way of our fathers, married Herod [Antipas], her husband's brother by the same father, who was tetrarch of Galilee; to do this she parted from a living husband (*Ant.* 18:136)."[90] Jesus' saying in Mark 10:12 can thus be linked to Herodias's divorce of Philip in order to marry Herod Antipas, a marriage which led to the execution of John the Baptizer. In this case, the divorce in 10:12 was not necessarily related to a common divorce law, but Jesus' criticism of the divorces initiated in both Herodias and Herod Antipas against their former spouses.[91]

It is interesting to note that the question on divorce was raised just after the return of Jesus to the "Jordan" (10:1), the territory of John the Baptizer (1:4–9). Those who question Jesus are the Pharisees, who earlier plotted with the Herodians to destroy him (3:6). It is possible that the Pharisees were really provoking Jesus to say what John once said against Herod so that the king would execute Jesus just as he did to John. Given this scenario, Mark's reference to divorce does not necessarily refer to the Roman divorce

---

89. Moloney, *Mark*, 14–15.

90. Josephus's disapproval of the marriage between Herod Antipas and Herodias was probably based on the Hebrew scripture: "You shall not uncover the nakedness of your brother's wife; she is your brother's nakedness" (Lev 18:16; cf. Lev 20:21).

91. According to Josephus (*Ant.* 18:109–111), when Herod Antipas fell in love with Herodias and proposed marriage to her, Herodias accepted on the condition that he divorce his wife, who was a daughter of Aretas, king of Petra. Herod Antipas fulfilled that condition and married Herodias. Hence the two divorced their former spouses. See also Lane, *Gospel according to Mark*, 358.

law, but rather it reflects a particular divorce involving king Herod Antipas. Thus the idea that the text on divorce supports Rome as the place of origin of the Gospel is misleading.

Senior's argument in favor of Rome as Mark's origin based on power abuse is also not convincing. As he himself has indicated, abuse of power was not a practice of the Romans alone. The Jewish authorities as well used their power abusively. For example, the Pharisees and the Herodians conspired to destroy Jesus (3:6); the scribes exploited the widows (12:40); Herod Antipas executed John (6:16, 27). These Jewish leaders did not care for the needs of their people, hence causing them appear "like sheep without a shepherd" (6:34). In another context, the Jewish authorities sent their agents with "swords and clubs" to arrest Jesus (14:43); handed Jesus over to Pilate (15:1); and before Pilate they incited the crowd to demand Jesus' crucifixion (15:10–14). Even when the Romans abused their power, they did so not only in Rome, but also elsewhere in the empire including Judea. Pilate ordered Jesus' crucifixion in Judea (15:15; cf. 13:9–11), and other Roman procurators authorized killings and crucifixions of so many Jews in Judea (e.g., *J.W.* 2:223–224, 253, 260, 263, 270, 272, 305–307). Hence, locating Mark's Gospel in Rome based on the abuse of power is both inadequate and misleading.

As I have argued above, the arguments used in favor of Rome as the place of origin of Mark's Gospel are unsatisfactory. Rather, a location in the East, Syria or Palestine fits better as the origin of Mark's Gospel. In the following paragraphs, I examine the Gospel's origin in a place in the East.

A Document from the East: A City's Document?

Joel Marcus is one of the advocates of the East as the place of origin of Mark's Gospel. According to him, the Gospel came from a geographical proximity of the Roman-Jewish War of 66–70 CE[92] and was written to a community that was primarily Gentile.[93] Marcus's emphasis on Mark's community as primarily Gentile excludes Palestine from being a place of origin of the Gospel. He specifically indicates that the Gospel was composed "in one of the Hellenistic cities that Josephus tells us were attacked at the beginning of the war."[94] Marcus's argument is based on the assumption that there is a close link between Mark's account of the destruction of the temple (13:1–2) and the actual event (cf. *J.W.* 7:1), and between Mark's account of Jesus'

---

92. Marcus, "Jewish War," 441, 446–47.
93. Ibid., 460–61.
94. Ibid., 461.

entry into Jerusalem and his actions in the temple (11:1–18), on the one hand; and the events of the war, on the other (*J.W.* 4:574–578). He also assumes that the references to both the "abomination of desolation" (13:14) and "den of brigands (11:17) allude to the occupation of the temple by the Zealots in the beginning of the winter of 67–68 CE (*J.W.* 4:151–557). Moreover, Marcus links the "false christs" (13:5–6, 21–22) and the messianic hopes that accelerated the revolt (e.g., *J.W.* 6:313) with the way in which this link illuminates the ambivalent attitude toward Davidic messianic hopes (10:47–48; 11:9–10; 12:35–37). Finally, Marcus believes there was a credible sociological correlation between the Jew-Gentile tension in Syria which promoted the revolt; and Mark's friendly attitude toward Gentiles and his criticism against Jewish leaders.[95]

Marcus's argument is compelling and has much to offer for the origin of the Gospel. However, the argument is not without weaknesses. First, the argument that Mark's community was primarily Gentile is doubtful because it fails to explain the references to Jewish Scriptures that have dominated Mark's Gospel. There would be no reason for Mark to write to a community dominated by Gentiles with so many references to Jewish Scriptures and traditions. Second, Marcus's location for Mark also fails to explain Mark's interest in rural settings.[96]

Collins, too, locates Mark's Gospel in a Syrian city and assumes Antioch was the place where the Gospel originated. She prefers Antioch because both Aramaic and Latin were spoken there, and hence the translation of Aramaic into Greek and use of Latin in the Gospel.[97] But this location does not conform to Josephus's report that Antioch was not among the Syrian cities which experienced violence resulting from conflicts between Jews and Gentiles. According to Josephus, Jews and their sympathizers were subjected to persecution by Gentiles in all Syrian cities except in Antioch, Sidon, and Apamea. Of all the Syrian cities, only these cities "spared the residents and refused either to kill or to imprison a single Jew" (*J.W.* 2:479).[98] The location in Antioch for Mark's Gospel fails to account for the threat of persecution of Christians depicted in the Gospel (13:9–13). A rural location

---

95. Ibid., 447–62.

96. See Dewey, "Gospel of Mark," 149; and Kee, *Community*, 103–4, 176, who locates Mark's origin in Syria as well, but differs from Marcus and Collins in that he prefers a rural setting in southern Syria.

97. Collins, *Mark*, 101.

98. Some of the Syrian cities and villages where violence occurred resulting from conflicts between Jews and Gentiles include Philadelphia, Heshbon, Gerasa, Pella, Scythopolis, and Kedasa, a Tyrian village (*J.W.* 2:458–459, 463, 466–67, 482). See also Kee, *Community*, 99.

fits much better as the place of origin of Mark's Gospel than a city. I now turn to arguments in support of this claim.

"The Gospel Breathes a Rural Air"

Mark's Gospel shows special interest in rural settings rather than urban settings. Dewey has made a significant point concerning the rural setting of the Gospel. In favor of a mostly rural imagery, she observes that: "The Gospel of Mark breaths a rural air. It assumes a rural setting, rather than an urban one."[99] Jesus himself avoids going into Galilean cities.[100] In his analysis of the social location of the audience of Mark's Gospel, Richard Rohrbaugh has shown that the Gospel reflects an ancient peasant society where a few ruling elites and their retainers accumulate wealth on the expense of others and enjoy life in cities while the majority poor live in villages and rural areas working the land.[101]

The authorities in Mark's Gospel belong to the urban elite group, while Jesus' disciples, including the women who follow him and the crowd, collectively represent the majority poor from rural villages and rural areas.[102] That is, Mark's audience was not comprised of urban poor, but peasants working the land in rural areas. In contrast to the authorities who are characterized as opponents of Jesus, Mark's story of Jesus is primarily in favor of these peasants and marginalized in society: the degraded, unclean, and expendables such as beggars, laborers, and outcasts.[103] Rohrbaugh notes further that only a very small number among Mark's audience were literate and that were the ones expected to "read the Gospel aloud for nonliterates."[104] Richard Horsley echoes Rohrbaugh's view about literacy of Mark's audience when he states that Mark's Gospel originates from an oral peasant village setting.[105] The Gospel's interest in rural settings points to southern Syria and/or Upper Galilee as the most probable locations for the origin of Mark's Gospel.

---

99. Dewey, "Gospel of Mark," 149.
100. Kee, *Community*, 103.
101. Rohrbaugh, "Social Location," 383, 388.
102. Ibid., 384, 389.
103. Ibid., 384, 387, 393.
104. Ibid., 382.
105. Horsley, *Hearing the Whole Story*, 49–51.

Rural Southern Syria

Howard C. Kee is one of the proponents of rural southern Syria as the place of origin of Mark's Gospel. His argument for this location is primarily based on the geographical errors (e.g., 5:1; 7:31) that the Gospel presents. For him, these errors do not favor a rural place in Palestine, but one in southern Syria. He correctly observes that the reference to the eastern shore of the lake as the country of Gerasenes (5:1) is inaccurate. He also rightly views that the description of the journey from Tyre to Decapolis through the Sea of Galilee (7:31) is unrealistic. Kee observes that an itinerary "from Tyre in the south to Sidon in the north to the Sea of Galilee through Decapolis, which lies east of the lake" is not credible. As a result, he argues that the author of Mark's Gospel "does not know Galilean topography accurately,"[106] and therefore he locates the Gospel "in rural and small-town southern Syria."[107]

Against Kee's view, Roskam has convincingly argued for the credibility of the author's geographical description related to Galilee. Roskam notes that the geographical description in the region of Galilee in Mark 1–4 and 8–9 are credible and without errors.[108] Although he admits the geographical errors in Mark 5:1 and 7:31, he points out that the errors are not indicators for Mark's unfamiliarity with Galilee, but rather unfamiliarity with places outside Galilee. He notes that while Mark 5:1 shows Mark's unfamiliarity with the geography of Transjordan,[109] Mark 7:31 indicates the author's lack of knowledge of the proper location of Sidon in relation to Tyre and the Galilean Sea.[110] Beyond that, the assumption that Mark would know precisely about the whole geography around Galilee is dubious.[111] In our own time it is common to find people who live in a certain region or city who do not know the whole geography of their own region or city.

Dewey also advocates rural southern Syria as the place of origin of Mark's Gospel. Her argument in favor of this place is primarily based on the Greek language. She contends that since the Gospel was written in Greek, it must have come from "Greek speaking areas" located "as close to Galilee as Bethsaida, especially if it had sufficient Greek speakers and mixed Jewish Gentile population."[112] Dewey strongly believes that the Greek language has

---

106. Kee, *Community*, 103, 176.
107. Ibid., 105.
108. Roskam, *Purpose of Mark*, 104, 108.
109. Ibid., 99–100.
110. Ibid., 108.
111. Collins, *Mark*, 8–9.
112. Dewey, "Gospel of Mark," 154.

a significant role in determining the origin of the Gospel. Elsewhere she says that if she can be shown of a village in Galilee where Greek was a common language, she is ready to change her mind in favor of a Galilean provenance.[113] According to Dewey, rural southern Syria fits best as the origin of Mark's Gospel for a number of reasons. The place helps to explains why the Gospel was written in Greek; it maintains the rural character of the Gospel; it conforms to oral context with some scribal influence; and it coheres with the narrative world of the Gospel as a whole.[114]

Although Dewey's argument for the Gospel's origin in rural Syria based on Greek language is compelling, it cannot go unchallenged. As Myers has pointed out, Mark's use of Greek to compose the Gospel might have been "the result of cultural (hence linguistic) colonization of his homeland by Hellenism since the time of Alexander the Great."[115] Mark might have composed the Gospel in Greek in order to reach a broader audience.[116] This point is credible in that it agrees with Mark's view that the good news he shares has to be proclaimed to all nations (13:10), the Greeks included. So, publishing the Gospel in Greek might have been in keeping with his view to spread the good news to all people. Myers reinforces this point with an example of African and Latin writers who write in French or English in order not only to critique "the colonizing culture" but also "to communicate with other oppressed linguistic groups in the imperial sphere."[117] Myers then concludes showing that the multicultural situation that involved Jews and Gentiles might have compelled Mark to use the Greek language to write the Gospel.[118] More significantly, Luke T. Johnson has observed that the use of Greek was prevalent in Galilee and reminds us of Aristotle's testimony preserved by Josephus in which he states that he met "a Jew of Coele-Syria . . . (who) not only spoke Greek, but had the soul of a Greek" (*Ag. Ap.* 1:179–81).[119] Although I do not completely ignore rural southern Syria as the origin of the Gospel, I maintain that this location cannot be taken for granted. The area can be considered but with some reservations.

---

113. Ibid., 155.
114. Ibid.
115. Myers, *Binding the Strong Man*, 95.
116. Ibid.
117. Ibid.
118. Ibid.
119. Johnson, *Writings of the New Testament*, 46.

Rural Galilee

Besides rural southern Syria, rural Galilee is another candidate for the origin of Mark's Gospel. Roskam is one of the advocates of this place. Mark's special interest in Galilee has moved him to argue for this location as the origin of the Gospel. Roskam demonstrates that most of Jesus' preaching and healing ministry occur in Galilee (Mark 1—10) and that in the passion narrative, Galilee plays a remarkable role (Mark 14—16).[120] The three women, "Mary Magdalene, Mary the mother of James the younger and Joses, and Salome" who watch Jesus' crucifixion from a distance are Galileans and had been supporters of Jesus' ministry there (15:40-41). These women and many other women accompanied Jesus to Jerusalem from Galilee. Mary Magdalene and Mary the mother of Joses, witnessed the place where Jesus was buried (15:47). The three women from Galilee were the first witnesses of Jesus' resurrection (16:1-8). Mark's use of women from Galilee as witnesses of Jesus' resurrection suggests that Galilee was the place where the author of the Gospel lived. The fact that one of the women is identified as "Mary, the mother of James the younger and of Joses" (15:40), suggests that hearers of the Gospel knew this Mary as well as her sons, James the younger and Joses. Otherwise, it would be meaningless for Mark to identify an unknown Mary by referring to James and Joses. This as well links Mark's community with Galilee, hence the evidence that the Gospel originates from this area.[121]

The reference to persecution (13:9-13) supports Roskam's argument for Galilee. Roskam believes that 13:9 reflects the actual situation of Mark's community, whose members lived under threats of persecution because of their faith. Christians were persecuted by Jewish authorities and handed over to the Roman and Jewish authorities—the "governors and kings" (13:9).[122] Roskam contends that the designation of these authorities is especially important if the community of Mark lived in Galilee. At the time Mark's Gospel was composed, Galilee was divided into two parts: the eastern part of Galilee administered by King Agrippa II, and the western part of Galilee, known as Upper Galilee under the Roman governors. Upper Galilee and Judea were administered by a Roman governor or *procurator* supervised by a Roman legate of Syria. After the war, Upper Galilee became part of a new Roman province of Judea, hence under the administration of a Roman legate, who was also the general of the tenth Legion.

---

120. Roskam, *Purpose of Mark*, 101.
121. Ibid., 103.
122. Ibid., 112.

The proper title for legates in Greek is *hēgemon*.¹²³ Given this administrative situation in Galilee during the composition of Mark's Gospel, the portrayal of persecution of Christians by "governors and kings" suggests that Mark's community was located in Galilee, hence an indication that the Gospel originated from this place.

Another piece of evidence in favor of Galilee as the origin of Mark's Gospel relates to the story about the young man at the tomb (16:1-8). When the women from Galilee arrived at the tomb where Jesus was laid and found the tomb empty, the young man in the tomb told the three women to go and tell Jesus' disciples and Peter that Jesus "is going before you to Galilee" where "you will see him, as he told you" (16:7). The young man's words recall Jesus' words to his disciples: "after I am raised up, I will go before you to Galilee" (14:28).¹²⁴ The mention of Galilee as the place where Jesus meets his disciples reinforces Roskam's argument that this is the place where Mark's community resided and a place where the Gospel was written.

Galilee as the place of origin of Mark's Gospel has not been safe from challenges. Scholars who locate the Gospel in Syria reject this place for different reasons. Collins, for example, challenges Galilee as the origin of the Gospel on financial grounds. She claims that since in the earliest period no "major Christian community" existed in Galilee that could finance the production of the Gospel, Galilee cannot be the place of origin of the Gospel.¹²⁵ But this argument is not convincing for several reasons. First, in the ancient world very few people could read and write. In this regard, Mark's Gospel was originally composed for the purpose of being heard rather than read. Horsley makes this point clear when he asserts that the Gospel "was composed in an oral communication environment and would originally have repeatedly performed orally to communities of listeners."¹²⁶ It was put in a written form only later by those who had the resources to do so.

Second, Mark's Gospel itself provides important evidence that promotion of Israelite cultural tradition was oral. For example, traditions such as Jesus' entry into Jerusalem on a donkey (11:2-8); David's plucking of grain (2:23-28); sayings of characters in the story (10:4; 11:9-10; 12:36); and the tradition about honoring father and mother (7:9-10; 10:19) come from

---

123. Ibid., 112-13.

124. Ibid., 103.

125. Collins, *Mark*, 101.

126. Horsley, *Hearing the Whole Story*, xi. Rhoads, *Reading Mark*, 35, captures Horsley's point of view when he notes that "the Gospels were written to be performed to audiences in a predominantly nonliterate culture," and that "all the narratives of the New Testament were written to be performed aloud to a listening audience." See also Dewey, "Survival of Mark's Gospel," 498-99.

memory, not from a written text. Even when Mark makes explicit citations, the words come from memory. One clear example of this is Mark's citation allegedly from Isaiah (1:2–3), which in fact starts with a quotation from Exodus 23:20 and Malachi 3:1. Such a combined citation may be explained as a result of popular cultivation of Israelite prophetic tradition rather than written texts.[127] Third, even if the Gospel was intended to be read, Mark has shown that from the very early stages of Jesus' ministry, there were already women who supported the ministry (15:41). Now, if at such an early stage of the good news there were support for the ministry, how much more about 40 years after Easter! As Dewey has pointed out, lack of financial resources is not a valid argument to put the Gospel away from Galilee.[128]

Dewey, nevertheless, rejects Galilee as the place of origin of the Gospel, again, based on its use of the Greek language. Although she acknowledges and appreciates the Jewishness, rural setting, peasant and marginalized social location,[129] and oral nature of Mark's Gospel as reflecting Galilean location, she nevertheless argues that the combination of these factors "suggests but does not require a Palestinian provenance."[130] But on the basis of Myer's argument concerning the Greek language in relation to the composition of Mark's Gospel noted elsewhere earlier, Galilee cannot be completely ignored or ruled out as a place of the Gospel's origin.

Given the significant role that Galilee plays in Mark's story of Jesus and Dewey's arguments for southern Syria as the origins of Mark's Gospel, I argue that the Gospel was composed in one of these locations. Probably the Gospel was written in an area where rural residents from both northern Galilee and southern Syria were the immediate hearers. If the Gospel did not originate from Galilee, then, it must have been composed in a village or town in southern Syria by a refuge from Galilee. I contend that Mark wrote the Gospel with firsthand knowledge of most of the events of the war in Galilee and that for the case of the war events in Jerusalem, he heard through a word of mouth from people who had escaped the war from the holy city. Whether the author wrote from rural Galilee or from rural southern Syria, the audience must have been the residents of both locations. The two places have the necessary conditions which complement each other in favor of the Gospel's origin from a rural place in northern Galilee and/or southern Syria.

---

127. For further examples of Mark's references to Israelite traditions that come from memory rather than from written texts, see Horsley, *Hearing the Whole Story*, 60–61.

128. Dewey, "Gospel of Mark," 141n3.

129. Ibid., 149.

130. Ibid., 150.

Conclusion

The purpose of this chapter was to determine the date and place of origin of Mark's Gospel. In regard to the date, evidence have shown that the Gospel was composed shortly after the fall of Jerusalem and the temple in 70 CE. As for the location of the Gospel's origin, I have established that the Gospel came from a rural area in northern Galilee and/or southern Syria. The Gospel's rural character, its special interest in Galilee, its composition in Greek, the mixed nature of the community of Mark, and the war situation that the Gospel expresses all support this location. Since this study associates Mark's Gospel with the Roman-Jewish War of 66–70 CE, it is important that I put the events of the war in perspective. The following chapter deals with this subject matter.

3

The Use and Bias of Josephus

Introduction

JOSEPHUS'S WORKS ARE AMONG the primary sources used in this study. These works provide significant and useful information about the Roman-Jewish War of 66–70 CE. They are especially important because Josephus, the person who composed them, was an eyewitness of, and an active participant in, most of the events he describes.[1] Given Josephus' importance, efforts must be made to know more about his person. In this chapter, I therefore seek to present a brief discussion about Josephus's person and career within his social contexts, the course and causes of the war.

The significance of this chapter is that it provides us with the necessary ground for interpreting specific passages from Josephus's works that are closely related to the texts in Mark's Gospel. It must be made clear that the relationship between Mark and Josephus does not lie on Mark's literary dependence of Josephus, but on the events that Josephus depicts. Since Josephus wrote some years later than Mark, it would be impossible for Mark to have read Josephus. Writing from Rome, Josephus tells us of the events of the war. People in and around Palestine would know about these events, having just lived through them. Since Mark wrote the Gospel in Palestine, his hearers heard him in the context of and in relation to these events. This is how Mark will be read in light of Josephus's accounts about the war.

---

1. Cf. Rhoads, *Israel in Revolution*, 1, who considers Josephus a major source for first-century political events, particularly for Jewish revolt since he was an active participant in the initial stages of the war and an eyewitness to the destruction of Jerusalem and its temple.

The Person and Career of Josephus

Lineage, Youth, and Education

Josephus ben Mathias was born in 37 CE into a noble Jewish priestly ancestry. He was thus a member of the aristocratic upper class in Palestine (*Life* 1-2). From his mother's side, Josephus shared a "royal blood" linked to the Hasmonean (Maccabees') high priest Jonathan (*Life* 2, 4).[2] This noble birth links Josephus with the aristocratic priestly ruling class in Israel, one that directly collaborated with the Romans and whose members feared war with Rome the most because they did not want to lose their wealth and positions of power.[3]

Describing his youth and education, Josephus presents himself as an intelligent and ambitious young man. He claims that at age fourteen he possessed extraordinary knowledge of the Torah, so much that chief priests and important men of Jerusalem sought advice from him (*Life* 8).[4] At age sixteen, he got advanced training in the major Jewish philosophical schools of the Pharisees, Sadducees, and Essenes, before he attended a three-year program of ascetic life in the wilderness under Bannus; and at age nineteen,

---

2. Although Josephus links his royal heritage to his mother's ancestors, who for a long time had been officials of a king and of a high priest (*Life* 2), the genealogy he presents to support his claim is nevertheless traced through his father, and not through his mother. Moreover, elsewhere Josephus reports that the Hasmoneans did not assume the title "king" until Aristoblus in 104 BCE (*Ant.* 13:301), the time after his ancestor's marriage, revealing one instance of his problems of inconsistency. Despite the inconsistency, it is accepted that Josephus was a descendant of a royal and priestly ancestry of the Hasmoneans because his priestly and pro-Hasmonean biases also appear in places where he does not speak about his ancestry. Cf. Mason, *Josephus*, 38–39.

3. Here again Josephus's inconsistency is observed. He claims he started his advanced education at sixteen and that he completed it at nineteen, implying that his training was a three-year program. But he also asserts that he was with Bannus in the desert for three years (*Life* 12), thus leaving a very limited time for his training in the Pharisaic, Sadducean, and Essene schools. In another context, Josephus tells his readers that to become a full member of the Essene community alone one would have to undergo training for three years (*J.W.* 2:137–142). Indeed, these are obvious inconsistencies. Despite these inconsistencies, I do assume that, as a member of an aristocratic family, Josephus was well educated and highly informed in matters of the Pharisees, Sadducees, and Essenes. The statements about his education in *Life* are not to be taken at face value; they should rather "be taken with a grain of salt." See Mason, *Josephus*, 41; Cohen, *Josephus in Galilee*, 184.

4. In his own words, Josephus boasts, saying, "While still a mere boy, about fourteen years old, I won universal applause for my love of letters; insomuch that chief priests and the leading men of the city used constantly to come to me for precise information on some particular in our ordinances" (*Life* 8).

he served as Pharisee in Jerusalem (*Life* 10–12).[5] When he was twenty-six years old, he made a diplomatic trip to Rome to negotiate the release of certain Jewish priests who had been imprisoned by Nero based on petty crimes (*Life* 13–16). The trip exposed Josephus to the wealth, culture, and might of Rome, an experience that might have influenced his political ambition within Judaism and perhaps even his position on the war with Rome. His attempt to dissuade Jews who supported the war with Rome in 66 CE by reminding them of Rome's power (*Life* 17) and his advice to the moderate chief priests and Pharisees (*Life* 12) to go for a peaceful solution with Rome when Cestius led his troops to stop the revolt (*Life* 22) serve as evidence in support of this view.[6]

Josephus as General of Galilee

According to the account in his *Jewish War*, Josephus served as an outstanding and ingenious general of Galilee. At the outbreak of the war he was appointed general of Galilee. Following the revolutionaries' initial victory against Cestius and his troops in Jerusalem, Jews were inspired to join the war against the Romans. An interim government led by the chief priests was formed (*J.W.* 2:562–565) and generals tasked with controlling the war in various regions of Palestine were appointed. Josephus became the general of Upper and Lower Galilee (*J.W.* 2:568).[7]

Throughout the *Jewish War*, Josephus describes himself as a daring, inventive, and beloved leader. For example, he claims that he fortified Galilean cities to prepare for the war with the Romans (*J.W.* 2:572–576); trained his forces in the manner of the Romans (*J.W.* 2:577–582); handled internal conflicts by one trick after another (*J.W.* 2:585–646); and fought against Vespasian in Galilee (*J.W.* 3:153–154) even causing injury to the Roman general (*J.W.* 3:236). Josephus claims further that when he had entered Jotapata, Vespasian regarded that development as a great fortune since "the

---

5. Mason, *Josephus*, 41, has made an interesting observation regarding Josephus's account of his youth when he states that the account prepares Josephus for "divine service" in the tradition of "the biblical-Jewish theme of desert-sojourn."

6. Cf. Rhoads, *Israel in Revolution*, 6.

7. Josephus's account here contradicts the one he presents elsewhere in which he indicates that he was sent to Galilee, not as a general to command the preparations for the war, but as one appointed by the leading men (*synedrion*) in Jerusalem to stop Galilee from joining the revolt against Rome (*Life* 28–29). See Cohen, *Josephus in Galilee*, 200; McLaren, *Turbulent Times?*, 72–73; Rhoads, *Israel in Revolution*, 6–7. The contradiction on this matter has led Herst ("Treachery of Josephus Flavius," 82–88) to conclude that Josephus's mission in Galilee was not primarily to fight but to defuse the war.

most sagacious of his enemies had thus deliberately entered a prison" (*J.W.* 3:143). Moreover, Josephus describes with abundant self-admiration his clever defense of Jotapata, including pouring boiling oil on the soldiers and boiled fenugreek on the Romans gangplanks to make the soldiers slip and stumble backward (*J.W.* 3:171–175, 190–192, 271–282).

Nevertheless, when Jotapata was besieged, Josephus surrendered to the Romans (*J.W.* 3:354, 392) despite a strong opposition from his colleagues in the cave. Refusing to give up and preferring suicide to capitulation, his fellow captives threatened to kill him in order to prevent his surrender (*J.W.* 3:356–361). Josephus argued against committing suicide (*J.W.* 3:369–370) and successfully persuaded the other captives to die by lot (*J.W.* 3:387–390). Whether by coincidence or maneuver, Josephus was one of the last two. He convinced the other not to kill one another, and both surrendered to the Romans (*J.W.* 3:391). It is questionable, however, whether the suicide event actually happened,[8] since there is no evidence to confirm the events described to have happened in the cave.[9]

Josephus's role as an army general in Galilee highlights diverse perspectives. On the one hand, his actions reflect a strong anti-Roman attitude. He fought against the loyalist forces of King Agrippa II (*Life* 114–19, 398–406), against Vespasian's legions (*J.W.* 3:60–63), and attacked pro-Roman cities (*J.W.* 3:61; *Life* 115–173, 373–389, 394–396). On the other hand, his behavior reflects elements of a pro-Roman perspective. For example, he refused to distribute the booty seized from the caravan of Agrippa's wife (*Life* 126–54; cf. *J.W.* 2:595–613) and opposed John of Gischala (*J.W.* 2:585–637); meanwhile, his fellow Jews accused him of being a tyrant (*Life* 260, 302; *J.W.* 2:626), a coward, and a traitor (*J.W.* 2:595–599; 3:439, 355; *Life* 129, 135), who desired absolute power for himself through deceit (*Life* 314; *J.W.* 2:602). Josephus's constant conflicts with the Jewish revolutionaries who opposed Rome, also reveal his pro-Roman bias.[10] Despite these contradicting perspectives, Josephus truly fought the Romans in Galilee until he surrendered to them (*J.W.* 3:354–405, 406). His conflicting attitude can be explained to have been the result of an ambiguous situation that he faced and in relation to his roles both as a general and negotiator for peace.

---

8. Cohen, "Masada," 397. He believes Josephus's suicide account at Jotapata is suspect.

9. Roberto, "Flavius Josephus and the Jewish Wars," para. 11.

10. Rhoads, *Israel in Revolution*, 7.

Josephus the Prophet

Josephus not only was an army general, he was also a "prophet." His prophetic role is primarily associated with his prophecy that Vespasian would become an emperor. Following the siege of Jotapata by the Romans in July 67 CE, Josephus, inspired by "some divine providence" escaped to a cave with forty others (*J.W.* 3:341–342). He claims that as he was contemplating Vespasian's second offer of safety should he surrender, a divine intervention visited him. Nightly dreams in which God had revealed to him the imminent doom of the Jews and the fortunes of the Roman sovereigns came into his mind (*J.W.* 3:351). With such divine aid, Josephus resolved to capitulate to the Romans.

Standing before Vespasian, who was ready to send him to Rome to appear before Nero as a prisoner of war, Josephus claims he prophesied about Vespasian's future. He told the Roman general, saying:

> You imagine, Vespasian, that in the person of Josephus you have taken a mere captive; but I came to you as a messenger of greater destinies. Had I not been sent on this errand by God, I knew the law of the Jews and how it becomes a general to die. To Nero do you send me? Why then? Think you that [Nero and] those who before your accession succeed him will continue? You will be Caesar, Vespasian, you will be emperor, you and your son here. Bind me then yet more securely in chains and keep me for yourself; for you, Caesar, are the master not of me only, but of the land and sea and the whole human race. For myself, I ask to be punished by stricter custody, if I have dared to trifle with the words of God. (*J.W.* 3:400–402)[11]

---

11. Mason, *Josephus*, 50–51, proposes four possibilities in regard to whether Josephus truly prophesied or whether it was just his own innovation: (1) Josephus had some supernatural insight; (2) Josephus made a lucky guess on what he knew about the political situation of the time (opposition against Nero, and Vespasian's likelihood to succeed him, especially because by then the general was on Jewish soil and was viewed in the light of Dan 9:26); (3) Josephus did not *predict* but brought the "prophecy" after Vespasian was proclaimed emperor by his troops. The release of Josephus from chains after Vespasian was announced emperor (*J.W.* 4:623–629), Vespasian's need for legitimization, and Josephus's need to cover up his cowardly behavior manifested in his surrender all seem to favor this view; and (4) Josephus encountered Vespasian two times; in the first, at his capture, Josephus told Vespasian about the Jewish prophecy that suggested that God would permit the Romans to rule the world. That Josephus was not sent to Nero suggests Vespasian saw him as a useful informant. Thus, after Vespasian was proclaimed emperor, Josephus stated that the prophecy signified Vespasian personally (*J.W.* 6:313). Josephus himself gives the impression that even while he told Vespasian the story of the prophecy, Vespasian thought of Josephus's prediction as "a nonsensical invention of the prisoner to avert the storm which he has raised" (*J.W.* 3:406). Since

Intrigued by this prediction, Vespasian spared Josephus's life, keeping him in chains but with special treatment, including precious gifts (*J. W.* 3:4–408). When Vespasian was acclaimed emperor in 69 CE (*J.W.* 4:601, 618–620, 655), Josephus was liberated from bonds (*J.W.* 4:622–629). From then on, he served the Romans, working as Titus's interpreter and spokesperson to the Jews during the siege of Jerusalem (*J.W.* 5:362–419).

Josephus understood himself as God's messenger appointed to announce some key historical events. In a passage where he describes his experience shortly before he surrendered to Vespasian, Josephus demonstrates his awareness of his divine call. He relates of himself in the third person thus:

> . . . suddenly there came back into his mind those dreams, in which God foretold to him the impending fate of the Jews and the destinies of the Roman sovereigns. He was an interpreter of dreams and skilled in divining the meaning of ambiguous utterances of the Deity; a priest himself and priestly descent, he was not ignorant of prophecies in the sacred books. At that hour he was inspired to read their meaning, and he offered up a silent prayer to God. "Since it pleases thee . . . who didst create the Jewish nation, to break thy work, since fortune has wholly passed to the Romans, and since hast made choice of my spirit to announce the things that are to come, I willingly surrender to the Romans and consent to live; but I take thee to witness that I go, not as a traitor, but as thy minister." (*J.W.* 3:351–354)

According to this account, Josephus foresaw the imminent destruction of the Jewish nation by the Romans and Vespasian's rise to the imperial throne. His trip to Rome, which exposed him to the might of Rome (*Life* 17–19), and his own defeat by the Romans in Galilee might have reinforced his prophetic certainty of the fall of his nation (*J.W.* 4:388; 6:311).[12]

Josephus attributes his ability to prophesy to various factors. He credits his gift to predict to his skills of interpreting dreams and God's oracles, and to his priestly heritage and training (*J.W.*3:351–353). As a priest and member of a priestly ancestry, Josephus had knowledge of the prophecies in the Jewish sacred books. Such knowledge contributed to his interpretation of an ambiguous oracle (*J.W.* 3:352)[13] preserved in the Old Testament: "a

---

rivals doubted Josephus's prophetic ability before Vespasian was proclaimed emperor, it is possible that even after Vespasian became the emperor they continued to believe that the prediction account was Josephus's invention intended to legitimate Vespasian's reign.

12. Rhoads, *Israel in Revolution*, 9–10.
13. Ibid., 10.

star shall come out of Jacob, and a scepter shall rise of Israel; it shall crush the borderland of Moab, and the territory of all the Shethites. Edom will become a possession, Seir a possession of its enemies, while Israel does valiantly. One out of Jacob shall rule, and destroy the survivor of Ir" (Num 24:17–19). While almost all the Jews, including the revolutionaries believed that the prophecy referred to the Messiah who would come from their own race, Josephus presented a contrasting interpretation. For him, the "ambiguous oracle" signified Vespasian's rise to the imperial throne, a claim supported by the fact that Vespasian was proclaimed emperor on the Jewish soil (*J.W.* 6:312–314). Josephus's reference to the ancient Jewish prophecy confirms his reliance on his Jewish prophetic heritage. Since he believes that he possessed special knowledge of the sacred scriptures, he considered his interpretation as credible and reliable, and strongly rejected that of the revolutionaries. The Roman historians, Tacitus and Suetonius also independently provide a similar interpretation to that of Josephus.[14]

Josephus's role as a prophet is also demonstrated in his speech when Jerusalem was under siege. Considering himself a prophet in the mode of Jeremiah, he calls the Jews to submit to the Romans in order to save themselves:

> When the king of Babylon laid siege to this city, our king Zedekiah having, contrary to the prophetic warnings of Jeremiah, given him battle, was himself taken prisoner and saw the town and the temple leveled to the ground . . . Yet, how much more moderate was that monarch than your leaders, and his subjects than you! For though Jeremiah loudly proclaimed that they were hateful to God for their transgression against Him, and would be taken captive unless they surrendered the city, neither the king nor the people put him to death. But you . . . assail with abuse and missiles me who exhort you to save yourselves, exasperated at being reminded of your sins and intolerable of any mention of these crimes which you actually perpetrate every day. (*J.W.* 5:391–393)

---

14. Tacitus writes, "The majority firmly believed that their ancient priestly writings contained the prophecy that this was the very time when the East should grow strong and that men starting from Judea should possess the world. This mysterious prophecy . . . pointed to Vespasian and Titus, but the common people, as the way of human ambition, interpreted these great destinies in their own favor, and could not be turned to the truth even by adversary" (*Hist.* 5:13). Suetonius's version reads, "There had spread over all the Orient an old and established belief, that it was fated at that time for men coming from Judea to rule the world. This prediction, referring to the emperor of Rome, as afterwards appeared from the event, the people of Judea took to themselves; accordingly they revolted." (*Vesp.* 4).

Unfortunately, his fellow Jews did not heed to his call to submit. As a result, in 70 CE, Josephus himself witnessed the destruction of Jerusalem and its temple.

Josephus the Historian

In addition to his career as an army general and a seer, Josephus was also a great historian. According to Louis H. Feldman, Josephus was a "historian whose writings constitute important sources for our understanding of biblical and of the political history of Roman Palestine in the 1st century C.E."[15] When the war was over and Jerusalem and its temple were no more, Josephus accompanied Titus to Rome, where he received many awards from the Flavian imperial family. In Rome, Josephus was granted citizenship, pension, and a mansion formerly occupied by Vespasian.[16] He also enjoyed several other privileges and favors, including a piece of land in Judea, protection against his opponents (some of whom were executed by the imperial family), and tax exemption for his property in Judea (*Life* 422–29). Finally, Josephus assumed the name "Flavius" from Flavian, Emperor Vespasian's family name. It was while in Rome enjoying all these privileges that Josephus was entrusted by the Flavians to write an official account of the war (*Life* 364). Josephus then spent the rest of his life in Rome writing.[17]

Josephus's career as a historian is demonstrated in his works, which serve as an important source for the history of the Jewish people in the first century under the Roman Empire. Josephus's writings include four major works, the *Jewish War* (75–79 CE),[18] *Jewish Antiquities* (93–94 CE),[19] *Life* (before 96 CE),[20] and *Against Apion*. Let me give a brief comment on the last three works before I concentrate on Josephus's *Jewish War*, which is the major source for this work.

The *Jewish Antiquities*, which appear in two volumes, narrates the history of the Jewish nation from its origin to the beginning of the Jewish revolt

---

15. Feldman, "Josephus," 981.

16. Rhoads, *Israel in Revolution*, 7–8. Rhoads indicates that Josephus resided in "Titus's former house," but the primary source shows that it was Vespasian who lived in the house before he became emperor. For Josephus's privileges in Rome, see also Mason, *Josephus*, 53.

17. Rhoads, *Israel in Revolution*, 8.

18. Mason, *Josephus*, 64; Contra Brighton, *Sicarii*, 41, who dates the book between 75 and 81 CE. See also Cohen, *Josephus in Galilee*, 90, who suggests a later date for *Jewish War* but before 81 CE.

19. Cohen, *Josephus in Galilee*, 170; cf. Mason, *Josephus*, 99.

20. Cohen, *Josephus in Galilee*, 180.

in 66 CE. Josephus's goal in this work is primarily "to defend his nation against widespread slanders about Jewish origins and early history.[21] The third book, *Life* is primarily an autobiographical work recounted in the first-person covering Josephus's career as an army general in Galilee until his life in Rome. It presents Josephus's response to Justus of Tiberias, who wrote a contrasting account of the war events in Galilee (*Life* 40, 338). Justus had accused Josephus of causing a revolt in Tiberius (*Life* 340)[22] and of being a brutal (*Life* 171–73) and greedy tyrant who desired to have absolute power for himself through deceit (*Life* 302). Josephus wrote the *Life* in order to refute Justus's account of the Galilean war and to prove his character based on public service.[23] The fourth book, *Against Apion,* provides information about the revolt. Not only does it present Josephus's refutation, but also highlights the spread of Jewish customs in the whole world (*Ag. Ap.* 1:1–5, 219; 2:144; 2:282–83, 196).[24]

Josephus's *Jewish War* describes the events of the Roman-Jewish War of 66–70 CE. Written under imperial patronage and appearing in seven volumes, it addresses Jews in the East.[25] Through this work, Josephus seeks to warn Jews from any attempt to resist the Romans after the conquest and destruction of their nation. The *Jewish War*, therefore, serves as a pro-Roman propaganda tool intended to prevent further threat to the empire, particularly from the Parthian Empire which hosted many of the Jews in the diaspora.[26] Josephus insists to his Jewish readers that the conquest of their nation by the Romans is evidence that God has shifted from the Jewish side to that of the Romans. His portrayal of the Roman troops as extraordinary powerful suggests that he wanted to warn the Jews not to attempt revolt

21. Mason, *Josephus*, 99–121. The citation is from page 100. Mason credits this to Henry St. John Thackery, *Josephus*, 52.

22. Cohen, *Josephus in Galilee*, 115–20.

23. Mason, *Josephus*, 122, 131. Josephus's outstanding pedigree and scholarly credentials favor this view.

24. Ibid., 132–3.

25. Contra Brighton, *Sicarii*, 41, 47, who believes that the war was "aimed primarily at a non-Jewish Roman audience." Similarly Mason, *Josephus*, 97–98, concludes that Josephus's main audience for this work was around him in Rome. Goodman, *Ruling Class*, 6, argues that Josephus wrote the *Jewish War* to a Gentile audience for apologetic purposes. He states that Josephus wrote in order to convince his readers that "Jews of the richer class like himself were, despite the revolt, just like other aristocrats in the Greek East of the Empire . . . [Hence they] should be entrusted again with the Jerusalem Temple and the flourishing Judaean society of which they had lost control."

26. Rhoads, *Israel in Revolution*, 12; Contra Mason, *Josephus*, 98, who argues that Josephus's goal for the war was to seek "broad sympathy from his audience for the plight of the Judean aristocrats, walking the well-travelled tightropes between pleasing the mob and saying unpopular things, between submission and national self-respect."

because that would lead to a catastrophic and horrific destruction. Hence, Josephus wrote the *Jewish War* in order to promote total loyalty of the Jewish people to Rome, for he believed loyalty was the only way that would guarantee the survival of the Jews (*J.W.* 3:108–109, 136).[27]

It is important to note that Josephus's pro-Roman perspective was not meant to be an abandonment of Judaism. In the *Jewish War*, Josephus demonstrates his defense of his nation. For example, he credits the fall of Jerusalem and its temple not to the military strength of Rome, but to God whose fortune aided the Romans (*J.W.* 5:367). He shows that Titus served only as God's agent to purge, defeat, and to destroy Jerusalem and the temple; that Vespasian became emperor based on the Jewish prophecies (*J.W.* 6:312–313). Josephus places blame for the war on the Jewish revolutionaries whom he labels as brigands, bandits, and madmen, and not on the whole Jewish nation (*J.W.* 1:27; 5:444; 6:251).[28] The Jewish aristocrats, a class to which Josephus belonged, are exempt from blame because they opposed the war.[29]

In the *Jewish War*, Josephus also counsels and consoles the Jews for the conquest of their nation. He explicitly counsels them neither to put blame on themselves for the war nor to give credit to the might of Rome for the fall of their nation, because the Romans' victory was a result of God's aid. Josephus writes: "Do not attach the blame on yourselves, nor the credit to the Romans, that this war with them has been the ruin of us all; for it was not their might that brought these things to pass, but the intervention of some more powerful cause has afforded them the semblance of victory" (*J.W.* 7:360). In this respect, Josephus shows his pride and concern for his nation. He offers guidance and consolation to his fellow Jews for the conquest of their nation (*J.W.* 3:108–109, 136; 6:267).[30] It is therefore clear that Josephus wrote the *Jewish War* not only to warn the Jews about the consequence of the revolt, but also to defend their long history and nobility before the Romans.[31]

---

27. Rhoads, *Israel in Revolution*, 11.

28. Ibid., 12–13; cf. Mason, *Josephus*, 85–86. In regard to the fall of the temple, Mason states very forcefully that in the *Jewish War*, Josephus persistently indicates that "not the Romans, not even Titus, but the Jewish God destroyed the temple" (ibid., 86).

29. Cohen, *Josephus in Galilee*, 234.

30. Rhoads, *Israel in Revolution*, 13.

31. Brighton, *Sicarii*, 23, insists that at first Josephus was thought to have written the *Jewish War* as a Roman propaganda tool to warn about the consequences of revolt, but that now it is thought that he wrote the Romans on behalf of the Jews in order to defend their long history and nobility. I personally think that the two views regarding Josephus's purpose for writing the book have to be taken together.

Credibility of Josephus

Reading Josephus's works, one observes not only the biases of his histories, but also the contradictions, exaggerations, and inventions in his accounts. For example, in the case of his bias, because he belonged to an aristocratic priestly and royal ancestry (*Life* 1–6), he puts blame of the war on the revolutionaries and not on his own class (*J.W.* 1:10; 4:318); as a Jew, he desires Judaism to survive and to be accepted in the Hellenistic world;[32] and as a beneficiary of Rome and her emperors, Josephus writes in praise of Rome and the Flavian family.[33]

Josephus's accounts are also marked with contradictions. For example, he gives contradicting accounts about his involvement in the war in Galilee. In one context, he claims he was sent to Galilee to lead the war against Rome (*J.W.* 2:568–576), while in another he says that he and two other priests were sent to Galilee to promote peace with Rome (*Life* 28–29, 77–78). Other examples of Josephus's inconsistencies relate to his accounts about the destruction of the temple and the total number of troops he recruited in Galilee. About the former, Josephus claims that Titus had no desire to destroy the temple (*J.W.* 1:10; 6:127–128, 236–243)[34] and that he even tried to save it (*J.W.* 6:254–266). But he contradicts this account when he states elsewhere that Titus ordered the destruction of the temple (*J.W.* 6:228; 7:1).[35] In regard to the number of troops he recruited in Galilee, Josephus says that the total was one hundred thousand (*J.W.* 2:576) or sixty thousand troops (*J.W.* 2:583), contrary to a total of ten thousand troops he gives elsewhere (*Life* 321, 331).

The total number of troops that Josephus says he recruited in Galilee, not only represents his inconsistence but also his exaggerations, a common feature of his accounts. The total number of six thousand Jews killed by Titus during the war (*J.W.* 4:106–111, 115), the 115,880 corpses removed at one of the gates during the war (*J.W.* 4:567), the Galilean population of more than three million (*J.W.* 3:43; cf. *Life* 235),[36] and the accounts about the Roman

---

32. Rhoads, *Israel in Revolution*, 12–13.

33. Mason, *Josephus*, 24–25.

34. Cf. Introduction to *J.W.* 2: xxiv–xxv.

35. For further discussion on Titus's involvement in the destruction of the temple, see Alon, "Burning of the Temple," 252–68; Yavetz, "Reflection on Titus," 411–23; Leoni, "'Against Caesar's Wishes,'" 39–51; Spilsbury, "Josephus on the Burning of the Temple," 306–27.

36. For a detailed discussion about Josephus's exaggerations, see Cohen, *Josephus in Galilee*, 90, 202nn40–41; Reed, *Archaeology and the Galilean Jesus*, 69–70; Byatt, "Josephus and Population Numbers," 51–60; Brandon, *Fall of Jerusalem*, 165; Broshi, "Population," 6; Avi-Yonah, *Holy Land*, 211, says, "Josephus in particular tends to generalize

devastations of villages and cities such as that of Sepphoris (*J. W.* 3:62–63),[37] represent Josephus's gross exaggerations. In addition to exaggerations and inconsistencies, Josephus is also known for his inventions of some events of the war such as the suicide accounts at Jotapata and Masada.[38]

The observations just noted have led some scholars to question Josephus's credibility. Cohen, for example, asserts that Josephus is so unreliable that our knowledge about the events of the 66–70 CE is very defective. He points out that since Josephus gives contradicting accounts and because we lack external control, we can never be sure of the underlying events.[39] Roberto goes even further in that he completely dismisses Josephus as a source. Note his remark: "Josephus's accounts cannot be corroborated by other sources. The archaeological evidence contradicts some of Josephus's accounts. The author's own writings contradict themselves. And Josephus's 'histories' were self-serving, containing several examples of embellishing by the author. It is within the light of these facts that we should disregard Josephus as a source in his entirety."[40]

By contrast, Magen Broshi has defended the credibility of Josephus. Although he agrees that the historian is not always correct, he maintains that most of his details are accurate.[41] Broshi states that "In many instances, numerous details provided by Josephus can be checked, including architectural data, and their accuracy confirmed."[42] He adds that Josephus's geographical data are also accurate.[43] The accuracy of Josephus's reliable data is credited to

---

or exaggerate."

37. Cf. Faulkner, *Apocalypse*, 201–2.

38. Cohen, "Masada," 404, states that "Josephus created his Masada story," and that the Jotapata suicide account is very suspect (ibid., 397). Similarly, Roberto, "Josephus and Jewish Wars," paras 11 and 15 rejects the credibility of these suicide stories.

39. Cohen, *Josephus in Galilee*," 181.

40. Roberto, "Josephus and the Jewish Wars," argues further saying, "Despite the fact that some of Josephus' physical descriptions can be confirmed, it is clear from evidence presented . . . that Josephus, at least embellished his accounts, and at the very worst, out and out lied. The mere fact that historians have suggested that 'Josephus [be taken] with a grain of salt,' should be enough to discredit him."

41. Broshi, "Credibility of Josephus," 383, acknowledges that Josephus's "inaccuracies range from vagueness to blatant exaggerations" and goes even further to assert that even if it is agreed that the copyists were responsible for the mistakes found in Josephus's writings, one cannot reject the fact that Josephus "was by nature somewhat negligent."

42. Ibid., 379.

43. Ibid., 380.

the commentaries of imperial commanders (*Life* 358, 342; *Ag. Ap.* 56)[44] and his own memory for the events he himself witnessed.[45]

Given these contrasting arguments about the credibility of Josephus, one is alerted not to take Josephus at face value. In this regard, Rhoads's suggestion on how to read Josephus is worth noting. Rhoads writes: "Anyone who reads Josephus's works in order to construct historical events must persistently keep in mind the person of the author and the point of view from which those events are described."[46] Considering the situation that faced Josephus and the context in which he wrote his histories, I also concur with Mason's proposal that Josephus's accounts; particularly those in the *Jewish War* should be read as "ironic."[47]

In this section, it was not my intention to prove or disapprove Josephus's credibility. Rather to show how other scholars have attempted to judge him. Personally, I feel that Josephus is generally credible. He could not so distort events and make up or give account that would have no credibility. Most of the people to whom he wrote had witnessed or heard through word of mouth the events of the war from those who had first-hand experience of those events. Such a situation could not give room for Josephus to tell much lies. For example, Josephus could not have invented all the events of the war in Galilee, the civil war in Jerusalem, Menachem's triumphal march from Masada to Jerusalem, and the destruction of Jerusalem and its temple. The killings and devastations of cities and villages as narrated by him are reliable.[48] In this respect, with caution, we assume that much of the underlying events occurred despite exaggerations, distortions, and embellishments. The events Josephus reports are those that the populace of Palestine would be well aware of. Thus despite his exaggerations, inconsistency, and some inventions, Josephus deserves to be used as a reliable source because he was an eyewitness of most of the events he narrates. Having dealt with the person of Josephus, his career, and his credibility, I now pay attention to the course and causes of the war.

---

44. Ibid., 381.
45. Ibid., 383.
46. Rhoads, *Israel in Revolution*, 14.
47. Mason, *Josephus*, 87.
48. Cf. Safri, "Description of the Land of Israel," 308, who argues that Josephus's "description of Vespasian's campaigns in Palestine seems to be exact and based on correct information. The portrayal of the battles in Galilee appears reliable and, likewise, the many other geographic details in this context."

Course and Causes of the War

Most scholars have seen that Mark reacts to the fact of the war.[49] For example, Boring mentions some important events associated with the Roman-Jewish War of 66–70 CE: the destruction of Jerusalem and its temple, Vespasian's rise to the throne, and the triumphal procession in Rome. After the listing of these events, Boring concludes: "At some point in this chaotic time Mark was written. The readers live in the time when the Holy City and the temple had just been destroyed or when its destruction was imminent and certain."[50] Similarly, Rhoads sees Mark as responding to the fact of the war. He writes: "In that war, the Jewish nation revolted against the Roman overlords. The Romans defeated the Jews, conquering Jerusalem and destroying the Temple. Mark wrote about Jesus to show that any attempt to dominate by force—either by Rome or Israel—was contrary to the values God calls forth from people in the rule of God.[51] Although these scholars acknowledge the fact that the war influenced the composition of Mark's Gospel, they do not, however, provide details of the full historical context of the Gospel. In the following sections, I attempt to fill out the historical context that will help to show that Mark is also addressing the course and causes of the war.

Pre-War Conditions

Scholars identify the year 6 CE as the starting point of the historical period that culminated in the Roman-Jewish War of 66–70 CE.[52] In that year, two major events occurred in the land of Israel including the establishment of Roman direct rule and the revolt against Rome. Josephus blames the revolt of 6 CE on Judas the Galilean and states that his revolt "sowed the seed" that resulted into later conflicts (*Ant.* 18:8).[53] Judah's revolt and the other later conflicts occurred as a response to the Roman imperial situation that began since Pompey's conquest of Israel in 63 BCE which involved the

---

49. Cf. Marcus, *Mark*, 37–39; Boring, *Mark*, 15; Hooker, *Mark*, 8, 297–98, who states that Mark was written subsequent to 70 CE, and that "Mark 13 reflects the trauma of those who had assumed that the temple's destruction was a sign which heralded the end of the era" (ibid., 8).

50. Boring, *Mark*, 15.

51. Rhoads, *Reading Mark*, 61.

52. Rhoads, *Israel in Revolution*, 20. See also Brandon, *Jesus and the Zealots*, 65; Nikiprowetzky, "Josephus and the Revolutionary Parties," 229; Goodman, *Ruling Class*, 1.

53. Cf. Rhoads, *Israel in Revolution*, 20.

destruction of Jerusalem and the violation of the temple's holy of holies (*Ant.* 14:105). Pompey's conquest of Palestine subjected the Jews under the payment of tribute to Rome. The refusal to pay such tribute was regarded as nothing less than a rebellion. After Pompey's reign, any attempt at revolt resulted in repeated destruction of the Jewish land, extraordinary taxes, and general social turmoil. The Romans treated the Jews brutally in order to compel them to submit (*Ant.* 14:120, 272–275; *J. W.* 1:180, 219–220; *Ant.* 17:288–289, 295).

Some scholars link the roots of the pre-war period specifically to Herod the Great, who ruled as a Roman client king of Judea from 37 to 4 BCE. Rhoads, for example, observes that the "pre-war period had its roots in the time of Herod."[54] Similarly, Moshe Aberbach and David Aberbach state that "Herod's rule helped to create conditions for the revolt."[55] The reason the pre-war period is linked to Herod the Great is the fact that his rule was characterized by tyranny. Herod weakened the power of the Jewish Sanhedrin and controlled his subjects using foreigners loyal to himself. He appointed and removed high priests at his will (*Ant.* 15:40–41) and killed whoever seemed to be a threat to him, even members of his own family (*Ant.* 15:50–56, 87, 222, 232–240, 247–252, 284–291; cf. Matt 2). In order to cover expenses for his extensive building projects within and outside Palestine (*J. W.* 1:524; 2:85–86; *Ant.* 16:149–159; 17:302–314) and his administrative costs, Herod imposed taxes on the poor Jewish peasantry. Such a situation forced the peasantry into landlessness, indebtedness, and severe poverty.[56] The drought and famine that occurred during his reign exacerbated the hardship among the poor peasantry (*Ant.* 15:121, 299–302; *J. W.* 1:370).[57]

Besides the economic hardship that Herod caused to his people, he also favored and promoted the Hellenistic culture against the Jewish culture. For example, he used foreign advisers who knew Greek culture; he built Hellenistic cities and temples within Palestine in honor of Caesar (*J. W.* 1:410–421; *Ant.* 16:136–145); he introduced pagan games (*Ant.* 15:267–276); and placed a golden eagle (the symbol of the Roman Empire) above the temple's gate in Jerusalem (*Ant.* 15:380–425). These things not only demonstrated Herod's love of the Hellenistic culture, but also his disregard

---

54. Rhoads, "Zealots," 1046–47.

55 Aberbach and Aberbach, *Roman-Jewish Wars*, 25. They also note that Herod's rule (37–4 BCE) and "the annexation of Judaea as a province in 6 CE were turning points for worse in Roman-Jewish relations" (ibid., 23).

56. The taxes that Herod exacted were over and above the tribute paid to Rome (*Ant.* 14:74) and the Jewish tithes and temple tax. See Horsley and Hanson, *Bandits*, 58.

57. Rhoads, *Israel in Revolution*, 23–24.

of the Jewish law and customs. His love of foreign culture, his birth status as a "half-Jew," his ruthless and oppressive rule, and collaboration with Rome (*Ant.* 15:368–371; 17:41–45) attracted Jewish opposition against him.[58] But since he ruled with an iron hand, he tolerated no resistance or rebellion (*J.W.* 1:304–314; *Ant.* 14:413–430). He controlled the people such that there was no opportunity for protests (*Ant.* 15:365–369).[59] This explains why we hear little of rebellion or unrest under his rule.

The deep and long suppressed discontent erupted shortly after the death of Herod the Great in 4 BCE. The rebellion began "first in daring acts of defiance of the dying tyrant and then in spontaneous popular revolts in every district of the kingdom."[60] In Jerusalem, people demanded reduction of taxes, abolition of duties, liberation of prisoners, and election of a new priest (*J.W.* 2:5–7; *Ant.* 204–212). Archelaus, Herod's son, killed about three thousand people who demonstrated to demand the truth about his killing of two teachers of the law who incited people to destroy the golden eagle erected at the gate of the temple (*J.W.* 2:8–13; *Ant.* 17:213–218).[61] In another incident, Varus, the Roman legate of Syria, captured Sepphoris, burned the city, sold its inhabitants into slavery (*J.W.* 2:68; *Ant.* 17:288–289),[62] and in Jerusalem he crucified about two thousand rebels (*J.W.* 2:75; *Ant.* 17:295).

When Herod the Great died in 4 BCE, his kingdom was divided up among his three sons: Archelaus, Herod Antipas, and Philip. Archelaus ruled Judea and Samaria until 6 CE when the Romans removed him from power due to his failure to govern (*J.W.* 2:111). Herod Antipas was given Galilee and Perea and ruled until his death in 39 CE. Philip ruled the area northeast of Galilee (*J.W.* 2:93–97). The removal of Archelaus and the accompanying replacement of a Roman governor marked the beginning of the Roman direct rule in Palestine (cf. *J.W.* 2:117).

Shortly after the Romans established their direct rule in Judea in 6 CE, a series of revolts occurred. The first revolt was that of Judas the Galilean

---

58. Horsley and Hanson, *Bandits*, 32–33. They note that Herod was considered a "half-Jew," hence, an illegitimate ruler of Israel because his father was an Idumean while his mother was an Arab.

59. Rhoads, *Israel in Revolution*, 25, has a similar view. He notes that Herod prevented a general outbreak of the people by "intimidation and manipulation."

60. Horsley and Hanson, *Bandits*, 33–34.

61. For more details, see Rhoads, *Israel in Revolution*, 25–27.

62. Faulkner, *Apocalypse*, 202, rightly comments that Josephus's account concerning the Roman devastation of Sepphoris is an exaggeration. He writes, "Josephus no doubt exaggerates the range of Roman devastation. But the general point stands: the fall of Sepphoris was a grievous loss, and this, together with the loyalists' threat at Tiberias, was a direct consequence of the governor's policy of prioritizing the defense of property over that of the revolution."

who resisted the payment of tribute to Rome which, for Jews, was a sign of recognition of Caesar as lord in the place of God (*J. W.* 2:118; *Ant.* 18:23). The Roman suppression of this revolt resulted into a relatively calm period that existed until the time when Pontius Pilate became governor of Judea (26–36 CE). Tacitus expresses this peaceful condition by telling that under Tiberius "all was quiet" (*Hist.* 5:9).[63] When Pilate was governor of Judea, the situation changed. He brought Caesar's standards in Jerusalem by night (*J. W.* 2:169) and plundered sacred money from the temple treasury for the construction of an aqueduct to bring water into Jerusalem (*J. W.* 2:175). These actions provoked uproar among the Jews. Pilate responded to the Jew's nonviolent protests with brutal repression (*J. W.* 2:176–177). Other series of protests occurred in early 40s CE following Emperor Caligula's attempt to erect his image in the Jerusalem temple (*J. W.* 2:184–207).

In 44 CE, the whole of Israel became a Roman province. This period witnessed few minor protests before a series of incidents that occurred in 44–66 CE leading to a deterioration of the Roman-Jewish relations. When Cumanus was procurator (48–52 CE), several riots took place that could lead to a series of protests. A Roman soldier made an obscene gesture that provoked a violent fight with the Jews; then a Jewish brigand attacked and robbed Caesar's slave; some Roman soldiers burnt a copy of the Torah, an action that triggered a riot; and Cumanus ignored a conflict between the Jews and the Samaritans (*J. W.* 2:223–244; *Ant.* 20:118–124). Although Cumanus was expelled from office due to misrule, brigandage developed in Palestine, a condition that subsequent procurators did little to alleviate. Josephus compares the spread of brigandage during this period as a disease in a human body. He writes:

> No sooner were these disorders reduced than the inflammation, as in a sick man's body, broke out again in another quarter. The impostor and brigands, banding together, incited numbers to revolt, exhorting them to assert their independence, and threatening to kill any who submitted to Roman domination and forcibly to suppress those who voluntarily accepted servitude. Distributing themselves in companies throughout the country, they looted the houses of the wealthy, murdered their owners, and set the villages on fire. The effects of their frenzy were thus felt throughout all Judea, and everyday saw this war being fanned into fiercer flame. (*J. W.* 2:264–265)

---

63. Rhoads, "Zealots," 1047, suggests that this peaceful situation was a result of the Jews' hope that the procuratorial arrangement would restore a Jewish autonomy under a high priest.

Further riots and rebellions took place after the expulsion of Cumanus. When Festus and Albinus were procurators of Judea in 60–62 CE and 62–64 CE respectively, the atmosphere in Jerusalem deteriorated. Conflicts arose among the Jewish high priestly factions because of the struggle to win over the procurator's favor. The state of terror resulting from the Sicariis' assassinations and killings exacerbated the situation (J.W. 2:272–277; Ant. 20:182–215). When Florus was governor (64–66 CE), he forced the Jewish people into open rebellion. During his rule, the Jewish people made repeated appeals and protests for their condition and treatment. In 64 CE, at a Passover in Jerusalem, they protested before the legate of Syria, accusing Florus of being a ruin to the country (J.W. 2:280). Rather than supporting the people's protests, the Jewish authorities sought military aid from the Romans and King Agrippa II in order to silence the people. Consequently, the people became desperate and determined to fight.

Course of the War

Beginning of the War in 66 CE

The war started in 66 CE when the procurator Florus attempted to plunder money from the temple treasury in Jerusalem. Shortly after the disturbance at Caesarea, Florus demanded 17 talents from the temple treasury. Initially Josephus indicates that the money was required for imperial service, but later he implies that Florus's greed was the prime motivation (J.W. 1:293–296). Whatever the motive, the Jews reacted angrily. In response, Florus ordered indiscriminate arrests and crucifixions among the Jews (J.W. 2:305–308). When Jerusalem became ungovernable due to increased riots, the procurator withdrew to Caesarea (J.W. 2:325–332). Agrippa II, a pro-Roman king attempted to persuade the Jews to restore the payment of tribute to Caesar, to repair the porticoes linking the temple and Antonia fortress, and to submit to Florus until his successor was appointed. His major concern was to have peace with Rome. The end result, however, was his own banishment from the holy city (J.W. 2:348–406).

King Agrippa's expulsion from Jerusalem was followed by the cessation of Gentile sacrifices offered on behalf of Caesar and the Roman Empire. Eleazar, son of Ananias the high priest successfully convinced the lower-class priests to stop receiving Gentile sacrifices. This action not only "laid the foundation of war with the Romans" (J.W. 2:409),[64] but also it expressed

---

64. Cf. Schäfer, *History of the Jews*, 121; Aberbach and Aberbach, *Roman-Jewish Wars*, 29–30.

the class-struggle between the lower-class priests and the traditional high priestly authorities.[65] In addition, that action marked a symbolic removal of the Roman's divine support of the God of Israel, and served as an act of purification of the temple from defilement caused by foreigners and pro-Roman high priests.[66] Commenting on this same action, Rhoads notes that the revolutionaries might have viewed this move as "a zealous act of cleansing the temple" or "a religious renewal of the temple cult based on a radical understanding of the prohibition of gentiles, which excluded also their gifts and sacrifices."[67]

Fearing that the cessation of Gentile sacrifices would lead into war with Rome, the Jewish authorities attempted to prevent it from happening. The ruling aristocracy, the chief priests, and the leading Pharisees tried to dissuade the lower-class priests and the revolutionaries from abandoning the Gentile sacrifices (J.W. 2:410–417). But the temple ministers rejected the proposal. Since the lower-class priests supported the revolutionaries, Josephus considers them to have been "instrumental in bringing about the war" (J.W. 2:418). Perceiving that they would not suppress the revolt and that they would be the first victims of the Romans' reaction, the ruling aristocracy sought military support from both Florus and Agrippa II (J.W. 2:419–421). This move resulted into a civil war.

The war was between the lower-class priests alongside the revolutionaries on the one side and the imperial and Jewish upper-class forces on the other. The former group fought to control the temple and to remove the Jewish aristocracy, the royal troops, and the Roman forces, all occupying the upper city (J.W. 2:422–424). Eleazar and his followers excluded their opponents from worship in the temple during the feast of wood carrying, but invited the Sicarii to join them. The Sicarii "carried a dagger in their bosom" and used them to terrorize and kill their opponents.[68] The royal troops were now outnumbered and hence forced out of the upper city. The revolutionaries burned the house of Ananias the high priest and the palaces of Agrippa II and Bernice. Public archives were burned in order "to destroy the money-lenders' bonds and to prevent the recovery of debts . . . (and) to win over a host of grateful debtors and to cause a rising of the poor against the rich, sure of impunity" (J.W. 2:426–427). The brutality of the Sicarii forced the Jewish "notables and high priests" to flee into hiding (J.W. 2:428).

65. Levine, "Jewish War," 841.
66. Schmidt, "Jewish War," 35.
67. Rhoads, *Israel in Revolution*, 99.
68. Ibid., 80.

Meanwhile Menachem, son of Judas, joined the revolt in Jerusalem. He first broke Herod's store of weapons at Masada, distributed arms among his men and marched to Jerusalem "like a veritable king." In Jerusalem he assumed leadership of the revolt and directed the siege of the palace (*J.W.* 2:433–434).[69] Now three groups, namely, that of Eleazar, of Menachem, and the Sicarii joined forces to fight against the Jewish upper-class that favored peace with Rome. With the aid of the Sicarii, Menachem defeated the ruling elite and Agrippa's troops. His murder of the high priest Ananias[70] led him to believe that he was without a rival in the city. He now became an intolerable tyrant (*J.W.* 2:444). When Menachem was put to death, some of his followers were also massacred, while others escaped to Masada (*J.W.* 2:445–448) where they remained until the Roman conquest in 74 CE.[71] Josephus identifies Menachem's followers as Sicarii,[72] the only Jewish revolutionary group that survived the war until they were destroyed at Masada.[73] Eleazar, son of Ananias, then assumed leadership of the revolution in Jerusalem and brutally murdered the Roman garrison except Metilius because he agreed to become a Jew by circumcision (*J.W.* 2:454, 450). Since the massacre took place on the Sabbath, their most sacred day, the Jews viewed the incident as "the prelude to their ruin" (*J.W.* 2:454, 456).

In November 66 CE, Cestius, the legate of Syria led a heavily armed Roman 12th Legion into Jerusalem in an attempt to reestablish Roman control of Palestine (*J.W.* 2:499–501). When he approached the city, the Jews abandoned the Feast of Tabernacle, took up arms and fought, even though the day was Sabbath, causing a great loss to the Roman troops (*J.W.* 2:517, 519). Because of the strong resistance from the Jewish revolutionaries (*J.W.* 2:453, 546–550) and the approaching winter (*J.W.* 2:523), Cestius's troops withdrew from the city. At a village near Beth-Horon, the imperial troops abandoned their military equipment because of the attack from Simon bar Gioras's men, which the latter seized and returned to Jerusalem, singing songs of triumph (*J.W.* 2:518, 554).[74]

---

69. Ibid., 114, comments that since "Anania, the high priestly head of state, was dead. Menahem was [therefore] filling the vacuum to exercise authority over temple and state."

70. Ibid., 122, contends that the murder of Ananias eliminated one of the most powerful opponents of the war in Jerusalem at that time.

71. Cf. Schäfer, *History of the Jews*, 122. After this incident, Menachem's followers played no further role in the war, which ended in 70 CE, until the Romans began the siege of Masada three years later.

72. See Rhoads, *Israel in Revolution*, 115, 117.

73. Ibid., 113.

74. Cf. Rhoads, "Zealots," 1047–48.

The Jews' triumph over Cestius motivated the Jerusalem pro-Roman elite and the populace to join the war against Rome.[75] Now the nation united to fight against Rome. The wealthy ruling elite, who formerly opposed the war because they were entrusted by the emperor to keep peace in the land and also to prevent their positions of power, joined the war against Rome. They did so probably to control the war and maintain their positions of power.[76] Soon a provisional government was formed under the leadership of the high priest Ananus (J.W. 2:562–568). This government thought it was responsible to undertake military strategy and preparations. Generals were appointed to command the war efforts in the different provinces of Judea. Josephus was appointed general of Galilee and Gamala (J.W. 2:566–568). His appointment without any military experience suggests that the provisional government expected the war would end quickly.[77] It is probable that the provisional government took part in the war primarily to control the revolutionaries and hence to protect their own interests, such as their positions of power, status, and wealth.[78]

The inhabitants of Galilee held varied views regarding the war with Rome. While the Jews living in cities opposed Josephus, the peasants from the countryside and villages supported him. Since hostility had existed between the poor peasantry and the powerful elite in the Galilean major cities, namely, Sepphoris, Tiberias, and Gabara, the countryside people needed very little excuse to attack the city dwellers. Their hostility can be credited not only to the long-lasting rural-urban tension, but also to their contrasting views on the war with Rome. The Galilean cities and towns that supported Josephus were Tarichaea, Jotapata, and Gamala. Tarichaea's anti-Roman attitude can be attributed to its residents' hostility to its neighboring city of Tiberias, which they viewed as a product of Roman-Herodian rule. Since Tarichaea was a settlement founded in 19–20 CE consisting of residents from different places, its collaboration with rural Galileans against Tiberias suggests a set of social issues: native residents against foreigners, rural against city, and a newer settlement against an old one.[79]

In Galilee, Josephus spent more time plotting against his opponents than preparing for the war with Rome. Although Josephus claims that he fortified Jotapata, Jopha, Tarichaea, Tiberias, Gamala, and other cities (J.W. 2:573–575; Life 187) and that he had a force of more than one hundred

---

75. Schäfer, *History of the Jews*, 122.
76. Rhoads, "Zealots." 1048.
77. Aberbach and Aberbach, *Roman-Jewish Wars*, 30.
78. Horsley, "Power Vacuum and Power Struggle," 91.
79. Levine, "Jewish War," 842.

thousand military men trained in the manner of the Romans (*J. W.* 2:576–584),[80] when the Romans came, he did not show any meaningful resistance. He spent most of the time plotting against his rivals with Agrippa II (*J. W.* 2:595–613; *Life* 126–32). John of Gischala was his major opponent in Galilee. John viewed Josephus not as truly anti-Rome, but as pro-Rome.[81] He suspected Josephus's goal was to negotiate peace with Rome rather than fight the Romans. In this case, John fought against Josephus in order to remove him from command (*J. W.* 2:585–646). In John's eyes, Josephus was a traitor who betrayed his country to the Romans (*J. W.* 2:593–594). This explains the reason why John proposed to the leaders of the provisional government in Jerusalem to denounce Josephus. John's proposal was intended to prevent Josephus from becoming a tyrant of the city (*J. W.* 2:627–631). Like Josephus, John of Gischala also did not provide strong resistance against the Romans; for Gischala, John's own home town was easily conquered in the summer of 67 CE (*J. W.* 4:97–106). The fall of the town of Gischala marked the Roman's complete conquest of the whole of Galilee.

Roman Military Operations in Galilee, 67 CE

The Jews' victory against Cestius in 67 CE compelled emperor Nero to commission Vespasian, a veteran general, to lead a campaign to stop the Jewish revolt (*J. W.* 3:64–69). Galilee was the first place where Vespasian began his military operation in Palestine. Josephus provided very little resistance against Vespasian in Galilee. When the city of Galilee was conquered, he escaped to Tiberias with other defenders (*J. W.* 3:115–131). Later, he took refuge at Jotapata (*J. W.* 3:142), a place where he later surrendered to the Romans (*J. W.* 3:339–344, 392–393) and prophesied about Vespasian's accession to the imperial throne (*J. W.* 3:400–402). Prior to the capture of Jotapata, the Romans had already devastated the city of Gadara. They "burnt all the villages and country towns" and reduced the residents to slavery (*J. W.* 3:133–134) causing the defenders of the city to flee to

---

80. The total number of one hundred thousand men that Josephus claims he recruited in preparation for the war in Galilee is an exaggeration. Elsewhere he gives different numbers of his soldiers: sixty thousand (*J. W.* 2:583), ten thousand (*Life* 321, 331), three thousand (*Life* 234), which was later enlarged to eight thousand (*Life* 212–13) or five thousand (*Life* 399). Sometimes he claims he had two thousand troops. This inconsistency in the number of his troops suggests that his army was not stable. The troops appeared and disappeared easily. Probably he had three thousand to five thousand men from whom he drew troops, but in daily activities not more than a few hundred. See Cohen, *Josephus in Galilee*, 201.

81. Schäfer, *History of the Jews*, 123.

Jotapata. Before Vespasian entered Jotapata to deal with the defenders, he first ordered his troops to prepare a broad highway leading to the town for easy passage of his forces (*J.W.* 3:141–145). When the construction was ready, his troops marched and surrounded Jotapata, seeking to starve its inhabitants in order to force them to surrender (*J.W.* 3:176–180). However, preferring death in battle to dying of hunger and thirsty, the Jews continued to fight (*J.W.* 3:189) until the Romans, finally, razed the city. At the capture of Jotapata, the Romans murdered whomever they found except for the women and children who were sold into slavery (*J.W.* 3:305). Josephus relates that the total number of Jews who died at Jotapata was forty thousand while that of the prisoners was 1,200. The fall of Jotapata took place on July 20, 67 CE (*J.W.* 3:336–339).

The next cities to be devastated by the Romans after Jotapata were Joppa and Scythopolis. After the fall of Jotapata, the Romans captured and destroyed Joppa (*J.W.* 3:427). A military camp was established there to defend Joppa from the revolutionaries continued pillage and destruction of the neighboring villages and towns. Every day Roman troops plundered and sacked the country until it was reduced to a desert (*J.W.* 3:428–431). With the fall of Joppa, the Romans advanced to Scythopolis, the largest city of Decapolis located close to the city of Tiberias (*J.W.* 5:444).[82] The city was also reduced to submission (*J.W.* 3:443–452) and its inhabitants received Vespasian "with acclamations, hailing him as their savior and benefactor" (*J.W.* 3:456–360). As a gesture of gratitude to Agrippa's hospitality, Vespasian spared the city from pillage and violence.

After the Roman subjugation of Scythopolis, Tarichaea was the next city to be dealt with. Most revolutionaries had taken refuge in this city. The city's strength and proximity to Lake Gennesar near the Gennesareth region, gave the rebels confidence that they would be safe. But it did not take long to realize that such hopes were in vain. Titus led the attacks against the defenders. Despite their initial resistance, the Jews were overpowered and subdued. Most of the Jews who attempted to escape were murdered before they boarded their boats; and those in the town were indiscriminately slaughtered. The town itself was put under Roman control (*J.W.* 3:497–502). Many Jews were slain at Lake Gennesaret such that the lake turned "red with blood and covered with corpses" (*J.W.* 3:529). Josephus reports that the total number of Jews who died in defense of Tarichaea was 6,700. The captives from the city were brought before Vespasian, who

---

82. The city of Tiberias was itself disaffected by the revolt (*J.W.* 3:445). The revolt at Scythopolis was led by Jesus ben Saphat, "the ringleader of this band of brigands" (*J.W.* 3:450–52), but was quickly crushed, forcing the residents to surrender, and Jesus and his party to flee to Tarichaea (*J.W.* 3:453–58).

refused to grant them amnesty. Among them, two hundred old and unserviceable men were executed, six thousand youths were sent to Nero, and 30,400 were sold or given as gifts to Agrippa because they were formerly subjects of his kingdom. Agrippa then sold them (*J.W.* 3:528–552). All the events of killing and shedding of so much blood likely occurred, but the numbers are exaggerations, often to show the superior strength of the Romans in conquering so many people.

The Romans' victory over Tarichaea reduced the number of Galilean-resisting cities to two: Gischala and Gamala. Gamala, situated on the other side of Lake Gennesar and opposite Tarichaea, was a city in Gaulanitis, Agrippa's territory. Unlike the cities of Sogane and Seleucia in the same region, which had submitted to Agrippa early in the revolt, Gamala supported the revolt and refused to surrender (*J.W.* 4:4). When Vespasian brought his troops into the city, Jews tried to resist, but they were not successful (*J.W.* 4:28–32, 39–49). The Roman commander, Placidus forced the defenders of Gamala to surrender (*J.W.* 4:61). Upon the arrival of Titus and Vespasian in the city, no life was spared, even that of the infants. A total of 5,400 Jews perished, and the city itself fell into the hands of the Romans (*J.W.* 4:80–83).

Gischala was the last city to be pacified by the Romans. Josephus blames John of Gischala for the revolt in Gischala. He accuses him of having incited the residents of the city to revolt "in order to attain supreme power" for himself (*J.W.* 4:84–85). Titus attempted to argue the defenders of Gischala to surrender, but without success. Instead, John proposed to him to delay the fight in order to allow the Jews to observe the Sabbath (*J.W.* 4:99–101). Actually, the proposal was John's trick to give him room for escape. By night, John escaped to Jerusalem along with his armed forces and many unarmed Jews (*J.W.* 4:106). When Titus came on the next day to complete the treaty, he found John had already gone. The residents of Gischala received and hailed him both "as benefactor and liberator of their town from bondage" under John (*J.W.* 4:112–113).

Being embarrassed by John's trick, Titus determined to pursue his enemy. He dispatched a squadron that destroyed many of John's followers. Some six thousand of John's followers were instantly murdered and three thousand women and children were also killed by Titus (*J.W.* 4:115). As far as the city of Gischala is concerned, not much destruction was done other than the pulling down part of the city's wall as a token of capture. Titus established there a garrison in order to keep peace in the city in his absence. The capture of Gischala completed the Roman military operations in Galilee. By the end of 67 CE, the whole of Galilee was under the Romans (*J.W.*

4:120). Thereafter, Roman garrisons were established throughout Galilee for the purpose of keeping peace.[83]

Generally speaking, all the events of the war reported by Josephus occurred even though the numbers of those who were killed or taken into slavery are exaggerations, often to show the superior strength of the Romans to conquer so many people. The Roman military operations in Galilee were marked with terror and tyranny. Murder, plunder of possessions, burning of homes and villages characterized the Roman troops. Describing the Roman military activities in Galilee Josephus states that the Romans moved from one city to another to devastate and "to pillage the property of the country-folk, invariably killing all capable of bearing arms and reducing the inefficient to servitude. Galilee from end to end became a scene of fire and blood; from no misery, no calamity was it exempt" (J.W. 3:63). The purpose of all this was to terrorize people so that they would not attempt another revolt.

Civil Wars in Jerusalem 68–69 CE

The years 68–69 CE were marked with strife and civil wars among Jews. The civil war exploded in Jerusalem among various Jewish factions including the Zealots, the Sicarii, John of Gischala's group, Simon bar Gioras's group, the Idumaeans,[84] and the provisional government (e.g., J.W. 4:305–333, 366–376).[85] There were wars between pro-Roman Jewish aristocrats and the revolutionaries (e.g., J.W. 4:335–336, 342–343, 357–365), and among the different Jewish revolutionary factions. The Zealot faction was formed in the winter of 67–68 CE under the leadership of Eleazar, son of Ananias, who directed the cessation of the Gentile sacrifices. The group consisted of Eleazar's followers and the brigands from the countryside who entered the city after the defeat of Cestius (J.W. 4:135, 138).

Under the leadership of Eleazar ben Simon,[86] the Zealots took control of the temple. The group chose Phanni ben Samuel to be their high priest

---

83. Schäfer, *History of the Jews*, 124.

84. Faulkner, *Apocalypse*, 266–67, notes that these people lived on a "dry barren land, mixed small-scale cultivation with extensive pastoralism, cross-border raising and social banditry. The Herodians had their origins in Idumaea, the family still owned estates there, and it had in the past been a recruiting ground for the royal armies. But overall Idumaea was not a region of big estates—there was not enough good land—and landlordism was less developed here than elsewhere in Palestine." The Idumaeans were notorious for independence and violence. Josephus says of them that by nature they were "most barbarous and bloodthirsty."

85. Schäfer, *History of the Jews*, 126; Cline, *Jerusalem Besieged*, 117–18.

86. Other than Eleazar ben Ananias. See Rhoads, *Israel in Revolution*, 102–4, who

by lot, thereby forming their own government. Phanni ben Samuel was a peasant who not only was not from a high priestly ancestry but also ignorant of what the high priestly office meant (*J.W.* 4:147–148, 153–157).[87] The election of a high priest by lot was probably an effort by the Zealots to reestablish an older and more legitimate line of high priestly descendants to conduct the cultic worship.[88] From the aristocracy's point of view, that is, from the standpoint of the high priests and leaders of the provisional government, the election of a high priest by lot was not only a "monstrous impiety," but also a degradation of "the sacred honor" (*J.W.* 4:157). The high priests Ananus ben Ananus and Jesus ben Gamalas strongly opposed the move, persuading the populace to join in the war against the Zealots but without success (*J.W.* 4:161, 163–193).

The Zealots made the temple their headquarters, stronghold, and center of their tyranny. This was a strategy for their defense in case the people would turn against them due to their terrorist actions in the city (*J.W.* 4:151–152). From the temple they murdered and imprisoned many of the aristocracy, the royalists and anyone they suspected was pro-Roman (*J.W.* 4:138–146, 335–336). Their control of the sacred space was important not only because it served as their fortress, but also because the temple was the headquarters of the national government. As such the Zealots were strongly

---

based on *J.W.* 2:564–565, observes that since he was an influential figure among the populace in Jerusalem (*J.W.* 4:225), he probably had his origin in the city. Rhoads notes further that this Eleazar was a priest and an active member of the priestly-lay coalition under Eleazar, son of Ananias, which stopped the sacrifices from Gentiles. Eleazar might have "emerged as a revolutionary leader during the defense of the city against Cestius, since he subsequently controlled the spoils from the rout of Cestius." In this regard, Rhoads contends that Eleazar was "a link between the earlier priestly-lay group and the Zealots party" that was founded in the winter of 67–68 CE and he caused the Zealots to split from the people and to withdraw into the holy temple (*J.W.* 5:5).

87. Rhoads, *Israel in Revolution*, 105, suggests that the act of choosing a high priest by lot was an expression of a democratic process against the traditional way of appointing a high priest: "[The Zealots] initiated their own 'democratic' government with the choice of a high priest by lot—an innovation acceptable both to lower priests and the Judean peasants."

88. Schäfer, *History of the Jews*, 125, views the Zealots' appointment of the high priest by lot not as a mockery or simply a parody of a time-honored institution, but as "an attempt to revive the office of the High Priest. The ruling high-priestly families since the time of Herod were, as non-Zadokites, no more qualified for the High Priesthood than any other class of priest and, moreover, were politically compromised. So, if the Zealots arranged for the appointment of a High Priest from another family, their aim was clearly to override the privileged aristocratic priestly families and possibly even to reinstate the Zadokites as the sole high-priestly dynasty. In choosing the High Priest by lot, they were very probably intentionally introducing a democratic element into the appointment which, while not laid down by tradition, was hardly less legitimate than the sharing of the office amongst a few privileged families."

opposed by the high priests Ananus ben Ananus and Jesus ben Gamalas. That opposition from the high priests led to a bloody war between the Zealots and the provisional government. The Zealots were finally overpowered and withdrew into the inner court of the temple (*J.W.* 4:204).

Thereafter, the Zealots sought support from the Idumaeans (*J.W.* 4:228–229). The Idumaeans agreed to fight alongside the Zealots because they wanted to defend the freedom of Jerusalem, the temple and the Jewish nation against the Romans and their Jewish collaborators (*J.W.* 4:234–235, 282). The high priests, however, prevented them from entering the city. A nighttime rainstorm provided opportunity for some Zealots to escape and open the gates for the Idumaeans. Now with the help of the Idumaeans, the Zealots continued their reign of terror in the city. All of the guards of Ananus were murdered (*J.W.* 4:305, 310) such that the entire outer court of the temple was flooded with blood and eight thousand five hundred corpses (*J.W.* 4:313). The chief priests Ananus and Jesus were among the dead (*J.W.* 4:325).

The murder of Ananus marked the beginning of the fall of Jerusalem. Josephus reports that "the capture of the city began with the death of Ananus . . . the overthrow of the walls and the downfall of the Jewish state dated from the day on which the Jews beheld their high priest, the captain of their salvation, butchered in the heart of Jerusalem" (*J.W.* 4:318). Since then John of Gischala assumed leadership of the Zealots. Under his leadership, the Zealots took control of the city and instituted their own Sanhedrin, which conducted trials of prominent leading citizens, the wealthy, and the powerful who were accused of treason. One of the victims of this kangaroo court was Zacharias ben Baris. Being accused of betraying the nation by keeping contact with Vespasian, Zacharias appeared before this court and was murdered at the center of the temple (*J.W.* 4:334–343).

The unity between the Zealots under the leadership of John of Gischala and the Idumaeans did not last long. Due to John's terror and tyranny, the Idumaeans withdrew their support and split from the Zealots (*J.W.* 4:566). Prior to their departure from the city, they liberated about two thousand prisoners, who quickly joined Simon bar Gioras (*J.W.* 4:353).[89] Meanwhile, the Zealots under John of Gischala and some few remaining Idumaeans continued their reign of terror in the city against all the persons of power

---

89. It is not clear why the liberated prisoners joined bar Gioras's group and not those who liberated them. A possible assumption, however, is that they joined Simon bar Gioras because they were motivated by his ideology that promised a reward to the liberated (*J.W.* 4:508). It is also possible that the freed prisoners did not join the Idumaeans because the latter really had no leader, but were just a contingent of Jews from Idumaea.

and authority in order to ensure their own security. Their acts of terror in the city involved plunder and destruction of the houses of the wealthy, murder of men and rape of women (*J.W.* 4:560). Gurion and Niger of Peraea were among the victims of the Zealots' terrorism in the city (*J.W.* 4:354-365). Apart from the war against the provisional government, the Zealots also fought against Simon bar Gioras, who terrorized the countryside and threatened to take control of Jerusalem (*J.W.* 4:514-555).

Soon after the withdrawal of the Idumaeans from Jerusalem, John of Gischala also withdrew from the coalition with the Zealots, the motive being to have absolute power for himself. In Josephus's words, John formed a faction because he wanted to have "despotic" or "absolute sovereignty" (*J.W.* 4:389-391). Even though John's faction separated from the Zealots, the two groups seldom fought against each other (*J.W.* 4:397). All these events occurred in 68 CE.

In early 69 CE, while John of Gischala continued his tyrannical rule in Jerusalem (*J.W.* 4:558-565), Simon bar Gioras founded another group of revolutionaries. This group started in the countryside and comprised of the peasantry primarily from Acrabetene and Idumaea (*J.W.* 4:503-544). Josephus indentifies Simon bar Gioras's followers as a group of "brigands," suggesting that they were active and violent revolutionaries (*J.W.* 2:652-654). Simon bar Gioras, however, had a social program that proclaimed liberty for slaves and rewards for the liberated (*J.W.* 4:508), most of whom joined his faction.[90] His program attracted even the aristocrats from the local population and from Jerusalem (*J.W.* 4:353, 510). The program contained a messianic element in that followers were obedient to Simon bar Gioras's "command as to a king" (*J.W.* 4:510).

In addition, Simon bar Gioras's program consisted of a messianic claim as well. For example, shortly after the fall of the temple, he made a messianic pretention. Dressed in white robes, he emerged from the ground at the area where the temple formerly stood (*J.W.* 7:28-29),[91] suggesting that he was

---

90. Rhoads, *Israel in Revolution*, 141, rightly observes that Simon bar Gioras "expanded his social program of opposing the rich and championing the poor to include the freeing of slaves, many of whom joined him." Cf. Isa 61:1-2; Price, *Jerusalem under Siege*, 118.

91. Rhoads, *Israel in Revolution*, 143, 147. He states that although Josephus's comment that Simon bar Gioras was obeyed by his followers like a king seems to indicate the he was a "messianic pretender," there is no clear evidence to show that Simon bar Gioras really aspired to royalty. First, Simon never made messianic claims as did Menachem, who dressed in royal robes to the temple. Second, bar Gioras's origin as a son of a proselyte would not have permitted him to claim a royal heritage. Rhoads adds that if Simon bar Gioras had any messianic consciousness, then that would not have been from the Davidic tradition but probably from the "strong man" tradition, which

the messiah. When he entered Jerusalem to liberate the city from John's terror in the early Spring of 69 CE (J.W. 4:572–577),[92] the populace hailed him as "their savior and protector" (J.W. 4:575). Even though Josephus claims that Simon bar Gioras's "sole concern was to secure his own authority" (J.W. 4:576), the messianic element still stands.

In April/May 69 CE, Simon bar Gioras became "master of Jerusalem" (J.W. 4:577).[93] His successful conquests in the countryside convinced the Idumaeans that he would provide the best leadership in the nation's struggle against the Romans.[94] On the other hand, his presence in the city generated a new civil war between his faction and that of John, which included the Zealots. Each group struggled for power to control the city but neither of them succeeded in gaining much ground. Simon bar Gioras and his forces controlled the upper city, while John's forces controlled the Temple Mount (J.W. 4:578–584; 5:11). Both groups terrorized the populace, plundered possessions, and killed both the rich and anyone suspected of treason (J.W. 5:29–30, 439–441).

Meanwhile, John of Gischala's faction suffered still another split. The Zealots under the leadership of Eleazar, son of Simon (the one who earlier led a revolt against the provisional government and withdrew into the temple) deserted from John's faction (J.W. 5:5).[95] The reason for their withdrawal was John's brutality and murderous career. Josephus, however, gives a contrasting view in that he says that Eleazar broke from John because he himself desired absolute power for himself. Because he could not accept "submission to a junior to himself," Eleazar, alongside other influential figures and a considerable number of the Zealots' followers, seceded from John (J.W. 5:5–7). Although elsewhere Josephus seems to put blame on John as

---

put more emphasis on "the mighty warrior." In regard to Simon's emergence from the ground dressed in white robes, Rhoads suggests that this might have been a gesture of sharing the consequences of the war with the Jews who were faithful to him. In this regard, Rhoads observes, "the white robes would symbolize the role of a martyr who gives up his life for his people."

92. Price, *Jerusalem under Siege*, 104, suggests that the Idumaeans invited Simon bar Gioras into the city in order to overthrow John and the Zealots so they could gain power for themselves: "The Idumaeans and high priests would have hoped to use Simon to dislodge John and the Zealots and then install themselves in power."

93. Rhoads, "Zealots," 1050, points out that Simon bar Gioras's arrival "in Jerusalem prevented John from gaining control over the whole city."

94. Cf. Rhoads, *Israel in Revolution*, 139, 145.

95. Cf. J.W. 4:225, where Eleazar is identified as a son of Gion and is described as the most influential figure among the Zealots and as a member of an ancestral priestly family. He once appealed to the Idumaeans to provide military support for the defense of Jerusalem in order to prevent Ananus's proposal to betray the city to the Romans as well as to rescue the revolutionaries imprisoned in the temple (see J.W. 4:228–229).

one who desired absolute authority and power for himself, what is evident here was a struggle for power even on the part of Eleazar. Eleazar separated from John because he wanted to have power above John. Both John and Eleazar struggled for absolute power for oneself.

Under Eleazar's leadership, the Zealots took control of the inner temple (*J.W.* 5:7), thus increasing a third strong Jewish faction struggling for power in the city in addition to those of John and Simon bar Gioras. The three factions fiercely fought against each other causing deaths not only to those who fought, but also to those who favored peace and in need of deliverance. In their fight among each other, the Jewish factions burned stores and destroyed whatever the city had provided against a siege, over and above "severing the sinews of their own" (*J.W.* 5:21–26). Since the calamities brought about by this civil war were unbearable, some prayed for the coming of the Romans with the hope that the external war would liberate them from their internal enemies (*J.W.* 5:28).

On the Passover day in 70 CE, the Zealots under Eleazar lost control of the inner court of the temple. This occurred when Eleazar admitted the citizens into the temple to worship and celebrate the Passover. John used that opportunity to his advantage. With his followers, he entered the temple with concealed weapons and indiscriminately attacked the worshipers, causing confusion and disorder in the temple. The result was that the Zealots lost control of the inner court of the temple. John then took control of the place and all the stores it contained. At this point, the two factions reunited under John's command. Their union reduced the number of factions in the city from three to two: John's group and that of Simon bar Gioras (*J.W.* 5:98–105). The two factions continued to fight against each other until Titus began the siege of the city in 70 CE.[96] Throughout the war period, the Jewish factions fought against one another; and they formed coalitions only in the presence of the Romans, their common enemy.[97]

During the Jewish civil war in Jerusalem in 68–69 CE, Vespasian delayed his operations in the city (*J.W.* 4:486–90).[98] Two factors may have contributed to that delay. First, Vespasian might have done so as his military strategy to let the Jews weaken themselves for his easy victory. Josephus re-

---

96. Price, *Jerusalem under Siege*, 115.

97. Rhoads, "Zealots," 1051; Price, *Jerusalem under Siege*, 107, has offered a similar observation: "While the Romans hesitated for two years [to attack the Jews in Jerusalem] because of their own civil war, the Jews in Jerusalem remained preoccupied with bloody power struggles. The results were the loss of many able-bodied men through war or desertion, the destruction of crucial food supplies and the ruin of some vital parts of the city. Divided energies meant lost opportunities."

98. Cf. Cline, *Jerusalem Besieged*, 118.

ports that the Roman generals viewed the strife among the Jews as "Divine providence" for their advantage and determined to use that opportunity to ambush and defeat their enemy as the Jews fought among themselves. Josephus supports this view when he comments that Vespasian postponed attacks against Jerusalem in order to let Jews "continue their own destruction" until they "had wasted their numbers in sedition" (*J.W.* 4:366–376). In effect, Vespasian's plan worked. The civil war caused losses of lives and desertions of those who could fight against the Romans, thus weakening their own military strength (*J.W.* 4:377–388). Further, the prolonged civil war involved burning of food stored in fear of the siege, destruction of the things the city had provided against a siege, and wastage of the energy of the fighters (*J.W.* 5:24–25).[99] As a result, the strength of the Jews was weakened giving room for the Romans' easy victory.

The second factor for Vespasian's suspension of his military operations in Jerusalem was the civil war in Rome.[100] The civil war in the capital of the empire occurred following the death of Nero in June 68 CE (*J.W.* 4:491). Vespasian learned of Nero's death while at Caesarea, when he was getting ready to advance to Jerusalem to crush the revolt (*J.W.* 4:491). As a result, Vespasian deferred his mission to Jerusalem in order to wait to hear who would be the next emperor, and hence further instructions concerning the war (*J.W.* 4:497–498). Nero's death led to a period of sedition and civil war in Rome (*J.W.* 4:545) that witnessed four competing emperors occupying the throne in quick successions: Galba, Otho, Vitellius, and finally Vespasian (*J.W.* 4:491, 494–495, 499, 548–549, 588–589, 650–653).[101]

---

99. Cf. Tacitus, *Hist.* 5.12.3, similarly reports that during the civil war, there "were constant battles, treachery and arson among them [the Jews], and a large store of grain was burnt." See also Price, *Jerusalem under Siege*, 105. Price comments that the burning of food stores by the different Jewish factions was meant to weaken each one's opponents and hence contributed to the weakening of the city even before the arrival of the Romans. This situation led the city to famine, just as Josephus relates that the Jews "were conquered by famine, which could not have happened had they not prepared it for themselves" (*J.W.* 5:26).

100. Cf. Rhoads, "Zealots," 1048, also comments that in 67–68 CE, Vespasian withdrew from besieging Jerusalem because of the unrest that occurred in Rome.

101. Cf. Cline, *Jerusalem Besieged*, 118; Price, *Jerusalem under Siege*, 107, has made a good observation: the failure of the Jews to utilize for their advantage the civil war in Rome contributed to their defeat by the Romans. Instead of fighting against one another for power, they could have organized themselves to fight their common enemy. Especially when Vespasian postponed his attacks in 68–69 CE partly due to Nero's death and the civil war in Rome, "the Jews could have tried to regain conquered territory, to spread revolution through the areas still volatile, or at least to ambush the Roman army as it moved through unfamiliar country. Yet they did none of this and greatly eased the task of the Romans."

Vespasian's accession to the imperial throne restored peace in Rome (*J.W.* 4:655; cf. 4:601, 616–621). Since Vespasian had to leave for Rome to occupy the imperial throne, he entrusted the task of crushing the revolt in Jerusalem to his son Titus (*J.W.* 4:656–658).[102] It is therefore to be concluded that the strife and civil war in Rome contributed to the Romans' delay in putting down the revolt in Jerusalem.

The Siege of Jerusalem, 70 CE

Titus began the siege of Jerusalem a few days before the Passover of 70 CE. To accomplish this crucial task, Titus had at his disposal the Roman's strongest and best equipped forces: the fifth, tenth, and the fifteenth legions. He also had the 12th legion, whose defeat under Cestius had inflamed the war in 66 CE (*J.W.* 5:41).[103] With these forces he left Caesarea and advanced to Jerusalem to begin the siege. Before he began the siege, Titus set up a military camp a few miles away from the city (*J.W.* 5:39–53), and stationed the tenth legion on the Mount of Olives (*J.W.* 5:69–70, 135). Meanwhile, the Jewish revolutionary groups of John Gischala and Simon bar Gioras formed a coalition to fight against Titus. Many Jews joined the war against the Romans and fought courageously, hoping that they would be the victors of the entire war (*J.W.* 5:71–80). The revolutionary forces attempted to prevent Titus from taking over and destroying the city of Jerusalem, but they were not successful (*J.W.* 5:303–330). Titus began the siege of Jerusalem by destroying its outermost walls (*J.W.* 5:331), and continued until he captured the fortress of Antonia in early August 70 CE (*J.W.* 6:68–93).

Titus's capture of Antonia led to a suspension of the daily sacrifice. The Jews boycotted the offering of the daily sacrifice in the temple. As Titus's spokesperson, Josephus attempted to persuade the Jews to restore the sacrifice and to surrender in order to prevent their nation from further destruction. His efforts, however, proved fruitless. The defenders of Jerusalem refused to surrender saying that they were afraid of capture since the city belonged to God (*J.W.* 6:93–99), implying that they were ready to die in defense of God's city. Titus then had no choice but to resume the siege (*J.W.* 6:129–130). On August 28, 70 CE, he captured and burned the temple to the ground.[104] The carnage in the temple during this final capture was hor-

---

102. Aberbach and Aberbach, *Roman-Jewish Wars*, 32.

103. Cf. Tacitus, *Hist.* 5:1, who has also kept a record of the strength of the Roman troops at Titus's disposal for the war with the Jews.

104. Cline, *Jerusalem Besieged*, 127. On page 330, in note 87, Cline observes that Josephus's statement that the temple was destroyed on "the tenth of the month of Lous

rendous. Killings were done around the altar and the blood of the victims flooded the sanctuary. Josephus describes the incidence thus:

> The impetuosity of the legionaries, when they joined the fray, neither exhortation nor threat could restrain; passion was for all the only leader. Crushed together about the entrances, many were trampled down by their companions; many, stumbling on the still hot and smoldering ruins of the porticoes, suffered the fate of the vanquished. As they drew near to the sanctuary they pretended not even to hear Caesar's orders and shouted to those in front of them to throw the firebrands. The insurgents, for their part, were now powerless to help; and on all sides was carnage and flight. Most of the slain were civilians, weak and unarmed people, each butchered where he was caught. Around the altar a pile of corpses was accumulating; down the steps of the sanctuary flowed a stream of blood, and the bodies of the victims killed above went sliding to the bottom. (J.W. 6:257–259)

This horrific bloody massacre in the holy place was followed by the destruction and desecration of the temple itself. Whether willingly (J.W. 6:229; 7:1; cf. Ant. 20:250) or unwillingly (J.W. 6:266), Titus authorized the burning of the temple.[105] As the fire continued to consume the sanctuary, the Roman soldiers plundered whatever they saw and killed whoever

---

[Ab]" (J.W. 6:250) contradicts the ninth month traditionally held to be the time Solomon's temple fell.

105. Scholars give contradicting views regarding Titus's role in the burning of the temple. While some think that Titus deliberately ordered the destruction of the temple, others exonerate the Roman general of the deliberate burning of the temple (thus favoring Josephus's account that the temple was burned against his wishes). The following scholars hold Titus as responsible for the destruction of the temple: Alon, "Burning of the Temple," 253–68; Spilsbury, "Burning of the Temple," 304–27; Price, *Jerusalem under Siege*, 170n28; Goodman, *Ruling Class*, 237–38, notes that the Jerusalem temple was deliberately destroyed despite Josephus's attempt to shift the blame from his patron Titus; Rives, "Flavian Religious Policy," 150, suspects that "Josephus's account of Titus' role in the Temple's destruction is misleading"; Mason, "Figured Speech," 257, views the account as part of Josephus's "ironic scheme." The following scholars are among those who exonerate Titus of direct responsibility in the burning of the temple: Rajak, *Josephus*, 206–11, concludes: "As long as it cannot be convincingly impugned, Josephus' story, the best we have, is the one that should stand." Also Leoni, "'Against Caesar's Wishes,'" 48–49, 51, states that "Josephus's narrative appears unequivocally clear . . . Right from the starting paragraphs of Book 1 it is explicitly stated that the Sanctuary was burnt down against Caesar's wishes . . . Therefore . . . until we have proof to the contrary, the order of publication should at least guarantee the internal coherence of the report." He concludes, "Josephus's relation on the burning of the Sanctuary proves to be substantially trustworthy." Leoni includes a detailed bibliography for both positions. See pages 42–45 of his article.

they caught. People of every class and age, the elderly people, children, lay and priests, were indiscriminately massacred (*J.W.* 6:271–272). A total number of people who died in the temple that day, either by fire or sword was six thousand. In addition to this huge loss of life, the treasury chambers with huge amount of money and other valuables were also reduced to ashes (*J.W.* 6:281–285). On top of this desecration of the holy place, the Romans committed further serious sacrilegious acts in the temple. Against the Jewish customs, they brought their standards into the temple court, set them opposite the eastern gate, and offered sacrifices to them. Moreover, at that holy ground, the Roman soldiers acclaimed Titus as imperator (*J.W.* 6:316), and the temple treasures were delivered up to Caesar (*J.W.* 6:387–391).[106] For the Jews, such actions at the holy place, were not only blasphemous, they were also a great humiliation.

The burning of the temple was not the conclusion of Roman conquest of Israel. The Romans' complete conquest of the Jews climaxed in the siege of the whole city of Jerusalem. The end of the conquest was marked by the destruction of the strongly fortified upper city (*J.W.* 6:374–377). The final events of the war in the streets of the upper city were unbearable on the part of the Jews. Josephus reports of this event in a painful detail that the Roman troops:

> massacred indiscriminately all whom they met, and burnt the houses with all who had taken refuge within. Often in the course of their raids, on entering the houses for loot, they would find whole families dead and rooms filled with the victims of the famine . . . while they pitied those who had thus perished, they had no similar feelings for the living, but, running everyone through who fell in their way, they choked the alleys with corpses and deluged the whole city with blood, insomuch that many of the fires were extinguished by the gory stream. (*J.W.* 6:403–406; cf. 6:353–355, 363–369)

---

106. According to Josephus, the sacred treasures were handed over to the Romans by the priest Jesus ben Thebuthi and Phineas, the treasurer of the temple, in exchange for protection from Caesar. Thebuthi delivered the following sacred treasures to the Romans: the massive golden vessels including two lampstands, tables, bowls, and platters; the veils, the priests' vestments, precious stones, and many other things used in public worship. Phineas handed over such items as the tunics and girdles worn by the priests; bundles of purple and scarlet preserved for necessary repair of the temple veil; a mass of cinnamon and cassia, spices used for daily burning as incense to God; numerous sacred ornaments and other treasures (cf. *J.W.* 7:161). If the whole temple was burned, as Josephus claims, how were all these things saved? I consider Josephus's statement that the temple was burned to the ground to be a gross exaggeration.

These events concluded the Roman conquest of the whole of Jerusalem. With the exception of Herod's palace, the tower of Phasael, Mariamme, and Hippicus, and part of the wall on the west, all of Jerusalem was now destroyed. Both the city and the temple were leveled to the ground such that visitors would not believe that the place had ever been inhabited.[107] The towers and walls that were left standing were meant to serve as a memorial to the strong defenses of the city and Titus's victory, and as protection for the Roman garrison stationed there to keep peace in the city (*J.W.* 7:1–3; 6:413).[108]

Generally, the Roman-Jewish war brought a horrible destruction to human life. The inhabitants of Jerusalem were either killed or taken into captivity.[109] Josephus reports that ninety-seven thousand Jews were taken prisoners during the entire war, and that eleven thousand of them died of starvation during the final stage of the siege (*J.W.* 6:419). The total of those who died during the siege was one milion one hundred thousand, most of them being Jews (*J.W.* 6:420).[110] The Jewish generals, John of Gischala and Simon bar Gioras surrendered and were then taken to Rome. While John of Gischala received life imprisonment, Simon bar Gioras was executed as the

---

107. Archaeological excavations have revealed that Josephus's statement on this matter is an exaggeration. Archaeologist Ben-Dov, *In the Shadow*, 185, writes this: "Standing there on a street from the Second Temple period with the ashlars of Herod's monumental walls at my feet—stones that had been torn out of the wall by ramping soldiers—I could almost feel the horror and savagery of those days of destruction when Jerusalem and the Temple Mount, the jewels at its center, were laid low." See also Geva, "Searching" 35–37; Cline, *Jerusalem Besieged*, 130. Mark's view that the temple stones were pulled down (13:2) agrees with this archaeological evidence, and hence is to be taken as a more credible account compared to Josephus's.

108. Schäfer, *History of the Jews*, 128.

109. Elsewhere Josephus relates that among the prisoners of war, the old, the weak, the seditious, and brigands were killed; the tallest young men were reserved for the triumph in Rome. The rest were either sold into slavery or given to provinces to serve as entertainment tools in theaters where they met their death either by the sword or by wild beasts (*J.W.* 6:414–419; cf. 7:24).

110. Cline, *Jerusalem Besieged*, 129, views this number as an exaggeration because after the siege "there were still sufficient Judeans left to defy the Romans over the next thirty years." Although he doubts the number over a million casualties, he believes that the Jews lost a substantial number of their population during the siege. A similar view is held by Grabbe, *Judaism*, 495–60, who comments on Josephus's exaggerations thus: "The noncombatants within the city suffered from famine and from the militants. Exactly how the many atrocities against innocent victims, often leaders and nobles, that are reported by Josephus are to be evaluated is problematic. If Josephus is to be believed, they must all have perished several times over: on several occasions his narrative describes things so that no one among the citizenry could have been left alive, yet the next episode reports more victims."

chief commander of the Jews (*J. W.* 6:433–434; 7:153–154, 36).[111] The Romans' capture of Jerusalem on the 26th of September, 70 CE not only marked the end of the siege (*J. W.* 6:442) and "the end of the political power of Judaism,"[112] it also sealed the Roman imperial domination over the Jews.

In Rome, Titus's victory in the war was marked with a triumph. After his successful completion of the military assignment in Jerusalem, Titus returned to Rome in 71 CE. There he celebrated a triumph with his father, Vespasian and his brother, Domitian. In the triumph, the Jewish prisoners of war, including John of Gischala and Simon bar Gioras were paraded (*J. W.* 7:118–119) and, the temple objects from Jerusalem were displayed (*J. W.* 7:148–152). The triumph processions were completed by the execution of Simon bar Gioras on the Forum in the vicinity of the temple of Jupiter Capitolinus (*J. W.* 7:152–157). The triumph sealed the end of the Roman-Jewish War of 66–70 CE.

Causes of the War

The causes of the Jewish revolt against Rome were many. Josephus, however, highlights only a few of them while downplaying the rest. He puts blame for the war primarily on the Jewish revolutionaries (*J. W.* 1:10; 7:113; *Ant.* 18:6–10), whom he repeatedly accuses of forcing peaceful Jews to revolt (*J. W.* 3:454–455; 492–493, 500; 4:84–86). He particularly mentions the "Fourth Philosophy" as the group most responsible for the war (*J. W.* 1:10; 6:113; *Ant.* 18:1–10, 23–25) and refers to them as having "sowed the seed of every kind of misery, which so afflicted the nation that words are inadequate (to explain)" (*Ant.* 18:6). Josephus stresses that the Fourth Philosophy initiated brigandage in Judea and "sowed the seed from which sprang strife between factions and the slaughter of fellow citizens" that climaxed in the destruction of the "very temple of God" by the Romans (*Ant.* 18:7–8). Certainly Josephus suggests that the war occurred partly due to the revolutionaries' activities in Israel prior to the war that operated between 6 and 66 CE.[113]

The Fourth Philosophy, also known as the Sicarii, held an ideology that emphasized the lordship of God alone over Israel. The group advocated that there is "no lord but God" (*J. W.* 7:323; cf. 7:411; Lev 25:18–25; Deut 15:4–6) and that "God alone is their leader and master" (*Ant.* 18:23).

---

111. Rhoads, *Israel in Revolution*, 147; Schäfer, *History of the Jews*, 128.

112. Aberbach and Aberbach. *Roman-Jewish Wars*, 32.

113. For a detailed discussion about the situation in Palestine and the revolutionary activities in the years 6–66 CE, see Rhoads, *Israel in Revolution*, 47–93; cf. Bilde, "Causes of the Jewish War," 187.

The implication of this ideology was that Caesar had no right to rule over Israel.[114] In order to promote rebellion against Rome, the Sicarii employed terrorist methods including murder, pillage, burning of homes, and kidnappings (*J.W.* 1:10).

Josephus also attributes the revolt to the hostility between Jews and Gentiles. The quarrel between the Jews and the Gentiles manifested itself in their violent conflict in Caesarea. That conflict led to the outbreak of revolt in Jerusalem (*J.W.* 2:284–286; *Ant.* 20:184). Josephus shows that the incompetence, brutality, and corrupt behavior of some of the Roman procurators were also factors for the war. Such behavior and incompetence of some of the Roman procurators contributed to the outbreak of the revolt (cf. *J.W.* 2:272–276). Tacitus reinforces this view when he states that the outbreak of the war was due to the harsh and careless behavior of the procurators such as Felix and Florus (*Hist.* 5.9.3–5; 10.1). Rabbinic literature, however, disregard these historical factors in favor of moralistic concerns involving social hostility, breakdown of values, and excessive materialistic concerns (*Tosefta Menahot* 13:22; *b. Git.* 55b–56a).[115]

Modern scholars have given additional causes of the war that Josephus seems to ignore. Such additional factors for the war are diverse and range from political, socioeconomic, and religious factors. The political factors relate to Roman domination in Judea and the imposition of Hellenism upon the Jews. The Roman control of Israel started when Pompey conquered the land in 63 BCE. In 37 BCE, Herod the Great became a puppet king of the Romans. During his reign priority was given to his personal and imperial needs while the needs of the Jewish people were made secondary (*Ant.* 15:328); the Jewish Sanhedrin lost its power; high priests were appointed and removed at his will, and most of them were foreigners from Alexandria and Babylonia (*Ant.* 15:40–41). The only high priest from Palestine was Joseph bar Ellem, who held the office for only a day (*Ant.* 17:166). For the 33 years of his reign, Herod the Great appointed not less than seven high priests.[116] This situation created a condition that would latter lead to the revolt on the part of the Jews.

During the reign of Herod the Great, the socio-economic condition of the Jewish people was harsh. The king bled the poor citizens by heavy taxes (*J.W.* 1:524; 2:85–86; *Ant.* 16:149–159; 17:302–314; cf. Tacitus, *Ann.* 2:42), which he used to cover costs for his administration, maintenance of his foreign military, to pay tribute to Rome, and to promote foreign culture

---

114. Rhoads, *Israel in Revolution*, 113, 119.
115. Levine, "Jewish War," 839.
116. Goodman, *Ruling Class*, 41.

through extensive building programs. The building programs involved the construction of Hellenistic cities, palaces, and temples in Palestine in honor of Caesar (*J.W.* 1:403–421; *Ant.* 16:136–145). When he built the temple in Jerusalem (*J.W.* 1:401–402; *Ant.* 15:380–425), the king violated the Jewish traditions by erecting a golden eagle (a symbol of the Roman empire) at the entrance gate (*Ant.* 15:267; 16:1–5). Some of the Hellenistic cities he constructed turned into being the source of hostility between Jews and Greeks, and finally led to the outbreak of the war (*J.W.* 2:266–267). Herod's brutality and control of his citizens[117] prevented a general eruption during his reign (*Ant.* 14:27, 315; 15:326).

The political factor for the war is also evident in actions of the Roman emperors, Caligula and Nero. Emperor Caligula attempted to erect his image in the temple in 40 CE (*J.W.* 2:184–207), an act that symbolized the Roman imperial domination in Palestine. It reminded the Jews of Pompey's similar violation of the temple's holy of holies in the past (*Ant.* 14:105). The Jews would thus not resist reviving negative attitude toward the Romans, and hence the feeling that could later lead to a revolt. Nero's decision in favor of Greeks in their conflict with the Jews at Caesarea created still another atmosphere that could result into war (*J.W.* 2:284).[118]

Furthermore, the brutality, incompetence, maladministration, and corrupt behavior of the Roman procurators also contributed to the situation that led to the outbreak of the war. Governors such as Crassus, Sabinus, Pilate, and Cumanus were hostile to the Jews. Their tyranny and brutality forced the Jews to take up arms to fight for their freedom. Sabinus, for example, was responsible for the riot that occurred after the death of Herod the Great in 4 BCE (*J.W.* 2:41, 49–50; *Ant.* 17:252–254, 257, 264). Pontius Pilate expressed his brutality when he responded violently toward the Jews' protests against his attempt to bring the Roman standards into Jerusalem (*J.W.* 2:169–174) and his plunder of the sacred money from the temple treasury for the construction of an aqueduct to bring water in Jerusalem. Pilate also ordered the murder of the Jewish nonviolent protesters (*J.W.* 2:176–177; *Ant.* 18:60–67). The crucifixion of Jesus (15:1–24) is another proof of Pilate's brutality and abuse of power.

The political factors for the war were expressed in other ways. The use of offices by some procurators as means of gaining wealth and high rank (*Ant.* 18:172–178); appointments of high priesthood contrary to Jewish customs; and the use of foreign military forces made up of ethnic groups hostile

---

117. Cf. *J.W.* 1:304–14, 648–55; *Ant.* 14:13–14; 15:368–71, 267–291; 17:41–61, 149–167.

118. See also *Ant.* 20:182–184.

to Jews, also contributed to the political situation that led to the war.[119] In any case, this situation provided the condition for the emergence of revolutionary groups to fight against foreign domination in order to attain their freedom.[120] Because of such a situation Judea this time was like "the top of a volcano of Jewish nationalism which might erupt at any moment."[121]

Socioeconomic factors also contributed to the outbreak of the Jewish revolt. According to Applebaum, the Jewish revolt of 66 CE emerged primarily due to "the reaction of rural Judaism to social injustice."[122] Menahem Stern underscores Applebaum's observation when he states that as Jerusalem prospered economically, poverty, hardship, heavy taxation, debt, and crime also flourished. Heavy taxation led to borrowing. Failure to pay the debt led to loss of land, and finally, to landlessness and severe poverty among peasants.[123] Landlessness became the source of conflicts and public disturbances. Stern views that the revolt "bore all the signs of an inner social upheaval." Since he considers Menachem and Simon bar Gioras as radical social revolutionaries, and John of Gischala as one of the wealthy Jews who supported the revolt, Stern concludes that there was a widespread interest in the revolt among Jews of all classes.[124]

Similarly, Rhoads believes that socioeconomic factors contributed to the outbreak of the war. Like Stern, he considers heavy taxation was a major problem among the peasant Jews under the imperial power. But he adds that the famine of the late 40s CE and unemployment that arose due to the completion of the construction of the Jerusalem temple in 64 CE created an atmosphere that led to the war. Rhoads argues that these factors forced the peasants into indebtedness, landlessness, and urbanization. These resulted into overpopulation, and to a widespread banditry and terrorism among the vulnerable peasants against the wealthy and upper class ruling elite. This

119. Rhoads, "Zealots,"1051.

120. Contra Goodman, "First Jewish Revolt,"426, who argues that the primary cause of the war was not "the cruel imperialism of the Roman enemy" but the social inequality within the Judean community that resulted due to the excessive wealth that flooded into the holy city of Jerusalem.

121. Smallwood, "Jews and Romans." 316.

122. Applebaum, "Economic Life in Palestine," 663.

123. Contra Udoh, *To Caesar What Is Caesar's*, 180, 243, who rejects the idea that taxation was severe during Roman imperial rule in Judea, and hence that taxation was one of the causes of the Jewish revolt. Udoh sees no evidence for excessive taxation in Judea before 70 CE, no evidence for its related impact on other parts of the empire or on individual lives. He concludes: "one cannot speak with dogmatic certitude about the role that the levels of taxation played in the Jewish revolt of 66 C.E."

124. Stern, *Aspects of Jewish Society*, 574–80; cf. Harter, "Causes and Course of the Jewish Revolt," 58–60.

situation climaxed in the Jewish revolt against the Romans.[125] The burning of the archive containing debts records by the Jerusalem populace after the defeat of the Romans strongly supports the view that socioeconomic factors contributed to the outbreak of the revolt.

Horsley and Hanson support the idea that socioeconomic factors were part of the causes of the war but they put particular emphasis on banditry. They argue that excessive taxation gave birth to banditry in Palestine, but insist that it was banditry which was the primary cause of "the outbreak of the massive revolt against the Romans."[126] I contend that both the heavy taxation and banditry have to be taken together as part of the contributing social economic factors for the war. It is misleading to take only one of them. The two complement one another.

Religious factors also contributed to the conflict between Jews and the Romans. Marcus Borg considers this aspect to have been the primary cause of the war. Borg asserts that the "quest for holiness" among the Jews was the primary cause of the war with Rome.[127] Borg's emphasis is drawn from the Sicarii's ideology that stated there is "no lord but God." With this ideology, the Sicarii questioned the right for Caesar to rule over Israel. For Borg, the Sicarii viewed that the Romans brought pollution in Israel and that in order to purify the land they had to remove them by force.[128] In this case, Borg agrees with Rhoads who argues that since the Roman domination of Israel contradicted the belief that God alone is the Lord of Israel, the revolutionaries committed themselves to revolt in order to free Israel from foreign power; to defend the law; and to purify the holy land, the city, and the temple from the pollution brought by Gentiles, thereby ensuring freedom and prosperity of their nation.[129]

The revolutionaries believed that their commitment to war against Rome would receive divine approval. They were confident that by taking up arms to defend the holy land and the temple against Rome, God would give them favor, and hence ability to free their land from foreign domination.

---

125. Rhoads, "Zealots," 1051; see also Goodman, "Jewish Revolt," 423–26; Feldman, "Josephus," 984; Horsley, *Jesus and the Spiral of Violence*, 77–89; Horsley and Hanson, *Bandits*, 49–50, who argue that social bandits occur when the state or rulers dictate unjust and intolerable social economic conditions among poor peasants who cannot cope with the excessive taxes which force them to landlessness, and thus compelling them to an alternative means for their livelihood. Then they conclude stating that in Israel, "Expanding banditry became a major factor leading to the outbreak of the massive revolt against the Romans."

126. Horsley and Hanson, *Bandits*, 69, 77.

127. Borg, *Conflict*, 87.

128. Ibid., 80.

129. Rhoads, "Zealots," 1051.

The eschatological expectation of the coming of the messiah (cf. *J.W.* 6:312) gave them confidence that God would soon intervene. Their victory against Cestius at the beginning of the war and the strife in Rome were seen by many Jews as signs that God was working on their favor and that Rome would soon fall. The Jewish coins minted during the revolt with the inscriptions "the Redemption of Zion" and "Jerusalem the Holy," vividly demonstrate the religious nature of the Jewish war against the Romans.[130]

Each of the causes presented in this part is essential for explaining the outbreak of the Roman-Jewish War. No single factor by itself is sufficient to explain the war. It is therefore important to consider all of them together as the causes of the outbreak of the Jewish revolt.

Conclusion

In this chapter I have attempted to examine the person and career of Josephus, the course, and causes of the war. I have shown that Josephus belonged to a royal and priestly ancestry; was trained in the Torah, and served as a priest in Jerusalem. I have also shown that he also served as a military general of Galilee, a prophet, and a historian who wrote the history of the war while enjoying benefits from the Roman imperial family in Rome. Despite the biases, exaggerations, contradictions, and some inventions in his histories, Josephus deserves to be used as a source especially because the war and most of the events he reports truly happened and himself was an eyewitness of most of the events he narrates about.

From Josephus's account of the war, we have observed the Romans' military campaign to stop the revolt in Judea started in Galilee before it culminated with the siege of Jerusalem and the temple. Serving for the interests of Rome, Vespasian led a strong army that violently devastated Judea. The Romans not only caused a great loss of life, they also sent many Jews into forced servitude while forcing many others into becoming refuges. We have also learnt that the war occurred due to a combination of causes involving political, socioeconomic, and religious factors. The heart of all these was Roman imperialism and its related values, namely, wealth, status, and power. The Roman imperial domination created a situation that led to the war. The Jewish authorities and the urban elites imitated the Roman imperial values in that they oppressed and exploited the rural peasants through heavy taxations and oppressive purity rules, some of which associated the Romans with pollution of Israel. In response to the Roman imperial domination and oppression, the Jewish revolutionaries fought the Romans in

130. Ibid., 1051–52.

order to achieve freedom and to remove pollution in Israel. Coming from among the exploited and oppressed rural peasants, the revolutionaries also fought against the oppressive and exploitative Jewish authorities and urban elites who collaborated with the Romans. The revolutionaries' motive was to end injustices and foreign domination.

It is clear from this chapter that many of the events of the war that Josephus reports are closely related to Mark's story of Jesus. One major example relates to Vespasian's rise to the imperial power. Vespasian was proclaimed emperor in accordance to Jewish oracles. In this case, he became ruler by divine assistance. The report about him that he was the new emperor and his entrances in cities were received as good news, and the populous hailed him as savior and benefactor. The oracles associated with his rise to the imperial throne predicted a ruler who would be "lord of land and sea" and "ruler of the whole human race," the titles that were appropriate only for God. Hence, these titles not only legitimized Vespasian's imperial power, but also elevated him to a divine status. There are other important events of the war that link Mark and the war, but I just mention them in passing. They include the civil war in Jerusalem where various Jewish groups fought each other in a struggle for power to control the city; the messianic pretentions associated with Menachem and Simon bar Gioras; killings in the temple on the Sabbath; occupation of the temple by the revolutionaries and fighting from there; and the destruction of Jerusalem and its temple, to mention just a few.

The insights from Josephus are crucial for the study of Mark's Gospel. Such insights give us some light as to what Mark's hearers might have known and associated them in their evaluation of the Gospel. In the subsequent chapters, I primarily use three main themes from Josephus's report on the war: Vespasian's rise to the imperial power, his military campaign in Galilee, and the Roman imperial values that might have led to the war. These three themes provided insights that are a rich source of material to which Mark offers ironic parallels or contrasts. For example, Vespasian's rise to the imperial power based on Jewish oracles, his entrances in cities, and the accompanying good news give ironic parallels to Mark's opening that begins with an announcement of the good news of Jesus Messiah, Son of God and his appearance. I use the insights in chapter four where I deal with the onset of God's empire in Mark. Second, Vespasian's military campaign in Galilee parallels Jesus' public ministry in Galilee. In this case, I use insights from Vespasian's war campaign in Galilee in chapter five where I examine Jesus' life-giving campaign in Galilee. Finally, the Roman imperial values, the main causes of the war serve as a foil for Jesus' teaching on the values of God's empire. I use these insights in chapter six where I focus on contrast of values.

It should be made clear that the insights that have not been specifically included in the three themes are neither meant to be regarded as less important nor ignored. They are important and will be used in this book when and where they are relevant and necessary.

4

The Onset of Empires

Introduction

IN THE ANCIENT WORLD, the advent of an emperor not only marked the onset of an empire or the beginning of a new era, but also was partly the source of good news. In the article, "Imperial Ideology and Paul's Eschatology in 1 Thessalonians," Helmut Koester enumerates important features related to the appearance of the emperor in the ancient world. He observes that the emperor's arrival in a city was associated with several events: preparations on the part of the community to be visited; a messenger who heralded the coming of the emperor when his arrival draws near; the delegation of a city that goes out to meet and greet the emperor when he arrives; a joyous reception of the emperor at his arrival; and finally, the benefits (security, prosperity, salvation) associated with the coming of the emperor into the city.[1] Adolph Deissmann adds other features that can be included here. For him, the advent of the emperor not only marked the beginning of a new era, but also involved the minting of the advent-coins after the arrival of the emperor and the giving of advent-sacrifices (speeches on entering a place).[2]

The idea that the advent of the emperor marked the inauguration of a new era or the beginning of an empire is crucial for this study.[3] In relation to Mark's story, that observation provides the basis for considering the prologue (1:1–13) as dealing with an onset of God's empire. Although Mark's prologue does not exhibit every feature of the advent of the emperor noted above, it manifests a number of them. The features present in Mark's

---

1. Koester, "Imperial Ideology," 158–62.
2. Deissmann, *Light*, 368, 371–72.
3. For the view that 1:1–13 form Mark's prologue, see Matera, "Prologue," 4–6; Donahue and Harrington, *Gospel of Mark*, 59–70; Moloney, *Mark*, 27–41; Wilhelm, *Preaching the Gospel of Mark*, 3–14; Tolbert, *Sowing the Gospel*, 108–20. Other scholars consider that the prologue ends at 1:15. See for example, Boring, *Mark*, 29–53; Keck, "Introduction to Mark's Gospel," 362–68; Guellich, *Mark*, 3–5; Guijarro, "Why Does the Gospel of Mark Begin as It Does?" 28, 34; Thurston, *Preaching Mark*, 13–17.

prologue include the reference to "Jesus Messiah, Son of God" (1:1) and to "the Lord" who stands on the place of the emperor; John as the messenger who not only prepares the way of Jesus (1:3), but also heralds the coming of Jesus whom he identifies as the "one who is stronger than I" (1:7); and the people from Judea and Jerusalem who serve as the community coming out to prepare for the coming of the Lord (1:5).

Moreover, there is also the appearance of Jesus from Nazareth of Galilee and his reception by John who baptizes him in the Jordan River. At his baptism, Jesus received the power of the Holy Spirit and heard God's voice endorsing him as "God's Son, the Beloved" (1:9-11). Jesus' baptism served as a ritual of divine enthronement of Jesus to be God's agent to lead God's people. The descent of the Holy Spirit upon Jesus and God's decree that Jesus is his Son: "You are my Son" (1:10-11) symbolize the anointed and installation of Jesus as one who is entrusted to rule God's people on behalf of God (cf. Ps 2:7).[4] The ripping apart of the heavens as well reinforces the idea that Jesus' installation marked the beginning of a new era[5] or the establishment of God's empire on earth. Furthermore, Mark's prologue suggests Jesus' victory in his encounter with Satan in the wilderness (1:12-13). The report about Jesus' return from the wilderness to "Galilee proclaiming the good news of God" about the arrival of God's empire (1:14-15), which appears immediately after an account of his encounter with Satan, signals Jesus' victory against Satan.[6] Such victory might have been the source of the good news (1:1) for those who would receive him.

Considering Mark's opening (1:1-13) is concerned with the onset of God's empire, I read the passage in the light of the onset of the Roman Empire under Vespasian seeking to explore the first hearers' possible understanding of Mark's use of the imperial language. To achieve this goal, I first put the context of Mark's hearers in perspective. I imagine what Mark's hearers knew. In Palestine, they had recently experienced the entrances of the military conqueror Vespasian (and his son Titus), who has just become Emperor. They have a sense of how he went through Galilee conquering towns and cities, disarming the populace, and decimating the countryside. They know Vespasian became the Emperor and are living with the devastations

---

4. Van Iersel, *Mark*, 101. Cf. Marcus, *Way of the Lord*, 71, who argues that the divine address expresses not only Jesus' royal task but also "the supernatural power necessary to accomplish that task that is in view in the bestowal of the title 'Son of God.'"

5. Moloney, *Mark*, 36.

6. Cf. Marcus, *Way of the Lord*, 72, who points out that as Son of God, Jesus shares in God's empire, "his kingly power, and becomes the instrument of its extension into every corner of the creation through his defeat of the demonic cosmic forces that twist and destroy human life."

he brought with him. In such a context, how might they evaluate Mark's opening loaded with features common in the Roman imperial cult: the good news, the divine titles, and the entrances? My proposal is that Mark's hearers evaluated 1:1–14 in terms of an onset of God's empire that contrasted the onset of Vespasian's imperial rule. I now turn my focus on the divinity, good news, and appearances in the context of the Roman imperial cult.

The Onset of the Roman Empire

Divinity of the Emperor

The opening sentence of Mark's Gospel reads: "The beginning of the good news of Jesus Messiah, Son of God" (1:1). This opening verse of Mark's Gospel finds parallels in the Priene inscription written in honor of Emperor Augustus in 8 BCE. The relevant section of the inscription reads:

> It seemed good to the Greeks of Asia, in the opinion of the high priest Apollonius of Menophilus Azanitus: "Since Providence, which has ordered all things and is deeply interested in our life, has set in most perfect order by giving us Augustus, whom she filled with virtue that he might benefit humankind, sending him as a savior [σωτήρ], both for us and for our descendants, that he might end war and arrange all things, and since he, Caesar, by his appearance [ἐπιφανεῖν] (*exceeded the hopes of former good news*), surpassing all previous benefactors, and not even leaving to posterity any hope of surpassing what he has done, and since the birthday of the god Augustus was the beginning of the good tidings for the world that came by reason of him . . . which Asia resolved in Smyrna." (*OGIS* 458)[7]

The inscription is loaded with references to the good news, the divinity, and appearance of the emperor, which also appear in Mark's opening but with reference to Jesus. It affirms that the Roman emperor was recognized as a divine savior to whom honor and worship were to be directed. The inscription depicts Caesar Augustus as the "savior," "benefactor," and a "god" whose birthday was the "beginning of the good news for the world."

---

7. Cited in Evans, "Mark's Incipit," para. 2. Italics are added and replace the original translation that reads, "excelled even our former anticipation." The following scholars also cite this inscription, though with some slight differences in translations and length: Horsley, *Jesus and Empire*, 23–24; Crossan and Reed, *In Search of Paul*, 239–40; Witherington, *Gospel of Mark*, 69. For the Greek text of the entire inscription, see Dittenberger, *Orientis Graecae Inscriptiones*, 48–60; Taylor, *Divinity*, 273.

Although the inscription depicts Augustus as a "god," other inscriptions dedicate him as "son of god," hence providing a vivid parallelism between Jesus and the emperor. Tiberius mentions the emperor as "god Caesar son of god, Zeus the liberator, Augustus, savior of freedom" (*SEG XI* 922–3). Elsewhere, he is honored as "Caesar son of god, Emperor" (*P. Teb.* 382) and "Emperor Caesar son of god, Zeus the liberator, Augustus" (*P. Oslo* 26; *SB* 8824).[8] Augustus promoted myths and stories as his propaganda tool to publicize a belief that he was divine, the son of a god or "god the son of the god Caesar," a title that became his official name.[9]

The reference to the term "appearance" serves to intensify the divinity of the emperor. The emperor's advent was sometimes regarded as the inauguration of a new era, as it is depicted in Virgil's poem where the emperor Augustus is said to be one "who shall again set up a Golden Age" (*Aen.* 6.791–793). The emperor was believed to effect a new era due to the fact that he had a link with heaven. This idea is associated with Alexander the Great who viewed himself as a mediator between heaven and earth. Plutarch says of Alexander that he believed: "he came as a heaven-sent governor (*theothen armostēs*) to all, and a mediator (*diallaktēs*) for the whole world . . . He brought together all people everywhere, uniting and mixing in one great loving-cup, as it were, people's lives, their characters, their marriages, their very habits of life" (*Mor.* 329c).

The dedication of Caesar as divine did not apply only for Augustus. Many other Roman emperors who came after him were also honored as divine. Emperor Tiberius (14–37 CE was recognized as "son of god" (*SB* 8318); Gaius Caligula (37–41 CE) was dedicated as a "new god" (*IGR* 4:1094) and Josephus says of him that he personally "wished to be considered a god and to be hailed as such" (*J.W.* 2:184; cf. *Ant.* 18:256).[10] Emperor Claudius (41–54 CE) also bore the divine title "god" (*PSI* 1235; P.Oxy. 713, 808. 1021; P.Mich. 224) and "lord" (*GOA* 1038; *SB* 4331). Moreover, Emperor Nero under whose reign the Jewish revolt occurred was described as the "good god of the inhabited world, the beginning and existence of all good things" (P.Oxy. 1021), "the son of the greatest of the gods" (*IM* 157b), and the "lord of the whole world" (*SIG* 814).

More significantly, Vespasian (69–79 CE under whose imperial rule Mark's Gospel was composed also bore divine titles. He was honored as

---

8. See Kim, "Anarthrous," 232.

9. Ehrenberg and Jones, *Documents*, 93n118; cf. Brent, *Imperial Cult*, 72; Samuel, *Postcolonial*, 91; cf. Collins, "Mark and His Readers," 95.

10. Cf. Philo, *Embassy*, 353, 357, too, records the self-proclamation of Emperor Gaius as a god.

a "god" (P.Oxy. 257, 112), was called "Divine Vespasian" (*CPL* 104)[11] and "lord" (P.Oxy 1439; *SB* 1927, 3563; *GOA* 439).[12] Suetonius reports that when Vespasian was on his death bed he said of himself that he was "returning into a god" (*Vesp.* 23:4). Josephus provides further evidence for Vespasian's divinity when he speaks of him as lord. He reports that after the capture of Jerusalem, the Sicarii in Egypt refused to confess Caesar as lord because they believed that there was "no lord but God" (*Ant.* 8:23; *J.W.* 2:118; cf. Exod 20:3). Rather than acknowledge Caesar as lord, the Sicarii willingly submitted to torture and tearing of their bodies (*J.W.* 7:418-19).[13]

The Sicarii belief that the title lord was reserved for God alone demonstrates that the title had a divine overtone. David Rhoads has made this point clear when he states that the Sicarii ideology was an expression of rejection of the emperor's claim of divinity using the title "Lord."[14] Similarly, Virgil, the great Roman poet, gives the impression that confessing Caesar as lord was no less than recognizing the emperor as divine. For example, in his prayer to Octavian (Augustus) he refers to the emperor as god and a veritable lord of land and sea (*Georg.* 1.25-42).[15] Given the evidence presented here, it can be concluded that as Roman emperor, Vespasian was recognized as divine.[16]

---

11. Cf. Atwill, *Caesar's Messiah*, 24-25. He observes that an Arch of Titus built in honor of his military victory over the Jews acknowledges the divinity of Vespasian thus: "The Senate and the People of Rome, to the divine Titus, son of the divine Vespasian."

12. See Evans, *Mark*, lxxxii-lxxxiii; Cf. Kim, "Anarthrous," 235. For a detailed list of inscriptions recording divine honors of Roman Caesars, see Taylor, *Divinity*, 267-83; and Roetzel, *World that Shaped the New Testament*, 112-14.

13. Cf. Deissmann, *Light*, 355-56. Josephus does not name the Caesar involved in this case. But since his account speaks of an event that occurred shortly after the capture of Jerusalem, the emperor who was to be confessed as lord was no doubt Vespasian.

14. Rhoads, *Israel in Revolution*, 49.

15. Virgil's prayer reads as follows: "Yea, and thou, O Caesar, who we know not what company of the gods shall receive thee as the giver of increase and lord of the seasons . . . whether thou come as god (*deus*) of the boundless sea and sailors worship thy deity (*numina*) alone . . . or whether thou add thyself as a new star to the lingering months . . . even now to hearken to our prayers!"

16. Vespasian's divinity should also be viewed in terms of acclamations he received: "benefactor," "savior," etc. Cf. Roetzel, *World that Shaped the New Testament*, 112-13, who views the acclamations "benefactor," and "savior," as expressions of the divinity of an emperor, just like the titles "lord," and "god." He observes that the "titles like savior, and the eponyms of god (epiphanies), benefactor, and lord also confirm the king's divine status." See also Evans, *Mark*, xci, who states that "only Caesar was recognized as God, savior, lord, and 'benefactor'"; Kim, "Anarthrous," 237, points out that people seriously referred to Emperor Augustus as "Savior, lord, god, benefactor"; Chow, "Patronage in Roman Corinth," 105n5.

The Good News in the Roman Imperial Cult

The reference to good news was already in use in the Hellenistic world before Christianity was born. When Christianity arose, the term was adopted by the Christian faith so that such faith may be understood in the world in which it was being proclaimed. In the secular Greek world, the term was applied in the military context, in relation to the emperor's birthday, and with respect to an accession to the imperial throne. In the military context, the word was associated with military conquests or victory. Plutarch uses the term in this sense when he relates that "a number of people sailed for Lesbos, wishing to announce to Cornelia the good news that the war was over" (*Pomp.* 66.3). Good news was therefore an announcement of victory from a battlefield, which extended to mean "the good news of peace and prosperity, the good life resulting from military victory."[17] The victory as such and the resulting good life were associated with the imperial peace and the emperor.

In the Roman imperial cult, good news also expressed the news of an emperor's birth, his coming of legal age, and then his accession to the throne.[18] Moloney indicates that Greek authors used the term "to announce a military victory, a royal birth, or a political triumph."[19] In the honors paid to Hellenistic rulers, and after them the Roman emperors, good news received an additional cultic meaning. Whatever the emperor did or said as a divine figure, became the content of the good news. Hence the coming of legal age, or accession to the throne, and the birth of the successor to the throne, was considered good news.[20] The Priene inscription noted above testifies to this truth. It describes the birth of Augustus as "the beginning of good news" for the world.

The announcement of Caesar's birthday as a message of good news had a universal significance. Strecker writes that the good news "was valid throughout the empire; even the cosmos was influenced by this message, for it meant peace and well being for the whole world."[21] Upon receiving the "good news" associated with the heir's coming of age, cities celebrated and offered sacrifices to the gods. Commenting on an inscription consisting of an official decree that established a change of a calendar of the cities in Asia to honor Augustus's birthday as the beginning of everything (*SEG* 4:490), John D. Crossan and Jonathan L. Reed have stated that since Caesar Augustus

---

17. Boring, *Mark*, 30.
18. Fredrich, "*euangelion*," 269. Cf. Strecker, *Theology*, 337.
19. Moloney, *Mark*, 31; Guelich, *Mark*, 13.
20. Strecker, *Theology*, 337.
21. Ibid.

exceeded all the emperors before and after him, there would never again be good news outshining that which announced his birth. "In every city of rich Roman Asia there was decreed, for all time past, present, and future, but one overwhelming gospel, the good news of Augustus's advent, epiphany, and presence, the good news of a global Lord, divine Son, and cosmic Savior."[22]

In the context of the Roman imperial cult, the good news was also associated with an accession to the throne. For example, the proclamation of Gaius Julius Verus Maximus Augustus as emperor was received as good news. An Egyptian author of a papyrus from the third century expresses his receipt of such "good news" and calls for a procession in honor of the new emperor.[23] Thus the idea that the emperor's accession to the throne was recognized and celebrated as good news is affirmed. The emperor's accession to the throne was good news for his subjects.[24]

The power of the Roman emperors was often rejuvenated by acclamations of good news of victory of Rome in wars. Through victory, the empire was both founded and maintained. It was the theology of victory that established the imperial reigns of the Julio-Claudians and the Flavian dynasty. Since the beginning of the principate, Victoria Augusta assumed a central place as an essential tool for expansion and expression of Roman imperial power. Victories in battles were celebrated as the manifestations of Victoria. Octavia's victories were not only proclaimed as good news, they were also celebrated as epiphanies of a particular Victoria, namely, Victoria Augusta.[25] In times of war, Victoria was personified in Octavia and other emperors such as Vespasian. Peace and salvation were viewed as products of such victories.[26] Tacitus asserts that Vespasian's accession to the imperial throne was a result of divine favor, and that the emperor served as an agent of divine blessings (*Hist.* 1:10; 2:69, 82; 4:26, 47; cf. Suetonius, *Vesp.* 5:2–6; Dio, *Rom. Hist.* 64.9.1; 65.1.2–4). This implies that victory in wars was a result of divine assistance.

The actions of emperors were recognized as epiphanies of the gods that brought salvation and prosperity to the entire human race. Since victories of emperors resulted from divine aid, the proclamations of such victories were received as good news. The Priene inscription cited elsewhere indicates that Caesar Augustus was sent to be a "savior" who "might end war" and set all things in proper order. Kim concurs with this idea when he states that

---

22. Crossan and Reed, *In Search of Paul*, 241.
23. Evans, *Mark*, lxxxiv. See also Deissmann, *Light*, 367.
24. Fredrich, "*euangelion*," 269, 70.
25 Fears, "Theology of Victory at Rome," 736–826.
26. Ibid., 778–83, 787–812.

Caesar Augustus "put an end to the disorder and civil war and created a great empire in which people could live and prosper, the likes of which they had not known, spanning most of the known world in this period."[27]

The reception of Rome's victory as good news was not limited to the Romans as the victors. It also extended even to the conquered people. Crossan and Reed inform that the conquered people also accepted the Romans' victory as good news.[28] Acknowledgement of the conquered lands that Rome had a divine right to rule contributed to the peace of empire.[29] The conquered people received Rome's victory as good news because they believed that the wining Caesar "had saved their world from either the continual destruction of the Roman civil war or the final destruction of Roman imperial control."[30]

The Good News Associated with Vespasian

Josephus associates the good news with Vespasian's military victory over Judea and his accession to the imperial throne. When news spread that Vespasian had been proclaimed the new emperor of Rome, governors and cities in the east received such a report as good news. All cities in the area celebrated "for the good news and offered sacrifice on his (Vespasian's) behalf" (*J.W.* 4:618). In Alexandria, Governor Tiberius Alexander made preparations for the new emperor's arrival; the populace and legions under his control pledged allegiance to Vespasian as did the legions in Moesia and Pannonia (*J.W.* 4:619). In Beryrus, delegations from Syria and other provinces waited for Vespasian, and at his arrival they crowned him and gave congratulatory decrees from their cities. Mucianus, the governor of Berytus reported the city's pledge of allegiance to the new emperor (*J.W.* 4:621). In this context, the good news was associated with Vespasian's accession to the imperial throne, hence the establishment of his political rule.

In Josephus's works, the good news linked to military victory also relates to Mucianus's victory against Vitellius in Rome. Before he left for Rome to occupy his throne, Vespasian sent Mucianus to keep order in Italy. Mucianus successfully defeated Vitellius who also competed for the throne. Such victory became good news to both the citizens in Rome and to Vespasian who was still in Judea. Josephus states that upon Vespasian's arrival in Alexandria, he "was greeted by the good news from Rome and

27. Kim, "Anarthrous," 237.
28. Crossan and Reed, *In Search of Paul*, 58.
29. Ibid., 59.
30. Ibid., 270.

by embassies of congratulations from every quarter of the world, now his own... The whole empire being now secured and the Roman state saved beyond expectation, Vespasian turned his thought to what remained in Judea" (*J.W.* 4:656–57).

Mucianus's military victory in Rome was good news for two reasons. First, it was good news because of the overthrow of Vitellius. Second, it was good news because the victory served to cement Vespasian's establishment in imperial power. Josephus has expressed this point clearly when he states that people of Rome "acclaimed Vespasian emperor, and celebrated with one common festival both his establishment in power and overthrow of Vitellius" (*J.W.* 4:654–55). Hence, Mucianus's defeat of Vitellius marked twofold good news: the good news of victory and the good news due to Vespasian's establishment in imperial power.

The good news linked to Vespasian's accession to the throne should not be viewed apart from the general's own military achievement. Elsewhere Josephus has noted that the senate approved Vespasian's ascendance to the imperial throne because he had long military experience and good record of military achievements. Tired of civil wars, the people were confident that Vespasian would bring them everlasting security and prosperity. Because of Vespasian's military achievements, the army believed that he would bring them salvation and honor (*J.W.* 7:65–67). These expressions indicate that Josephus speaks of good news not only to refer to Vaspasian's accession to the throne, but also to an announcement of his military successes.[31] Since Vespasian became emperor based on his military victories, the good news associated with him involved shedding of blood of innocent people and loss of life, both in Judea and Rome.

Vespasian's Entries

Vespasian's entrances fulfilled most of the features related to the onset of an empire or entrances of the emperor introduced at the beginning of this chapter. Vespasian's first military campaign to crush the revolt in Judea started in Galilee. The general entered the area through Caesarea, the largest city in Judea, with a military mighty consisting of well equipped and heavily armed

---

31. Cf. *J.W.* 3:143, where the word is used with reference to the intelligence report about Josephus's movement at Jotapata given to Vespasian by a deserter from Josephus's group. Vespasian received the report as "good news." *J.W.* 3:503 speaks of the "good news" related to Titus's initial victory at Tarichaea. Josephus relates that "Titus dispatched a trooper to convey 'good news' of his achievement to his father." Other places where Josephus uses the word for good news or its cognates, include *Ant.* 2:277; 5:24, 5:282; 6:56; 7:245; 11:65; 15:209; 18:228, and so forth.

forces (*J.W.* 3:115–16). Since the city was primarily populated by Greeks, there was no resistance against him. The residents of the city received him and his troops "with blessings and congratulations of every description" (*J.W.* 3:409–10). The Tiberians likewise welcomed Vespasian with acclamations and hailed "him as savior and benefactor" (*J.W.* 3:459). Later, the people of Gischala, too, welcomed and hailed Titus, Vespasian's son "as benefactor and liberator of their town" (*J.W.* 4:112–13; cf. 3:117).

When Vespasian was proclaimed emperor, the residents of the cities he visited on his way to Rome to occupy his throne, received him with praise and acclamations (*J.W.* 7:21–22). Upon his arrival in Rome, people thronged on the road-sides and saluted him as "'benefactor,' 'savior,' and 'only worthy emperor of Rome'" (*J.W.* 7:71). At his arrival in the capital city of the empire, Vespasian offered sacrifices to the gods (*J.W.* 7:72–73). And when his son Titus also arrived in Rome after his victory over the Jews in Judea, ceremonies were held to celebrate their achievement (*J.W.* 7:119–22) involving the successful ending of the civil war in Rome, the crush of the Jewish revolt, and the establishment of the Flavian dynasty in the empire.

Vespasian's entrances were climaxed in a common triumphal procession with his sons in Rome (*J.W.* 7:119–22). That triumph not only marked Titus's victory over the Jews, but also affirmed Vespasian's ascendance to the throne. On the day of the triumph, Vespasian and his sons were crowned, dressed in purple robes, and were received by important men: the senate, the chief magistrates, and those of equestrian rank who had been waiting for their coming. Following Vespasian's brief speech to those who gathered to receive him, the Flavians offered sacrifices to the gods (*J.W.* 7:123–31).

Many other features associated with the emperor's advent noted by Koester and Deissmann are evident elsewhere in Josephus's accounts. According to Josephus, Vespasian's triumph in Rome involved the preparations prior to his arrival; the people who went to meet him; a joyous reception at his arrival; the benefits associated with his appearance (security, prosperity, and salvation); and feasts (*J.W.* 7:63–74). Josephus is silent about a messenger. However, it is very likely the messenger was involved because people could not have been aware of the emperor's coming and could not have participated in the preparations for his arrival without a herald having done his job.

Moreover, in addition to the features noted above, Josephus's triumphal account also represents an advent of the emperor as an inauguration of a new era. The account confirms Vespasian's inauguration of his imperial rule. Before Vespasian's arrival in Rome, people anticipated his arrival with the hope that his reign would bring "salvation," "security," and prosperity to the empire. When he arrived in Rome and assumed his throne, a new age of the empire was ushered in. Rome "rapidly advanced to great prosperity" (cf. *J.W.* 7:74), implying that there was security, salvation, and peace in the empire (cf. *J.W.* 7:157). Vespasian's appearance and reign formed the beginning of a new political order that was received as good news.[32] His entrance in Rome marked the beginning of his imperial power (*J.W.* 7:158). That beginning of a new era had a savior figure, Vespasian.[33]

Feasting as an element in the emperor's entrances was common in Vespasian's appearances. Josephus shows that Vespasian's entrances were characterized with lavish feasts. When Vespasian visited Agrippa's kingdom he feasted at Caesarea Philippi for twenty days (*J.W.* 3:443-44). Upon receiving news that Vespasian had been proclaimed emperor, cities held banquets in his honor (*J.W.* 4:618). When he arrived in Rome, Vespasian offered sacrifices to the gods, people held feasts and with libations prayed long life for his family (*J.W.* 7:72-73).[34] Apart from being a prelude to the triumphal ceremonies in honor of the Flavians's achievements, these feasts also affirmed people's loyalty to Rome and to the new imperial rule.[35] The lavish banquets suggest that expenses related to the arrival of the emperor were both massive and unimaginable.

In sum, in this part, I have established that in accordance to the Roman imperial cult, Vespasian as Caesar had divine status. I have shown that his military victory, entrances in cities, and establishment of his imperial rule were celebrated as good news. In this case, the onset of Vespasian's imperial power, rooted in his military achievements, was the source of the good news associated with him. With this background in mind, I examine Mark's opening, which seems to be concerned with the beginning of a new era involving God's empire.

---

32. Samuel, *Postcolonial*, 92.

33. Koester, "Jesus the Victim," 12-13. Based on the Priene inscription from 9 BCE, Koester writes about Augustus as the savior figure thus: "The new age has a savior figure, the greatest benefactor of all times . . . 'Son of God'—the victorious Augustus." The Greek transliteration is mine. This comment can also apply to Vespasian. Cf. Taylor, *Divinity*, 57, who, commenting on the Roman triumph, writes that "With the longing of the people for a savior went at the same time the growth of the power of individuals, chiefly the great generals, to whom was accorded the triumph that was the closest thing in Roman state ceremony to deification."

34. Drawing from Dio, Taylor, *Divinity of the Roman Emperor*, 151, indicates that the practice of libation started during the reign of Emperor Augustus. She states that libations were poured out in honor of the emperor at both public and private banquets.

35. Cf. Roetzel, *World that Shaped the New Testament*, 74, who observes that the celebrations "symbolically constructed a world with the Roman Empire at the center, and they legitimized the imperial rule."

The Onset of God's Empire

Mark's opening (1:1–13) exhibits the beginning of a new era of God's empire with Jesus as the divine agent. The opening starts with this announcement: "The beginning of the good news of Jesus Messiah, Son of God" (1:1). The good news here is the announcement that the human named Jesus is the "Messiah, Son of God." Following this announcement, the divine words spoken through the prophets (Mal 3:1; Exod 23:20; and Isa 40:3) are heard. God announces his plan to send his messenger and the one who is to come as the Lord. The role of the messenger will be to prepare a way of the Lord (1:2–3). Then, John appears in the wilderness as the messenger "proclaiming a baptism of repentance for the forgiveness of sins." As God's messenger, he also announces the coming of "the one who is more powerful" who will baptize by the Holy Spirit. John's activities affirm his role as the messenger (1:4–8). That is, John's activities mark the preparations of the way of the Lord.

Next, coming from Nazareth of Galilee, Jesus undergoes a baptism ritual administered by John in the river Jordan. At Jesus' baptism, the heavens rip apart, the Holy Spirit descends upon Jesus, and a voice from the heavens speaks to Jesus, "You are my Son, the Beloved; in you I am well pleased" (1:9–11). Finally, the Holy Spirit drives Jesus into the wilderness where he is tested by Satan for forty days. In the wilderness, Jesus was with the beasts, being served by angels (1:12–13). Hence the portrayal of Jesus as the expected Lord whose coming was foretold by the prophets (1:2–3) and proclaimed by John (1:7). In the following paragraphs, I examine Mark's concept of the good news, his portrayal of Jesus as a divine agent, and Jesus' entrance in Mark's prologue.

The Good News of Jesus

Mark's opening sentence announces "The beginning of the good news of Jesus Messiah, Son of God" (1:1). The statement forms the title of Mark's whole narrative.[36] It also presents a striking parallel with the last line of the Priene inscription referred to earlier: "the god Augustus was the beginning of the good tidings for the world . . ." The similarity is observed in the use of the words "beginning," "good news," and the reference to a divine agent. While the Priene inscription speaks of the Roman Empire that has Caesar

---

36. Cf. Matera, "Prorogue," 6; Hooker, *Mark*, 33; van Iersel, *Mark*, 88; Boring, *Mark*, 29–32.

Augustus as the divine agent, Mark's opening speaks of God's Empire and has Jesus Messiah, Son of God as the divine agent.

In the discussion about the Roman imperial cult in the previous section, I have shown that the good news was associated with military victory, birth of the emperor, and with a political achievement. I have also indicated that the emperor was recognized as divine. Vespasian in particular, was recognized as a divine agent; and his military achievements, ascension to the imperial throne, and entrances in cities, were celebrated as good news. It is now my duty to explore the possible responses of Mark's hearers with this imperial language used by Mark: the good news, Jesus' divine status, and entrance based on Mark's opening in 1:1–13.

In the Greek texts, it is unclear whether the good news referred to in Mark 1:1 is *about* Jesus Messiah (objective genitive) or that which Jesus Messiah himself announces (subjective genitive).[37] Both possibilities are possible in that the narrative seeks to proclaim the fullness of God in Jesus Messiah as well as the good news of God's empire that Jesus himself proclaimed (1:14–15). Thus, in Mark, the good news is both of and about Jesus Messiah, Son of God.[38]

Marcus reads Mark's story of Jesus from the perspective of Jewish scripture. He understands the good news in relation to Deutero-Isaiah[39] where the prophet links the good news to God's messenger (Isa 40:9; 41:27; 52:7; 60:6; 61:1). While in classical Greek, a messenger heralds a victory in a battle field, in Isaiah, a messenger announces God's victory over enemies of his people, Israel (Isa 41:27) and the arrival of God's rule that marks the time of salvation (Isa 40:9–11; 52:7).[40] So Isaiah's good news is the coming of God's victorious rule.[41] The good news in Mark's opening is closely linked to a quotation credited to Isaiah (1:2; cf. Isa 40:3), a verse that points to the one who heralds good news. This link suggests that Mark's reference to good news originates from Isaiah. Hence, it is possible Mark's good news refers to

---

37. Cf. Hay, "Son-of-God Christology," 109, who states that "to be God's son means to be both object and agent of the divine purpose."

38. Thurston, *Preaching Mark*, 14. Similarly, van Iersel, *Mark*, 90, states that "'the good news of Jesus Messiah' means the good news is both from and about Jesus." See also Hooker, *St. Mark*, 34, who even though she agrees that both the objective and the subjective senses are possible, puts more emphasis on the former. She writes, "Mark may well have had both meanings in mind, since the gospel proclaimed by the church is identical with the gospel proclaimed by Jesus. But the emphasis is probably on the former meaning here, since Jesus is certainly the content of Mark's Gospel."

39. Marcus, *Way of the Lord*, 18, notes that "the word 'gospel' itself . . . has its important background in Deutero-Isaiah." Cf. Hooker, *Gospel according to Saint Mark*, 33–34.

40 Van Iersel, *Mark*, 89.

41. Samuel, *Postcolonial*, 93.

the coming of Jesus as God's Messiah who proclaims God's victory over his enemies and heralds the onset of God's empire.[42]

Evans has presented an insightful argument about the good news expressed in Mark's Gospel. According to him, "the vision of Second Isaiah approximates the Roman Imperial cult's promise of a new order."[43] He views Mark's good news not only as the fulfillment of Isaiah's prophesied good news fulfilled in Jesus, but also as a response to the claims of the Roman imperial cult, in that it announced Jesus as Messiah, Son of God. In this case, Mark proclaims that Jesus Messiah, not Caesar, is the beginning or source of the good news.[44] In Mark, Jesus is also the content of the good news. Mark's good news is concerned with the announcement of the advent of God's anointed leader who heralds the arrival of God's empire.[45] Mark's hearers might have related the good news of and about Jesus with that about Vespasian. Hearing that a new era of God's rule was taking place through Jesus while living in the midst of Vespasian's imperial rule, Mark's hearers may have hoped that the Roman imperial rule was about to end.

Mark's reference to "good news" is also found elsewhere other than in the opening sentence. After his encounter with Satan in the wilderness, Jesus returns to Galilee proclaiming "the good news of God" (1:14) and calls people to trust in the "good news" (1:15). In this context, the good news relates to the arrival of God's empire. In another context, the good news is the determinant of the value of one's life. Jesus teaches that "those who lose their life . . . for the sake of the good news will save it" (8:35). People who leave family and possessions for the sake of the good news will receive in this age, family and house with persecution, and in the age to come, eternal life (10:29–30). Moreover, in Mark, the good news is universal in that it is for the whole world. As such, before the end comes, "the good news must be proclaimed to all nations" (13:10). In 13:10, the reference to good news is in the context of Jesus' warning about persecution in synagogues, and before kings and governors, implying that the good news associated with Jesus involves persecution of those who proclaim it.

Furthermore, in Mark, the good news is also linked to the proclamation of Jesus' death. With reference to the act of an unnamed woman who anointed Jesus with costly ointment, Jesus said to his disciples, "whenever the good news is proclaimed in the whole world, what she has done will be

---

42. Cf. Winn, *Mark*, 98.
43. Evans, "Mark's Incipit."
44. Ibid.
45. Myers, *Binding the Strong Man*, 123–24.

told in remembrance of her" (14:9).[46] It is important here to note that the act to remember is not the mere anointing, but the act that the anointing symbolizes. The woman's anointing symbolized the burial of Jesus (14:8), which implies death. This idea is reinforced by the fact that the anointing account is placed between two accounts that speak about the plots to destroy Jesus (14:1-2; 14:10-11).[47] In Mark's Gospel, there is a strong link between the good news, and persecution and death. The good news involves suffering and death of Jesus (cf. 8:31; 9:31; 10:33; 14:8; 15:28) and of those who trust in and proclaim the good news (cf. 8:35; 10:30; 13:9-10). This relationship between the good news and death differentiates the good news of Jesus from the good news associated with Vespasian. While the good news related to Vespasian involves destroying others, the good news associated with Jesus involves losing one's life for the liberating of others.

Jesus Messiah, Son of God

Mark's opening sentence introduces Jesus in divine terms, referring to him as "Messiah, Son of God" (1:1). The phrase "Jesus Messiah" appears to be a proper name.[48] The Greek word translated Messiah is *Christos*, the word usually translated Christ. But *christos* can also be rendered "anointed one." Hence, at the very beginning of his narrative, Mark introduces Jesus as Messiah, God's anointed. Mark here foreshadows Peter's declaration of Jesus as the Messiah (8:28). The reference to Messiah appears elsewhere in Mark's Gospel. It is used in relation to good treatment of those who bear the name of the Messiah. Anyone who treats the disciples well because they bear the name of the Messiah will be rewarded (9:41). In another context, Jesus accepts that he is the "Messiah, Son of the Blessed" (14:61-62). Moreover, Jesus warns his disciples against false "messiahs" (13:21-22), implying that he alone is the true Messiah. When Jesus was crucified on the cross, the chief priests and the scribes mocked him as "the

---

46. The reference to good news is linked to Jesus. Note that the anointing was a symbolic preparation for the burial of Jesus' body (14:8), and consider the fact that the account is located between the plot by the chief priests and scribes who arrest Jesus (14:1) and Judas Iscariot's conspiracy with the high priest in order to betray Jesus (14:10). This strongly supports the idea that the good news here is linked to Jesus' death.

47. The story about the anointing of Jesus (14:3-9) is preceded by an account concerning the high priest and scribes who plot to arrest and kill Jesus. Immediately after the account on Jesus' anointing follows the story about Judas, who betrays Jesus to the high priests.

48. Van Iersel, *Mark*, 90.

Messiah, the King of Israel" (15:32).⁴⁹ For Mark's hearers, however, the mockers were ironically proclaiming the truth confirming that Jesus was the King of the Jews (cf. 15:2, 9, 26).

From the Jewish perspective, the concept of messiah had varied meanings. It was used to refer to kings (e.g., 1 Sam 12:3, 5; 24:7–8; 16:3, 13; 2 Sam 2:4; 12:7) and high priests (Lev 4:5). After David, hopes for a royal messiah coming from the line of David developed (2 Sam 7:11–17; 2 Chr 6:42). The growing critical and negative attitude towards kings in the period of the prophets, the concept of the messiah was associated with the idealized figure of a "King to Come" (Jer 23:5–6; Ezek 34:23–24). Elsewhere in the Old Testament, the messianic king is recognize as a Son of God (e.g., 2 Sam 7:13–14; Pss 2; 110; Isa 9). Isaiah refers to the Persian emperor Cyrus as the LORD's Messiah (Isa 45:1). Also various Jewish non-canonical sources anticipated a messiah who would serve either as a high priest (1QSa = 1Q28a), or a powerful king (1 En. 37–71), or a judge, destroyer of the unrighteous rulers, and liberator of Israel from its enemies (Pss. Sol. 17:21–33; 18:3–9).⁵⁰

Mark, however, rejects the idea of Jesus being the royal messiah of the Davidic type, the warrior messiah (cf. 12:35–37).⁵¹ Rather, for him, Jesus is Messiah because he fulfils God's will to serve and liberate God's people even in the face of suffering and death (8:31; 9:31; 10:33–34, 45; 15:32). As Matera has correctly pointed out, "Jesus is Messiah because he is the son of God."⁵² This comment fits Mark's portrayal of Jesus as Messiah and Son of God (1:1; 14:61). "Son of the Blessed One" (14:61) is a circumlocution for Son of God. Jesus' status as the Messiah and Son of God is strongly implied in Mark's baptism account, where a voice from the heavens declares Jesus to be God's beloved Son (1:11). Such a declaration is fulfillment of a royal Psalm where the LORD tells the king of Israel, his anointed, "You are my son" (Ps 2:7). Mark's allusion to the royal Psalm suggests that God has anointed Jesus to be his Messiah.

The reference to Jesus as Son of God is prominent in Mark's Gospel. Besides its occurrence in its opening sentence, the phrase occurs elsewhere

---

49. Cf. Matera, *New Testament Christology,* 24–25.

50. Samuel, *Postcolonial,* 93–94. Cf. Collins, "Pre-Christian Jewish Messianism," 1–20.

51. Cf. Matera, *New Testament Theology,* 16, who states that rather than depict Jesus in the light of the traditional Davidic messianic hopes expressed in Pss. Sol. 17 and 18, Mark defines the messianic hopes in the light of God's redemptive work through Jesus. According to him, Pss. Sol. 17 and 18 "provide and excellent description of a royal Davidic messiah who would free Israel from oppression of its enemies and then rule Jerusalem in righteousness" (see his note 7).

52. Matera, *New Testament Christology,* 25.

in the narrative. At Jesus' baptism, God announces with respect to Jesus, "You are my Son, the Beloved; with you I am well pleased" (1:11). God's affirmation of Jesus as his beloved Son is repeated at Jesus' transfiguration where the announcement is addressed to Peter, James, and John. At the transfiguration scene, God declares with reference to Jesus: "This is my Son, the Beloved; listen to him" (9:7). The unclean spirits as well recognize Jesus as "Son of God" (3:11) or the "Son of the Most High God" (5:7).[53] Jesus' divine status is also implied in the parable of the vineyard where the tenants kill God's "beloved Son" (12:1–12). Before the Sanhedrin, Jesus is affirmed as "the Son of the Blessed One" (14:61–62). Moreover, shortly after Jesus' last breath, the Roman centurion declared Jesus truly "God's Son!" (15:39).[54] Jesus' status as the Son of God is also reflected when Jesus refers to God as his Father (8:38; 13:32; 14:36).

Among the Jews, the designation "Son of God" had diverse meanings. It was used to refer to angels (6:2, 4; Deut 32:8; Job 1:6–12; 1 En. 13:8; 106:5); people of Israel (Exod 4:22; Jer 31:9; Hos 11:1); kings of Israel (2 Sam 7:14; Pss. Sol. 2:7; 89:26–27); and to a righteous person (Sir 4:10b; Wis 2:18; 5:5).[55] As we have already noted elsewhere, in the Hellenistic world, emperors were also recognized as sons of a god.[56] However, Jesus' status as the Son of God in Mark is unique in that God himself addresses him alone as his "beloved Son" (1:11; 9:7). Drawing from E. Lipinski, Joel Marcus relates Jesus' baptism in 1:11 to Psalm 2:7 and argues that through baptism, Jesus was installed as the earthly king and received God's power to rule the world on God's behalf.[57]

The identification of Jesus as "Messiah, Son of God" may have had a great impact on Mark's hearers. They may have related Jesus' status as the Messiah and Son of God with the events of the war. Josephus shows that one of the things that motivated the Jewish revolutionaries to make war with the Romans was the Jewish prophecy that expected a world ruler to come from Judea (J.W. 6:312–13). He states clearly that the prophecy found its fulfillment in Vespasian because he was proclaimed emperor on the Jewish

---

53. Cf. Neyrey, *Render to God*, 30.

54. Kingsbury, *Christology*, 132, wrongly asserts that the centurion's confession signals his newfound Christian faith. For a critique of Kingsbury's view, see Kim, "Anarthrous," 221, who compares the confession to the unclean spirit's addressing Jesus as "the Son of God" (3:11; see note 3).

55. Cf. Samuel, *Postcolonial*, 95; Matera, *New Testament Theology*, 19; Hooker, *Mark*, 47.

56. Cf. Kim, "Anarthrous," 232. Collins, "Messiah as Son of God," 95; Winn, *Mark*, 101–2.

57. Marcus, *Way of the Lord*, 69.

soil. Vespasian used this prophecy to justify his own imperial rule and the divine status associated with the imperial office.[58] Mark's hearers may therefore have associated Jesus' divine identify with Vespasian's divine status and the claim that he was the fulfillment of the Jewish oracle. They may have considered Mark's message as a critique of the recognition of Vespasian's divinity and his claim that he was the world ruler in accordance to the Jewish prophecy. It is likely therefore, that they would reject Vespasian's claim to global rulership in favor of Jesus Messiah, Son of God, and hence, their identification with him.

Besides Mark's recognition of Jesus as Messiah and Son of God, Jesus' divine status is also expressed through his deeds of power. The acts of healings, exorcisms, raising of the dead, pardoning sins, and ability to feed thousands of people from scarcity of food were expressions of Jesus' divine status. Further, ability to prophesy about his own death, ability to walk on the water and to calm storms also signified Jesus' divine nature. Moreover, Mark's portrayal of Jesus as Lord (1:3),[59] a term that for Jews was reserved for God alone, also highlighted Jesus' divine status. Indeed, the omens at his baptism—the ripping apart of the heavens, descent of the Holy Spirit upon him, and the voice from the heavens (1:11); the transfiguration and the related events: turning dazzling white, the appearance of the ancient prophets of Israel, the voice from heaven (9:7); the ripping apart of the temple curtain at his death (15:38), and his advent that was foretold by prophets (1:2–3) reinforced and intensified Jesus' divine status.

Even though Mark uses expressions that portray Jesus as divine, care must be taken not to think of Jesus' divine nature as pre-existent. In Mark, Jesus is truly human. His divinity depends on his commitment and faithfulness to God's will. Waetjen has given an intriguing and compelling suggestion on how to understand Jesus' divine nature. He views Jesus as "the New Human Being" created to serve as God's viceregent to order the world. Waetjen writes: "God comes, as the Baptizer has promised, but instead of inaugurating the kingdom names a viceregent to reorder reality. Ironically,

---

58. For a detailed discussion on this matter, see Winn, *Mark*, 153–77.

59. Jesus is Lord of the Sabbath (2:28); the Gerasene demoniac recognizes Jesus as Lord in that when he is instructed to tell friends how much the Lord (God) had done for him (5:19), he goes and proclaims what mercy Jesus has shown him (5:20); the Syrophoenician woman addresses him as Lord (7:28); he is the Lord who needs a donkey (11:3); Jesus the Lord is greater than David (12:36–37); and Jesus refers to himself as Lord when he sends his disciples to prepare a room for the last Passover (14:14). Other references to *kyrios* in Mark refer to God (12:11, 29–30, 36) or ambiguously to either Jesus or God (5:19; 11:9; 13:20). Tolbert, *Sowing the Gospel*, 245, denies any reference to Jesus as Lord in Mark except when the word *kyrios* expresses a title of respect—"sir" or "master" in 7:28 and 11:3.

it is a carpenter from insignificant town of Nazareth in rural Galilee who is called into being as God's beloved offspring and therefore also as God's surrogate. His identification by the Heavenly Voice is simultaneously his commission. The reality of God's rule must now be constituted and the task is entrusted to him as the New Human Being."[60] Waitjen's identification of Jesus as "a carpenter from insignificant town of Nazareth in rural Galilee" is to be taken seriously. Such a statement portrays Jesus as truly human. As Helmut Koester also points out, "Jesus indeed is God, but only insofar as he represents fully God's moral purpose for humankind. Nothing in the ministry of Jesus documents Jesus' activity in the metaphysical or supernatural terms. Rather, this divinity in revealed because Jesus as a human being remained faithful to his vocation to the very end, in spite of the resistance and hatred of the word."[61]

Based on this discussion it is clear that Jesus is recognized as divine. He is the Messiah and Son of God. His divine status, however, is not pre-existent. It is rather grounded on his faithfulness to God's will. This is the reason God himself declared him as his beloved Son, with whom he is well pleased. Because of his faithfulness and obedience to God, Jesus was empowered by the Holy Spirit and entrusted to establish God's empire on earth.

Jesus' Entrances

Immediately after the announcement of the "beginning of the good news of Jesus Messiah, Son of God" (1:1), Mark cites a prophecy that he attributes to Isaiah (1:2–3). Actually, the prophecy he cites is a combination of prophecies from Exodus 23:20, Malachi 3:1, and Isaiah 40:3. Mark 1:2 is a combination of words from Exodus and Malachi. While the phrase, "See, I am sending my messenger ahead of you" (1:2) agrees with LXX of Exod 23, the phrase "prepare your way" (1:2) agrees with Malachi 3, but "me/my" being changed to "your." Mark 1:3 agrees with LXX version of Isa 40, with "for our God" being replaced by "his." As the story unfolds, hearers understand that John is the messenger who prepares the way of the Lord; and that Jesus is the Lord whose way John prepares (1:2–3; 4–8). Given this prophecy, we note that Jesus' coming was not just a coincidence, but one that God had planned and foretold through prophets.

Mark's language, "Prepare the way of the Lord, make his paths straight" (1:3, cf. 2c) is crucial, hence the need for special attention. Although the verbs "make ready" (1:2c) and "prepare" (1:3) come from different Greek words,

60. Waetjen, *Reordering of Power*, 71.
61. Koester, "Jesus the Victim," 3.

they however, express the same meaning. In the Roman imperial world, the phrase "prepared the way of the Lord, make his paths straight" would not simply mean the construction of the road. They would rather connote the sense of "making all the necessary arrangements to insure a fitting welcome and reception for the heralded king or conqueror."[62] In Mark, the prophetic proclamation, "prepare the way of the Lord," implies getting ready to receive Jesus who is the coming Lord. For Mark's audience, the announcement may have evoked memories of the events of the war. Josephus states that the Roman army consisted of pioneers whose roles were to "straighten sinuosities on the route, to level the rough places and to cut down obstructing woods, in order to spare the army the fatigues of a toilsome march" (*J.W.* 3:118). Josephus also reports that at one point Vespasian ordered his forces to level the road on a stony mountain leading to Jotapata before he entered and destroyed the city and its inhabitants (*J.W.* 3:141).

Hence, hearing the prophetic call to "prepare the way of the Lord," Mark's hearers would have recalled the war event of leveling of the road to Jotapata by the Romans for the purpose of destroying the city and its inhabitants. They would, however, also note the contrast between the construction of the road in the context of the war and Mark's call to prepare the Lord's way. While the making straight of the road by the Romans was physical, literal and meant for getting access to destroy life, the preparation of the way in Mark does not connote a physical and literal sense, but the making of the necessary preparation for a fitting reception of Jesus, who comes to inaugurate God's rule that involves liberation of people from demonic and human oppressive forces.

The appearance of Jesus was preceded by the coming of John, the forerunner. When John appeared in the wilderness, he proclaimed baptism, forgiveness, and repentance (1:4). It is interesting to note that many people flocked from Judea and Jerusalem to the Jordan River to repent and receive forgiveness. John offered God's forgiveness in the wilderness without the demand of temple sacrifices and without the need of the religious experts of Jerusalem.[63] This explains the fact that Mark wrote the Gospel after the fall of the temple. John's message suggests both renewal and fulfillment. This is demonstrated by the place of activity: the river Jordan, the entrance through which the Israelites entered the Promised Land, an expression pointing to the beginning of a new era. At the river Jordan, John announces the coming

---

62. Bratcher and Nida, *Handbook on the Gospel of Mark*, 6.

63. Wilhelm, *Preaching the Gospel of Mark*, 7. Cf. Witherington, *Mark*, 72, who states that John "seems to have been offering forgiveness without sacrifice being offered in the temple. He was offering remission of sins without connection to the hierarchical system in Jerusalem."

of "the one who is more powerful" (1:7), who will baptize with the Holy Spirit (1:8), manifesting his role of not only announcing the coming of the Lord, but also of preparing the way of the Lord (1:3).

John was not a man of the city, but a wilderness person. While he ate locusts and honey, he dressed in camel's hair and a belt around his waist (1:6). His ascetic life in the wilderness, dress, and diet associated him with similar prophetic figures in Israel (cf. Zech 13:4).[64] Except for the type of food he ate, his dress and lifestyle identify him with the prophet Elijah (2 Kgs 1:8).[65] His diet, the locusts and wild honey (1:6), reveals a very strong contrast to Vespasian's pompous feasts during his entrances. This contrast may not have gone unnoticed among Mark's hearers who were aware of Vespasian's entrances and his extravagant meals and celebrations. Mark's expression that multitudes of "people from the whole Judean countryside and all the people of Jerusalem" (1:5) flocked to the river Jordan to be baptized and to confess their sins is indeed hyperbole. Perhaps Mark used this expression as a rhetorical tool to express the effectiveness of John's ministry. Such an expression foreshadows the flocking of crowds of people to Jesus during his Galilean campaign[66] and the spread of the good news to the whole world (13:10).[67]

When the time of arrival of the Lord had come, an announcement was made and Jesus was baptized by John. Mark heralds, "In those days Jesus came from Nazareth of Galilee" (1:9). Now, it is clear that the Lord whose coming was foretold by God through the prophets is Jesus. As Jesus comes, he is baptized by John in the river Jordan. At his baptism, Jesus sees a vision involving such events as the ripping apart of the heavens, the descent of the Holy Spirit upon him like a dove, and heard a heavenly voice being addressed to him: "You are my Son, the Beloved; in you I am well pleased" (1:11). The tearing apart of the heavens not only "marks the beginning of a new era,"[68] but also symbolizes "God's coming down"[69] and foretells the ripping apart of the temple curtain when Jesus dies on the cross (15:37).[70] The tearing apart of the heavens and the temple curtain can be understood as an expression of God's presence everywhere on earth with his people.

---

64. Hooker, *Mark*, 37.

65. In Mark, John is presented as the model of Elijah the prophet (9:12–13; cf. Mal 4:5–6).

66. E.g., 1:33; 2:2, 13; 3:7–10, 20, 32; 4:1–2; 5:21, 24; 6:30–44, 54–56; 8:1–10.

67. Moloney, *Mark*, 34.

68. Ibid.

69. Thurston, *Preaching Mark*, 16.

70. In both occasions, Jesus is acknowledged as God's Son (1:11; 15:39).

The events show that since the coming of Jesus at the river Jordan, God's dwelling is no longer confined in heaven or in the temple, but that God is everywhere with his people. That is, through Jesus and the Holy Spirit, God has come to inaugurate his empire and to liberate his people.

Van Iersel observes that the divine address, "You are my Son" at Jesus' baptism was an enthronement formula used at the coronation of a king.[71] Based on this argument, Jesus' baptism may be viewed as Jesus' enthronement to be a leader of God's people. As Boring has pointed out, Mark's reference to Ps 2:7, suggests "the royal imagery and inauguration of a ceremony of the Judean king, who was declared to be God's son."[72] The key is therefore that through baptism, God not only has installed Jesus to be his agent, but also that he has approved and empowered him with the Holy Spirit to carry out his redemptive deeds among his people. In addition, Jesus' baptism signifies Jesus' solidarity with sinners.[73]

Announcing the coming of Jesus, John proclaimed that the one coming after him was stronger and more powerful than himself. He said: "The one who is more powerful than I is coming after me" (1:7). From the proclamation, it is evident that Jesus is more powerful than John. In Mark, Jesus' power is linked to the Holy Spirit who descended upon him at his baptism like a dove (1:10). After baptism, the Holy Spirit drives Jesus into the wilderness, and there empowers Jesus to battle with Satan.[74] Mark does not tell us the nature of the battle, nor does he tell about the victor. But the fact that Jesus is said to have returned to Galilee with the good news (1:14–15), suggests that Jesus worn the battle. In this case, the good news of and about Jesus involves victory in a battle against Satan.[75] Such victory over Satan is a prelude to Jesus' victories in the entire narrative,[76] including victory over the power of death on the cross. It is important to note that the battle that Jesus is involved in is nonviolent. It is neither a military battle nor a battle with humans. In Mark, Jesus battles against demonic forces, illnesses, powers of death, sin, life threatening natural forces such as hunger and storms, and so on.[77] Also in

71. Van Iersel, *Mark*, 101.

72. Boring, *Mark*, 45.

73. Thurston, *Preaching Mark*, 16.

74. Cf. Marcus, *Mark*, 157–58: "Jesus' strength is concerned with baptism in the Spirit . . . the Spirit is above all the divine power that enables Jesus . . . to do battle with the *evil* spirits" (italics original).

75. Ibid., 170.

76. Cf. Guijaro, "Gospel of Mark," 34: "Jesus' relation to the Spirit and his confrontation with Satan in the early stage of the Gospel prefigure his later confrontations with the evil spirits."

77. A detailed discussion on how Jesus uses power and authority from God to

Mark, Jesus never uses his power from God to coerce, manipulate, control, or destroy human beings. Instead, he uses power from God to liberate others and "to give his whole life as a ransom" (10:45).

The descent of the Spirit upon Jesus like a dove needs close attention. The dove imagery may have evoked memories of the war among Mark's audience. This birdlike imagery may have been related to the Roman's eagle emblem which also consisted of an image of a bird. Describing Vespasian's entrance in Galilee with his troops, Josephus shows that among other things, the procession involved the eagle, the bravest of all the birds which the Romans considered it to be the symbol of empire, and in battle fields, an omen of victory (*J.W.* 3:123). This implies that the Romans believed the eagle to be the source of their strength and victory. It is interesting to note that Mark, too, depicts the Spirit that descends like a dove, as Jesus' source of power and victory over Satan (1:12–13). Mark's hearers may have viewed Mark's use of the dove imagery for the Spirit that descends upon Jesus as a contrast to the Roman's use of the eagle emblem.[78] Dorothy R. Willette argues that during the time of Jesus, the dove symbolism was rich of meanings including being a symbol for the "atoning sacrifice (cf. Gen 15:9; Lev 5:7–11), suffering, a sign from God, fertility, the spirit of God" and a symbol of peace.[79] Hence, while the Roman eagle emblem symbolized destruction, the dove imagery symbolized an atoning sacrifice for others, the value embodied in God's empire that Jesus proclaims its arrival.

Jesus' experience in the wilderness as well, may have invoked hope and courage among Mark's hearers. First, hearers may have viewed Jesus' testing as a model for their struggles. Marcus's proposal on the matter is worth noting. Referring to Mark's first hearers, Marcus states that: "Whatever demonic powers they confront, they would know that they, like Jesus before

---

liberate people is presented in a chapter on campaigns in Galilee.

78. Cf. Incigneri, *Gospel to the Romans*, 261, who notes that, "The Roman eagle may have rested on Vespasian and Titus, who promised peace and a new beginning for Rome, but for Mark has the bird that proclaimed the end of an earlier calamity and beginning of a new era for the whole world (cf. Gen 8:8–12) come down upon Jesus."

79. Willette, "Enduring Symbolism of a Dove," paras. 4 and 8. Her arguments are based on biblical texts and archaeological findings. The idea of peace originates from the Genesis flood narrative: "In Gen 8:8–12, after the ark has landed on the mountains of Ararat, Noah sends out a dove three times to see how far the flood waters have receded. The first time is found nothing and it returned to the ark. The second time it brought back an olive leaf, so Noah could see that God's punishment was over and life had begun again on earth. (The image of a dove holding an olive branch continues to be a symbol of peace to this day). The third time, the dove did not return, and Noah knew that it was safe to leave the ark." Cf. Incigneri, *Gospel to the Romans*, 161n29, who comments that the "dove was used as a symbol of peace in early Christian funerary inscriptions."

them, had been impelled into the fray by the Spirit and were armed with its power, so that they need not be afraid. Moreover, the narrative linkage between Jesus' baptism (1:9-11) and his Spirit-filled contention with Satan (1:12-13) might well remind them of their own baptism, in which they were equipped with the Spirit to fight demonic powers.[80]

Mark's first hearers would remember that through baptism they were clothed with Holy Spirit and therefore that in their time of trials and confrontation with demonic powers they would not be afraid, for like Jesus they were empowered to conquer their enemies. Moreover, Mark's expression that Jesus was with the "wild beasts" (1:13) may still have another powerful impact on the hearers. Many interpreters relate the expression with the restoration of original creation. Moloney, for example, says that by that expression Mark demonstrates that God "has restored the original order of God's creation."[81] In addition to this interpretation I think that Mark's hearers may also have related this expression with the events of the war. Hearing of beasts may have evoked memories among Mark's hearers of the Jewish prisoners who died violently in spectacles in which they were forced to fight with wild beasts.

Shortly after the Roman-Jewish War, multitudes of Jewish prisoners perished in games with wild beasts. Titus sent many Jews captured during the siege of Jerusalem "to various provinces, to be destroyed in theatres by the sword or by wild beasts (*J.W.* 6:418). At Caesarea Philippi and Caesarea Maritima masses of Jewish prisoners of war were killed in contests with "wild beasts" as part of Titus entertainment (*J.W.* 7:23-24, 38).[82] Many other prisoners died in the same manner at Berytus and in the Syrian cities that Titus visited as he travelled back to Rome after the war (*J.W.* 7:39, 96). Given the overwhelming occasions where masses of Jewish prisoners perished in games with wild beasts, the reference to beasts in Mark must have reminded Mark's first hearers of the violent deaths of their fellow Jews just after the fall of Jerusalem and the temple. The hearers may as well have noticed the con-

80. Marcus, *Mark*, 170.

81. Moloney, *Mark*, 39. Cf. Guelich, *Mark*, 38-39; Marcus, *Mark*, 168.

82. In other cases, Josephus speaks of beasts to express a vicious behavior. For example, because of their tyranny, he refers to the Zealots as beasts or monsters (*J.W.* 4:262); he says of Simon bar Gioras's march to Jerusalem to rescue his wife from the hands of the Zealots to have been "like some wounded beasts" (*J.W.* 4:540); the civil war in Jerusalem is said to have been "like some beast for lack of other food [that] at length preyed upon its own flesh" (*J.W.* 5:4). In another context, dogs and beasts are said to have devoured the dead bodies of the high priests Ananus and Jesus, who were murdered by the Idumaeans during the civil war in Jerusalem (*J.W.* 4:324). For details about games involving humans and wild beasts in the ancient Roman Empire, see Kyle, *Spectacles of Death*, 8, 76-127.

trast between the wild beasts in the context of the war and those mentioned in Mark. They may have understood that while the beasts in the context of the war symbolized destruction, the wild beasts with Jesus symbolized a peaceful situation that signaled the presence of God's rule among his people and the restoration of God's original creation (cf. Isa 11:1–9).

Conclusion

In this chapter I have studied 1:1–13 as an account about the onset of God's empire in the light of the onset of the Roman Empire under Vespasian. In examining the subject of onset of empires, I primarily focused on the meaning of the good news, the presence of a divine agent, and entrance of the divine agent. Jesus and Vespasian were the focus of this study in that they respectively represented the onset of God's empire and that of the Roman Empire. The two were the divine agents of their respective empires. The results are summarized as shown below.

I begin with the aspect of the good news. In the context of Roman imperial cult, the good news was associated with military victory, the political achievements, and entrances of the emperor in cities. Since my investigation focused on Vespasian as the divine agent of the Roman Empire, a summary about the good news in the Roman imperial cult is restricted to him. The good news related to Vespasian was associated with his military victory, his accession to the imperial throne, and entrances in cities. Vespasian's military achievements, the proclamation of him as the emperor, his entrances in cities, and his enthronement were celebrated as good news. Since the good news associated with Vespasian was founded on military success, it is fair to conclude that this good news was basically about destruction. In Mark, the good news is associated with Jesus. It is about the coming of God's rule which Jesus spreads, not by violent means but by proclamation. Where the good news about Jesus in Mark involves a battle, that battle is neither against humans nor with a sword. When Jesus battles, he does so against Satan. His victory over Satan in the wilderness is a prelude to his victories over demonic powers, illnesses, death, hunger, sin, and oppressive forces of nature. Given the social location of Mark's hearers, the good news about Jesus may have had positive impact among them because it sanctified life, unlike the good news about Vespasian that glorified destruction of their own people and nation.

Another aspect considered in this chapter related to the divine nature of the agent of the empire. My investigation has revealed that Vespasian, the agent of the Roman Empire, was recognized as divine. Besides his own claim that he was a god, people recognized and hailed him in divine terms as lord, savior, benefactor, lord of land and sea, and bringer of new life. Vespasian's claim to possess a divine status was based on oracles, omens associated with him, and his ability to perform miracles of healing. These claims were primarily used as propaganda tools to legitimize his imperial power. In Mark, Jesus also possessed a divine status. From the outset of Mark's story, he is identified in divine terms. He is the "Messiah," "Son of God," "Lord," and "the one more powerful." Like Vespasian, his divine status is associated with prophecy (1:2-3) and omens at his baptism (and at his transfiguration). Unlike Vespasian, however, God himself declares Jesus as his Son. More importantly, God declares Jesus as his "Beloved Son" (1:11; cf. 9:7), an expression that demonstrates Jesus' unique relationship with God. Thus for Mark's hearers, rather than Vespasian who claims to be the fulfillment of a Jewish oracle that expected a world ruler from Judea, the true world ruler is "Jesus Messiah, Son of God." As God's Messiah, Jesus faithfully and responsibly fulfils his redemptive role that God had entrusted him. It is ironic that although Jesus saves[83] on land and sea and reigns the whole world as God's Messiah, he is never addressed as savior, benefactor, lord of land and sea, or as a world ruler.

There are other marks that distinguish the entrance of Jesus from those of Vespasian. Before Jesus inaugurates God's empire, he first undergoes a ritual of baptism through which God endorses him as his beloved Son and empowers him with the Holy Spirit who becomes the source of power that he uses to liberate God's people as the story unfolds. The first time the power of the Holy Spirit is demonstrated was in the struggle against Satan. Jesus' victory against Satan foretells Jesus' victories soon to be revealed in his Galilean campaigns against illnesses, demonic forces, and all forces that oppress people or operate against God's will. Moreover, unlike Vespasian's entrances that are focused in cities, Jesus' entrances were focused in Galilean villages and towns. In Galilee, crowds of people from villages followed Jesus in desert places, beside the sea, and at market places to receive from him the blessings of God's empire. It is also important to note that while Vespasian feasted with the elite, Jesus ate with the poor, the oppressed, and the marginalized such as the unclean and outcasts.

---

83. E.g., Mark 5:23, 28, 34; 6:56; 10:26, 52; 13:13; 15:31.

5

Campaigns in Galilee
Vespasian and Jesus

Introduction

IN THIS CHAPTER, I examine Jesus' campaign in Galilee in light of Vespasian's military conquests of Galilee. I seek to present the contrasts between Jesus' life-giving campaign in Galilee as depicted in Mark's Gospel and Vespasian's destructive military campaigns in that territory. Since we do not know what Mark's Gospel really intended to be, I assume that when Mark's hearers heard the story about Jesus' redemptive campaign in Galilee, they brought with them their life experiences and memories of Vespasian's campaigns in the area. Before I discuss Jesus' life-giving campaign, I first put Vespasian's Galilean military campaign in perspective.

Vespasian's Military Campaign in Galilee

The Romans' Military Power

As an experienced military general, Vespasian was appointed by Nero to suppress the revolt in Judea (*J.W.* 3:1–8). The general left Rome, the centre of the empire, crossed the Hellespont, and marched on land to Antioch, before he proceeded to Ptolemais in Syria.[1] From Ptolemais Vespasian advanced to Galilee with a total of sixty thousand troops, including the best three Roman legions: the fifth, tenth, and fifteenth legions (*J.W.* 3:8, 64–69, 115). The huge number of forces, though perhaps an exaggeration,[2] clearly expresses the strength and power of the Roman army that was to deal with the Jewish revolt.[3]

---

1. Antioch was the capital of Syria while Ptolemais was a city located in Southern Syria on the cost of the Mediterranean Sea very close to the west side of Galilee.

2. Cf. Faulkner, *Apocalypse*, 191.

3. Goodman, *Rome and Jerusalem*, 425, notes that such a huge number of forces

Along with the military equipment, Vespasian's troops carried with them "the eagle" emblem and the trumpets. The Romans considered the eagle not only as "the king and bravest of all the birds" but also as "the symbol of empire." During war times they considered the eagle emblem as "an omen of victory" (*J.W.* 3:120–123), suggesting that they believed it to be the source of their power and victory. In the customary marching order of the Roman armies (*J.W.* 3:115–126),[4] the eagle emblem came before every legion while followed by the trumpeters (*J.W.* 3:124).[5] The trumpets were used to scare, threaten, and to terrify the enemy in the battlefield. The trumpeters may also have served as heralds responsible for announcing the good news of victory in battle when such an achievement was attained (cf. *J.W.* 3:92). The eagle emblem and the trumpets were therefore important instruments for the Roman troops.

Vespasian began his campaign to crush the revolt in Galilee before he proceeded to Jerusalem. His strategy was to subdue the countryside first before he began the siege of the Holy City. This would ensure that there was no attack from behind as his troops advanced to the capital and holy city of the Jews. Perhaps he learned from Cestius Gallus, whose mistake of undermining the strength of the Jewish rebellion as a riot of some outlaws led to his shameful defeat (*J.W.* 2:513–55). As a result, Vespasian took the Jewish revolt very seriously. Recognizing the Jewish revolutionaries as determined guerrilla fighters committed to defend their land and holy city, he avoided rushing to Jerusalem. Rather, he planned to start his military campaign with the devastation of Galilee as a strategy to prevent attacks from behind as he advanced to Jerusalem. Faulkner has made a remarkable and insightful observation about this matter that is worth noting. He writes:

---

was necessary for three major reasons. The first was the huge loss of troops and military equipment during Cestius's engagement with the Jews in Jerusalem in the summer of 66 CE. This required a large force to punish the Jews who caused such a shameful loss. Second, the rebellion of the Jews was viewed as a major threat to the empire that needed to be severely dealt with. Third, Vespasian was given such a huge force simply because the troops were available in the region. Following the end of the campaign against Armenia and Parthia, troops were left unemployed; so when the Jewish revolt occurred, they had to be effectively used. According to Goodman, this explanation is the most plausible.

4. For a detailed description of the order in which they marched from Ptolemais into Galilee, see *J.W.* 3:115–26; Faulkner, *Apocalypse*, 206–17.

5. Trumpeters issued commands for meals, sleep, duty, rising, breakfast, and for attacking or retreating on a battlefield (*J.W.* 3:85–92; 2:579). As trumpets sounded, "the troops raised a terrific shout, [and] at a given signal arrows poured from all quarters" (*J.W.* 3:265). Cf. Krentz, "Paul, Games, and the Military," 350, who states that trumpets were used in the Roman army to make the voice of command in the battlefield more audible.

Vespasian's strategy was to fight a long war, each move carefully staged, avoiding undue risk, reducing the rebel bit by bit through a succession of skirmishes and sieges, while destroying their infrastructure and will to fight with a ruthless application of fire and sword to villages and farmland. It was to be a terrible war of attrition and annihilation. With such a strategy, the first objective had to be the destruction of revolutionary Galilee, which would restore full communications with Herod Agrippa's territories in the northern Transjordan, relieve the Decapolis cities of any Jewish threat, and secure the Roman rear for an advance through Judea to the revolutionary capital (Jerusalem).[6]

Vespasian's strategy was successful in that after the devastation of Galilee there were no attacks from behind as he advanced to Jerusalem.

Campaigns in Fortified Cities, Starvation, and Attack at the Last Hour of the Night

Vespasian's Galilean campaign was primarily based on fortified cities. Vespasian conquered one city or town after another. Starting with Garis, a town near Sepphoris (*J.W.* 3:127–30),[7] he then captured Gabara (*J.W.* 3:132–34), Japha (*J.W.* 3:289–306), and Jotapata (*J.W.* 3:141–288, 316–408), a city that upon its fall, Josephus prophesied that Vespasian would become emperor (*J.W.* 3:400–402). After the fall of Jotapata, Tiberias surrendered, and its inhabitants hailed Vespasian as "saviour and benefactor" (*J.W.* 3:453–461). Thereafter, Vespasian conquered Tarichaea (*J.W.* 3:462–502), Gamala (*J.W.* 4:9–83), Mount Tabor (*J.W.* 4:54–61), and finally, the city of Gischala (*J.W.* 4:92–120). The conquest of Gischala brought the entire Galilee under Vespasian's control, hence, under the Roman imperial domination.[8]

In order to achieve victory in his war operations in Galilee, Vespasian used a variety of strategies. Here I highlight only two of them: attacking the enemy at the last hour of the night and starving the enemy. These strategies

---

6. Faulkner, *Apocalypse*, 218.

7. Sepphoris was the largest city in Galilee. Its inhabitants were the only people in Galilee who did not resist the Romans (*J.W.* 3:30–34). Josephus's attempt to capture it before the arrival of Vespasian in the city caused serious Roman hostilities against those in the countryside. Roman troops led by Placius responded harshly. Day and night they devastated the plains and pillaged "the property of the country-folk, invariably killing all capable of bearing arms and reducing the inefficient to servitude. Galilee from end to end became a scene of fire and blood; from no misery, no calamity was it exempt" (*J.W.* 3:60–63).

8. Schäfer, *History of the Jews*, 123–24.

are important because they highlight links with Mark's story of Jesus. The former strategy relates to Jesus' walking on water the event that manifested his identity and authority as an agent of God entrusted to announce and reveal God's empire (6:45–51).[9] The latter strategy parallels, though ironically, Mark's feeding stories depicted at 6:30–44 and 8:1–9. The Romans applied both these strategies against their opponents at Jotapata.

At Jotapata, Vespasian's forces met strong resistance from the Jewish forces under Josephus. The Roman general was therefore forced to develop a strategy that would help him achieve his goal to win the war. Since the city lacked springs of water, it depended on rain-water falling in summer (the same time Jotapata was engaged in war), and Vespasian believed he could use such a situation to his advantage. Rather than fight, Vespasian ordered his troops to block and starve the city in order to force the defendants to surrender (*J.W.* 3:178–80, 185). Unfortunately, the plan was not successful for two reasons. First, the defenders had plenty of corn and other necessary supplies in store, except salt. Second, although the defenders lacked spring water in the city, a water rationing system helped them prolong the use of water available. In addition, even if water and food supplies would not be available, Jews "preferred death in battle to perishing of hunger and thirst" (*J.W.* 3:181–89).[10] Due to these factors, the Romans were not able to capture Jotapata until an alternative strategy was employed.

Since the starvation strategy did not produce the expected results, Vespasian used an alternative tactic. This was to attack the enemy at the last hour of the night. The approach, however, did not originate from Vespasian himself. It is credited to a deserter from Jotapata who provided intelligence information to the Roman general. The deserter revealed to Vespasian both the strength of the defense of the city and the hour of the night when the tired defenders fell asleep. Josephus says of this deserter that he "stated that about the last watch of the night . . . when jaded men easily succumb to morning slumber—the sentinels used to drop asleep; and that was the hour when he advised the Romans to attack" (*J.W.* 3:316–319). Taking advantage of this military intelligence report, Vespasian dispatched Titus and Domitius Sabinus with some men of the fifteenth legion to attack the city at the very hour that the defenders slept. Titus's troops,

---

9. Another incident in Mark relating to "the last hour of the night" appears outside the locality of Galilee. This incident concerns Jesus' warning to keep watch because of the unknown hour when the lord of the house will come (13:32–37). Note especially v. 35: "for you do not know when the lord of the house will come, in the evening, or at midnight, or at cockcrow, or at dawn." For further explanation about the division of time in the ancient world, see Marcus, *Mark*, 920.

10. Cf. Faulkner, *Apocalypse*, 224.

along with those under the command of Sextus Calvarius and Placidus, caught the Jewish fighters by surprise, most of them in a state of tiredness and asleep. The Romans conquered Jotapata and put it under their control (*J.W.* 3:324–328). The attack at the last hour of the night resulted in the Roman victory against the Jews at Jotapata.

Outcomes of Vespasian's Campaign

Vespasian's military campaigns in Galilee were destructive and catastrophic. The campaigns were marked with losses of life, pillage, and plundering of property. In some cases, the campaigns resulted in enslavements and displacements. In every city or town that attempted to resist against Rome received indiscriminate killings, pillage, and destruction of people's possessions. Josephus gives numerous accounts about the destructive effects of the Roman troops under Vespasian's command in Galilee. He shows that when Vespasian captured Gabara not only did he mercilessly and indiscriminately massacre and enslave its inhabitants, but also reduced the neighboring villages and towns to ashes (*J.W.* 3:132–34). A similar principle was applied at Jotapata where the Romans also massacred forty thousand residents, enslaving 1,200 Jews, and burning the city to the ground (*J.W.* 3:336–339). No doubt the numbers are expressive of Josephus's gross exaggerations. However, the general point stands that the Romans caused a great loss of life at Jotapata over and above the devastation of the city itself. The Roman cavalry encamped at Joppa had a devastating effect as well. It "daily scoured the country, pillaging and reducing it to an utter desert" (*J.W.* 3:428–431). In addition, in the city of Tiberias, Vespasian ordered the execution of 1,200 captives; sending multitudes in slavery (*J.W.* 3:539–541). Sometimes the means of execution was crucifixion as was the case for the Jewish prisoner who refused to betray his town to the enemy even under the ordeal of fire (*J.W.* 3:321).

The losses of life that Vespasian's military campaign brought with it upon the Galileans was horrendous. Josephus provides huge figures of those who perished in each of the Galilean cities as a result of Vespasian's military campaign. According to him, 15,000 Jews died at Jappha (*J.W.* 3:305), 40,000 perished at Jotapata (*J.W.* 3:338), and 6,700 died at Tarichaea (*J.W.* 3:531). Josephus reports further that 1,200 died in Tiberias (*J.W.* 4:540–41), more than 9,000 at Gamala (*J.W.* 4:80), and finally, that 6,000 died at Gischala (*J.W.* 4:115). Although Josephus exaggerates the numbers, the fact remains that Vespasian's campaign caused a great loss of life among Jews in Galilee.

Besides the losses of life, Vespasian's military campaign in Galilee also led many Jews into slavery. According to Josephus, Vespasian sent or sold a number of Galilean war captives into slavery. For example, he shows that Vespasian sold infants and women captives from Jappa into slavery (*J.W.* 3:304) and that the inhabitants of some towns near Gabara were also reduced to slavery (*J.W.* 3:134). In another context, Josephus indicates that Vespasian sent multitudes of Jewish captives from Tarichaea to Rome to serve as Nero's slaves while he gave others to Agrippa who also sold them into slavery (*J.W.* 3:540–541).

In addition to losses of life and enslavements, Vespasian's campaign also forced some Galileans into becoming refugees. The evidence of this is Josephus's remark that when Vespasian had entered the devastated neighboring towns of Gadara he found some of those towns completely deserted (*J.W.* 3:134), implying that the inhabitants left their town and took refuge somewhere else. Mark's audience may have been part of those who had been displaced as a result of Vespasian's military campaign. Faulkner has underscored the overall outcome of the Roman military campaign when he points out that the Romans had a principle they followed whenever they conquered a city. He states that whenever the Romans forces enter a city:

> Men of fighting age would be cut down, sometimes along with women, children, old people and even animals; women would be gang-raped; all moveable property of value would be plundered; and buildings and possessions would be ransacked and vandalized . . . (By the order of officers) [m]en of fighting age might be mutilated and cast adrift, or tortured and executed, or sold to the slave dealers. Women, children and old men would usually be enslaved, except for the decrepit, who might be executed or left to fend for themselves.[11]

It is therefore undeniable that Vespasian's military campaign in Galilee brought about devastating effects upon the Galilean people. The campaign was so destructive that it led to a great loss of life and property, enslavements, mutilations, violation of women, displacement, etc.

Vespasian's Rest at Caesarea Philippi

After his tiring but successful military campaign in Galilee, Vespasian had rest at Caesarea Philippi (*J.W.* 3:443–444). The rest took place shortly after he was informed of the prophecy that he would become Caesar. The

---

11. Faulkner, *Apocalypse*, 220–21.

prophecy was made between the time of the fall of Jotapata and that of Tarichaea. Since Jotapata fell in July 67 CE (*J.W.* 3:339) and Tarichaea in September 67 CE (*J.W.* 3:542), it follows that Vespasian heard about the prophecy (*J.W.* 3:400–402) the time between July and September. If this observation is accepted, it is therefore intriguing to note that Vespasian's visit at Caesarea Philippi is also connected to the prophecy about his accession to the imperial throne.

Vespasian visited Caesarea Philippi at the invitation of King Agrippa II. The king hosted him for two purposes: to entertain the general and his troops and to seek help to stop the revolts at Tiberias and Tarichaea, the cities that were part of his kingdom. Vespasian rested at Caesarea Philippi for twenty days. While there, he gave thank-offerings to God for his successful campaign in Galilee. As payback for the hospitality and generosity he received from Agrippa, Vespasian assisted the king to pacify revolts in cities of Tarichaeae and Tiberia (*J.W.* 3:443–446). This account highlights, among other things, one of the important aspects of Vespasian's entrances, namely, the reception. At Caesarea Philippi, Vespasian is received and hosted by a king who displaced on his behalf "all the wealth of his royal household" (*J.W.* 3:443).

The reception at Caesarea Philippi, recalls two other receptions that Vespasian received in Syrian cities, Antioch and Ptolemais when he was on his way to crush the revolt in Judea (*J.W.* 3:29–30). At Antioch, the general was received by kings including Agrippa II (*J.W.* 3:29). This reception parallels that at Caesarea Philippi in that those who received Vespasian were kings. The welcome expressed to Vespasian at Ptolemais by the deputation from Sepphoris (*J.W.* 3:30, 32) parallels that at Caesarea Philippi in that, like king Agrippa, the deputation sought for military support from the general against their fellow citizens (*J.W.* 3:33–34). In all cases, Vespasian was received by men of power. Another important point worth noting about Vespasian's rest at Caesarea Philippi relates to the lavish banquet prepared in his honor. It is ironic that while he starved others at Jotapata, Vespasian fêted himself with lavish feasts at Caesarea Philippi. Note that Vespasian enjoyed the banquet worth "all the wealth" of the king's family.

Vespasian Fought to Consolidate the Roman Empire

Vespasian made the military campaign on behalf of the Roman Empire seeking to consolidate the empire. Normally the Romans made wars in order to expand their empire. At one point, Josephus indicates that Vespasian told his troops that the Romans "make war not from necessity, but to increase empire" (*J. W.* 3:210). In his long speech in which he tries to dissuade the Jews from making war with Rome, King Agrippa II is cited as mentioning many great states that had been subdued by the Romans: Athens, Greece, Macedonia, Asia, Gaul, Spain, Germany, Britain, Egypt, and others (*J. W.* 2:358–368). The mention of these states strongly supports Vespasian's claim that Rome made war in order to expand their empire. In the present time, Horsley has also argued in support of this claim. He states that ancient Romans used military power to expand and consolidate their empire. In support of his point, Horsley uses an example of Pompey whose victorious campaign against the pirates in central Asia Minor inaugurated the expansion of Roman imperialism.[12] He also argues that the Romans conquered other nations with their superior military power in order to ensure their own security and to achieve loyalty from the conquered people in terms of submission.[13]

The Roman military response to the Jewish revolt of 66 CE as well was meant to maintain their control of Judea and thereby to ensure security of the empire. Judea played a significant role for Rome in that it served as a buffer zone against the Parthian Empire in the east. The Parthian Empire was a formidable threat to the Romans. Parthia once controlled Israel from 40 to 37 BCE and had hosted large Jewish communities since the Babylonian exile. The Parthians considered Judea as their potential supporter in war with Rome. Similarly, when Judea revolted against Rome in 66 CE, Jews hoped to receive aid from their Jewish friends in Parthia. They expected that Parthia would persuade the Parthians to wage war against the Romans (*J. W.* 6:341–43; 2:388–389), but this dream never happened. So, Rome responded to the Jewish revolt with its full military strength both to maintain control over Judea and to ensure security of its empire against the Parthians (*J. W.* 2:91).[14]

It was also characteristic of the Romans to use military forces to terrorize for the purpose of maintaining control of the subject states. Faulkner argues that the military power with which the Romans responded to the Jewish revolt was "for the sake of terror" (Polybius, *Hist.* 10.15–17; cf. Dio Cassius, *Rom. Hist.* 68.6.1–2).[15] Such terror was meant to maintain the

12. Horsley, *Jesus and Empire*, 18–19.

13. Ibid., 27.

14. Rhoads, *Israel in Revolution*, 27. Highlighting the importance of Judea for the security of the Roman Empire, Rhoads says, "The province of Judea was too important to the Roman Empire as a protection on the eastern front for the rebellion to be treated lightly" (ibid., 151).

15. Cf. Faulkner, *Apocalypse*, 221. He notes that the sack was not just a moment of madness and bloodlust, and emphasizes that it was an ordered and purposeful action

Roman control over Judea through keeping the subject people submissive to Caesar. This would then ensure security and peace for the whole empire. Their conquest of Judea would send a message to other parts of the empire that any attempt at revolt against Rome was very risky. In this regard, Vespasian's military campaign in Judea may have been viewed as a purposeful action to terrorize the Jews in order to force them to submit and pay loyalty to Caesar. The key is that Vespasian made the military campaign in Galilee to serve the interests of Rome and to consolidate the empire to which he soon became emperor.

Vespasian Proclaimed Emperor

Shortly after the capture of Jotapata, Vespasian heard of a prophecy that he would become emperor. Josephus, his prisoner of war prophesied of him that he would be ruler "of land and sea and the whole human race" (*J.W.* 3:400–402). In 69 CE, Vespasian was proclaimed emperor by his troops while he was still on the Jewish soil. Consequently, Josephus claimed that Vespasian became emperor in accordance with a Jewish prophecy that expected a world ruler to come from Judea (*J.W.* 6:312–13; cf. Num 24:17–19). This would imply that Vespasian was the fulfillment of the expected Jewish Messiah[16] and hence also his possession of a divine status. The title of ruler or master of "land and sea"[17] may also have elevated Vespasian to the level of a divine figure,[18] an honor also expressed by the Tiberians when they hailed him as "savior and benefactor" (*J.W.* 3:459–460). The people of Tiberias praised Vespasian as savior because he saved their city from falling into the rebels'

---

intended to "inspire terror." Its purpose was to destroy the will to resist or to rebel.

16. Winn, *Mark*, 160.

17. This or a similar phrase was common imperial propaganda of the Roman emperors. For example, the expression was used in praise of Augustus's achievements when he ended wars waged by pirates from Europe and Asia (Philo, *Legat.* 145–147). See also Deissmann, *Light*, 347, figure 64, where Augustus is praised as "overseer of every land and sea" (Pergamum No. 381); Seneca uses a similar phrase to praise Nero for the prevailing peace on land and sea (*De clementia* 4). Critics of the imperium as well used this phrase to expose the evils of the empire. See for example, Plutarch, *Pomp.* 70; Petronius, *Sat.* 119.1–3; Tacitus, *Agric.* 30.5.

18. Cf. Koester, "Jesus the Victim," 12–13. Based on the Priene inscription from 9 BCE (*OGIS* no. 458), Koester observes a number of features of the Roman imperial order. Such features include (a) the advent of a new age as the fulfillment of prophecy; (b) the involvement in the new age of both the earth and the heavens, ruled by god Apollo-Helios; (c) the universal inclusion in the new age of all nations; (d) the presence in the new age of a "savior figure, the greatest benefactor of all times," identified as the "Son of God."

hands (*J.W.* 3:449–452), which implied salvation from destruction by the Romans. During his military campaign in Galilee, Vespasian was also hailed as bringer of "new life." The people of Tiberias addressed him as such because he rescued their city from the effects of sedition (*J.W.* 3:461).[19] Like the other honors that elevated Vespasian to a divine status, the honor as bringer of "new life," also lifted him up to a divine status.[20] Suetonius refers to him as one who "lacked prestige and a certain divinity . . . since he was an unexpected and still new-made emperor" (*Vesp.* 7:2). Therefore, since the new emperor was low born, a person who in normal circumstances would not be expected to become emperor, these divine titles may have been used as propaganda machinery to legitimate his imperial rule. Josephus's prophecy in particular, not only legitimated Vespasian's accession to the throne, it also suggested that even the God of the Jews approved him to be emperor.

The idea that an emperor had the power to bring life was not uncommon in the ancient Roman world. As propaganda machinery, providences set the emperor in a very positive light. For example, Augustus's honor as "the beginning of good news" developed into subsequent emperors being viewed as "the source of all good things" as was the case on Nero's accession (P.Oxy. 1021.5–13). According to Seneca, the emperor was also capable of bringing life from the dead. Highlighting the tremendous power of Nero, the Caesar who sent Vespasian to suppress the Jewish revolt, Seneca writes: "To give safety to many and *to recall them to life from the very brink of death* and to earn civic crown through clemency—that is happiness . . . This is divine power, to save in mobs and states; but to kill many and indiscriminately is the power of conflagration and collapse" (*Clem.* 1.26.5).[21] But all these were propaganda tools intended to promote the emperor's positive image before his subjects. Vespasian's divine titles have to be viewed in the same manner. The divine titles associated with him were used to consolidate his imperial power. The proclamation of him as emperor in 69 CE consolidated

---

19. Tiberias was one of the cities in Agrippa's kingdom whose elders and principal citizens were pro-Roman. While Jesus son of Saphat tried to resist the Romans, these elders and principal citizens of the city with the approval of Agrippa marched to Vespasian and sued for peace. Their pro-Roman attitude must have been one of the contributing factors for the fall of the city. Since the city belonged to Agrippa's realm and because its principal citizens also were pro-Roman, after its capture, it was spared from destruction. Vespasian strictly forbade any pillage, violence, or destruction of the city walls, opposing his usual practice in the cities he captured, as a compliment to Agrippa for the king's hospitality as well as for the people's commitment to loyalty to the Romans (*J.W.* 460–461).

20. Roetzel, *World that Shaped the New Testament*, 74, 112, 114: the titles "savior . . . benefactor, and lord . . . confirmed the king's divine status" (ibid., 112).

21. Italics are mine.

his rule and the continuation of Roman domination and oppression over the Jews. This may have been the view of the Galileans who knew about his destructive military campaign in Galilee and the imperial oppression associated with his rule.

The claim that Vespasian had ability to bring new life can be associated with another claim that he had ability to heal. Although Josephus does not associate Vespasian with healing activities, other ancient sources indicate that Vespasian performed two miraculous healings: the restoration of sight and of a withered hand. Tacitus describes at length Vespasian's healings performed at Alexandria, Egypt in 69 CE. He writes:

> During the months while Vespasian was waiting at Alexandria for the regular season of the summer winds and a settled sea, many marvels occurred to mark the favor of heaven and a certain partiality of the gods toward him. One of the common people of Alexandria, well known for his loss of sight, threw himself before Vespasian's knees, praying him with groans to cure his blindness, being so directed by the god Serapis, whom this most superstitious of nations worships before all others; and he besought the emperor to design to moisten his cheeks and eyes with his spittle. Another, whose hand was useless, prompted by the same god, begged Caesar to step and trample on it. Vespasian at first ridiculed these appeals and treated them with scorn; then, when the men persisted, he began at one moment to fear the discredit of failure, at another to be inspired with hopes of success by the appeals of the suppliants and the flattery of his courtiers: finally, he directed the physicians to give their opinion as to whether such blindness and infirmity could be overcome by human aid. Their reply treated the two cases differently: they said that in the first the power of sight had not been completely eaten away and it would return if the obstacles were removed; in the other, the joints had slipped and become displaced, but they could be restored if a healing pressure were applied to them. Such perhaps was the wish of the gods, and it might be that the emperor had been chosen for this divine service; in any case, if a cure were obtained, the glory would be Caesar's, but in the event of failure, ridicule would fall only on the poor suppliants. So Vespasian, believing that his good fortune was capable of anything and that nothing was any longer incredible, with a smiling countenance, and amid intense excitement on the part of the bystanders, did as he was asked to do. The hand was instantly restored to use, and the day again shone for the blind man. Both

facts are told by eye-witnesses even now when falsehood brings no reward (*Hist.* 4.81).²²

Although the healing events described in this account did not occur during Vespasian's military campaign in Galilee, it is important to note them here because they may have been associated with his ability to bring life. Galileans who were aware of these healings may have associated them with Jesus' related healings.

In sum, Vespasian came from Rome to crush the revolt in Judea on behalf of the Roman Empire. With a powerful military force, he invaded Galilee and devastated fortified cities and towns one after another. The results of his campaign were devastating upon the Galileans. So many Jews lost their lives and possessions while many others were sent into slavery. In order to win the war, sometimes Vespasian starved his enemies or attacked them at the last hour of the night. Overall, Vespasian's military campaign was destructive and was intended to consolidate the Roman Empire by putting Judea under the Roman's ongoing domination and control. Since Vespasian was proclaimed emperor while he was still in Judea, Josephus claimed that the new emperor was a fulfillment of the Jewish prophecy, hence perhaps carrying the status of the "messiah."

By contrast, Jesus' campaign in Galilee was life-giving. It started with Jesus' coming from Nazareth, the margin of the empire, to the wilderness, and finally to the villages and town of Galilee and its neighboring regions. Initially, Jesus gathered the twelve to be with him in the campaign that he made on behalf of God's empire. In the villages or towns of Galilee and its neighboring regions, Jesus campaigned against demonic powers, illnesses, hunger, and other oppressive and life-threatening forces of nature. So, while Vespasian's campaign was based in fortified cities, Jesus' campaign was focused on rural villages and towns. Unlike Vespasian who starved people during his military campaign, Jesus gave food to the hungry; instead of

---

22. Suetonius has preserved a similar account in his *Vesp.* 7:2–3. He writes, "A man of the people who was blind, and another who was lame, came to him [Vespasian] together as he sat on the tribunal, begging for the help for their disorder which Serapis had promised in a dream; for the god declared that Vespasian would restore the eyes, if he would spit upon them, and give strength to the leg, if he would deign to touch it with his heel. Though he had hardly any faith that this could possibly succeed, and therefore shrank even from the attempt, he was at last prevailed upon by his friends and tried both things in public before a large crowd; and with success. At this same time, by the direction of certain soothsayers, some vases of antique workmanship were dug up in a consecrated spot at Tegea in Arcadia and on them was an image very like Vespasian." Although Suetonius's account differs from that of Tacitus in that he replaces the hand referred to by Tacitus with a leg, the general idea of Vespasian's ability to heal and the mode of healing remain the same.

attacking and killing at the last hour of the night, Jesus saved his disciples from the threat of death due to the sea storms. Also while Vespasian was being welcomed by kings and delegations of powerful men of the cities, Jesus was rejected by the authorities who also challenged his campaign. Instead, Jesus received and served crowds of the people, the oppressed, marginalized peasants and outcasts, who flocked to him in large numbers. Indeed, while Vespasian led a violent and destructive campaign, Jesus led a non-violent and redemptive campaign.

Besides the contrasts highlighted above, Jesus' Galilean campaign also parallels Vespasian's campaign. Apart from the fact that both campaigns started in Galilee before they each culminated in Jerusalem, both Vespasian and Jesus visited Caesarea Philippi, and each of the visits was associated with a messianic claim. Vespasian rested at Caesarea Philippi shortly after it was prophesied that he would be emperor, a status that was later associated with the Jewish oracle that expected a world ruler to come from Judea. Jesus was also proclaimed the Messiah in the villages of Caesarea Philippi, a place not far from the location known for emperor worship and where Vespasian visited shortly after he received an oracle that he would be emperor.

Jesus' Life-Giving Campaign in Galilee according to Mark's Gospel

Jesus' Overall Campaign

Unlike Vespasian's military campaign that was primarily focused on Galilean fortified cities, Jesus' Galilean campaign was primarily rural-based. Jesus avoided entering cities like Tiberias and Sepphoris.[23] He focused his life-giving ministry in the periphery until the time when he went to the center in Jerusalem where he was arrested (14:46) and crucified (15:20, 24-25). He started his campaign in Galilee in order to get support from the peasants, before he advanced to the center in Jerusalem. This strategy demonstrates that Jesus' movement in Mark is indeed a peasant movement whose goal was to bring renewal in Israel's local communities. Before Jesus started his campaign, he travelled from Nazareth of Galilee to the Judean desert where he was baptized by John in the river Jordan (1:9). From there, after his testing in the wilderness, Jesus returned to Galilee where he inaugurated his campaign proclaiming the good news about the arrival of God's empire (1:14-15).

Before the campaign gained root, Jesus gathered his close followers. Starting with the calling of the fishermen (1:16-20) and tax collectors

---

23. These were the major Galilean cities, but Mark never mentions them.

(2:14–15), he appointed the twelve to be with him (3:13–19). He recruited the twelve in order to give them authority over unclean spirits, to preach repentance, to drive out demons, and to anoint and heal the sick (6:7–13). Jesus' recruitment of the twelve ironically parallels Vespasian's gathering of his armies before he started his destructive campaign in Galilee. While Vespasian gathered troops in order to conquer violently and to subject Jews under the Roman Empire, Jesus recruited the twelve in order to be with him and to liberate people from oppressive human and natural forces and to invite them into God's empire. Note that the twelve did not destroy life or force people to enter God's empire; rather, they conquered demons and liberated people from related oppressive supernatural forces.

The center of Jesus' Galilean campaign was Capernaum.[24] Jesus moved in and out of this place. From there, he went out throughout the villages of Galilee and the neighboring regions conducting his life-giving campaign in synagogues (1:21–28, 38–39; 6:2), in a house or at home (1:29–31, 32–34;; 2:1–12, 15–16; 3:1–6; 3:19–27; 9:33), beside the sea (1:16–20; 2:13–14; 3:7–12; 4:1–20; 5:21), on a mountain (3:14–19; 6:45–51), among villages (6:6, 7–13), and in desert places (6:30–44; 8:1–10). Sometimes Jesus made his liberative campaign while crossing the sea (4:35–41; 6:45–51) or while in a boat (4:1; 5:21; 8:14–21). Jesus' crossing of the sea (4:35; 5:1, 21; 6:51–53; 8:10, 13) may have reminded Mark's hearers of the Roman troops that came from Rome through the Mediterranean Sea to conquer Judea. Because of Jesus' successful campaign, his fame spread "throughout the surrounding region of Galilee" (1:28). As a result, crowds of people from beyond Galilee came to him. They came from "Judea, Jerusalem, Idumea, beyond the Jordan, and the region around Tyre and Sidon" (3:7–8). Except for Judea, Jesus latter visited and preached in these places (7:24, 31–37; 10:1).[25] Jesus' Galilean campaign culminated in the villages of Caesarea Philippi, the place where he was proclaimed the Messiah (8:27–30).

Mark's presentation of Jesus' overall campaign provides some ironies when compared with Vespasian's campaign in Galilee. For example, while Vespasian goes into cities and kills, Jesus goes in villages and helps people

24. Malbon, "Galilee and Jerusalem," 259. With reference to Capernaum as the center of Jesus' ministry, she writes, "From the centre, movements radiate outwards, and to the centre they return. As broadly as Jesus travels, his name and fame travel further, borne on the lips of those who come to him from as far as far away as Syrophoenicia (7:26) in the north and Idumea (3:8) in the south and who go away from him not only through Galilee (1:28) to the west but also throughout the Decapolis (5:20) to the east. During his Galilean ministry, Jesus moves not only throughout Galilee but to Judea and to foreign regions as well, and persons from each of these three major areas come to him."

25. Cf. ibid., 258–59.

in their needs; while Vespasian is met with kings and the great men (*J. W.* 3:8, 29–32) when he enters cities, those who come to Jesus are the *'amme ha-arets*—the ordinary people, the poor and oppressed peasants from the Galilean villages and of the neighboring regions. Moreover, while Vespasian, who although he kills and enslaves people and destroys cities and property is hailed savior and liberator; Jesus is never addressed savior or liberator even though he liberates people from oppressive forces through his works of power. Furthermore, while Vespasian used military power to campaign for the consolidation of the Roman Emperor, Jesus campaigned for God's empire without violence by proclamation of the good news of God.

Recruitment of the Twelve

In Mark, the first thing Jesus did after his announcement of God's empire was to recruit his disciples. He started with the calling of four fishermen: Simon (Peter), Andrew, James, and John (1:16–20); and then, Levi the tax collector (2:13–14). Thereafter, on a mountain, he appointed the twelve to be with him, to be sent to proclaim the good news, to heal, and to drive out demons (3:13–19). Then, Jesus fulfilled his promise of making those whom he chose to be "fishers for people" (1:17) by sending the twelve in two to proclaim and to heal (6:6–13). The followers who make up the twelve are ordinary people from among the Jewish peasantry from rural Galilee. Jesus himself belonged to the peasant class, for he was a carpenter from the village of Nazareth (6:3; cf. 1:9).

The major role of the twelve was to proclaim the good news and thereby to expand God's empire. In order for the campaign to be successful, the twelve had to be mobile and not static. As such, they must leave everything that would make them stationary and delay the progress of their mission. They had to leave their possessions, families, homes, and lands (e.g., 1:16–20; 2:14; 10:28). As they campaigned on behalf of God's empire around the Galilean villages, they were to travel lightly. They had to take nothing: no bread, no bag, and no money, except to wear sandals and a tunic, but no extra tunic (6:8–9).[26] The prohibitions suggest that the twelve were to depend entirely upon the hospitality of those whom they were sent to serve.[27] These prohibitions reinforced the mobility nature of the mission in that the twelve had to travel and move easily from village to village proclaiming the

---

26. Cf. Blount, *Go Preach*, 49, who states that "The mission of the twelve is so important that they are not to weigh themselves down with unnecessary baggage. They must move quickly."

27. Rhoads, *Reading Mark*, 101.

good news of God. Generally, the mission of the twelve was modeled after Jesus' campaign. Like Jesus, the twelve proclaimed (3:14; 6:12; cf. 1:14), called people to repent (6:12; cf. 1:15), drove out demons, and healed the sick (6:13; cf. 1:34). In this way, the twelve manifested God's compassion to people exactly as Jesus did. They utilized the power authorized by Jesus to bring life to people over against the demonic forces and illnesses.

The twelve were recruited in order to bring renewal in local communities of Israel. They were to serve as alternative to the ruling authorities in Jerusalem whose leadership was a failure. But this does not mean that Jesus' intention was to overthrow the government in Jerusalem and replace it with the twelve. Rather, Jesus believed that God would be the judge and bringer of an alternative rule, the empire of God among his people. This idea is made explicit in the parable of the vineyard in 12:1-12. Because the authorities, who are the tenants beat, insult, and kill God's servants (12:3-6), God, the owner of the vineyard "will come and destroy the tenants and give the vineyard to others" (12:9). So it is God who will judge and establish an alternative rule through Jesus as his agent. Jesus' vision was not to establish God's empire by force, but by proclamation of the good news of God. Entrance into God's empire was to be voluntary through the acceptance of the good news proclaimed by the twelve. Thus, Jesus' appointment of the twelve signaled the establishment of God's rule that would bring renewal in local communities of Israel.

Jesus' recruitment of the twelve provides an ironic parallel to Vespasian's gathering of troops to suppress the Jewish revolt. The parallelism exists in the sense that both Jesus and Vespasian recruited people who would serve as aides in their respective campaigns. The irony, however, is that while Vespasian gathered a huge military force to conduct a violent and destructive campaign on behalf of the Roman Empire, Jesus recruited the twelve to conduct a non-violent and life-giving campaign on behalf of God's empire. Another irony is that while Vespasian recruited well-trained soldiers including kings to crush the Jewish revolt with sophisticated weapons, Jesus recruited the twelve from among the uneducated rural peasants to win over the nations by the proclamation of the good news of God's empire.

Jesus' campaign involving the twelve did not have room for any form of revenge. When Jesus commissioned the twelve to proclaim the good news of God's empire, he instructed them not to exercise vengeance against those who would refuse to accept them. Instead of a revenge, he instructed them to "shake off the dust" from their "feet as testimony against" those who reject them (6:11). The shaking off of dust from the feet is not revenge, but a symbolic action of the disciples' testimony against those who rejected the good news. As Morna Hooker has stated: "Shaking the dust from the feet was a symbolic action normally performed by a Jew who had been abroad on his re-entry into Palestine: foreign dust must not contaminate Jewish soil . . . Such an action on the part of the disciples was clearly meant to indicate that the village or town which had rejected them was no longer to be regarded as part of the Jewish nation."[28]

Hooker's explanation suggests that the act of shaking dust off the feet implies a threatening judgment. However, a careful observation indicates that it is not the twelve who are to make the judgment, but God. The twelve only play the role of witnesses. This understanding makes the contrast between Jesus' campaign and Vespasian's military operations in Galilee even more evident. While Vespasian's troops killed people and plundered their cities, towns, and possessions as a revenge for the Galileans' refusal to submit to Caesar, the twelve were instructed to avoid any act of revenge against those who rejected them and God's empire embodied in the good news they proclaimed.

Campaign against Demonic Powers

One of the major characteristics of Jesus' Galilean campaign in Mark relates to the driving out of the unclean spirits or the demonic powers. For example, in a synagogue at Capernaum on the Sabbath, Jesus drives out a demon that identifies him as "the Holy One of God" (1:21–29). On the evening of the same day, while in Simon's house, all who were "possessed with demons" were brought to Jesus who "cast out many demons" (1:32–34). Because of Jesus' authority, demons fell down before him every time they met him: "Whenever the unclean spirits saw him, they fell down before him and shouted, 'You are the Son of God!'" (3:11). When the scribes accused him of being out of his mind, that is, of being possessed by Beelzebul, and of operating under the influence of "the ruler of the demons" (3:21–22), Jesus responded indicating that he had power or authority to bind the strong man, namely Satan, and to plunder his possessions. In his own words, Mark's Jesus says: "How can Satan cast out Satan? If a kingdom is divided against itself, that kingdom cannot stand. And if a house is divided against itself, that house will not be able to stand. And if Satan has risen up against himself and is divided, he cannot stand, but his end has come. But no one can enter a strong man's house and plunder his property without first tying

---

28. Hooker, *Mark*, 157. Cf. Lane, *Mark*, 209, who understands that the act of shaking dust "is a prophetic act designed to provoke thought on the part of the rejecting villagers." Lane also views the act as signaling judgment against those who refuse to accept the twelve and their message.

the strong man; then indeed the house can be plundered." (3:23-27).The most dramatic story about Jesus' dealing with demonic powers during his Galilean campaign in Mark is that of the Gerasene demoniac (5:1-20).[29] My exploration of Jesus' dealings with demonic powers does not cover all the stories related to demonic powers in Mark. It primarily focuses on Jesus' encounter with the Gerasene demoniac or the legion story.

Jesus' encounter with the Gerasene demoniac took place in a Gentile region of the Gerasenes, the other side of the sea (3:1) with respect to the Galilean villages and towns (2:1-4:35). Mark depicts the man with an unclean spirit as being in a pathetic condition. The man is possessed by a "legion," an expression of an army of demons; he lives among tombs, an unclean place because of the dead bodies there; and he dwells in the soil inhabited by an army of unclean pigs.[30] In addition, the demoniac also lives among tombs naked, as is implied by the expression that after his liberation from the legion he was found clothed (5:15). Such description intensifies the man's terrible condition. That the man lives among the tombs implies that he has been exiled from the world of the living, the community that makes human life possible, to live in the world of the dead.[31] In this case, his restoration is a return to life from among the dead.

By driving out the legion, not only has Jesus freed the man from the oppressive and destructive demons, but also he has brought the man back to life. The man's wholeness, being, and dignity have been restored. The man is transformed. He can no longer live among tombs in the world of the dead, but can now return to his community where he can actively

---

29. Outside his Galilean campaign, Jesus drives out demons only once. This incident relates to the liberation of a boy who has been oppressed by a demon from his childhood (9:14-29).

30. Marcus, *Mark*, 347.

31. For a detailed discussion about the "Legion" in relation to the Gerasene demoniac, see Aus, *My Name Is "Legion,"* 1-99. Aus notes that during the time of Jesus a complete Roman legion consisted of about six thousand foot soldiers, in addition to a number of cavalry and auxiliary troops with special tasks (ibid., 16). He also shows that a Roman legion "had a wild boar as part of its military standards. The wild boar as a pig was an unclean animal for the Jews (Lev 11:7; Deut 14:8) and stood metaphorically for a ravaging, destructive power (Ps 80:14)." According to Aus, Jews in Palestine considered a Roman legion unclean for several reasons: (1) Gentiles by definition were unclean (2) the Tenth Legion, Frentesis, had as a part of its insignia a wild boar, an unclean animal; and (3) it carried with it human scalps, unclean, probably as charms in war. This explains why the Gerasene demoniac (Mark 5:1-20), whose name is Legion, requests to enter a herd of swine, unclean animals (ibid., 17-18). Aus states further that the demoniac's "impurity is not only due to his living in tombs (5:2-3, 5), causing him to have uncleanness due to contact with the dead . . . The spirit(s) within him are also those of 'uncleanness'" (ibid., 24).

participate in all social and religious activities. This is demonstrated by the man's active participation in the proclamation of God's mercy manifested in his healing (5:20). The man is now able to experience a renewal of his identity. As Derrett has pointed out, "Jesus is actually saving a man from the world of the dead, bringing him back to life, 'clothed and in his right mind.'"[32] Mark's hearers may have understood Jesus' campaign against the demoniac powers as part of Jesus' program of establishing God's empire that brings freedom from demonic powers.

Horsley understands the Gerasene demoniac in terms of the Roman oppression. He argues that "Demonic possession . . . of the manically violent man among the Gerasenes can be understood as a combination of the effect of Roman imperial violence, a displaced protest against it, and a self-protection against a suicidal counterattack against the Romans . . . [T]he demoniac became the repository of the community's resentment of the violent effects of the Roman domination."[33] Even though Horsley does not believe that Mark's Gospel was written as a response to the Roman-Jewish War of 66–70 CE, his insight can be applied even for the situation during and after the war. In this regard, Mark's audience may have heard the story of demonic possession in light of the Roman imperial domination and oppression. This view is intensified by the military expressions present in the legion story.

Mark's use of military language is so pervasive that his hearers would not miss the link between the legion story and the events of the war. First, the word "legion" (5:9, 15) is a military term associated with the Roman imperial power that depended on its armies (e.g., *J.W.* 3:8, 65, 97, 120, 233, 289; 5:39–43, 67–70).[34] Mark's hearers may have heard the legion story as an obvious parallel to Vespasian's military campaign. Vespasian was renowned for his military experience and power. He controlled and commanded the best and powerful Roman legions. Mark's legion story depicts Jesus as one who commands the demonic legions. So, while Vespasian commands the

---

32. Derrett, "Contributions," 4.

33. Horsley, *Hearing the Whole Story*, 145. He also notes not only that the name Legion symbolizes the Roman army as "the cause of the possessed man's violent and destructive behavior, but that the man also is symbolic of the whole society that is possessed by the demonic imperial violence to their persons and communities" (ibid., 140).

34. In the first century a Roman legion was composed of between five thousand and six thousand soldiers. While Marcus, *Mark*, 344–45, holds that a legion comprised five thousand soldiers, and Guelich, *Mark*, 281, asserts that a legion includes six thousand soldiers, Kennedy, "Roman Army," 789–90, argues for both possibilities. For scholars who read Mark's story of the Gerasene demoniac in light of the Roman imperial power, see Myers, *Binding the Strong Man*, 190–92; Crossan, *Historical Jesus*, 314; Marcus, *Mark*, 251–52; and Horsley, *Hearing the Whole Story*, 140–41.

armies of the physical sphere, Jesus commands armies of supernatural sphere. Hence, as Winn has observed, Mark's legion story may have been heard as a "response to Vespasian's awesome military might, one of the compelling features of the new emperor's credential. Because Jesus' credential clearly lacks such military prestige, Mark cleverly takes Jesus' power as an exorcist and portrays it through a military motif. Unlike Vespasian, Jesus never commanded military legions, but more impressively, he did command legions of powerful demons."[35] The reference to the sea in which the pigs possessed by demons perished supports the association between the "legion" and the Roman army in that it provides a link with the Mediterranean Sea from which the Roman armies had come to suppress the revolt and thereby consolidate the Roman imperial domination.[36]

Another element that associates Mark's account about Jesus' casting out of the "legion" and the Roman military is the use of the word "sent" (5:10). The word has a military overtone in that it connotes "dispatch" as an officer sends troops.[37] Josephus uses the term often times in the military context. The use of the term "herd" (5:11), also has a military association. Although the word is not appropriate for pigs, it is, however, applied to troops of military recruits.[38] The Greek terms for "permitted" (5:13) also means "dismiss," which is a military expression. Further, the Greek word for "rushed" (5:13), has a military overtone in that it expresses "troops rushing into battle."[39] Next, the sexual expression, "so that they may enter them" (5:12) has a military nuance in that in the ancient times the armies "were famous for rape."[40]

---

35. Winn, *Mark*, 184.

36. Horsley, *Hearing the Whole Story*, 50.

37. Mark has Herod use this word when he sends his "soldier of the guard" to behead John (5:27). The author of Maccabees also uses the word in a military context (1 Macc 3:35).

38. Boring, *Mark*, 151; note that Josephus uses the word in the context of the war where people are butchered like a herd of pigs (*J.W.* 4:326).

39. Derrett, "Contributions," 5; Horsley, *Hearing the Whole Story*, 140–41.

40. Brownmiller, *Against Our Will*, 31–113; Marcus, *Mark*, 352. Cf. *J.W.* 2:465, where Josephus suggests rape in the wake of the Jewish revolt against the Romans. Describing a massacre, Josephus states that among the dead bodies one could see "poor women stripped of their last covering of modesty." In another context, he says of the Zealots that "the violation of women [was] their sport" (*J.W.* 4:561). In our own time, a good example of incidents of rape in the context of war are the sexual violations in the war-torn Democratic Republic of Congo. In its report released in 2014, Human Rights Watch (HRW) accuses both the Congolese army and the rebel groups of brutal gang rape against women. See Human Rights Watch, "Democratic Republic of Congo: Ending Impunity for Sexual Violence."

Joshua Garroway gives still further evidence in support of the association between the Roman forces and demons depicted in Mark's legion story. Garroway identifies three more associations between the demons and the Roman troops: the demons' address of Jesus as "Son of the Most High God" (5:7), the demons' violent behavior, and the demons' request not to be sent out of the country (5:10).[41] As for the demons' address of Jesus as "Son of the Most High God," Garroway states that the latter part is a Hellenistic expression for God common among Gentiles,[42] thus suggesting that the address is associated with the Romans. Concerning the demons' violent behavior, Garroway argues that the demons symbolized the legion because they behave like them. He notes that when they see Jesus from a distance, they run aggressively toward him seeking to confront and drive him away rather than submit to him.[43]

Concerning the demons' request not to be "sent out of the country" (5:10), Garroway has made two important observations. First, he notes that the demons make petition on their own initiative because Jesus has not issued any threat of expulsion. In his second observation, he indicates that in exorcism literature it is unusual for demons to beg not to be driven out.[44] Then Garroway concludes that the story of the Gerasene demoniac represents "a confrontation between Jesus and a Roman Legion, between a man and an occupying army."[45] This conclusion agrees with Myers's argument that the demons symbolize the "Roman military power."[46] Based on the evidence presented here, the legion story has to be located in the context of Roman imperial rule in Palestine, particularly with respect to the Roman-Jewish War of 66–70 CE. In this context, Mark's hearers may have heard the account about the man possessed by the legion in the light of the Roman imperial domination and oppression.[47]

---

41. Garroway, "Invasion," 64.

42. Ibid. Garroway adopts this view from Collins, *Mark*, 268, who observes that the title "Son of the Most High God" contains the phrase "Most High," *Hypsistos*, which is a title both for the God of Israel (*LXX*, Deut 32:8; 1QapGen 21:2) and a Gentile god, Zeus.

43. Ibid.

44. Ibid., notes that "demons recognize they are in a place they should not be and desperately wish to remain—precisely how one would expect those under Roman hegemony to describe their invading foes."

45. Ibid., 66.

46. Myers, *Binding the Strong Man*, 192. Cf. Theissen, *Miracle Stories*, 255, who also notes that the military "allusion to Roman occupation is unmistakable."

47. Baird, "Gerasene Demoniac," 189.

The military expressions in the exorcism of the demons in 5:1–20 may have had an impact in Mark's hearers. The hearers may have associated Jesus' driving out of the legion with their own experience in relation to the recent war and their life under the Roman imperial domination.[48] The military vocabularies in the story may have evoked memories of the crisis of the war and its results. Especially, with regard to the term "legion," this may have evoked memories of the Roman troops that had recently been involved in attacks, burning of their villages and houses, plundering their possessions, killing and enslaving people. There may have been feelings that the violent attacks of the Roman troops resulted into the man's violent and destructive behavior, in which he injures and disrupts his community.[49] The self destruction of the demoniac may have been interpreted in the light of the suicide events of the Jews at Masada[50] and Jotapata, and even in the light of the civil war in Jerusalem shortly before the siege of the Holy City by the Romans.

The term "legion" would also have reminded hearers, of the presence of the Roman tenth legion or *Frentesis* in Palestine, even after the war. Josephus has explicitly indicated that after the war, the Romans left their tenth legion in Jerusalem in order to keep watch lest another revolt occurred (*J. W.* 7:5, 17).[51] The link between the legion and the pigs may have evoked memories of the Roman forces in that the tenth legion had an emblem of a wild boar on its banners.[52] Mark's hearers who knew that the legion represented a company of the Roman army may have remembered the massacres and mass enslavements done by the Romans as well as their current status as people conquered by the Roman armies.

---

48. Such a political reading of Mark 5:1–20 has become common in the New Testament scholarship. See for example Baird, "Gadarene Demoniac," 189; Derrett, "Contributions," 2–17; Hollenbach, "Jesus, Demoniacs, and Public Authorities," 567–88; Myers, *Binding the Strong Man*, 190–94; Marcus, *Mark*, 341–53; Waetjen, *Reordering of Power*, 115–18; Theissen, *Miracle Stories*, 255–56; Dormandy, "Expulsion of Legion," 335–37; Crossan, *Historical Jesus*, 314–18; Horsley, *Hearing the Whole Story*, 140–41; Horsley, *Jesus and Empire*, 100–108; Staley, "'Clothed and in Her Right Mind'"; Newheart, *"My Name is Legion,"* 70–85.

49. Horsley, *Hearing the Whole Story*, 140.

50. Cf. Dormandy, "Expulsion of Legion," 336.

51. Cf. Garroway, "Invasion," 63, who observes, "During the Jewish War . . . a host of legions and auxiliary forces roamed the land; after it, one legion remained stationed in Jerusalem (*X Frentesis*); before it, the forces in the region comprised mainly auxiliary regiments stationed in Caesarea (with a much larger assembly in Syria)." See also Geva, "Camp of the Tenth Legion," 239–54.

52. Theissen, *Gospels in Context*, 110.

The reference to the Gerasene territory in the legion story may also have evoked memories of the war among Mark's hearers. According to Josephus, shortly before the siege of Jerusalem, Vespasian dispatched troops under the command of Lucius Annius to besiege Gerasa. That operation involved destroying the city, killing the youth, imprisoning of women and children, plundering property, burning houses, and destroying the surrounding villages (J.W. 4:486–89). Thus, hearing of the expulsion of the legion in the region of the Gerasenes, Mark's hearers may have remembered the events of the war that took place in the area that was familiar to them.

Moreover, Jesus' dealing with the man possessed by the legion represents an invasion into an alien territory to reclaim it for God's empire. Mark indicates that the demoniac recognized Jesus. As the demonic saw Jesus from a distance, he ran and knelt before him, suggesting his acknowledgement of Jesus' authority and power.[53] The question, "What have you to do with me?" (5:7) also indicates that the unclean spirit recognized Jesus as one belonging to a realm different from its own. While Jesus belonged to God's sphere and operated in the power of the Holy Spirit, the unclean spirit belonged to Satan's sphere and operated under the influence of demons. That the unclean spirits called Jesus, "Son of the Most High God: (5:7) demonstrates that they knew that Jesus had divine origin and dignity.[54] The unclean spirits therefore saw the coming of Jesus as an invasion intended to disrupt and overthrow their empire. As Boring has observed, God's empire was confronting the empire of Satan, the strong man (cf. 3:22–27).[55] Jesus' defeat of the legion may likely have suggested to the hearers that Jesus was subjugating the oppressive demonic forces that possessed and oppressed people, thereby manifesting God's empire.[56] They may have viewed that through his expulsion of the legion, Jesus not only demonstrated his power over demons but also the establishment of God's empire among people. The legion exorcism story likely instilled confidence in, and loyalty to Jesus among the hearers.

There is still another point that needs to be noted concerning the impact of the legion story among the hearers of Mark. Mark reports that when the liberated demoniac begged to be with Jesus, the later told him, "Go home to your friends, and tell them how much the Lord has done for you, and how he has shown mercy on you" (5:19). Jesus' words here may have

---

53. Collins, *Mark*, 267.

54. Lane, *Mark*, 183.

55. Boring, *Mark*, 150; Lane, *Mark*, 184n17, where he cites Herbert Preisker, who suggests that the term "Legion" does not express anti-Roman sentiment, but rather "the struggle between the forces of God and those of Satan."

56. Horsley, *Hearing the Whole Story*, 141, 146.

been received as an invitation of Mark's hearers to focus on God's healing rather than fear of demonic reprisals. Mark's hearers may also have noted Jesus' status as Lord. For, while Jesus spoke of the Lord with reference to God, the liberated demoniac proclaimed in the Decapolis what Jesus did to him: "he went away and began to proclaim in the Decapolis how much Jesus had done for him" (5:20). The identification of Jesus with the liberating God is unmistakable and complete.[57] Mark's hearers may have recognized Jesus as the true Lord, and not Vespasian who also claimed to be lord. In this case, they may have been encouraged to resist the lordship of Vespasian in favor of the Lordship of Jesus.

Campaign against Illnesses

A campaign against illness is another major mark of Jesus' liberative activities in Mark's Gospel. During the Galilean campaign, Jesus performed various types of healings. His healing campaign included the healing of Peter's mother-in-law from fever (1:29–31); the healing of many people from various diseases (1:31–34; 3:7–12; 6:53–56); the cleansing of a leper (1:40–45); the restoration of a man from paralysis (2:1–12) and another man from a withered hand (3:1–6). Also Jesus' healing campaign involved the healing of a woman with a flow of blood (5:24–34); the raising of Jairus's daughter from the dead (5:21, 35–43); the healing of the Syrophoenician woman (7:24–30); and the restoration of sight of a blind man (8:21–26).[58] Indeed, Jesus' healing campaign involved healing of various maladies: fever, skin diseases, paralysis, blindness, deafness, deformity, and even the rising of a girl from among the dead.

Although Jesus healed different kinds of illnesses, based on the geographical proximity criterion, a particular intention is paid to the healing of the Syrophoenician woman's daughter in the region of Tyre (7:24–30). This healing story will be supplemented by Jesus' healing of a man with a withered hand (3:1–6), that of a man with hearing and speech difficulties (7:31–37), and the healing of blindness (8:22–26). These additional healing stories are important because they have close association with Vespasian's healings of a blind man and that of a withered hand mentioned by Tacitus (*Hist.* 4:81) and referred to earlier.

---

57. Dormandy, "Expulsion of Legion," 337.

58. Outside the Galilean campaign, Jesus' healing activities are very rare. The only healing incident that takes place outside the Galilean campaign relates to the restoration of Bartimaeus's sight (10:46–52).

The suppliant in the story of the Syrophoenician woman is unnamed. She is introduced as "a Greek, a Syrophoenician by birth" (7:26). The term "Syrophoenician" distinguishes Phoenicians from Syria, Carthage, and Libya. While the designation "Syrophoenician" underscores the woman's race, the reference to her as "a Greek" highlights her political and socio-cultural affiliation that she is a Gentile.[59] The woman, therefore, is not just a non-Jew, she is also from a pagan background. From the Jewish perspective, she is "unclean" by birth, a female, a daughter, and a foreigner. Since her daughter is possessed by an unclean spirit she is also "untouchable."[60] As Marcus has also noted, the fact that she is a Gentile means that the woman is also "ritually impure."[61]

Despite the negative status she may have received from the Jewish perspective, the Syrophoenician woman was affluent. This idea is suggested in Mark's portrayal of her that she had in her house a "bed" (7:30), not a "mat" (2:11) usually used by poor people. The woman is referred to as "a Greek," a "privileged group of the Hellenes."[62] Hence, as Boring has pointed out, this woman is not a representative of "the 'poor and outcast . . . one of the poorest of the poor,' but a dominant, oppressive group."[63] Having heard about Jesus that he was in Tyre, her homeland (7:24), the woman approached Jesus, fell down at his feet and begged him to expel the demon from her daughter (7:25). Since Mark has already indicated that there were people from Tyre who flocked to Jesus (3:8), it is likely that the woman had knowledge about Jesus even before he visited Tyre.[64] Mark does not say what the woman had heard about Jesus, but we assume it was the news about Jesus' ability to heal and to drive out demons (cf. 1:28; 3:8).

---

59. Rhoads, *Reading Mark*, 72, observes that the absence of the woman's name underlines her status as a Gentile. But this reason is questionable because not all Jewish characters in Mark are identified by their names. Note for example, the leper (1:40–45), the man whose sins are forgiven (2:1–12), the girl who is raised from the death (5:21–24, 35–43), the woman with the issues of blood (5:25–33), the poor widow who out of her poverty gives to the temple treasury everything she has (12:41–44), the woman who anoints Jesus (14:3–9), "a woman who carries a jar of water" and "the owner of the house" where Jesus plans to have the Passover meal with his disciples (14:13–15), the man who cut off the ear of a slave of the high priest with a sword at the arrest of Jesus (14:47), and the young man who runs naked to escape capture by though who come to arrest Jesus (14:51). All these characters seem to be Jews but their names are not mentioned.

60. Kinukawa, *Women in Mark*, 55.

61. Marcus, *Mark*, 467.

62. Theissen, *Gospels in Context*, 71–72.

63. Boring, *Mark*, 209.

64. Rhoads, *Reading Mark*, 72.

Mark indicates that as the Syrophoenician woman approached Jesus, "she came and bowed at his feet" (7:25). Kinukawa observes that in a patriarchal society, the act of bowing expressed one's inferior position. She emphasizes that the practice, however, was done only among men. Kinukawa suggests that since in Mark's story it is a woman who falls before a man, that act is not viewed as an expression of honor but a serious misdeed against Jesus. Kinukawa, however, quickly argues that the woman made a courageous action:

> Though "bowing down at his feet" may show one's inferior position in the social relationships in the patriarchal society, it is an action only accepted among men. Her bowing down is not considered to honor the status of Jesus as a male teacher. On the contrary, it is a serious misdeed which brings disgrace on him. Women of the time are not expected to come out of their homes where they have their role, much less to make a plea in a public setting . . . her invasive solicitation would make a man lose his face in the culture of honor and shame. It is something very unusual for an anonymous woman, unknown and unrelated to the Jews, to dare to break his privacy. Nevertheless, she does.[65]

The woman's courage to fall down at the feet of a male Jew against her culture suggests that her daughter was in a desperate condition that needed immediate care. The Syrophoenician woman might have been aware that her action would humiliate, dishonor and even defile Jesus. But the condition of her daughter, which also reflected her own, forced her to act against her culture. She loved her daughter dearly and wanted her to be freed from the demon. Kinukawa has made an important observation about the relationship between the mother and her daughter: "Daughter's issues are mothers' issues. They are both thus triply polluted, female, demon-possessed."[66] Such a situation compelled the Syrophoenician woman to fall down at Jesus' feet seeking help from the great healer.

Jesus' initial response to the woman's request is very rude, shocking, and discouraging.[67] Jesus said to the woman, "Let the children be fed

---

65. Kinukawa, *Women in Mark*, 54–55.
66. Ibid., 55.
67. Marcus, *Mark*, 470–71, has rightly observed that nowhere else does Mark depict Jesus as using such rude, dishonoring, and humiliating language: "There is nothing quite like this elsewhere in the Gospel. Indeed it is surprising in a Gospel that pictures Jesus as in constant conflict with leaders of Judaism and has just depicted him challenging the basis of its communal life, the Law (7:19); that portrays Judaism itself as an old wineskin incapable of accommodating the new wine of the gospel (2:21–22); that foreshadows and foretells the destruction of Judaism's central institution, the Temple,

first, for it is not right to take children's bread and throw it to the dogs" (7:27). While the term "children" stands for Jews, "dogs" is a designation for Gentiles.[68] The Syrophoenician woman and her daughter have become the "dogs." Given Jesus' positive response to women (1:29–30; 5:21–43; 14:3–9), Gentiles (5:1–20; 8:1–9; 11:17), and wealthy people in authority (5:21–24, 35–43; 10:17–22) throughout Mark's Gospel, this response is extremely harsh. Scholars have described this response with diverse expressions. They have viewed it as an insult,[69] a provocative means of evoking a deeper response from the woman,[70] a test of the woman's faith,[71] and as a way of dismissing the woman's request with a joke.[72] On the basis of the use of the term "first," Boring has stated that Jesus' reply reflected the priority of his ministry to Israel. He states: "Jesus' statement maintains the priority of Israel without excluding Gentiles."[73] Whatever description one gives to Jesus' response, it was an expression that Jews used to refer to Gentiles during the first century CE.[74]

The image of "bread" encompasses not only the teaching of Jesus but also all that he has to offer. It incorporates all the benefits available in God's empire such as exorcisms, healings, restorations, raising people from the dead, giving food to the hungry, and so on.[75] Here the woman's request for exorcism is encompassed by the metaphor. Mark has been showing that Jesus provides bread to those in need but now, when a Greek woman begs for help, he reveals that the bread is for the children (Israel) and should not be thrown to the dogs (the Greeks). Jesus reveals that the primary focus of his campaign was to remove unclean spirits from amongst Israel, rather than from amongst Greeks.

Despite the harsh and discouraging response from Jesus, the woman persisted. Her persistence suggests that she had a serious need and that she

---

and of those who control it (11:12–15; 12:1–9; 13:1–2; 15:38); and that depicts the Jewish multitude as joining their leaders in calling Jesus' crucifixion (15:11–14). Elsewhere in the Gospel, Jesus shows great solicitude for Gentiles, as in the continuation of our own passage and in 7:31; 13:10; and 15:39."

68. Collins, *Mark*, 366. She states that "The contrast between the 'children' and the 'dogs' represents a contrast Jews and Gentiles" for which the designation of the woman as 'a Greek' has prepared. See also van Iersel, *Mark*, 250–51.

69. Witherington, *Mark*, 232; Rhoads, *Reading Mark*, 78.

70. Boring, *Mark*, 211, citing France, *Gospel of Mark*, 296.

71. Marcus, *Mark*, 468; Lane, *Mark*, 262.

72. Van Iersel, *Mark*, 250.

73. Boring, *Mark*, 211.

74. Collins, *Mark*, 367.

75. Cf. Rhoads, *Reading Mark*, 77.

trusted that Jesus had power to provide for her need. Since she is caught up between life and death, she has to be aggressive if she and her daughter are to survive. Hence, without opposing what Jesus has said, she replies using the same metaphor that Jesus used, but to her advantage: "Yes Lord; yet even the dogs under the table eat the children's crumbs" (7:28). From her perspective, dogs are domestic animals and part of the family. She is therefore ready to accept even the crumbs that fall under the table just as dogs do. The woman seems to tell Jesus: "You are the one who provides bread for the needy; so even though I may be a dog I am ready to eat the crumbs."

Being impressed by the woman's response, Jesus changed his mind and announced the liberation of the woman's daughter from the demon (7:29). As the woman went home, she found her daughter lying in bed, free from the demon (7:30). The girl's deliverance from the demon was proof that Jesus had crossed racial barriers to bring the benefits and blessings of God's empire to non-Jews. The persistence of the Syrophoenician woman in seeking help on behalf of her daughter, which is understood as faith,[76] has compelled Jesus to break and cross racial and cultural boundaries in order to bring life to Gentiles, thereby extending God's empire and its blessings to people of all nations.

The impact of this story on the hearers can be made clear only if we set the Gospel into appropriate historical context. As I have noted earlier, Mark's Gospel was written in rural Galilee or southern Syria shortly after the Roman-Jewish War of 66–70 CE. In the region of Tyre there had been tension between Jews and Gentiles which led up to and accompanied the war. According to Josephus, the Tyrians were the notoriously "bitterest enemies" of the Jews (*Ag. Ap.* 1:70). At the beginning of the Jewish revolt Tyrians assaulted the Jews and put many of them in chains (*J. W.* 2:478); and their army attacked and destroyed the town of Gischala by fire (*Life* 44). Towards the end of Vespasian's war campaign in Galilee, Titus encamped his troops at Cydasa (probably Kedasa, *J. W.* 2:459), an inland Tyrian village that was "always at feud and strife with the Galileans" (*J. W.* 4:104–105). It is very likely that Mark's story is linked to the hostility between Jews and Tyrian Gentiles existing at that time and probably also the fear and suspicion that Jews might avenge the lengthy oppression against them.[77]

Economically, there is evidence that Tyre depended on Galilee for food. Tyre was a rich city famous for metal work, making of purple dye (cf. Pliny the Elder, *Nat. Hist.* 5.17.76; Strabo, *Geogr.* 16.2.23), and extensive trade with

---

76. Ibid., 81–83.

77. Theissen, *Gospels in Context*, 77–78; Rhoads, *Reading Mark*, 93–94; Boring, *Mark*, 209; and Marcus, *Mark*, 471.

the entire Mediterranean region. The major problem with Tyre, however, was its location. Being located on an island, it lacked enough land for farming, hence its dependence on imports for food products (*Ant.* 8:141; 14:190–216).[78] The book of Acts provides further evidence for the dependence of Tyre and Sidon on food products from Galilee. The relevant texts reads thus: "Now Herod (Agrippa I, ruled about 41–44 CE) was angry with the people of Tyre and Sidon; and they came to him in a body, and having persuaded Blastus, the king's chamberlain, they asked for peace because their country depended on the king's country for food" (Acts 12:20).

Given the evidence shown above, it is evident that rural Galilee was the "breadbasket" of the metropolis of Tyre. Galilean peasants often had feelings that they worked the land for the rich city-dwellers while they themselves were in great need. Gerd Theissesn's citation from Galen offers a clear picture of the related sentiment:

> The people who, as is customary, store up enough food in summer to last the whole year, take all the wheat from the fields together with the barley, beans and lentils, and leave for the country people nothing but the remaining pulses, although they themselves even take the greater part of that, too, into the cities. The country people then, when they used up their winter supplies, have only unhealthful nourishment through the entire summer. In that period these country people eat the shoots and suckers of unhealthful plants.[79]

Locating Jesus' words in Mark 7:27 in the context reflected in this citation, Theissen sees that Jesus' statement would evoke among Mark's hearers an association with this expression: "First let the poor people in the Jewish rural areas be satisfied. For it is not good to take poor people's food and throw it to the rich Gentiles in the cities." Theissen further relates that, "when people mentioned food in the border regions of Tyre and Galilee, and also spoke of children (= Jews) and dogs (= Gentiles), they simultaneously addressed the general economic situation, determined by a clear hierarchy that was just as clearly reversed by Jesus' words. Perhaps Jesus, in replying, was able to make connections with a well-known saying shaped by this situation."[80] Theissen's observation on the economic relations between the Galileans and the Tyrians expressed here is crucial. I concur with him that Jesus' statement to the woman that the bread intended for children cannot be given to the dogs was

---

78. Some examples from the Old Testament include 1 Kgs 5:11; 17:7–16; and Ezek 27:17.

79. Theissen, *Gospels in Context*, 75.

80. Ibid.

connected to the reality of the economic relations existing between the poor Galileans and the rich Syrians.

The healing of a Greek girl not only put Jesus in parallel with the Caesars but also as a superior healer. Philo, for example, depicts Emperor Augustus as a Caesar "who healed the pestilences common to Greeks and barbarians" (*Embassy* 145). However, unlike Augustus's healing which was purely metaphorical, Jesus' healing was an actual event that involved a real person.[81] Therefore, the healing of the Greek girl highlights Jesus' superiority to the Roman Caesars. The story may also have suggested to Mark's Jewish hearers that there should be no room for revenge against Gentiles. Such story may have been received and interpreted as a call to be open to heal and treat Gentiles with love and not seek revenge against them.

Besides the story of Jesus' healing of the Syrophoenician woman's daughter, there are three healing stories that need special attention. These stories relate to Jesus' restoration of a man's hand in a synagogue at Capernaum (3:1-6), his restoration of a man's hearing and speech in the region of the Decapolis (7:31-37), and his restoration of sight of a blind man at Bethsaida (8:22-26).[82] These stories are important because they have direct parallels with Vespasian's two healings performed in Alexandria: the restoration of a blind man's sight and of a man's withered hand (Tacitus, *Hist.* 4:81).[83] In restoring a man's withered hand, Jesus used a word of command. He commanded the man, "Stretch out your hand" (3:5) and immediately after the man did as he was instructed, his hand was restored. This event occurred on the Sabbath in a synagogue at Capernaum (3:1-2).

Concerning the healing of the man with hearing and speech impediments, Jesus employed saliva, touch, and a verbal command, *ephphatha*, which means, "Be opened" (7:33-34). The healing was done in privacy and was instant (7:33). The man's "ears were opened, his tongue was released, and he spoke plainly" (7:35). People said of Jesus, "He has done everything well; he even makes the deaf to hear and the mute to speak" (7:37). Hearers

---

81. Cf. Lane, *Mark*, 262, insists that unlike in the miracles of "divine men," in Jesus' healing, God's power is "properly released not in superstition and magic but in response to faith."

82. Bethsaida was a city build by Herod. Philip the Tetrarch renamed it Julia in honor of Caesar Augustus's daughter Julia (*Ant.* 18:28; *J.W.* 2:515). It then became the capital of Gaulanitis. According to Lane, *Mark*, 284, Bethsaida was located "on the northeastern shore of the Sea of Galilee in the Territory of Herod Philip" (*J.W.* 6:45). This was one of the large sites on the lake that had the size of a city but the organization of a village, and Mark's designation of it as in verse 23 is precise. In Matthew and Luke, Bethsaida is mentioned together with Chorazin as cities that refused to respond to Jesus' "mighty works" done among them (Matt 11:20-24; Luke 10:13-15).

83. Cf. Suetonius, *Vesp.* 7:2-3; and Dio Cassius, *Rom. Hist.* 65.8.1.

may have understood the acclamations, "He has done everything well," which echoes God's view of his creation that all things he created are very good (Gen 1:31; cf. Sir 39:16) in the sense that Jesus was truly "the agent of God in the eschatological renewal of creation."[84] As for the healing of blindness at Bethsaida, this took place in privacy. The mode of healing was by touch and use of saliva. Jesus "took the blind man by hand . . . led him out of the village . . . put saliva on his eyes . . . (and) laid his hands on him" (8:23). The healing did not occur instantly. Consequently, "Jesus laid his hands on his eyes again; and he looked intently and his sight was restored, and he saw everything clearly" (8:25).[85] The restoration of sight occurred during Jesus' second attempt.

Jesus' ability to restore a withered hand, sight, hearing, and speech demonstrates that he bears the status of being God's Messiah. In the Old Testament such kind of healings are associated with God's Messiah (Isa 35:3, 5-6). In early Judaism, God's Messiah was expected to have power to give "sight to the blind" (4Q521).[86] Even the Rabbis believed that only God and his Messiah could cure blindness.[87] Since Jesus performed healings associated with God and his Messiah, it is clear evidence that he is truly God's Messiah. Hence, it is not a coincidence that Peter declared Jesus, "You are the Messiah" (8:29).

Jesus' healing of a withered hand, blindness, and hearing and speech impediments, both parallel and contrast the healings associated with Vespasian in various ways. First, both Jesus and Vespasian dealt with a man with a withered hand and a man with blindness and each of them has a status of a ruler. Second, both Jesus and Vespasian used a touch and saliva as a mode of their healing. Jesus restored a man's hearing using spittle and touch. Vespasian, too, used saliva to restore a man's sight[88] and touch to restore a

---

84. Collins, *Mark*, 376.

85. In the ancient world, restoration of sight was difficult. Therefore ancient sources attribute the healing of blindness to the gods. An inscription from the temple of Asclepius at Epidaurus shows that the healing god Asclepius frequently dealt with eye conditions. The inscription closest to the cure of blindness in Mark 8:22-26 reads, "Acletas of Halieis. This man, saw a dream. It seemed to him that the god came towards him and drew open his eyes with his fingers, and he first saw the trees in the sanctuary" (Stele A18), recorded in LiDonnic, *Epidaurian Miracle Inscriptions*, 99. See also Kee, *Medicine, Miracle and Magic*, 67.

86. Marcus, *Mark*, 599.

87. Witherington, *Mark*, 239; cf. Matt 11:2-6//Luke 7:18-23; 4:18.

88. Concerning the use of saliva for healing in the ancient world, see Pliny the Elder, who writes that saliva has healing power and that it was used to treat various problems—including venom poisoning and superficial ailments (*Nat. Hist.* 28.7.37), mental anxiety if put upon the ear with one's finger (*Nat. Hist.* 28.5.25), and to deflect

man's withered hand. Despite these parallels, Jesus' healings contrast those of Vespasian. For example, Vespasian's healing involved suppliants who were sent to him by the god Serapis, consultation with the doctors, and was performed after he was assured that he would receive glory if he succeeded and that in the event of failure he would not share the blame (Tacitus, *Hist.* 4:81). By contrast, in Jesus' healing the suppliants were brought by other people and were not sent by a god (7:32; 8:22); and Jesus himself made no consultation with health professionals.

In other cases, Jesus used a word of command to heal (3:5; 7:34) while Vespasian never healed using a word of command. While Jesus restored the sight of the blind man in private, Vespasian restored a man's sight in public, perhaps as propaganda to validate his imperial rule. As Suetonius has pointed out, Vespasian became emperor unexpectedly since he did not possess appropriate traditional qualification required for the office. Suetonius writes that Vespasian "lacked prestige and a certain divinity . . . he was an unexpected and still new-made emperor" (*Vesp.* 7:2). This situation could have forced Vespasian to make propaganda such as that public healing in order to legitimate his imperial rule.

Hearers who were aware of Vespasian's miraculous healings may have linked Jesus' healings to those of the Roman emperor. Since Jesus healed without the help from the professional doctors, Mark's hearers may have interpreted Jesus' ability to heal as a contrast to Vespasian's claim to possess a divine status. Indeed, they would have recognized Jesus as having superior power than Vespasian, and hence, as one whose primary concern was not to destroy but to give life to people.

Campaign to Eliminate Hunger

Over and above the campaigns against illnesses and demonic powers, Jesus' Galilean campaign also involved elimination of hunger through provision of food to the hungry. Mark provides two major feeding accounts that depict Jesus as feeding multitudes of hungry people with meager resources of food: the feeding of five thousand and of four thosand people (6:30-44; 8:1-10).[89] These two stories fall in the category of the verbal parallels crite-

---

witchcraft. Pliny also recommends that people with epilepsy be spit upon when they have a seizure (*Nat. Hist.* 28.4.35-39) and emphasizes that saliva is used in healing according to custom (*Nat. Hist.* 28.7.36), suggesting that it was commonly used.

89. In addition to these feeding stories, Mark presents numerous food and eating motifs. For example, John eats locusts and wild honey in a desert (1:6); the angels serve Jesus in a desert (1:13); Peter's mother-in-law's service is assumed to include meals (1:31); Jesus eats with tax collectors and sinners (2:15-17); Jesus speaks of eating with

rion in that the terms employed in the narratives parallel the military terms or expressions. So, I use these stories as representatives of all other eating motifs in Mark.

According to Boring, food is the most basic need for human survival. Commenting on the feeding of the five thousand people, Boring says:

> Food is a primal human need. Eating is a matter of life and death, to be deprived of food is to be deprived of life; hunger not only kills, it dehumanizes. To receive food is not only to survive, but to have one's humanity maintained or restored. Eating together is a sharing of humanity at the most fundamental level. In this scene, Jesus represents God who grants authentic life, and the story represents not only what happened on a particular day in the life Jesus, but the act of God in the Christ event as such.[90]

In the light of Boring's description, Jesus' provision of food to the hungry people in the wilderness was a matter of urgency. The motivation behind Jesus' feeding was compassion (6:34; 8:2).[91] Jesus had compassion for people because they were in need of food[92] and for the Jews in particular, because they were "like sheep without a shepherd" (6:35). The phrase "like sheep

---

the bridegroom at a wedding (2:18-20); the disciples eat grain on the Sabbath, and Jesus references David, who entered the temple and ate the bread of the Presence reserved for priests only (2:23-28); Jesus and the twelve fail to eat because of the crowd (2:30); and Jesus orders food be given to Jairus's daughter, who has just been raised from the dead (5:43). Other food or eating motifs relate to Jesus' order to the twelve not to take bread when they are sent out to preach (6:8); king Herod's birthday banquet (6:21-22); the mention of loaves (6:52); the mention of food laws (7:1-8); Jesus' teaching on defilement and his declaration that "all foods are clean" (7:14-23); children's food that cannot be thrown to dogs (7:27-28); and the lack of bread in a boats, which happens as Jesus warns against the yeast of the Pharisees and of Herod (8:13-21). The food and eating motifs are recognized in the references to a cup of water (9:41); to the cup that Jesus drinks (10:38-40; cf. 14:36); to the hunger that leads Jesus to look for figs and then to curse the fig tree because it is fruitless (11:12-14); and the banquet where scribes want to occupy the best seats (12:39-40). Moreover, eating and food motifs arise with the arrival of Passover and the festival of Unleavened Bread (14:1-2); they continue when Jesus sits at table in the house of Simon the leper at Bethany and in Jesus' teaching on giving to the poor (14:3-9); food and eating motifs persist through Jesus' Passover meal with his disciples (14:12-22); the festival (15:6); when wine is given to Jesus when he is crucified (15:23, 26). Finally the women's provisions for Jesus while in Galilee also suggest a motif of food (15:41). Cf. Fowler, *Loaves and Fishes*, 132-36.

90. Boring, *Mark*, 182.

91. Mark's reference to Jesus' compassion in these texts recalls Jesus' compassion on the leper at Capernaum (1:41), and anticipates the request of the father of the boy with an unclean spirit, to whom Jesus would show compassion and give help (9:22).

92. Moloney, *Mark*, 153.

without a shepherd" implied that people lacked responsible leadership to care for them in the time of their need.

The expression "sheep without a shepherd" can better be understood in terms of the Old Testament perspective. In the Old Testament, the expression recalls the exodus where God tells Moses that "the Lord's community may not be like sheep without a shepherd" (Numb 27:17).[93] While the term "sheep" stands for God's people, Israel (e.g., Ps 100:3; Isa 53:6), the term "shepherd" is a metaphor for a royal figure (e.g., 2 Sam 5:2; 7:7; Ps 78:71). The kings of Israel and Judea were entrusted to represent God's rule among Israel, but their kingship failed. God himself is the true shepherd of Israel (e.g., Ps 23:1; 28:9; Isa 40:11) and will replace the failed human shepherds (Jer 23:1–4; Ezek 34) by establishing his own kingship in power, either by coming himself or by sending an eschatological king or shepherd (Isa 40:11; 49:9–10; Jer 31:10; Ezek 34:5, 8, 23–24; Mic 5:1–4; Matt 2:6). Since Jesus cares for the neglected people by giving them food, he may have been viewed as the expected good shepherd sent by God to care for his people.

In the context of Mark, King Herod Antipas is a representative of failed shepherds of Israel. While he enjoys banqueting with privileged people of high status (6:21), he does not care for the majority poor and marginalized village and town people who now flock to Jesus. Herod Antipas hosts a banquet in his own honor, inviting only the prestigious members of society: his political officers, the courtiers, and the leading men of Galilee (6:21). The royal banquet ends with the execution of John (6:25–28). By contrast, Jesus is depicted as a compassionate good shepherd who cares for others. He blesses bread in God's name and gives food to the hungry (6:41; 8:6). Unlike Herod Antipas who permits the execution of John to satisfy his wife and her daughter and to maintain his honor before his guests, Jesus commands his disciples to serve others—to "give them something to eat" (6:37; 8:6–7) and "to set (bread and fish) before the people" (6:41; 8:7).

There is still another contrast between Jesus' feeding and Herod Antipas's banquet. Unlike Herod Antipas's banquet, which concludes with John's head on a platter, Jesus' feeding ends with everyone's satisfaction and the gathering of twelve baskets full of food left over (6:42–43; 8:8). Contrary to Herod's banquet that involves destruction of life, Jesus' feeding is purely life-giving. Using the expression from Boring cited above, by giving food to the hungry, Jesus not only enables them to survive but also restores their humanity and dignity. Jesus truly represents God who grants life. When his disciples suggest that the crowd should be sent away hungry (6:36), Jesus gives food to the hungry crowd. Instead of plundering and

---

93. See also Ezek 34:5–6.

killing God's sheep as Herod Antipas has done to John, Jesus, as a good shepherd, provides people with food to restore their lives, their humanity, and their dignity.

Jesus' feeding campaign may have evoked memories of the recent war among Mark's hearers who were familiar with Vespasian's campaign in Galilee. Mark's account about the feeding of the five thousand may have evoked memories of the war in many different ways. The reference to "rest" (6:31) accompanied with the feeding (6:37, 41–42), for example, may have reminded them of Vespasian's rest and feast he had with his troops at Caesarea Philippi. Just as Vespasian had rest with his troops, Jesus, too, called the twelve to have rest (6:31). The contrast, however, is clear. While Vespasian and his troops rested after a destructive military campaign, Jesus and the twelve rested after a life-giving campaign that involved healing, driving out demons, feeding of the hungry, raising of a dead girl, saving of the disciples from the dangerous sea storms, and so on. Another parallel between Vespasian's rest at Caesarea Philippi and Jesus' rest with his disciples in the wilderness relates to giving thanks to the divine. Vespasian gave thanks to a god for the successes of his destructive military campaign in the Galilean cities and countryside. Jesus, too, took bread and fish and looked up to heaven (6:41). The act of looking up to heaven may be seen as Jesus' symbolic action of giving thanks to God for his willingness to feed his flock. So, both Vespasian and Jesus gave thanks to the divine when each rested with his aides.

The eating motif provides further parallels between the two accounts. Like Herod Antipas's banquet with his notables, Vespasian and his troops feasted on meals prepared by the royal family. Similarly, Jesus, his disciples, and the crowd held meals. The contrasts, however, are also obvious. While Vespasian had meals with a king, a feast that was held out of abundance, Jesus ate with the lowly and fed them out of scarcity. Even though he had at his disposal only a few loaves and fish, Jesus was able to feed thousands of people to their satisfaction such that they even collected baskets of leftovers (6:42–43; 8:8).[94] In this regard, Jesus demonstrated that he was indeed a shepherd who provided for all who were in desperate need. In addition, while Agrippa provided for Vespasian because of both the already received and anticipated military support to suppress the revolt in his kingdom (cf. *J.W.* 3:446), Jesus provided to people out of compassion and expected nothing in return from those whom he fed. Moreover, while the banquet prepared by King Agrippa

---

94. Witherington, *Mark*, 220: "God's provision was more than abundant, and was collected so it would not be wasted."

II in honor of Vespasian was partly for entertainment purposes, Jesus' feeding was provided out of necessity or desperate need.

The eating motif manifests still another contrasting parallel. As I have noted elsewhere, Vespasian used starvation as a strategy to achieve victory in war. At Jotapata, for example, he starved the Jewish revolutionaries in order to compel them to surrender. Starvation can also be viewed in terms of plundering of property, devastating and destruction of villages and towns. These actions were another way of starving people because they led to lack of food, famine, and then to loss of lives. Killings and enslavements as well denied the Galileans manpower that could work the land and produce food for their own survival and for the survival of their families and relatives. By contrast, Jesus provided food out of generosity in order that the Galileans might survive and have life. Mark's hearers may have interpreted Jesus' provisions of food as a means of manifesting the presence of God's empire, a sphere where people's needs are met.

Furthermore, Mark's use of military imagery in the feeding of five thousand may have reminded Mark's hearers of the war that had just ended. The crowd was arranged in the order modeling the military. The people were made to sit in companies, group by group, in groups of hundreds and of fifties (6:39-40). According to the Biblical tradition, Moses arranged the Israelites in military camps in hundreds and fifties in the wilderness (Exod 18:21, 25; Deut 1:15). Mark's hearers who were familiar with the military language as such may have linked the feeding story to their own experience of the war. More significantly, the number of five thousand people who were fed by Jesus may have recalled the number of troops that Josephus gathered in order to engage Placidus, one of Vespasian's commanders in Galilee (*Life* 212-13). Mark's hearers may have therefore understood Jesus' feeding story of the five thousand people in terms of the war events with which they were familiar.

The feeding of four thousand people demonstrated Jesus' caring for Gentiles. Mark refers to the beneficiaries of Jesus' feeding as having "come (from) a great distance" (8:3). This expression suggests that those people were Gentiles.[95] The episode therefore recalls the theme present in 7:24-30 and 7:31-37 where Jesus deals with Gentiles. From the Jewish perspective, Gentiles are spoken of as coming from distant lands (e.g., Jos 9:6, 9; Isa 60:4).[96] The use of Greek words, *eucharistēsas* (8:6) instead of *eulogēsen* (6:41) for blessing, and *spyridas* (8:8) instead of *kophinōn* (6:43) for baskets,

---

95. Lane, *Mark*, 236. Contra Hooker, *Mark*, 188, who argues that the expression "have come from a distance" suggests that they came from Galilee.

96. Cf. Guelich, *Mark*, 404; Marcus, *Mark*, 487.

also supports the idea that people whom Jesus fed were Gentiles. Moloney has shown that the usage of the Greek terms for blessing differ in that the former carries the sense of "giving thanks" while the latter connotes the sense of Hebrew *berakah*, "blessing." With respect to the Greek terms for baskets, he shows that the word *spyris* denotes a larger basket familiar to wider cultural settings, while the term *kophinos* refers to a small basket used by Jews to carry various things.[97] Given these observations, I concur with Witherington who proposes that Mark's focus on Gentiles in this passage "foreshadows the mission of the church to the Gentiles."[98] Jesus' feeding was a manifestation of Jesus' dealing with and inclusion of Gentiles in God's empire that he called people to enter.

Jesus' feeding of the four thousand Gentiles (8:1–10) may have had a great impact on Mark's hearers. Jesus' compassion and provision of food to the hungry people may have reminded Mark's hearers of Vespasian's actions which denied people of their basic need for their survival during his war campaign in Galilee. While Jesus provided food to the hungry, Vespasian not only starved his enemies but also plundered and destroyed their possessions. By starving his opponents, Vespasian denied them food, the very basic need for human survival. The feeding of non-Jews in the wilderness demonstrated that Jesus, a Jew, had enough to feed the Gentiles. The rhetorical impact of this story to Mark's hearers may have been a challenge not to contemplate revenge against Gentiles. They may have interpreted the feeding story as an invitation of Jews to treat Gentiles well following the example of Jesus who fed them out of generosity and compassion.

Mark's feeding narratives (6:30–44; 8:1–10) clearly demonstrated Jesus' role as a benefactor. Scholars have associated these stories with the eschatological heavenly manna (2 Bar. 29:8; *Mek. Exod.* 16:25; *Eccl. Rab.* 1:9),[99] Elisha's feeding of the one hundred people with a few pieces of bread (2 Kgs 4:42–44) and last supper (14:17–25).[100] But to my knowledge no one has read these episodes in terms of Jesus as the ideal benefactor. In both accounts, Jesus provides food to people who are in desperate need of it, demonstrating that he is indeed a benefactor. So although Mark never uses verbal expressions about Jesus' role as a benefactor, he explicitly and vividly underscores Jesus' deeds of benefaction. Such portrayal of Jesus as a benefactor may have reminded Mark's hearers of Vespasian who, during

---

97. Moloney, *Mark*, 154–55; cf. Witherington, *Mark*, 236; Boring, *Mark*, 221.
98. Witherington, *Mark*, 236.
99. Marcus, *Mark*, 410.
100. Fowler, *Loaves and Fishes*, 134; see the similarities between the feeding of the thousands people the Eucharist meal based on the expression in 6:41, 8:6, and 14:22.

his campaign in Galilee, was hailed as benefactor even though he starved people and plundered their possessions. They may have considered Jesus' feeding campaign not only as a contrast to Vespasian's military campaign but also as a powerful testimony that Jesus was indeed the ideal and powerful benefactor.

Campaign against Life-Threatening Forces of Nature

Along with the campaigns against illnesses, demonic powers, and hunger, Jesus' campaign in Galilee also involved dealing with life-threatening forces of nature. In Mark, the life threatening forces of nature relate to the sea storms (4:35-41; 6:45-52). In relation to these forces of nature, Jesus calmed the violent storms either by a verbal command (4:35-41) or by his mere presence (6:45-52).

Jesus' campaign against the violent sea storms occurred on the Sea of Galilee. The first incident occurred as Jesus and his disciples were crossing the Galilean sea (4:35) to go to the land of the Gerasenes (5:1). Jesus initiated the journey from the Jewish side of the sea by inviting his disciples to go with him "across to the other side" (4:350. As they were crossing the sea by boat, a violent storm occurred (4:37). Meanwhile, Jesus "was in the stern, asleep on the cushion" (4:38). Because of fear of death, the disciples woke Jesus up saying to him, "Teacher, do you not care that we are perishing?" (4:38). Waking up, Jesus rebuked the violent wind and commanded the sea to be still. Consequently, the violent storm immediately calmed down and "there was a dead calm" (4:39) such that the disciples wondered at Jesus saying to one another: "Who is this, that even the wind and the sea obey him?" (4:41).

The other incident of Jesus' campaign against life-threatening natural forces took place during the crossing of the Galilean sea to go to Bethsaida (6:45-52). The journey had started immediately after the feeding of the five thousand. Jesus had permitted the disciples to cross the sea to go to Bethsaida by boat while he remained on the land (6:45-47). While the disciples were crossing the sea, a strong wind came that threatened their lives (6:48a). Seeing his disciples in such a great danger, Jesus quickly came to their rescue "about the fourth watch of the night . . . walking on the sea" (6:48b). By his mere presence, the strong wind ceased (6:51). Thus, both in 4:35-41 and 6:45-52, Mark's Jesus demonstrated his ability to subdue the sea storms.

Both sea storms narratives underscore Jesus' divine power. First, his ability to calm the sea storms by a word of command (4:39) and by his mere presence (6:51) revealed that Jesus truly acted on God's behalf. In the Old

Testament, God is depicted as the Lord of history and nature. He has authority over "waters of sea" (Ps 33:7); he silences the roaring of seas and their waves (Ps 65:7); waters fear him and the deep trembles before God (Ps 65:7); and God "rebukes the sea" (Nah 1:4). Job understands God as having power to control the waters: "If (God) withholds the waters, they dry up; if he sends them out, they overwhelm the land" (Job 12:15). The biblical God also has power to control wind and to still the storm (Ps 107:25–30; 147:18; cf. Prov 30:4; Amos 4:13; Nah 1:3–4). The exodus event through which God allowed the Israelites to cross on a dry land in the Red Sea is a revealing example of God's power over the waters and sea (Exod 14:15–31). In Mark, Jesus does what God does. He rebukes the wind and the sea obeys him and becomes still (4:39). This demonstrates that Jesus is truly God's agent who operates under the influence of the divine power.

Second, Jesus' ability to walk on the sea (6:48) manifested his divine power. In the ancient world, walking on the sea was a manifestation of divine power.[101] Adela Y. Collins has shown quite convincingly that numerous Greco-Roman sources give evidence that only the divine men, god-gifted rulers, and the gods had the ability to walk on the sea.[102] Since Jesus can walk on the sea, then it is clear evidence that he has divine power. That Jesus has divine power is also demonstrated in his words to the disciples. When the disciples become terrified because they think he is a ghost (6:49), Jesus says to them, "Take heart, I AM; have no fear" (6:50). In the Old Testament, "I AM" is YAHWEH's self-address in the theophany scene (Exod 3:14). The I AM says to his people, Israel, do not be afraid (e.g., Isa 41:14), and I can "trample the waves of the Sea" and still the waters of chaos and death (e.g., Job 9:8; cf. Ps 74:12–17; Isa 51:9–11).[103] The theophany imagery allusion in this episode vividly suggests that Jesus is a ruler who is able to "trample the waves and walk on the Sea" because he is the "I AM." Jesus has therefore demonstrated that he is the "lord of land and sea." Unlike Vespasian who is also referred to as "lord of land and sea," Jesus is more than just a divine figure. He is indeed God's representative, a reliable ruler, and true bringer of peace and life because he calmed the winds on the sea and saved his disciples from the danger of death.

Jesus' ability to pacify the wind and sea was not only an illustration of power, but also an epiphany through which he revealed his role as the

---

101. Combs, "Ghost on Water?," 358. He rightly views "Jesus' walking on the sea in terms of divine manifestation."

102. Collins, "Rulers," 207–27. Other sources that treat the subject of Jesus' walk on the sea include Heil, *Jesus Walking on the Sea*; and Stegner, "Jesus' Walking on the Water," 212–34.

103. Cf. Collins, "Rulers," 212–13.

savior. He demonstrated his role as the Savior in the midst of threat and serious danger when he saved his disciples from the threat of death caused by the sea storms. Mark's hearers may have interpreted Jesus' act of saving his disciples from the dangerous storms as a sign of Jesus' saving presence in their own suffering on account of the good news (13:9–13). It is therefore not a coincidence that early Christian art portrays the Church as a boat sailing on a death-threatening sea with Jesus in their midst, but with nothing to be afraid of.[104]

The ability of Jesus to save his disciples from drowning in the sea in 4:35–41 and 6:45–51 respectively recalls and anticipates the drowning of the herd of two thousand pigs in the sea (5:13). The pigs drowned as a result of the legion that had entered them (5:9–13). In this case, as the swine perished so also the legion. Since the legion symbolized the Roman troops, the drowning of pigs implies the drowning of the Roman troops. That may connote that Jesus had power over the armies belonging to Caesar who claimed to be the lord of land, to the extent that he could command and cause them to perish in the sea. This shows that Jesus has power even over the strong imperial military power. However, Jesus does not conquer the imperial military power using violent military means, but rather he uses the word of command. Mark indicates that having being permitted by Jesus to leave the Gerasene demoniac the legion entered two thousand swine and "rushed down the steep bank into the sea, and were drowned in the sea" (5:13). There is no element of force in Jesus' dealing with the legion. This demonstrated that Jesus does not use violent means to confront domination and oppression. While the legion perished in the sea, the Gerasene demoniac was liberated (5:19), demonstrating that Jesus uses his power from God to liberate the oppressed.

Mark's hearers may have associated Jesus' dealing with the sea storms with the events of the war at many points. First, Jesus' crossing of the sea with his disciples may have evoked memories of Vespasian's crossing of the Mediterranean Sea with his troops from Rome to bring destruction in Judea. Here Mark's hearers may have noted the contrast between Vespasian and Jesus. While Vespasian crossed the sea leading his troops to destroy life, Jesus crossed the Galilean sea in order to bring life to people. Second, Jesus' ability to save his disciples from a dangerous sea storm on the Sea of Galilee "early in the morning" or "about the fourth watch of the night" (6:48b) as expressed in the Revised Standard Version, may have reminded Mark's hearers of the events of the war that occurred at Jotapata, Joppa, and Gamala. At Jotapata Vespasian attacked the defenders at "the

104. Lane, *Mark*, 178.

last hour of the night" (*J.W.* 3:318–319) destroying the wall "towards the hour of the morning watch" (*J.W.* 3:251). At Joppa, with the help of a strong storm that occurred "towards dawn" (*J.W.* 3:421–422), Vespasian's troops destroyed all the enemies by throwing them alive on the shore of the sea (*J.W.* 3:426). At Gamala, Vespasian's troops destroyed the tower at "the time of the morning watch" (*J.W.* 4:62–464).[105] Hence, Mark's reference to the time "early in the morning" or "about the fourth watch of the night" may have evoked among his hearers memories of these events of the war which also occurred at that time.

Third, Jesus' rescue of his disciples from the deadly storm may also have evoked memories of the events of the war on the Sea of Galilee and at Joppa along the coast of the Mediterranean Sea. During Vespasian's campaign at Joppa, the Jewish rebels took refuge in their ship on the Mediterranean Sea. When the storm occurred on the sea many of them perished as a result of it. Those who were thrown alive on the seashore were killed by the Roman troops (*J.W.* 3:414–427). The contrasts between Vespasian's campaign and Jesus' campaign are clear. While Vespasian did nothing to stop the sea storm, Jesus calmed the sea storms. Again, while Vespasian caused people to die in the severe storm and killed those whom the waves threw them alive onto the shore, Jesus saved his disciples from the threat of death due to the sea storm. Hence, unlike Vespasian's campaign which destroyed life, Jesus' campaign promoted life.

Furthermore, Jesus' power to calm the sea storm not only may have associated Jesus with Vespasian as the chief commander of the Roman armies in Galilee, but also Vespasian as the emperor. The Roman imperial propaganda proclaimed the emperor as lord of land and sea. An inscription from Pergamum praises Augustus as "overseer of every land and sea" (No. 381).[106] Seneca, too, depicts Claudius as one who "made peace by land and sea" (*Apol.* 10); and he applies a similar phrase when he appeals to Nero for the existing peace on land and sea (*Clem.* 4). Second Maccabees shows that some Greco-Roman rulers claimed to have power to command the seas (2 Macc 9:8). When Josephus prophesied that Vespasian would be emperor, he also said that Vespasian would be master of "land and sea" (*J.W.* 3:402).

---

105. The expressions of time—"the fourth watch of the night," "the last watch of the night," "the hour of the morning watch," "towards the dawn," and "the time of the morning watch"—all speak of the same time, which is the time from 3 a.m. to 6 a.m. This was in accordance to the Roman way of dividing time between 6 p.m. and 6 a.m. into four watches. See Marcus, *Mark*, 423; Boring, *Mark*, 189. Mark therefore expressed time according to the Roman custom (cf. 13:34).

106. Cited in Deissman, *Light*, 347, figure 64.

The title "lord of sea and land," expressed the emperors's military power that served to consolidate their imperial rule.

Critics of the Roman Empire, however, used the title to expose the greed and thirst of Rome to conquer and plunder. Ancient Roman historians, Tacitus and Petronius are representatives of those critics of the Roman Empire. According to Petronius, "The conquering now held the whole world, sea and land and the course of sun and moon. But he was not satisfied. Now the waters were stirred and trouble by his loaded ships" (*Sat.* 119.1-3; cf. 4-18, 27-36). Similarly, citing Calgacus, Tacitus writes, "To plunder, butcher, steal, these things they misname empire: they make desolation and they call it peace" (*Agric.* 30.5). This description is expressive of Vespasian's military campaign in Galilee and Judea in general. Vespasian left Rome and crossed the Mediterranean Sea in order to bring destruction in Judea. On the Mediterranean Sea near Joppa, for example, he was unable to control the sea storms and his troops mercilessly massacred the Jews who tried to escape death due to the storm on the sea (*J.W.* 3:426-427).

By contrast, Jesus calmed the sea storms and saved his disciples from the threat of death due to the severe sea storm. In so doing Jesus demonstrated that his power was superior to that of any of the Roman Caesars.[107] Mark's hearers may therefore have recognized Jesus, not Vespasian, as the true "Lord of land and sea," and "ruler of the whole world." As Cotter has pointed out: "In the stilling of the storm, Jesus' command to the wind and the sea would suggest to the first-century audience that he is Lord of the sea. Metaphorically, since the sea symbolizes life's unsettled and dangerous character, Jesus' authority as the Lord of the sea signals to the attentive listener that just as surely as he commands the elements such as wind and sea, so too he can control other life-threatening events."[108] The original hearers of Mark may indeed have regarded Jesus' lordship as superior to that of Caesar Vespasian. The ability of Jesus to command and to calm the sea storms, his ability to walk on the sea, and to save his disciples from the threats of death on the sea may have led the hearers to put faith in Jesus with the hope that he would calm the storms threatening their own lives and grant them salvation as he did to his disciples.

---

107. For a detailed discussion on Jesus' superiority over the Roman Caesars in the context of the storm stories, see Strelan, "Greater Than Caesar," 166-79. Concluding his article, Strelan writes, "Jesus is the protector of his people, the controller of their destiny. In contrast to Lucan's view of the gods, Mark's Jesus is not removed, not distant, not unconcerned. He is in the same boat as his fearful followers in their transition and speaks with authority over the forces that threaten" (ibid., 179).

108. Cotter, "Cosmology and the Jesus Miracles," 127.

In sum, Jesus' campaign in Galilee was very successful. Many people from the villages of Galilee and the neighboring regions benefited from Jesus' life-giving campaign that manifested the presence of God's empire among them. Many were freed from oppressive demonic forces and illnesses; the hungry were given food to eat; the dead girl was restored to life; and the disciples were saved from the life-threatening sea storms. During Jesus' Galilean campaign, the disciples witnessed all of his liberative works of power. Consequently, just as Vespasian was proclaimed emperor on the Jewish soil, so also Jesus was proclaimed Messiah in the villages of Caesarea Philippi. In the next section, I examine more closely Peter's declaration of Jesus as the Messiah.

Jesus Proclaimed Messiah at Caesarea Philippi

Peter's confession of Jesus as the Messiah culminates Jesus' Galilean campaign. The incident takes place in Caesarea Philippi (8:27-30). Having healed the blind man at Bethsaida (8:22), Jesus led his disciples to the villages of Caesarea Philippi (8:27a). While on the way, he asked his disciples about the public opinion concerning his identity: "Who do people say I am?" The answers to this question were diverse. They included John the Baptist, Elijah, and one of the prophets (8:27b-28) probably based on rumors circulating following the death of John (6:14-15). Then Jesus asked the disciples about their own understanding of him: "But who do you say that I am?" a question to which Peter responded, "You are the Messiah" (8:29). Following Peter's reply, Jesus forbad the disciples to tell anyone about his identity (8:30).

To understand Peter's proclamation of Jesus as Messiah we need to place that proclamation in its appropriate social setting. Caesarea Philippi, the place where Jesus is proclaimed the Messiah was a major Gentile city in the district of Iturea, located in a territory north of the Sea of Galilee. The city was built at the source of the Jordan River near the foot of Mount Hermon. In the ancient times, the place was called Paneas in honor of a Greek god called Pan. Herod the Great had erected there a temple near a cave which he dedicated to Emperor Augustus (*J.W.* 1:404-406; *Ant.* 15:363-364). Previously, the place had been a site where an oracular god Baal, identified with Zeus, was worshiped. The rebuilding of Paneas is attributed to Herod Philip who made the city his capital and renamed it Caesarea Philippi in honor of Caesar (*J.W.* 2:168; *Ant.* 18:28).[109] Herod Agrippa II enlarged the city and

---

109. Waetjen, *Reordering of Power*, 143, describes Caesarea as "the citadel of political power, constructed under the Herodian King Philip and named in honor of the

renamed it Neronias in honor of Emperor Nero (*Ant.* 20:211). During his reign, the temple there continued to serve as a place for emperor worship.[110] Moreover, Caesarea Philippi was associated with visionary activity and ascent to heavenly Temple (1 En. 12–16 and *T. Levi* 2–7). According to the Babylonian Talmud, the miraculous fall of a gate in Paneas served as a sign of the coming of the messiah (*b. Sanh.* 98a).[111]

Given the historical facts about Caesarea Philippi noted above, the place was therefore an appropriate setting for the revelation of an important aspect of Jesus' identity. As indicated above, the place was associated with false gods, Baal and Pan; vision and ascent into heavenly temple; messianic hopes; and imperial power. In the midst of a city dedicated to false gods, Jesus' true identity is revealed countering not only the ancient gods, but also the claims that an emperor is a god and lord.[112] Locating Peter's declaration of Jesus as the Messiah at Caesarea Philippi makes the point, for those aware of the imperial cult practiced there, that Jesus and not the Roman emperor is the agent of the supreme deity.[113] Witherington rightly states that by declaring "Jesus Messiah, Peter sees Jesus as God's anointed, and so most blessed, one.[114]

Caesarea Philippi is also linked to the events of the Jewish revolt against Rome. At the initial stages of the war, many Jews living in the city were massacred (*Life* 54). By the order of King Agrippa II, Jews were imprisoned there following the defeat of Castius Gallus, the governor of Syria (*Life* 74; cf. *Life* 24–25). More significant for the hearers of Mark is that Vespasian rested at Caesarea Philippi with his troops for twenty days, being entertained by King Agrippa II. At this very place, Vespasian gave thank-offering to the gods for his success in suppressing the rebellion in Galilee (*J.W.* 3:443–444). It is worth mentioning that immediately after the fall of Jerusalem and the destruction of the temple, Titus also rested at Caesarea Philippi, with his troops being entertained with games in which many Jewish prisoners of war died violently as they fought with wild beasts or with one another (*J.W.* 7:23–24; 37–38). Hence, as Marcus has observed, Caesarea Philippi was a city "associated with imperial rule, messianic hopes, and violent death-all of which make it a fitting backdrop for our story."[115] Hearers of Mark who were

---

Roman emperor."

110. See Lane, *Mark,* 289; Witherington, *Mark,* 240; Marcus, *Mark,* 602–3.

111. See www.come-and-hear.com/sanhedrin/sanhedrin_98.html/.

112. Witherington, *Mark,* 240; Lane, *Mark,* 289; Collins, *Mark,* 400.

113. Collins, *Mark,* 400–401.

114. Witherington, *Mark,* 240.

115. Marcus, *Mark,* 603. The reference to "our story" here refers to the story about

familiar with the events of the war may have related Peter's proclamation of Jesus as the Messiah to Vespasian's rest at Caesarea Philippi shortly after Josephus had prophesied about him that he would be emperor at Jotapata, a place very close to Caesarea Philippi. Hearers may also have associated Jesus' visit at Caesarea with Titus' visit after the war about the same time Mark was composing the Gospel.

The link between the events at Caesarea Philippi that were connected to the war and Mark's report on Jesus as the Messiah highlights the ironic contrast between Jesus and Vespasian. The parallels between the two figures are evident. Both of them are associated with messianic claims and both visited Caesarea Philippi. Vespasian was claimed to be the fulfillment of the Jewish prophecy that expected the coming of a messiah[116] and visited Caesarea Philippi. Jesus was declared the Messiah in the villages of Caesarea Philippi. The irony, however, is that while the messianic claims associated with Vespasian involved violence and destruction, the declaration of Jesus as the Messiah is based on his deeds of mercy to the marginalized and the oppressed people. Given these facts, Mark's hearers may have evaluated Peter's announcement of Jesus as the Messiah as a valid contrast to the claim that Vespasian was the fulfillment of the Jewish expectation of the messiah. This story may have reinforced the hearers' loyalty to Jesus as God's true Messiah rather than to Vespasian, who had just become emperor. The story may also have reminded the Jewish hearers of the betrayal of Josephus who set up Vespasian's accession to the imperial power at Jotapata, a place very close to Caesarea Philippi.

Peter's confession of Jesus as the Messiah may also have evoked memories of the Jewish messianic claimants who were active during the Jewish war with the Romans. According to Josephus, Menachem (*J.W.* 2:44, 433-434) and Simon bar Gioras (*J.W.* 4:508; cf. 4:510, 575-576; 7:26-36) made messianic pretensions during the war. Mark's hearers may have linked the reference to Jesus as the Messiah to the activities of these messianic pretenders. Marcus has made this point clear when he states that Mark's "hearers are aware of the catalytic role by [these] messianic claimants in the Jewish War against the Romans, and perhaps [are] even being persecuted because of their refusal to accept these claims (13:6-9, 21-22), the assurance that Jesus

---

Peter's confession of Jesus as the Messiah (8:27-30).

116. Cf. Winn, *Mark*, 164: "the tradition claiming Vespasian to be the fulfillment of the Jewish messianic prophecy—a tradition found in the writings of Josephus, Tacitus, and Suetonius—reflects Flavian propaganda that was used to legitimatize the emperor's power."

and no other is the Messiah would come as a powerful encouragement to maintain fidelity to him alone."[117]

Jesus' identity as the Messiah was not to be used as a tool for public propaganda. After Peter's declaration of Jesus as the Messiah, Jesus prohibited his disciples not to publicize his identity (8:30). Commanding people to silence is Jesus' common characteristic in Mark. Jesus orders the unclean spirits to silence because they know him and call him Son of God (1:25; 3:11–12); he tells the leper to "say nothing to anyone" (1:44) and does the same to the crowd after the healing of a man with hearing and speech difficulties in the Decapolis (7:36). Moreover, after he raises Jairus's daughter from the dead, Jesus strictly charges the witnesses, including his three disciples Peter, James, and John, not to make the event known (5:37, 43). Jesus' order to silence among his disciples is closely linked to Jesus' order to silence directed to the demons because they know him (1:34; 3:11–12).

Jesus' command to silence at Caesarea Philippi needs close attention. This may have been necessitated by the disciples' lack of knowledge that the messianic nature of Jesus would also involve suffering and death. The prohibition was therefore necessary in order to safeguard Jesus' identity from any danger of misunderstanding that might arise as a result of the disciples' "overemphasis on authority and their disregard of his sacrificial servanthood."[118] It is also possible that Jesus ordered his disciples not to publicize about him in order to keep his messianic identity anonymous so as to avoid any understanding of him in terms of the messianic pretenders.[119] In addition, the command to silence may also have served to highlight that Jesus did not have an agenda for personal publicity. For Mark's hearers, this last point may have underscored the contrast between Jesus and Vespasian. While Vespasian used Josephus's prophecy about him as the "coming messiah" as propaganda tool to legitimatize his imperial power, Jesus avoided publicizing his identity as the Messiah.

Conclusion

The goal of this chapter was to read and examine Jesus' campaign in Galilee in the light of Vespasian's military campaign in Galilee, seeking to show the contrasts between the two campaigns. My examination has revealed a number of contrasts, but I highlight only a few of them. As for Vespasian's campaign, the general came from Rome (the capital of the

---

117. Marcus, *Mark*, 612.
118. Santos, *Slave of All*, 158.
119. Blount, *Go Preach*, 143, based on a citation from Boers, *Who Was Jesus?* 90.

empire) leading a powerful army seeking to devastate Judea and to put it under the imperial control, thereby consolidating the Roman Empire. By contrast, Jesus came from Nazareth of Galilee, the margin of the empire, and appointed the twelve to be with him to spread God's empire through proclamation without violence.

Moreover, Vespasian's campaign was primarily focused on fortified cities. When he entered the cities, he conquered them; was being received by kings and the powerful men, and the populous hailed him as savior and benefactor even though his campaigns involved loss of life, destruction of property, enslavement, displacement of people, and starvation. By contrast, Jesus' campaign was based on villages and the countryside. Jesus was rejected by the authorities and powerful who challenged his campaign. Rather than being hosted, Jesus made himself the host of multitudes who flocked toward him. He welcomed the poor and marginalized peasants including outcasts and untouchables in society. Even though his campaign was redemptive in that it involved healing, exorcisms, feeding, raising of the dead, and calming of life-threatening storms, Jesus was never hailed in divine terms as savior or benefactor.

Further, Vespasian crossed land and sea in order to subjugate Judea. For that matter Vespasian was considered lord of land and sea. To the contrary, although Jesus crossed land and Sea of Galilee to proclaim and liberate the Judeans, he was never addressed as lord of land and sea. Moreover, since Vespasian was proclaimed emperor on the Judean soil, he claimed to be the fulfillment of the Jewish prophecy concerning the coming messiah and used this as propaganda to legitimize his rule. By contrast, when Jesus is proclaimed Messiah at Caesarea Philippi, he does not publicize it. Rather, Jesus charges his disciples to tell no one about him. Given these contrasts, Mark's hearers may have chosen to identify themselves with Jesus, whose deeds demonstrated that he was truly God's agent sent to establish God's empire among his people.

6

Contrast of Values
Wealth, Status, and Power

Introduction

THE GOAL IN THIS chapter is to examine Mark's portrayal of the contrasts between the values of human empire represented by the Roman Empire and the values of God's empire based on the issues of wealth, status, and power in Mark's Gospel. In Mark, the values of human empire are represented by both the Roman and Jewish elites and sometimes Jesus' disciples while those of God's empire are embodied in the teaching of Jesus that he delivers as he journeys to Jerusalem with his disciples. As I deal with the contrast of values, I particularly pay attention to Mark's contrast to Rome, contrast to Jewish authorities, and contrast to Revolutionaries. I examine Mark's portrayal of the contrasting values in light of the crushing defeat of the war and the fact that the war was also a peasant rebellion against the Jewish elites. In order to realize the relevance of Mark's contrasts of values to his hearers, I first place Mark's hearers in perspective.

Richard L. Rohrbaugh has made a helpful study about the social location of Mark's first hearers. He locates Mark's original hearers in the framework of an advanced agrarian peasant society comprising of two major social classes: the upper and lower classes. According to him, the upper class included at the minimum, the ruler, the ruling elite, and their retainers, respectively covering 1 to 2 percent and 5 percent of the total population. The top members of this group lived in heavily fortified cities enjoying luxurious life at the expense of the rural peasants who worked the land. Power, privilege (wealth), and prestige (status and honor) rested in the hands of these few urban elites. The lower class, on the other hand, was formed by illiterate, urban non-elite (3 to 7 percent), rural peasants (75 percent), and the unclean and expendables (10 percent).[1] Except for the urban non-elites, most of the lower class lived in rural villages and small towns working the land.

---

1. Rohrbaugh, "Social Location," 381–84.

Although the peasants were the primary labor force, what they produced did not benefit them but the urban ruling class who exploited them in the form of rent for land and taxation.[2]

Rohrbaugh indicates that, in Mark, the disciples, the crowds, and Jesus himself belong to the peasant class.[3] While those who oppose Jesus belong to the ruling class, namely the high priests, the elders, Herod Antipas, Pilate, and their retainers including the scribes and the Pharisees, the Herodians, and the Roman soldiers;[4] most of those who come and seek help from Jesus are the unclean and expendables.[5] Thus, as Thurston has pointed out, "Mark is a realistic narrative with particularizing details... It is 'told' among the unofficial people" and it says nothing good about the 'official people,' whether Jewish or Roman."[6]

The social location of Mark's original hearers is a predominantly rural peasant class and fits the situation of first-century Palestine. Such a social location provides the reality of Mark's portrayal of contrast of values. Mark's Jesus opposes the values of the Judean and Gentile ruling elites and of their retainers in favor of the values that give life and dignity to those who suffered the most under Roman imperialism: the poor and marginalized peasants, the degraded, the unclean, and the expendables. In the period following the outbreak of the Jewish revolt in 66 CE, aristocrats controlled most of the fertile lands, leaving the majority of the peasants landless. Such ownership of land increased accumulation of wealth in the hands of a few ruling elite while it "pushed the peasant economic viability to the brink."[7] At the time the Gospel was written, Mark's hearers faced opposition from both the Roman and Judean authorities (13:9). They were in a situation in which they were challenged to choose God or Caesar (12:13–17). In other words, Mark's hearers had to choose either to practice the values of Caesar or the values of God. In this situation, Mark's Jesus promoted abandonment of the values of the elite in favor of the values of God's empire embodied in his life and teachings.

---

2. Kimondo, "Milking a Starving Cow?," 29.
3. Rohrbaugh, "Social Location," 384–86.
4. Ibid.
5. Ibid., 387–88.
6. Thurston, *Preaching Mark*, 6.
7. Rohrbaugh, "Social Location," 388.

Contrasts to Rome

Gaining the Whole World vs. Giving Up Everything for the Good News

One of Jesus' teaching about values of God's empire in Mark relates to giving up everything for the sake of the good news. This teaching occurs in the context of Jesus' first passion prediction. Mark has Jesus teach:

> If any wants to become my follower, let them deny themselves and take up their cross and follow me. For those who want to save their life will lose it, and those who lose their life for my sake, and for the sake of the good news, will save it. For what will it profit them to gain the whole world and forfeit their life? Indeed, what can they give in return for their life? Those who are ashamed of me and my words in this adulterous and generation, of them the Son of Humanity will also be ashamed when he comes in the glory of his Father with the holy angels (8:34–38).

This passage is dominated by economic terms: "profit," "gain," "loss," and "give in exchange," suggesting that Mark's Jesus here is primarily concerned with economic matters. In this section, I therefore primarily pay attention to the value related to wealth or possessions. In dealing with this matter, I first consider the value of wealth in the context of the Roman imperial world.

Material possessions or wealth was one of the core values of the Roman Empire. People in the empire desired to accumulate wealth for themselves. The emperor who was the supreme ruler and the urban elite used their political power to gain and accumulate wealth for themselves. Wealth was concentrated in the hands of a few urban elite while the greater majority of the population "lived at or close to, subsistence level."[8] One historian has underscored the economic situation of the rulers in the ancient world. He writes,

> The emperor's wealth did not consist alone in the accumulated riches of his families or predecessors or in the immense *latifundia* he inherited here and there in Africa and Asia, or in the fact that he everywhere annexed the bulk of partial or total confiscations decreed by judges. Over and above all this, nothing prevented his replenishing his private purse from the resources of the imperial Exchequer, into which poured the taxes levied for the maintenance of the soldiers, and none dared to suggests an audit of his accounts. He could dispose at will—with no need

---

8. Lenski, *Power and Privilege*, 267.

to render account to any man—of the revenue of Egypt, which was a personal possession of the Crown, and he could plunge open hands into booty of war.⁹

Such an accumulation of wealth of the emperor must be understood in accordance with what Lenski refers to as "*the proprietary theory of the state.*" According to this theory, the state is considered as a property that its owner uses for his personal benefit, including passing it on to one's heirs.¹⁰

Referring specifically to Vespasian who became emperor at the time Mark's Gospel was composed, Josephus writes: "Caesar [Vespasian] sent instructions to Bassus and Laberius Maximus, the procurator, to farm out all Jewish territory. For he founded no city there, reserving the country as *his private property*, except that he did assign to eight hundred veterans discharged from the army a place for habitation called Emmaus, distant thirty furlongs from Jerusalem" (*J.W.* 7:216–217).¹¹ According to Lenski, the ruling elite possessed at least twenty five percent of the total income of the empire, and the combined income of the ruler and the governing class ranged from 60 to 67 percent of the total wealth of the empire.¹²

Landownership and public office were the primary sources of income of the ruling elite.¹³ Lenski asserts that "*landownership, when divorced from public office, was valued chiefly as a means to obtain prestige and economic security, while public office was used primarily for political and economic advancement.*"¹⁴ Similarly, Carter expresses the significance of land in the Roman Empire and how Caesar, the governing class, and the urban elite benefited from it. He writes thus:

> The Roman Empire was an agrarian economy with land as the primary resource . . . [T]hroughout the empire, the small governing group of 2 to 3 percent of the population, often urban based, controlled most of the land and its production. They owned large estates worked by slaves. They collected rent, usually paid in kind, from peasants. They increased their holdings by

---

9. Carcopino, *Daily Life in Ancient Rome*, 68, cited in Lenski, *Power and Privilege*, 214.

10. Lenski, *Power and Privilege*, 214.

11. Italics added.

12. Lenski, *Power and Privilege*, 228.

13. Carter, *Roman Empire*, 100, states that the "Elites controlled the production, distribution (trade), and consumption of its products."

14. Lenski, *Power and Privilege*, 229. Italics are original. Cf. Garnsey and Saller, *Roman Empire*, 43, 44, who also argue that land was a good investment that provided security and stable income through agriculture, the main source of wealth. They also note that land was valued as a source of prestige and political power.

foreclosing on defaulted loans. They traded surplus for needed resources and profit. They redistributed peasant production to cities, to their own large estates and households, and to temples . . . Their economic control reflected their political power and exerted influence on how most of the population lived.[15]

Thus Mark's phrase, "acquire the whole world" directly expresses the Roman domination over the land of the conquered nations in order to gain wealth, status, and power to control others.[16] Caesar and his governing elite, whom he appointed to serve as political, military, and religious officials, used their political power to control the land—one of the chief sources of wealth. In return, landownership gave them power to control others.

Military conquests of other nations and taxes increased the wealth of the Roman elites. The Roman ruling elites used the military to "gain the whole world" (8:36), which implied gaining more material possessions. That means they used their military power to conquer other nations and thereby to acquire and accumulate wealth of the "whole world" for their personal benefits.[17] Victory in wars gave the Romans more power to control economic surplus. Their victory became "a prize that brought fabulous wealth and immense power."[18] When they conquered other nations, they confiscated land, subjugated the conquered people under their control, and forced them to pay tribute to Rome. For example, following the conquest of Judea in 70 CE, Vespasian confiscated land which he either farmed out or gave it as a gift to his veterans (*J.W.* 7:216) and friends like Josephus (*Life* 425).[19] Part of the confiscated land in Jerusalem was reserved for the tenth legion left there to protect the city and its surroundings from other possible revolt (*J.W.* 7:17; cf. *Life* 422).[20] It can therefore be

15. Carter, *Roman Empire*, 45–46.

16. Ibid., 3: "In the first century, Rome dominated the territory and people around the Mediterranean Sea. Its empire extended from Britain in the northwest, through (present-day) France and Spain to the west, across Europe to Turkey and Syria in the east, and along North Africa to the south. Rome ruled an estimated 60–65 million people of diverse ethnicities and cultures."

17. Cf. Moxnes, *Economy of the Kingdom*, 39, who writes that "One basic form for redistribution was warfare. Although wars were rarely fought for economic reasons, they resulted in a redistribution of wealth: winners in wars confiscated property and labor and redistributed land among soldiers."

18. Lenski, *Power and Privilege*, 212.

19. Titus, too, confiscated land in Judea and gave part of it to Josephus (*Life* 422). For a discussion concerning the nature of Vespasian's treatment of the Jewish land after the Roman-Jewish War of 66–70 CE, see Benjamin, "Judea after AD 70," 44–50.

20. For detailed discussion concerning the Roman Tenth Legion that was left in Jerusalem after the city's destruction, see Geva, "Camp of the Tenth Legion," 239–54.

said that the Roman's motive to conquer Judea was partly to advance and to protect the economic interest of the Roman Empire.

Collection of taxes from the dominated people served as a means of accumulating wealth for the Roman ruling elite. The ruling elite gained enormous wealth through taxes, rents, and tributes. Through taxes, wealth flowed from the margins of the empire to the center in Rome. As Moxnes has pointed out, "The center of power in the Roman Empire was Rome. Wealth was extracted from the provinces in the form of taxes, either directly through Roman officials and their soldiers or through vassal princes."[21] The taxes involved tribute to Caesar which expressed the loyalty of the conquered people to the emperor (*J.W.* 2:386, 404-405, 409): property tax (*Life* 429), rents based on the farmed out land, and the poll-tax (*J.W.* 7:216). In general, taxes and military power were the primary sources of the Roman Empire's "legionary economy."[22]

In Mark, people's desire to accumulate wealth in accordance to the Roman imperial values is expressive in various ways. Those who have possessions reject Jesus and the good news in favor of "gain(ing) the whole world" and wrongly think that they can gain profit and save their lives by keeping riches (8:35-36). The man who "had many possessions" grieved because he was told to share his wealth with the poor (10:20-22). The tenants of the vineyard seized, beat, insulted, and killed the slaves and a beloved son of the vineyard because they wanted to own the vineyard for themselves (12:1-12). More significantly, the Romans subjected the Jews under payment of tribute to Caesar (12:13-17). This tribute was a means of acknowledging Caesar as ruler of the conquered people. For Mark's hearers, this tribute may have been associated with Vespasian, the emperor at the time.

To ensure that tribute to Caesar was effectively paid, the emperor used Roman governors and soldiers to enforce it. In the Gospel, the governor who took charge of this role was Pontius Pilate, under whose tenure Jesus was crucified as a criminal who threatened the political and economic interests of the Roman Empire (cf. 15:24-27). "As a governor, Pilate represents and enforces the (Roman) empire's control through tours of his province, administering justice, *collecting taxes*, deploying troops, of

---

21. Moxnes, *Economy of the Kingdom*, 39-40.

22. Kautsky, *Politics of Aristocratic Empires*, 6, 144-55. Cf. Garnsey and Saller, *Roman Empire*, 8, who note that "Rome was essentially a parasite city, feeding off the manpower and wealth of Italy and the numerous provinces that made up the Roman Empire." See also Lenski, *Power and Privilege*, 206, 210, who states that in the Roman imperial world "there was a steady flow of *goods* from the peasant villages to the urban centers" that created in the empire "unequal distribution of power, privilege, and honor."

the province, and securing alliances with local *landowning* and religious elites."[23] Pilate's actions represent and demonstrate the Roman's way of doing things in terms of the values of "this adulterous and sinful generation" (8:38). In other words, the mind of Pilate is not set "on divine things but on human things" (8:33).

By contrast, Mark's Jesus embodies values of God's empire. He encourages people to abandon the economic values of the Roman Empire expressed by the Roman elite. Instead of accumulating wealth, Mark's Jesus urges his hearers to give up everything for the sake of the good news. Jesus presents this teaching in the context of his first passion prediction. He exhorts his disciples and the crowd to relinquish their lives in order to follow him and to gain life (8:34–35). Mark's Jesus also urges the rich man to share his possessions with the poor (10:21). In principle, Mark's Jesus wants people to renounce their self-centeredness in order to become God-centered. He wants people to live up to the values of God's empire and not in terms of the values of the Roman Empire.

The reason Mark's Jesus wanted people to relinquish possessions is because possessions are not truly profitable. They lead to loss of life. Possessions prevent people from following Jesus—the way that leads to eternal life. Jesus' rhetorical question, "what will it profit . . . to gain the whole world and lose life?" (8:36) implies that wealth is not comparable to life. The question suggests that life is invaluable compared to acquiring the entire world. Acquisition of wealth leads to loss of true life. Since wealth is associated with honor, the rich elites rejected Jesus and the good news because they wanted to maintain their honor and glory before people, thereby avoiding shame of being poor. Such behavior, however, will have negative consequences in the eschatological times. Jesus, who is the Son of Humanity, will also be ashamed of them when he comes in glory (8:38). Mark's Jesus calls people to relinquish wealth in favor of loyalty to him and to the good news in order to gain an authentic life in his glory (cf. 8:35). This teaching may have evoked hope among Mark's hearers in that Jesus' triumph in God's eschatological reign may have been regarded as an assurance for them that if they endure and faithfully remain loyal to Jesus and the good news even in the face of persecution, they would also share in Jesus' glory (cf. 13:9–13). True, it is not easy for humans to be saved, but as Jesus teaches, with "God everything is possible" (10:27). Only in sharing of wealth with the poor does one show trust in God for whom all things are possible.

Moreover, Mark's Jesus urged people to renounce possessions because they prevent people from becoming members in God's empire. This idea is

---

23. Carter, *Pontius Pilate*, 36. Italics are added.

clearly demonstrated in the story of the rich man (10:17–31). In that story, Jesus speaks three times of the impossibility for the rich to enter God's empire. Two times, Jesus says, "How hard it will be for those who have riches to enter God's empire!" (10:23, 25). The third time he says, "It is easier for a camel to go through the eye of a needle than for a rich man to enter God's empire" (10:25). These remarks clearly show how critical Mark's Jesus is on the trust in wealth. He criticizes reliance on possessions because they prevent people from following him and from committing themselves to doing God's will, thereby preventing them from entering and enjoying the blessings available in God's empire. The rich man rejected Jesus' call to sell his possessions, to give to the poor, and to follow Jesus because "he had many possessions" (10:22). The rich man was not willing to give up his possessions; he did not want to help the needy—a mark of his lack of love for the neighbor (12:31); and to become a disciple of Jesus. The motive behind the rich man's refusal was fear. He was afraid of losing his wealth and security, a situation that "would render him vulnerable to poverty and deprive him of the much-coveted opportunity to serve as a benefactor to others, garnering the attention and respect of his peers."[24] His own wealth had become an obstacle to discipleship.[25]

In Mark, giving up possessions for the sake of Jesus and the good news is gain, not a loss. This is because there is a reward promised for just doing that. Responding to Peter's sentiment concerning the compensation that the disciples would receive for giving up everything for the sake of the good news: "Look, we have left everything and followed you" (8:28), Jesus says that those who have abandoned their possessions for the sake of the good news will be rewarded a hundred times in this age "houses and brothers and sisters and mothers and children and lands, with possessions, and in the age to come eternal life" (10:29–30). So those who abandon their possessions in favor of loyalty to Jesus and the good news will not be losers but beneficiaries. Mark's hearers may have been challenged to view the teaching on giving up everything for Jesus and for the good news as a profitable investment.[26] On the other hand, however, they may have considered the desire to acquire wealth as an unprofitable investment because accumulation of wealth leads

---

24. Wilhelm, *Preaching Mark*, 178.
25. Donahue and Harrington, *Mark*, 307.
26. Cf. Wilhelm, *Preaching Mark*, 152–53: "There is no real profit if one gains the world and loses one's life; such forfeiture reveals a bad investment. But if we are willing to stake our lives on the gospel, that is, the good news of God's reign proclaimed by Jesus Christ, then our investment will prove priceless. Jesus' use of commercial language relates the realm of material life to spiritual reality and heightens our appreciation of both."

to loss of authentic life and away from God's empire. They would take this as a warning against the desire to accumulating wealth.

Jesus' teaching on giving up wealth parallels the position of some revolutionaries on issues of wealth. One of the causes of the Jewish revolt was the accumulation of wealth in the hands of a few elites while the majority peasants suffered in extreme poverty (cf. *J.W.* 2:426–429). The revolutionaries opposed such an imbalance of wealth among the Jews. Consequently, they took up arms to fight against the urban elites who exploited the rural peasants. The motive was to end exploitation and oppression. Mark's Jesus, however, does not advocate the use of force to end oppression and exploitation. He rather calls the rich to give up and to share their possessions with the poor. In this way, Jesus not only challenged the value of the Roman Empire based on accumulation of possessions but also both the rich Jews who accumulated wealth while others perished in poverty, and the revolutionaries who used force to end exploitation and oppression. Jesus' way of dealing with economic oppression was renewal of life based on an egalitarian form of shared wealth.

Being Greatest vs. Being Least of All

Another core value of God's empire that Mark's Jesus teaches while on the way to Jerusalem is based on the value of being great. Being great relates to one's status, honor, or social position in the society. This teaching appears in the context of Jesus' second passion prediction. Jesus offers his teaching following the disciples' argument among themselves about who is the greatest among them (9:34). Jesus tells his disciples: "Whoever wants to be first must be last of all and servant of all" (9:35). To demonstrate his point, Jesus took a child in his arms and said to the disciples, "Whoever welcomes one such a child in my name welcomes me, and whoever welcomes me welcomes not me but the one who sent me" (9:37). Before I go into details about Jesus' teaching on the issue of greatness, I first put the value of being great in the context of the Roman imperial world.

Desire for greatness was one of the core values of the Roman Empire. The Romans wished to become greatest among others. This is demonstrated in their struggle for power among themselves and their conquest of other nations. For example, the Romans conquered other nations because they wanted to be recognized as the greatest nation in the world. The conquest of such nations as Athens, Sparta, Macedon, Greece, Asia, Gaul, Spain, Germany, Britain, Parthia, Carthage, Egypt, Alexandria, and others (*J.W.* 2:358–388) clearly demonstrate the Romans' desire to be the greatest of all human beings. The civil war in Rome following the death of Nero in 68 CE is another evidence of the power struggle among the Romans. Galba, Otho, Vitellius, and Vespasian fought successively in order to become the greatest among the Romans (*J. W.* 4:491–502). This indicates that in the Roman imperial world power was sought after and often inspired envy. Plutarch shows that Thucydides said that power necessarily attracts envy (*Vit. pud.* 535E). Juvenal, too, says, "Even those who don't want to kill anybody would like to have power to do it" (*Sat.* 10.96–97). So in the Roman Empire people fight and destroy others in order to become the greatest. It so happened because "Power was a mark of honor."[27]

In the Roman Empire, the emperor was the supreme ruler with enormous power. Power and wealth of the empire were concentrated in his hands and a few governing elite. The majority of the population lacked access to power, wealth, and status. The emperor's position and power were derived from Jupiter and the gods. According to Virgil, Jupiter had declared the Romans as "lords of the world" who were entrusted with "an empire without end" (*Aen.* 1.254, 278–279, 282). Loyalty to the emperor was considered as a means to gain more wealth, power, and status among the elite.[28] As Warren Carter has observed, "Cooperation with the emperor leads to increased wealth, power, and status for members of the elite. Given that the benefits of power are so great, it is not surprising that members of the elite regularly conflict with others and with the emperor as they struggle for 'fabulous wealth and immense power . . . privilege, and prestige.'"[29]

When the term "first" is used with respect to people, it refers to people with power and authority. Josephus uses it to refer to "men of the highest standing" (*Ant.* 18:7, 64), people who lead others (*Ant.* 20:125, 130, 132, 135), "the magistrates" (*Life* 185), and "the leading counselors" (*Life* 381). Josephus also employs the term to refer to the king's "first friends" (*Ant.* 13:85, 146). Indeed, when this word is used with reference to people it connotes the "most important, most prominent (people)."[30] In other words, the term refers to people who have power and authority over others.

Mark as well employs the term "first" to express a high social rank or status. The people of high social status who attend Herod Antipas's birthday banquet are introduced as the "first ones" (6:21). Those who want to have high positions of honor among others are said to be wishing to be "first"

---

27. Watson, "*Life of Aesop,*" 708.
28. Carter, *Pontius Pilate*, 36–38.
29. Ibid., 36–37.
30. BDAG, "πρῶτος," 892. Cf. *Ant.* 15:398; 7:230; 11:141; 20:180. See also Michaelis, "πρῶτος," *TDNT*, 6:865.

(9:35). In other cases, Mark employs the Greek words *megas* and *meizon* to express positions of power in society. For example, the courtiers who are among the "first ones" at Herod Antipas's birthday banquet are the "great ones, *megistasin*" (6:21); the rulers of the Gentiles are the "great ones, *hoi megaloi*" (10:42); and the disciples argue among themselves about who of them is "the greatest, *meizon*" (9:34). In another context, Mark links the concept of prestige with the concept of authority. The "greatest ones" who rule over Gentiles not only "lord over," they also exercise authority over and tyrannize others (10:42).[31] This implies that the "first" and the "great ones" wished to be served and to have glory and honor among their peers.

In the Roman Empire, people wished to be "first" and to be "great" among others. They killed others in order to gain, maintain, and enhance their positions of power and honor. Vespasian and his troops crushed the Jewish revolt in order to force the Jews to serve the interests of the imperial Rome. He also used troops loyal to him to overthrow Vitellius in order to become the supreme ruler of the Roman Empire (*J.W.* 4:655). During and after the war in Judea, Vespasian and Titus degraded others by ordering their crucifixions, the most shameful and humiliating death reserved for slaves.[32] They did this to maintain their positions of power.

In Mark's Gospel, Pontius Pilate represents the values of Rome in Judea. As a representative of Rome, Pilate does everything to protect the Roman interests. For example, he ordered the execution of John to protect Rome's interests and to maintain his own honor before the people. He also ordered the crucifixion of Jesus because he wished "to satisfy the crowd" (15:15). As Samuel observes, "[Pilate] succumbs to popular outcry and prefers a crucifixion (of Jesus) in order to safeguard the imperial interest rather than preserve a colonial subject who, in his sight, committed no evil."[33] Pilate's action in this case demonstrates that he set his mind "not on divine things but on human things" (8:33). Hence, in Mark rulers of the Gentiles serve as a model of leaders who abuse their power and authority.

The Roman authorities in Judea use the military to protect the interests of the Roman Emperor. At Pilate's order, the Roman troops humiliated and degraded Jesus. The soldiers mocked, beat, spat upon, and crucified Jesus along with two brigands, and left him hanging naked on the cross (15:16–32). Their treatment of Jesus is typical of the Roman imperial armies' response toward local revolutionary figures of the conquered nations who

31. Domination as a value of the Roman Empire will be developed further in the next section.

32. See Watson, "*Life of Aesop*," 710–12. Cf. Malina and Rohrbaugh, *Social-Science Commentary on the Synoptic Gospels*, 272–76.

33. Samuel, *Postcolonial*, 150.

opposed the Roman domination (cf. *J. W.* 2:223–236).[34] They treated Jesus as a rebel who threatened the Roman imperial authority,[35] their positions of power, honor, and wealth which they accumulated through their acquisition of land, and the exploitative tribute and taxes extracted from the impoverished conquered people.

By contrast, Mark's Jesus turns the values of the Roman Empire upside down. Jesus teaches that anyone who wishes to become "first" and "great" must become "last" in status. When his disciples argue among themselves about who was the greatest among them, Jesus says, "Whoever wants to be first must be last of all and servant of all" (9:35o). To drive his point home, Jesus took in his arms a child, one of the least in society, and then stated that anyone who welcomes such a child in his name welcomes him, and that whoever welcomes him, welcomes God who sent him (9:37). In another context, Jesus teaches that "Whoever does not receive the kingdom of God as a little child will never enter it" (10:15). The key here is that Jesus used the insignificant, disrespected and one who was not a proper recipient of honor to be the model of greatness in God's empire. The Greek term for child, also stood for a slave,[36] a person who was considered powerless and with the lowest status in society.[37] It is therefore important to note that Mark's Jesus not only equates himself and God with a child, but also likens entrance into God's empire to the reception of a child. The hearers of Mark may have understood Jesus' teaching as a contrast especially to the values of the Roman Empire that emphasized greatness in terms of being "first," powerful, and of being served.

The Jesus of Mark contrasted the imperial concept of being "first" and of being "great" in terms of gaining honor and being served by urging people to become "last of all and servant of all" (9:35). Jesus, categorically invites anyone who desires to be "great" and to be "first" to become a "servant" and a "slave" of all (10:43–45). Mark's hears may have interpreted this teaching as a contrast to the Romans' behavior of enslaving others. The teaching may have especially evoked memories of the war when Vespasian and Titus sent multitudes of Jewish prisoners of war into slavery.

In Mark, Jesus did not just use mere words to teach about the value of being least and of being slave in the service of others. Whatever he taught in words, he demonstrated it in deeds. He equated himself with the least in society, the child; he served others by liberating them from oppressive human,

---

34. Cf. Hengel, *Crucifixion*, 22–38, 46–85.
35. Brandon, *Trial of Jesus*, 103.
36. BDAG, "παῖς, παιδός, ὁ or ἡ," 750. Cf. *Ant.* 18:192.
37. Watson, "*Life of Aesop*," 700.

demonic, and natural forces that threatened their lives. Unlike Vespasian who healed a man with a useless hand because he would receive glory (Tacitus, *Hist.* 4:81), Jesus served others freely without strings attached and without seeking glory for himself. In his campaign to serve others, Jesus made no claim for his personal gain. He avoided a self claim that he was the Messiah and Son of God until when it was necessary for him to do so.[38] Mark's Jesus frequently identified himself in the third person as the Son of Humanity, a designation that associates him with his authority to forgive sins (2:5, 9–10), authority over the Sabbath (2:28), resurrection from the dead (8:31; 9:31; 10:33–34; cf. 16:6), and his future coming with great power and in glory (13:26–27). More significantly, Jesus' self-renunciation and service for others reaches its peak when he willingly relinquishes his whole life on the cross as a ransom for others (10:45).

Rhoads, Dewey, and Michie have offered an intriguing summary about Jesus' self-renunciation to become least in the service of others. This insightful summary read thus:

> Jesus' ultimate self-renunciation occurs when he relinquishes his own safety and undergoes execution for the sake of the larger purposes of God's rule. In a sense, Jesus meets all the standards of his own teaching in his death. His willingness to die expresses his total faith in God for his salvation. His crucifixion is the ultimate consequence of a life of service and of his refusal to oppress others to save himself. And in this tragic execution—misunderstood, falsely accused, abandoned—he is least of all.[39]

Jesus' willingness to empty himself unto death on the cross truly demonstrated his commitment to serve others as his fulfillment of God's will. His teaching about the value of being least demonstrated in his own life and deeds clearly shows that in God's empire one's greatness and importance depends on serving others and not on being "first" and being "served." In God's empire, whoever wants to be "great," "first," important, or to have honor, must be willing to become least and a slave of everyone.[40] It is "only by service does

---

38. Jesus acknowledges that he is the Messiah only when he is directly confronted by Peter (8:29), and when he responds to a specific question raised by the high priest, who wants to know whether he is "Messiah, the Son of the Blessed One" (14:61).

39. Rhoads et al. *Mark as Story*, 110.

40. For a detailed study on servanthood in Mark's Gospel, see Santos, *Slave of All*. Elsewhere Santos defines a slave as "someone who has no authority or privilege at all, and who is expected to serve his master with no recognition or commendation," 206. Other works focusing on servanthood include Seeley, "Rulership and Service in Mark 10:41–45," 234–50; Weinfeld, "The King as the Servant of the People," 190–94; van Wahlde, "Authority that Serves," 49–67.

one become great."[41] Wilhelm echoes this view when she notes that Jesus' point is that "true greatness resides in being a slave of all."[42]

Domination vs. No Lording over Others

Another core value of the Roman Empire that Mark's Jesus contrasts relates to domination of others. In the context of Jesus' third passion prediction, James and John asked to be granted positions of honor in Jesus' glory. They said, "Grant us to sit, one at your right hand and one at your left, in your glory" (10:37). This request served as foil for Jesus' further teaching on the values of God's empire. In response Jesus taught his disciples saying: "You know that the Gentiles those whom they recognize as their rulers lord it over them, and their great ones are tyrants over them. But it is not so among you, but whoever wishes to become great among you must be your servant, and whoever wishes to be first among you must be slave of all. For the Son of Man came not to be served but to serve, and to give his whole life as a ransom" (10:42–45).

The key in this passage is that Jesus not only challenges the abuse of power and authority by Gentile rulers, but also proposes the proper use of the same. He explicitly shows that Gentile rulers use power to "lord over" and to "tyrannize over" others (10:42). The Gentile rulers referred to in this passage are the Roman authorities. The Roman imperial power was set to aggrandize those in positions of power and authority to maintain power, to secure wealth, and to advance their social standing or status. As Donahue and Harrington have noted, the Roman imperial power "exercised primarily through force, intimidation, and a network of patronage that tried to insure absolute loyalty to the emperor."[43]

In Judea, the Roman imperial power was made visible in the figures of the Roman governors or procurators and their military forces. Both the governors and the soldiers served the interests of Caesar and the empire. Most governors abused their power in dealing with the people over whom they had authority. Philo, for example, accuses some governors who served under Caesar Tiberius for their tyranny. He writes: "Some, indeed, of those

---

41. Lane, *Mark*, 382. See also Higginson, *Leadership*, 45, 46, who comments in relation to the Greek term *doulos* that even though in the New Testament the term is used for "servant," the most accurate translation is "slave." He adds that the word "really does indicate a willingness to assume the lowliest of positions and to endure hardship and suffering on behalf of other people." He cites Kouzes and Posner as saying that "serving others is the most glorious and rewarding of all leadership tasks."

42. Wilhelm, *Preaching Mark*, 185.

43. Donahue and Harrington, *Mark*, 316.

who held governorship in the time of Tiberius and his father Caesar, had perverted their office of guardian and protector into domination and tyranny and had spread hopeless misery through their territories with their venality, robbery, unjust, expulsion and banishment of quite innocent people, execution of magnates without trial" (*Flacc.* 105). Similarly, Tacitus says of Antonius Felix who was governor of Judea in 52–60 CE that he "practiced every kind of cruelty and lust, wielding the power of a king with all the instincts of a slave" (*Hist.* 5.9–10).

Josephus, too, writes of several Roman governors who abused their power. For example, he reports of Albinus who was procurator in 63–64 CE that:

> There was no form of villainy which he omitted to practice. Not only did he, in his official capacity, steal and plunder private property and burden the whole nation with extraordinary taxes, but he accepted ransoms from their relatives on behalf of those who had been imprisoned for robbery by the local councils or by former procurators; and the only persons left in gaol as malefactors were those who failed to pay. Now . . . the revolutionary party in Jerusalem was stimulated; the influential men among their number secured from Albinus, by means of bribes, immunity for their seditious practices. (*J.W.* 2:272–276)

Indeed, Albinus profited from the extra taxes he imposed upon the Jews, from stealing property, bribes, and from attacks on the rich people. However, comparing the character of Albinus with his successor Gessius Florus who was procurator in 64–66 CE, Albinus was an angel. Josephus states that when one compares the character of Albinus with that of Florus, the latter would appear as a "paragon of virtue" (*J.W.* 2:277). Describing Florus's character, Josephus writes:

> as though he had been sent as a hangman of condemned criminals, abstained from no form of robbery or violence . . . he was the most cruel of men; for shame, none more shameless than he . . . To make gain out of individuals seemed beneath him: he stripped whole cities, ruined entire populations, and almost went the length of proclaiming throughout the country that all were at liberty to practice brigandage, on condition that he received his share of the spoils. Certainly his avarice brought desolation upon all the cities, and caused many to desert their haunts and seek refuge in foreign provinces. (*J.W.* 2:278–279)

From this citation, Florus was surely a terrible and corrupt procurator. Besides ruling for the purpose of personal benefits through robbery, bribery, and exploitation, he promoted brigandage from which he got his share of spoils. As a result of his brutality and misrule, the Jews begged Cestius Gallus, governor of Syria "to have compassion on the calamities of the nation, and loudly denounced Florus as the ruin of the country" (*J.W.* 2:280). It was under Florus's governorship that the outbreak of the Roman-Jewish War of 66–70 CE occurred.

In another context, Josephus likens the Roman governors in Judea to blood sucking flies in relation to their oppression and exploitation. Commenting on Tiberius's tendency to keep governors in office for a long time, Josephus writes that the emperor claimed that he purposely did so:

> out of consideration for the feelings of the subject-peoples. For it was a law of nature that governors are prone to engage in extortion. When appointments were not permanent, but were for short terms, or liable to be cancelled without notice, the spur to peculation was even greater. If, on the contrary, those appointed kept their posts longer, they would be gorged with their robberies and would by the very bulk of them be more sluggish in pursuit of further gain. Let succession come rapidly, however, and those who were the destined spoil of the governors could never do enough, for there would be no intervals of relaxation in which those already glutted with their spoils might abate somewhat of their grasping avarice, since before that could happen the moment would come to depart. (*Ant.* 18:172–173)

Josephus continues to show how Tiberius demonstrated this point with the following fable:

> Once a man lay wounded, and a swarm of flies hovered about his wounds. A passer-by took pity on his evil plight and, in the belief that he did not raise a hand because he could not, was about to step up and shoo them off. The wounded man, however, begged him to think no more of doing anything about it. At this the man spoke up and asked him why he was not interested in escaping from his wretched condition. 'Why,' said he, 'you would put me in a worse position if you drove them off. For these flies have already had their fill of blood, they no longer feel such a pressing need to annoy me but are in some measure slack. But if others were to come with a fresh appetite, they would take over my now weakened body and that would indeed be the death of me.' . . . (Emperor Tiberius) said, for the same reason took the precaution of not dispatching governors continually to the subject-peoples who had been brought to ruin by so many thieves; for the governors would harry them utterly like flies.

Their natural appetite for plunder would be reinforced by their expectation of being speedily deprived of that pleasure. (*Ant.* 18:174–177)

From this fable we understand that the Roman governors in Judea were not only oppressive and exploitative; they were also very corrupt. Overall, the Roman governors in Judea exercised "enormous power in keeping order (i.e. submission to Rome), collecting taxes . . . commanding troops, administering justice (that protects Rome's elite interests against provincial troublemakers) . . . imposing death sentence on those who threatened Roman elite interests, and keeping local elite satisfied."[44] Such roles are expressive of how the Roman governors used their power and authority to defend and promote Roman interests in Judea.

The Roman rulers used the military to control others. The primary function of the army was to "enforce submission and to intimidate those who contemplated revolt."[45] The Roman's campaign to crush the revolt in Judea is a vivid evidence of how the army served to protect the interests of the Roman Empire. One of the ways the military fulfilled its role to terrorize, to intimidate, and to compel the conquered people to submission was the use of crucifixions, the most horrific and painful form of torture and execution (cf. *J.W.* 7:202–203).[46] The crucifixions were employed "as a means of waging war and securing peace, of wearing down rebellious cities under siege, of breaking the will of conquered peoples and the bringing mutinous troops or unruly provinces under control."[47] Indeed, crucifixion was used to strike fear among those who would dare to threaten the empire and its interests. A speech of a British chief recorded by Tacitus summarizes the Roman imperial domination, exploitation and tyranny. The British chief criticized the Roman imperial power saying, "Robbers of the world . . . to plunder, butcher, steal, these things they misname empire; they make a desolation and they call it peace . . . our goods and chattels go for tribute; our land and harvests in requisitions of gain; life and limb themselves are

---

44. Carter, *Roman Empire*, 38. Cf. Rhoads, *Israel in Revolution*, 28.

45. Carter, *Roman Empire*, 4–5. See also Neyrey, "Honour and Shame," 113–37; Hanson and Oakman, *Palestine in the Time of Jesus*, 85–87.

46. Josephus reports on a number of crucifixions administered by the Roman authorities in Judea. He reports on the crucifixion of two thousand Jews ordered by general Varus in 4 BCE (*J.W.* 2:71–72; *Ant.* 17:195), the crucifixions of the brigands ordered by Felix, the Roman procurator in Judea, in 52–60 CE (*J.W.* 2:353) and those ordered by Festus, the procurator in 60–62 CE (*J.W.* 2:271). See also Hengel, *Crucifixion*, 26, especially note 17. A further discussion of crucifixions related to the war will be made later in this study.

47. Hengel, *Crucifixion*, 46.

worn out in making roads through marsh and forest to accomplishment of gibes and blows" (*Agric.* 31.1–2).

The Roman imperial domination also expressed itself through the oppressive taxes imposed upon the conquered peoples. For example, as conquered people the Jews were forced to pay tribute to Rome. Failure to pay it was tantamount to rebellion against Rome.[48] Some passages from Josephus may help to clarify how failure to pay tribute to Caesar was equal to declaring war with Rome. When the Jews stopped sending tribute to Caesar and proposed to send an embassy to Emperor Nero to denounce Florus, King Agrippa II warned them not to make war with Rome. The Jews, however, cried out that "they were not taking up arms against the Romans, but against Florus, because of all the wrong that he had done them." King Agrippa II, however, responded stating that their refusal to pay tribute to Caesar was indeed an act of rebellion against Rome, and not against Florus as they claimed (*J.W.* 2:402–405). To avoid the Roman's actions for their non-payment of tribute, they heeded to the kings warning, and arrears of the total amount of forty talents were rapidly collected (*J.W.* 2:406).

Josephus's passage on King Agrippa's speech just referred to above is immediately followed by another passage that refers to a tax incident that triggered the war with Rome. That passage gives an account about the cessation of the sacrifices offered on behalf of Caesar. The passage reads:

> Eleazar, son of Ananias the high-priest, a very daring youth, then holding the position of captain, persuaded those who officiated in the Temple services to accept no gift or sacrifice from a foreigner. This action laid the foundation of the war with the Romans; for the sacrifices offered on behalf of that nation and the emperor were in consequence rejected. The chief priests and the notables earnestly besought them not to abandon the customary offering for their rulers, but the priests remained obdurate . . . Thereupon the principle citizens assembled with chief priests and the most notable Pharisees to deliberate on the

---

48. Carter, *Roman Empire*, 28; Horsley, "Jesus and Empire," 89, states that "Roman domination of subject peoples focused on the tribute. The Romans viewed failure to 'render to Caesar' as tantamount to rebellion, and were prepared to enforce their demand with punitive military action." Cf. Hooker, *Gospel according to Saint Mark*, 279, who remarks that "The imposition of the tax, like the arbitrary parceling out the Jewish territory to suit the convenience of Rome, was regarded by the Jews as an outrageous act of interference on the part of their foreign rulers. It caused the simmering hatred of Rome to boil over in the revolt under Judas referred to in Acts 5:37, and according to Josephus (*Ant.* 18:1–10, 23–24) it gave rise to the Zealot movement, and so led to the revolt of AD 70." See also Reiser, *Jesus in Solidarity with His People*, 127, who states, "To pay the poll tax, or any tax, implies an acknowledgment of the claims of some earthly authority."

position of affairs, now that they were faced with what seemed irreparable disaster. Deciding to try the effect of an appeal to the revolutionaries, they called the people together before the bronze gate—that of the inner Temple facing the eastward. They began expressing the keenest indignation at the audacity of this revolt and at their country being thus threatened with so serious a war. (*J.W.* 2:409–411).

These passages clearly demonstrate how serious non-payment of taxes and tribute to Rome was. It was immediately after the cessation of the tribute to Rome that the imperial power responded with its military might that led to the outbreak of the war in 66 CE.

When Vespasian became emperor, he too imposed a poll-tax upon all the Jews regardless of whether one participated in the war or not. "On all Jews, wheresoever resident, he imposed a poll-tax of two drachms, to be paid annually into the Capital as formerly contributed by them to the temple of Jerusalem" (*J.W.* 7:218). This kind of tax was over and above the property tax (cf. *Life* 429). The tax was not only a burden among the Jews but also caused distress among them in that it was used to reconstruct the temple Capitoline Jupiter. The use of the tax to support the imperial cult must have added salt on the wounds of Jews as a result of the fall of the temple in Jerusalem.

Emperor Vespasian was not immune from blame for his exploitative behavior. A Roman historian Suetonius accuses him of using his governors to accumulate his own wealth. He says: "He is even believed to have had the habit of designedly advancing the most rapacious of his procurators to higher posts, that they might be the richer when he later condemned them [and confiscated their wealth through fines]; in fact it was common talk that he used these men as sponges because he, so to speak, soaked them when they were dry and squeezed them when they were wet" (*Vesp.* 16). This passage is expressive of Vespasian's exploitative behavior. Vespasian used his power to appoint procurators who exploited the conquered peoples. In turn, when those procurators became richer, the emperor confiscated their wealth to increase his own. Hence, Vespasian used his power and authority to extract wealth from the dominated people using the exploitative procurators.

In Mark, the Roman domination and exploitation is expressed in various ways. For example, the Roman imperial power in Mark is represented by the emperor who is mentioned in the question about payment of tribute to Caesar (12:13–17); Pilate the Gentile governor who represents Caesar's authority in Judea (15:1–15); and the Roman soldiers who serve to maintain order in Judea for the benefit of Rome (15:16–24). The abuse of power by the Romans has been underscored in Jesus' words, and in the actions of both Pilate and the Roman soldiers. While Mark's Jesus highlights the tyranny of the Roman governors when he warns his disciples of the trials and persecutions before governors for his sake (13:9), Pilate demonstrates his tyranny when he authorizes the execution of Jesus (15:15).[49] The soldiers intimidate and terrorize people in order to safeguard the interests of the Roman Empire. Their role is explicit in their dealing with Jesus. They humiliate him in that they mock, beat, spit upon him, strip his garments, crucify, and finally leave him on the cross naked (15:16–24). They treated Jesus as if he were a criminal or a rebel who threatened the interests of the Roman imperial power. The soldiers' actions were meant to be a way to protect the imperial values over against the values of God's empire proclaimed and advocated by Jesus.

Based on the evidence shown above, it is evident that the Roman authorities operated against what God wills for people. Their values are based on "human things" (8:33). Not only do they lord over people, they also tyrannize them. Because of fear of losing their positions of power, status, and wealth, they use military power to intimidate, to control, and to kill others in order to protect their own positions of power, possessions, and honor.

By contrast, Jesus teaches that in God's empire, power is not to be used to lord over people. While the Gentile rulers lord over and tyrannize people, "it is not so among you (his disciples)" (10:43). In God's empire, power is not to be used to dominate and to oppress people the way the Gentile rulers do. Instead of using power and authority to lord over and to tyrannize people, those in positions of power are urged to refrain from the abuse of power, but use power to serve others instead. The disciples of Jesus are encouraged to take the role of a servant and of a slave in order to serve everyone, even to the point of risking their own lives.

In the Gospel of Mark, Jesus has power and authority from God and uses it to benefit people. Unlike the authorities who use their power and authority to lord over—to oppress, to exploit, to tyrannize, and to kill, Jesus uses his power to overcome oppressive nonhuman forces that oppress people. He uses his power from God to liberate in that he uses it to overcome illnesses, demons, hunger, and storms. Indeed, Jesus uses his power to heal, to drive out demons, to calm severe and dangerous storms, to raise the dead, to multiply fish and bread to feed thousands of hungry people, to forgive sins, and to remove uncleanness, but has no power to control people. Jesus uses his power from God to liberate people from the oppressive forces, and he never uses it to control humans. He cannot make people do what they

---

49. Cf. Senior, "Swords and Clubs," 16.

do not want to do. For example, he tells the healed leper to be quiet, but the healed leper proclaims freely (1:44–45); he tells the man freed from the legion to go home in the Gerasenes land to bear witness of the mercy that the Lord has shown him, but the man goes to the Decapolis and proclaims there (5:1, 19–20); and he warns people not to publicize the healing of the man who was deaf and mute, but people zealously proclaim it (7:36). Jesus does deeds of power only when people have faith, for in Nazareth he performs no works of power due to lack of faith (6:5).

Moreover, when Jesus calls for the fruits of the vineyard from the leaders of Israel he neither employs force nor punishes the farmers from their failure to produce fruits. He leaves the punishment with God (12:1–12). It follows from these observations that although Jesus has power, he does not use it to control, oppress, or to lord over others. Neither does he use power to acquire wealth and to gain honor for himself. Instead, Jesus uses power from God to serve and to liberate people. He exercises power and authority for the advantage of others.

In his teaching about power, Jesus calls for a completely different kind of leadership. He advocates and insists upon servitude to all people. Wilhelm offers an insightful and remarkable expression about Jesus' teaching about power in Mark when she writes that: "Jesus completely overturns all earthly perceptions of *power*, since he does not base his authority on lording it over others but on serving others. In a series of paradoxical statements, Jesus redefines the nature of leadership not in terms of patronage but servanthood, not according to privilege but slavery, not seeking economic advantage over others but offering his life as payment to secure the release of others."[50] This understanding of Jesus' teaching about and use of power is indeed compelling. It really underscores the core of Jesus' warning of his disciples not to exercise power in terms of worldly values. The disciples were to avoid using power and authority in terms of patronage, for personal privileges or economic gains, but to exercise servanthood leadership for the advantage of others.

Mark's Jesus opposed the use of violence in dealing with oppression. I have argued elsewhere that the Romans acquired land and wealth for their own benefits, and that they exercised power to lord over and tyrannize people. The Jewish authorities also imitated these Roman imperial values. They accumulated wealth in order to have status and to gain more power to lord over others. This is also true for the Jewish revolutionaries who fought the Romans. They also mimicked the Gentiles in that they wanted to establish their own territory. During the civil war in Jerusalem, each of the leaders of

---

50. Wilhelm, *Preaching Mark*, 185. Italics are original.

the Jewish groups struggled to have power to dominate others. They hated the Romans and wanted to remove them out of their holy land by force. They interpreted the ambiguous oracle to mean that the messiah was to be one among them and fought to force its fulfillment because they desired to have power for themselves. By contrast, even though Jesus also opposed the Romans, he did not use military force. Instead, he used non-violence means to resist the Romans. In this way, Jesus opposed and critiqued both the Romans and the Jewish revolutionaries. He opposed both the domination of others and the use of violence to deal with domination and oppression.

Jesus' teaching on not to lord over others would have an appealing impact on Mark's hearers. Being aware that domination was one of the factors for the war and that the revolutionaries' military response to alleviate the situation led to catastrophic results on the part of the Jews, they possibly conceded with Jesus' teaching. They may have understood that domination and lording over others as well as using force to deal with oppression and domination, all contradict the values of God's empire which Jesus was advocating. They may have been challenged to avoid any form of domination in favor of the role of a servant and of a slave in serving others.

Contrast to Jewish Authorities: Not Like the Gentile Rulers

In Mark, the Jewish authorities are presented in various groups of characters. They include King Herod Antipas, the Herodians, the chief priests, the Pharisees, the scribes, the elders, the Sadducees, and two individuals, Jairus who is a ruler of a synagogue and Joseph of Arimathea, a member of the council.[51] Except for the scribes who is said to be "not far from the kingdom of God" (12:34), Joseph of Arimathea who looked "for the kingdom of God" (15:43), and Jairus who trusted in Jesus for the restoration of his daughter from illness and death (5:21–24, 35–43), all the Jewish authorities appear as Jesus' opponents and reflect the values of the Roman Empire.

In the previous part I have indicated that wealth, power, and status were core values of the Roman Empire. I have shown that the Roman ruling authorities loved to accumulate wealth for themselves, to use power to lord over and tyrannize others, and to destroy others in order to save themselves and to protect their positions of power. It is evident from this part that the Roman authorities also desired to be great and to be first in order to be honored, and that they enslaved others in order to be served. As such, the Roman authorities operated to impress people and not according to God's will. As we shall see, the Jewish authorities mirrored these values of the Roman Empire.

---

51. Malbon, "Jewish Leaders in the Gospel of Mark," 263–64.

Herod and the Herodians

Herod Antipas ruled Galilee from 4 BCE to 39 CE as a puppet of the Romans. During his reign, he exercised the values of the Roman Empire. For example, because he did not have a royal title, he desired "a kingdom" in order to possess a high rank of a king, which would ensure him more power, glory, and wealth through ownership and control of land (*Ant.* 18:240–254).[52] As a ruler of Galilee, Antipas used his power to lord over people through oppressive taxes he collected to support his administration and to meet costs for his court, massive building projects, and lavish lifestyle (cf. 6:21).[53] Antipas's building construction included the cities of Tiberius in Galilee and Julia in Perea (*J.W.* 2:168). Naming the cities after the emperor and the emperor's mother respectively may be viewed as his way of impressing the emperor in order to gain some special favor from the imperial supreme ruler.

In Mark's Gospel, Herod Antipas appears as a ruler characterized by Roman imperial values. First, he models his court after the imperial pattern. At his birthday banquet, he invites only the high ranking people: "his courtiers and officers and the leading men of Galilee" (6:21) and the soldiers who guide his palace (6:27).[54] Next, Antipas has accumulated wealth that enables him to prepare an extravagant banquet he enjoys with important men in Galilee. The banquet suggests lifestyle of kings. Antipas's wealth is also expressed in the promise he makes to give half of his kingdom to his daughter, Herodias, because of her impressive dancing. Mark writes that "When his daughter Herodias came in and danced, she pleased Herod and

---

52. Josephus shows that following Emperor Gaius Caligula's appointment of Herod Agrippa II to be king over Trachonitis and Gaulanitis (once Philip's tetrarchy) and the tetrarchy of Lysania (*Ant.* 18:237, 106–108), Herodias provoked her husband, Antipas, to also seek a royal title. She pushed Antipas to go to Rome to request "the high position," "the acquisition of a kingdom," to seek "a throne at any cost" (*Ant.* 18:243–245). Unfortunately, Antipas's desire to gain a kingdom at any cost and become a king ended in his banishment to a foreign land. It is important to note that Mark's use of the title "king" in reference to Antipas (6:16, 22, 25. 26, 27) reflects local custom. The term also expresses an irony in that although Herod Antipas desires to be "king" and models his court after Rome, he is not a king in the real sense of the Roman perception of a king. Mark therefore identifies Antipas with the title that he failed to secure, his desire for which caused Emperor Caligula to send him into exile (*J.W.* 2:181–183). Antipas's desire to bear a royal title may have reflected his wish to gain more power, in order to be able to confiscate land from the peasants.

53. The taxes that Antipas collected were over and above the tribute to Caesar and the temple tax that was exacted in the form of tithes and offerings. See Horsley, "Jesus and Empire," 79.

54. The modeling of the court after the manner of Rome may have been motivated by his experience, for he grew up in Rome and received his education in the context of the imperial court. See Horsley, "Jesus and Empire," 79.

his guests; and the king said to the girl, 'Ask me for whatever you wish, and I will give it.' And he solemnly swore to her, 'Whatever you ask me, I will give you, even half of my kingdom'" (6:22-23). That the king promises to give whatever his daughter wished and the fact that he indicates that he owns a kingdom suggest that Herod Antipas had many possessions. While he spends his wealth in lavish feasts with distinguished and important figures of Galilee and promises to give half of his kingdom to his daughter, Herod Antipas cared less for the Galilean peasants who live "like sheep without a shepherd" (6:34).

In the Gospel of Mark, Herod Antipas also appears as a tyrannical ruler in that he uses his power to destroy innocent people. At his birthday banquet, he ordered the execution of John the Baptist (6:27) even though he had acknowledged that John was "a righteous and holy man" (6:20). Like the Roman authorities, he uses soldiers to kill people who threatened his interests (6:17-18, 27-28). Antipas's motive behind the execution of John was fear of losing honor before his important guests, the eminent and leading men of Galilee. He executed John to protect and maintain his own honor. His abuse of power expressed in the arrest and execution of John "a righteous and holy man" serves as a model of the kings before whom people would appear and be persecuted because of their loyalty to Jesus (13:9). Another important element related to Herod Antipas's imitation of the Roman imperial values relates to his making decisions to impress people. Like Pilate who ordered the crucifixion of Jesus to satisfy the crowd, Herod Antipas ordered the execution of John in order to satisfy the wishes of his wife and daughter (6:24-25). Herod Antipas did what people want against what God wants for people (8:33), hence manifesting the values of the Roman Empire.

Hearers of Mark's Gospel may have associated Herod Antipas's story with Herod Agrippa II for a number of reasons. First, both rulers bear the name of Herod. Since Mark uses only the family name, Herod, hearers may be free to associate the character with someone familiar to them bearing the same name. Second, the actions of the two rulers reveal a number of parallels. For example, both rulers served as puppets of the Romans; both kings hosted figures of high social standing with lavish banquets: Herod Agrippa II hosted Vespasian and his troops at Caesarea Philippi just as Antipas held his birthday banquet with his courtiers and leaders of Galilee. For Mark's hearers, the name Herod may have evoked memories of Herod Agrippa who had been ruler of Judea for the entire period of the war, and the events of the war associated with him.[55]

    55. For the role of King Agrippa II in relation to the Roman-Jewish War of 66-70 CE, see chapter 1, under the section on "Criterion on Correlation," particularly under "People and Empire" (pp. 20-26).

Regarding the Herodians, these were a group of people with authority and political power. They owned large land estates (cf. 12:1–12) and gave strong political support to Herod Antipas.[56] Like Herod Antipas, they also exhibit the values of imperial Rome. Early in Mark's story, the Herodians plot with the Pharisees how to destroy Jesus, because Jesus has saved life on the Sabbath (3:1–6); and latter they conspire with the Pharisees to entrap Jesus on the issues of payment of tribute to Caesar (12:13–17). They also plot to kill Jesus because they believe he is a threat to their positions of power. Due to the successful life-giving campaign in Galilee, Jesus' fame spread all over Galilee and the surrounding regions (cf. 3:1:28; 6:16). Consequently, crowds of people flocked toward Jesus from different places (cf. 3:7–8, 32; 4:1; 5:21, 24; 6:31, 34, 44; 8:1, 9, etc.). Perhaps because of Jesus' success in his campaign, the Herodians felt that their own fame and positions of power were in danger. Hence in order to protect their positions of power and honor, they plotted to eliminate him. Their actions are surely guarded by human desires to aggrandize themselves and not to do God's will as the Jesus of Mark sees it.

The Judean Priestly Aristocrats

The high priestly aristocrats served as the governing class of Judea under the watch of the Roman governor. Even though in some cases the high priests were appointed by a Roman governor (*Ant.* 18:26),[57] they were primarily appointed by the king of Judea (*Ant.* 20:247–251). After the death of the kings Herod the Great and his son Archelaus, "the priests were entrusted with the leadership of the nation" (*J. W.* 20:251). Since they were appointed into the office by kings who received their appointments from the emperor, they served the interests of both the king (*J. W.* 1:665; 2:94–97, 181, 214) and the emperor who put the king in power (*J. W.* 2:320–322, 352, 403–405).[58]

The priestly aristocrats also imitated the values of the imperial power. For example, as entrusted rulers, the high priests were responsible for keeping order in Judea and for ensuring that tribute to Rome was paid. This is the reason they opposed the cessation of tribute for Rome that Eleazar ben Ananias championed to stop. Josephus reports that although the chief priests and the notables earnestly besought the lower-class priests not to

---

56. Oakman, "Countryside in Luke-Acts," 164. He points out that the Herodians controlled land in Israel under oversight from the imperial agent, the Roman governor.

57. Here it is reported that the Roman governor of Syria, Quirinius, appointed Ananus to be high priest. Ananus held the office in the years 6–15 CE.

58. Cf. Mendels, *Rise and Fall of Jewish Nationalism*, 359.

stop sending tribute to Rome, the later refused (*J.W.* 2:410). Consequently, the high priests along with "the principal citizens" and "the most notable Pharisees" gathered to deliberate how to control the revolt in order to avoid the war with Rome (*J.W.* 2:411; cf. 2:405).[59]

Since the chief priests wished to save themselves—their positions of power, honor, and their property—they assembled to find ways to protect themselves. For example, when they perceived that the revolt was so inevitable and imminent, they assembled to seek a way to exonerate themselves from blame for failure to control it and thereby to protect their own positions of power and property. Josephus reports that: "The leading citizens, perceiving that it was now beyond their power to suppress the insurrection and that they would be the first victims of the vengeance of Rome, took steps to exonerate themselves from blame, and dispatched two deputations, one to Florus . . . and another to Agrippa . . . They besought them both to crush the revolt before it became insuperable" (*J.W.* 2:418–420). The leading citizens referred to in this passage are the chief priests who served as the rulers of the Jewish nation (*Ant.* 20:251). It is evident from this passage that they served the Roman interests as well as their own. The fact that they sought military support from the Roman governor Florus and King Agrippa II to crush the revolt because they believed they would be the first victims of the Romans' vengeance is strong evidence of their collaboration with the Romans against their own people. Their motive for seeking military support was also to save themselves, their positions of power, and their possessions. Horsley is therefore right when he states that the high priests "constituted the face of the Roman imperial rule in Judea."[60]

Further, the Judean priestly aristocrats also used their power to lord over people. Over and above the tribute to Caesar and the Herodian taxes, the high priestly aristocrats demanded revenues from the peasantry for their personal advantage.[61] They used "their positions of power to feather their own nests of privilege."[62] One of Josephus's priestly colleagues, for example, is said to have "amassed a large sum of money from tithes which they accepted as their priestly due" (*Life* 63). The revolt of the lower-class priests manifested in their cessation of gifts for Caesar, and the revolutionaries' burning of public archives in order "to destroy the money-lenders' bonds . . . to prevent the recovery of debts . . . to win over a host of grateful debtors and to cause a rising of the poor against the rich" (*J.W.* 2:427) vividly demonstrate that

---

59. Cf. Carter, *Pontius Pilate*, 38–39.
60. Horsley, "Jesus and Empire," 80.
61. Horsley, *Hearing the Whole Story*, 113. Carter, *Pontius Pilate*, 39.
62. Horsley, "Jesus and Empire," 80.

the high priestly elite were oppressive against their own people. Because of their abuse of power, the high priests along with the notables were among the targets of the revolutionaries' attacks. Josephus reports elsewhere that when the revolutionaries advanced against their enemies "the notables and chief priests" escaped in order to save their lives (J.W. 2:428).[63] Indeed, the chief priestly elite were the target of attacks because they used their power to oppress and to lord over people for their own advantage.

In Mark, the high priestly aristocrats involve the Pharisees, the scribes, the Sadducees, and the elders who serve as retainers of the governing elite. Together they form the Jewish national leadership.[64] As the aristocrats of Judea, they use their positions of power and authority to lord over and exercise tyranny over people. They plan to kill those who oppose them in order to maintain their status of honor. For example, the Pharisees plot with the Herodians to kill Jesus because he healed on the Sabbath (3:4, 6); the Pharisees and the scribes make oppressive laws and use them to harm others (2:24; 3:4), and they use the *corban* law to prevent people from caring for their parents (7:8-12). The chief priests and the scribes seek to destroy Jesus because of his teaching and actions in the temple (11:18). Although the chief priests, the scribes, and the elders recognize Jesus' authority, they question the source of that authority (11:27-33). This indeed is an allegory for them. They beat and kill the servants and the son of the vineyard owner because they want to control the vineyard of Israel for themselves. When they recognized that Jesus' parable is said against them, they attempt to arrest him, but fail to accomplish their plan because of the crowd which they fear (12:1-12).

The Pharisees also exemplify the Roman imperial values. With the Herodians, they plot to entrap Jesus on the question about tribute to Caesar (12:13-17). Since they pay the imperial tax (though as Jews do so reluctantly), they exercise the "politics of imperial power." They pay the imperial

---

63. Other examples from Josephus of the actions of revolutionaries against high priests, the Jewish elite, and the rich can be found. Consider, for instance, the murder of Jonathan the high priest by the Sicarii (J.W. 2:256); the looting of "the houses of the wealthy" and the killing of the rich (J.W. 2:265); the arrest and imprisonment of "the most eminent citizens," including Antipas (a relative of Agrippa II in charge of the public treasury) and Levias, one of the nobles, and Syphas ben Aregetes (both members of the royal family), and other persons of high social standing (J.W. 4:138-146); and the murder of all men of authority, including "Gurion, a person of exalted rank and birth" (J.W. 4:357); the list goes on.

64. Carter, *Pontius Pilate*, 39, notes that "When the gospels refer to chief priests, Sadducees, leading Pharisees, and scribes, with whom Jesus is in conflict, they refer to Jewish officials often based in Jerusalem and its Temple. They form the ruling aristocracy who in alliance with Rome has immense political, social, and economic power."

tax for fear of the outcome for resisting the Roman imperial power.[65] So the Pharisees do what humans want in order to keep their loyalty to Caesar and not to God as Mark sees it. Doing what Caesar wants is over and above their motive to destroy Jesus as suggested by their plot to trap him.

The scribes, too, embody the values of the Roman imperial power. They come down from Jerusalem to Galilee and accuse Jesus of being possessed by Beelzebul and of driving out demons by the power of the prince of demons (3:22). Their accusation was intended to divert people's attention from Jesus and his works of power, seeking to suppress Jesus' popularity and fame. This could be one of the strategies that the scribes used to protect their status and honor, which they saw was under threat due to the increase of Jesus' fame. Like the other Jewish elite, the scribes love to occupy positions of honor and to be honored. They want to be greeted at the market places, and to occupy the best seats in the synagogues and at banquets. They also exploit widows in order to accumulate wealth for themselves; and make long hypothetical prayers to attract honor from people (12:38-40). Their longer prayers may be viewed as their economic motivation to acquire wealth. Senior is therefore correct when he points out that the "scribes are condemned for their lust for prestige and their exploitation of widows."[66]

In Mark, the Judean authorities use their position of power against Jesus. The scribes and the chief priests together plotted to arrest and destroy Jesus (14:1).[67] After Jesus' arrest in the garden of Gethsemane by the agents of the chief priests and the scribes (14:43-50), the Sanhedrin meet to seek false testimony in order to destroy Jesus (14:53, 55), and then hands him over to Pilate (15:1), who finally delivers him up "to be crucified" (15:14-15). At the crucifixion, the chief priests and the scribes mock Jesus because "he cannot save himself" (15:31).[68] The Judean authorities did all these in order to maintain their positions of power to control others, to gain more wealth, and to advance their honor.

Fear was at the centre of the Judean authorities' motive to seek to maintain their positions of power and status (15:15). For example, Herod put

---

65. Reiser, *Jesus in Solidarity with His People*, 125, 127. His idea of "politics of compromise" is borrowed from Horsley, *Jesus and the Spiral of Violence*, 307-17.

66. Cf. Senior, "Swords and Clubs," 15.

67. The scribes' participation in the plot against Jesus might have been motivated by envy: Jesus, unlike them, taught people with authority (1:22).

68. Rhoads, *Reading Mark*, 47. See also Samuel, *Postcolonial*, 147, who observes that the way the Jewish authorities handled the trial of Jesus highlights their role of serving the interests of Rome. He notes that the Jewish authorities "are primarily instrumental for the arrest, the handing over and impending execution of Jesus by the Roman colonial authorities. The trial also exposes the corruption in the judicial system headed by the chief priest."

John the Baptist in jail and then executed him because he was afraid of him (6:20); the high priestly class delivered Jesus up because they were afraid of his popularity (11:18; 15:10). Because of Jesus' popularity, the authorities were afraid of losing their positions of power and authority (cf. 12:7), and hence the loss of their honor in the eyes of the people (6:26; 11:18; 12:12). In Jerusalem, the Judean governing aristocrats bent the law and arrested Jesus secretly (14:43–50); bribed witnesses "against Jesus to put him to death" (14:55–65); they called a kangaroo court (15:3); and then, incited the crowd to release Barabbas instead of Jesus (15:11). The motive for all these actions was the authorities' attempt to maintain and protect their power and status. Their desire was to protect their status and their authority over people just as was the case for the Jewish authorities during the war. Their fear was an expression of their lack of faith and trust in God. Unlike fear, faith in God promotes courage in the face of threat and loss.[69]

In general, the Jewish authorities in Mark use their power and authority to lord over and to terrorize people. Their power and authority guaranteed that taxes and tribute to Rome were paid. Their goal was to maintain their positions of power, honor, and control over people. Their opposition against Jesus who used power from God to liberate people demonstrated that they had no trust in God. Their actions were evidence of the fact that they had no love for God and for the neighbor (cf. 12:28–33). Clearly their authority did not represent God, but the human empire of Rome because they acted in human terms (8:33) "lording over people" (10:42).

By contrast, Jesus taught that in God's empire authorities are not to abuse their power. Contrary to the desire "to gain the whole world," Jesus taught his disciples to be willing to give up everything for the sake of the good news (8:35) and to share wealth with the poor (10:21). In contrast to the desire to be "great" and "first," Jesus urged his disciples to willingly become "least," "slaves," and servants of all (10:35, 43–45). Moreover, in contrast to the use of power and authority abusively, Jesus taught that those who wish to be rulers or leaders must become slaves and servants of those whom they have authority over them. Responding to the request of James and John who wished to be granted positions of power and honor in his glory, Jesus said: "You know that among the Gentiles those whom they recognize as their rulers lord it over them, and their great ones are tyrants over them. But it is not so among you; but whoever wishes to become great among you must be your servant, and whoever wishes to be first among you must be slave of all. For the Son of Man came not to be served but to serve, and to give his whole life for others" (10:42–45). Mark's hearers may

---

69. Rhoads, *Reading Mark*, 48.

have interpreted the expression "not so among you" as a direct contrast to the Jewish authorities who exercised their power and authority in terms of the values of the Roman authorities. Like the Roman authorities, the Jewish authorities lord over and terrorize others. By contrast, Mark's Jesus urges his disciples not to exercise power and authority in the manner of the Gentile rulers. He encourages his followers to use power and authority for serving everyone as slaves and servants do. Jesus' phrase "not so among you" may have been an indirect contrast to the Jewish authorities who imitated the values of the Roman imperial power.

Contrast to Jewish Revolutionaries

Take Up the Cross vs. Crucifixion

One of the contrasts that Mark makes to the Jewish revolutionaries relates to Jesus' call to take up the cross and follow him. In the context of the first passion prediction, Mark presents Jesus as telling his disciples and the crowd: "If any want to become my followers, let them deny themselves and take up their cross and follow me" (8:34). How might the call to carry the cross have been heard by Mark's hearers who were aware of the uses of crosses during the war? In this section, I deal with this question. I begin with a general view of crucifixion in the ancient world.

In the ancient world, "the cross was not just a matter of indifference, just any kind of death. It was an utterly offensive affair, 'obscene' in the original sense of the word."[70] This cruel form of punishment and execution was mainly reserved for serious crimes against the state and for high treason. Generally, crucifixion served as "a means of waging war and securing peace, of wearing down rebellious cities under siege, of breaking the will of the conquered peoples and bring mutinous troops or unruly provinces under control."[71] Particularly for the Romans, crucifixion was primarily administered to rebellious foreigners, mutinous troops, bandits, violent criminals, robbers, and slaves.[72] It was primarily applied to lower-class people. The Roman nobility and citizens were exempted from it.[73]

---

70. Hengel, *Crucifixion*, 22.
71. Ibid., 46.
72. Ibid., 46–46; van Iersel, *Mark*, 287; and O'Collins, "Crucifixion," 1207–10.
73. Hengel, *Crucifixion*, 46–63. Cicero (*Rab. Perd.* 16) associates the exemption of the nobility and the Roman citizen from crucifixion with the shameful nature of death by crucifixion. He writes, "the very word *cross* should be removed not only from the person of a Roman citizen and a free man but from his thoughts, his eyes and his ears. For it is not only the actual occurrence of these things or the endurance of them, but

The Romans used crucifixion as a means of terror and humiliation.⁷⁴ They used it to intimidate people not to attempt revolt. To make sure that the purpose of crucifixion was effective, the victims were crucifies in public places.⁷⁵ As Pseudo-Quintilian wrote, "Whenever we crucify the condemned, the most crowded roads are chosen, where most people can see and be moved by terror. For penalties relate not so much to retribution as to their exemplary effect" (*Decl.* 274).⁷⁶ Indeed, "Crucifixion was a shocking manifestation of the violence that could be inflicted when the more powerful of society felt threatened by their social subordinates."⁷⁷

The Roman domination in Judea was marked by crucifixions. The authority to administer the punishment of crucifixion in the provinces of the Roman Empire was left in the hands of the Roman governors. Hengel affirms this truth when he asserts that the "imposition of the crucifixion upon robbers and rebels in the provinces was under the free jurisdiction of the local governor, based on his *imperium* and right *of coercitio* to maintain peace and order."⁷⁸ Josephus provides extensive evidence on this matter. According to him, governor Tiberius Alexander ordered the crucifixion of James and Simon, the sons of Judas the Galilean for causing disorder (*Ant.* 20:102; cf. Acts 5:37); Varus crucified about two thousand Jews due to insurrection charges (*J.W.* 2:75; cf. *Ant.* 17:295); Quadratus, governor of Syria crucified Jews whom procurator Cumanus held captive for making a revenge against the Samaritans who had murdered a Galilean (*J.W.* 2:241; cf. *Ant.* 20:129); and procurator Felix crucified numerous brigands for ravaging the country (*J.W.* 2:253).

In the critical weeks shortly before the outbreak of the war in 66 CE, governor Florus did what Josephus understands "none had ever done before" (*J.W.* 2:308). As a response to the mock against him by Jews who carried a basket and begged copper on his behalf (*J.W.* 2:295), Florus ordered arrest of many peaceable Jews and "had them first scourged and then

---

liability to them, the expectation, nay, the mere mention of them, that is unworthy of a Roman citizen and a free man."

74. Watson, "*Life of Aesop*," 711. See also Hengel, *Crucifixion*, 87. Hengel describes the humiliating nature of crucifixion thus: "By the public display of a naked victim at a prominent place—at a crossroads, in the theatre, on high ground, at the place of his crime—crucifixion also represented his uttermost humiliation, which had a numinous dimension to it."

75. Horsley, *Jesus and Empire*, 28; Kyle, *Spectacle of Death*, 53: "For exemplary effect, crucifixions were held at well-travelled public roadways."

76. Cf. Hengel, *Crucifixion*, 50n14.

77. Watson, "*Life of Aesop*," 712.

78. Hengel, *Crucifixion*, 49.

crucified" (J. W. 2:306-308). Given this practice, Hengel is therefore correct when he relates that, "The excessive use made of crucifixion by the Romans in the pacification of Judaea meant that from the beginning of direct Roman rule crucifixion was taboo as a form of the Jewish death penalty."[79]

During the war period, crucifixions were widely exercised. The Romans used crucifixions to punish rebels and sometimes as a means to compel Jews to capitulate. For example, during the Galilean campaign, Vespasian tortured and crucified a Jewish captive at Jotapata (J. W. 3:321). In another context, Josephus gives a more detailed account about the fate of the Jewish war prisoners during the siege of Jerusalem. Josephus states that:

> When caught (by the Romans), they were driven to resist, and after a conflict it seemed too late to sue for mercy. They were accordingly scourged and subjected to torture of every description, before being killed, and then crucified opposite the walls. Titus indeed commiserated their fate, five hundred or sometimes more being captured daily; on the other hand, he recognized the risk of dismissing prisoners of war, and the custody of such numbers would amount to the imprisonment of their custodians; but his main reason for not stopping the crucifixions was the hope that the spectacle might perhaps induce the Jews to surrender, for fear that continued resistance would involve them in a similar fate. The soldiers out of rage and hatred amused themselves by nailing their prisoners in different postures; and so great was their number, that space could not be found for crosses nor the crosses for the bodies. (J. W. 5:449-451)

This passage not only highlights the magnitude of the victims of crucifixion during the siege of Jerusalem but also the motive of those crucifixions. The crucifixions were partly meant to terrorize and intimidate the Jews in order to compel them to surrender.[80] According to Josephus, Titus cruci-

---

79. Hengel, *Crucifixion*, 85.

80. There is a passage in which Josephus explicitly depicts the Roman crucifixions as a means to force Jews to surrender. The incident reported occurred at the end of the siege of Jerusalem. Josephus writes, "The [Roman] general[, Bassus,] having ordered him [Eleazar] to be stripped and carried to the spot most exposed to the view of the onlookers in the city and there severely scourged, the Jews were profoundly affected by the lad's fate, and the whole town burst into such wailing and lamentation as the misfortune of a mere individual seemed hardly to justify. Observing this, Bassus proceeded to practice a ruse upon the enemy, desiring so to intensify their distress as to compel them to purchase the man's life by the surrender of the fort; and in this hope he was not disappointed. For he ordered a cross to be erected, as though intending to have Eleazar instantly suspended; at which sight those in the fortress were seized with deeper dismay and with piercing shrieks exclaimed that the tragedy was intolerable. At this juncture, moreover, Eleazar besought them not to leave him to undergo the most

fied many other Jewish captives shortly after the war, three of whom were Josephus's friends. At Josephus's request Titus ordered the release of and "most careful treatment" to Josephus's friends. Unfortunately, however, only one of them survived while the other two died in the hands of the physicians (*Life* 420–421). Given the evidence available, it is not an exaggeration to say that the Romans used crucifixion excessively in order to pacify rebellious provincials.

In Mark, Jesus calls people to "take up their cross" and follow him. The call appears in the context where Jesus teaches about renouncing everything including one's self and possessions for his sake and for the sake of the good news (8:34–38). In the context of Mark's Gospel, the call to take up one's cross evokes Jesus' passion prediction about his persecution and death (8:31; 9:31; 10:33–34), and anticipates Jesus' execution on the cross (15:21–32). So, in Mark, to "take up their cross" is to be prepared to face any possible death. Elsewhere, Mark's Jesus warns his disciples to beware of the persecutions they would face before councils, in synagogues, and before governors and kings for the sake of the good news (13:9). This suggests that the cross represents the sufferings that result from the unavoidable persecution that followers of Jesus experience due to their faithful commitment to the good news.[81] To carry one's cross is to be willing to suffer the consequences of faithful living in relation to the good news.[82] Jesus' call to carry the cross "is an exhortation to remain faithful to Jesus and to the rule of God in the face of persecution by political leaders."[83]

---

pitiable of deaths, but to consult their own safety by yielding to the might and fortune of the Romans, now that all others had been subdued. Overcome by his appeals, which were backed by many interceders within—for he came of a distinguished and extremely numerous family—they yielded to a compassion contrary to their nature and hastily dispatched a deputation to discuss the surrender of the fortress, stipulating for permission to depart in safety, talking Eleazar with them (*J.W.* 7:200–203).

81. Rhoads, *Reading Mark*, 52–53. Rhoads warns us not to understand the call to bear the cross as authorizing God's agents "to use force to stop those who oppress." Rather, Rhoads asserts that "those who confront oppression may suffer persecution at the hands of at the oppressors they condemn, just as Jesus did." He insists that carrying the cross in Mark is the willingness to suffer because one has "chosen to live by the good news of the kingdom of God." In Mark, Jesus "calls people to proclaim the good news—*in spite of* the suffering that one may encounter because of this commitment." Similarly, Dewey, "'Let Them Renounce Themselves,'" 35–36, argues while commenting on 8:34 that Jesus' call to renounce self and to carry one's cross is not "an exhortation to suffering and victimage in general" and strongly warns not to read the "passage as encouraging individual suffering" because the passage "does not encourage suffering or self-sacrifice."

82. Wilhelm, *Preaching Mark*, 156.

83. Dewey, "'Let Them Renounce Themselves,'" 98.

Become Like Slaves vs. Slavery for Others

Another contrast to the Jewish revolutionaries that Mark highlights relates to Jesus' call to become a "slave for all." Responding to the request of James and John who asked him to grant them to sit one on his right and another on his left hand in his glory, Jesus said: "whoever wants to be first among you must be slave of all" (10:44). How might Mark's original hearers interpret this call to become a slave of all in light of the war? In the following paragraphs I discuss about this question. I first present an overview of slavery in the ancient world.

In the ancient world, slaves had no legal identity. They had neither a status of their own nor the right to own anything.[84] According to Aristotle, a slave was considered as a body owned by a master or a master's "living tool" (*Pol.* 1.2.3–5). Seneca states that the Romans treated slaves just as "beasts of burden" (*Ep.* 48.5). In this case, a slave is one at the bottom of hierarchy of social status under whom there is no one he/she can receive honor or service from. By definition, a slave does everything for the advantage and wellbeing of others.[85] Because of their inferior status, they were the subject of punishment by crucifixion. Based on the various ancient writers, Hengel concludes saying that "crucifixion was practiced above all as a deterrent against trouble among slaves and was to be found principally in contexts where the power of punishment of an individual householder ... were no longer sufficient."[86]

Under the Roman imperial domination, Jews served as slaves of the Romans. As such they were subjected to pay tribute to Rome (*J.W.* 2:404–406, 409; 5:405). Their servitude under the Roman imperial power is confirmed in King Agrippa II's pro-Roman speech he delivered in his attempt to dissuade the Jews from making war with Rome. Josephus cites the king's speech about the Jewish servitude to the Romans:

> Passing to your present passion for liberty, I say that it comes too late. The time is past when you ought to have striven never to lose it. For servitude is a painful experience and a struggle to avoid it once for all is just; but the man who having once accepted the yoke then tries to cast it off is a contumacious slave, not a lover of liberty. There was, to be sure, a time when you should have strained every nerve to keep out the Romans; that was when Pompey invaded this country. But our forefathers and

---

84. Kaminouchi, *Not So among You*, 135.

85. Cf. Lane, *Mark,* 382, who shows that a servant and a slave are people "whose activities are not directed toward their own interest but to those of others."

86. Hengel, *Crucifixion*, 54.

their kings, though in wealth and in vigor of body and soul far your superiors, yet failed to withstand a small faction of the Roman army; and will you, to whom thralldom is hereditary, you who in resources fall so far short of those who first tendered their submission, will you, I say, defy the whole Roman empire? (J.W. 2:356–357)

In this passage King Agrippa II affirms that Jews were under servitude since the time when Pompey had conquered Judea in 63 BCE.

One of the revolutionaries' motives for the war with Rome was to gain freedom from the imperial rule. There is overwhelming evidence to support this view. In the passage just cited above, King Agrippa II acknowledges (though he does not support the war with Rome) that revolutionaries want to fight the Romans because they have "passion for liberty" (J.W. 2:256). Elsewhere, Josephus blames the revolutionaries for inciting people "to resolve, exhorting them to assert their independence" (J.W. 2:264); and shows Titus telling his troops that Jews "face war for liberty" (J.W. 3:479). Simon bar Gioras, one of the revolutionary leaders, also had a program of "proclaiming liberty for slaves" (J.W. 4:508). These few examples are evidence that freedom from the Roman imperial domination was one of the revolutionaries' motives for the war with Rome. The revolutionaries took up arms in order to fight against the Romans for the purpose of gaining independence from the imperial domination.

The revolutionaries' violent means of dealing with Roman domination, oppression, and enslavement turned into the Roman-Jewish War of 66–70 CE. One of the results of that war was the enslavement of masses of Jewish captives. Josephus reports of so many Jewish captives who were sent or sold into slavery. He shows that the Jews who were captured at Gabara (J.W. 3:14), Japha (J.W. 3:304), Tarichaea (J.W. 3:540–541), and some of those captured during the siege of Jerusalem were either sold or sent into slavery (J.W. 6:418). In another context, Josephus states that when Titus left for Rome, he took with him Simon bar Gioras, John of Gischala, and seven hundred other prisoners to be marched in the triumph (J.W. 7:11). While he reports of Simon that he was executed as the general of the Jews at the end of the triumphal procession (J.W. 7:153–154), he is silent about the fate of John and the seven hundred prisoners. It is highly probable, that these prisoners whose fate is not stated were reduced to slavery.

The Jewish prisoners of war who were set into slavery did not become slaves by choice. Theirs was a forced servitude, for no one willed to become a slave voluntarily. This point agrees with Josephus's account that during the civil war in Jerusalem, Jews were not willing to become slaves of their own

Jews. Now, how much more would the Jews feel becoming slaves of foreigners! Josephus, however, indicates that not all Jews preferred war to servitude under the Romans. He shows that there were Jews who voluntarily accepted servitude. Josephus writes:

> No sooner were these disorders reduced than the inflammation, as in a sick man's body, broke out again in another quarter. The impostors and brigands, banding together, incited numbers to revolt, exhorting them to assert their independence, and threatening to kill any who submitted to Roman domination and forcibly to suppress those who voluntary accepted service. Distributing themselves companies throughout the country, they looted the houses of the wealthy, murdered their owners, and set the villages on fire. The effects of their frenzy were felt throughout all Judea, and every day saw this war being fanned into fiercer flame. (J.W. 2:264–265)

This account highlights the willingness of some Jews to become slaves of the Romans and also the unwillingness of revolutionaries to become slaves of the Romans. It is ironic, however, that while the revolutionaries refused to become slaves willingly, upon their capture during the war they were sent into slavery out of coercion. Another irony is that while they rejected the Roman enslavement, they enslaved others by forcing them to take up arms on their side against both the Roman and Jewish authorities.

Besides taking up arms to get rid of the imperial and foreign enslavement, the revolutionary leaders struggled for power to rule over the Jews. The civil war in Jerusalem is a good testimony in favor of this view. Before the Romans advanced into Jerusalem to crush the revolt, several Jewish groups fought each other, because the leaders of each group wanted to have power to control the city and to rule over other Jews. Five Jewish factions were involved in the struggle for power: the Zealots under Eleazar, John of Gischala's group, Simon bar Gioras's group, the Sicarii under Menachem, the Idumaeans, and the provisional government. Josephus says of John of Gischala that he aspired to have "despotic power" and "absolute sovereignty" (J.W. 4:389–390). He also says of Simon bar Gioras that "his sole concern was to secure his own authority" (J.W. 4:575–576). Leaders of the provisional government as well fought against the rest of the groups in order to maintain their positions of power in the service of the Romans. At the initial stages of the revolt, with the help of troops from both Florus and King Agrippa II, "the leading men, the chief priests and all the people who were in favor of peace" fought against the Zealots (J.W. 2:422–424). The civil war in Jerusalem confirms the desire of revolutionary leaders to form an alternative government to the Roman imperial rule in which they would rule over Jews and be served by them.

In contrast to the revolutionaries' use of arms and violence to remove the Romans in order to free themselves from the imperial domination and enslavement, Mark's Jesus teaches his disciples to become slave of all. Jesus teaches that anyone who wants to be "great" and "first" among his followers must be a servant or a slave of everyone. He says: "whoever wishes to become great among you must be your servant, and whoever wishes to be first among you must be slave of all" (10:43–44). The teaching implies that whoever wants to be a leader must be willing to serve others as a slave. It emphasizes that anyone who wishes to become great and important among others must embrace the lowest status in society and become a slave of all. Hence, in Mark, a slave is a model of greatness in God's empire.

Mark's Jesus still shows another contrast to the revolutionaries. While the revolutionaries refused to accept voluntary servitude or to die like slaves, Mark's Jesus called people to voluntary servitude. Unlike the revolutionaries, Jesus emphasizes servitude even if it leads to death. This view is reinforced by the fact that slaves in Mark perished at the hands of the tenants. Mark also mentions the slaves of the vineyard owner who the tenants seize, beat, insult, and kill when they are sent by the vineyard owner to collect the fruits of the vineyard for him (12:4–5). Further, "the slave of the high priest" who is among the agents of the Jewish authorities who are sent to arrest Jesus, his ear was cut off by one of those standing near Jesus (14:47). Slavery is therefore associated with suffering and death. In Mark, however, not all slaves receive punishment. The slaves of the man who goes on a journey are only "put in charge, each with his work" (13:34). But they must give account of their services when the master returns. Meanwhile they are instructed to keep watch for the coming of the master (13:34–37). Therefore, while the revolutionaries are not willing to become slaves and to die like slaves, Jesus teaches his followers to voluntarily become slaves and to die as they serve others.

In Mark, not only does Jesus teach others to become slaves of all, he also serves all. Mark's story is dominated with Jesus' deeds of service to others. Such deeds of services are evident in Jesus' acts of healing, exorcisms, the raising of the dead, feeding of the hungry, rescuing of his disciples from the threat of death due to sea storms, and in his teaching and proclamation of the good news. In the contexts of his journey to Jerusalem in particular, Jesus' deeds of service manifest themselves in the restoration of a boy possessed by a dumb and deaf spirit (9:14–29), and in the defense of the little ones who trust in him not to be led to sin (9:42). Jesus also demonstrates his service to others when he defends marriage and family against divorce

(10:2–9), when he welcomes and blesses children (10:14–16), and when he restores Bartimaeus's sight (10:46–52).

More significantly, the greatest service that Mark's Jesus renders to all humanity is understood in his commitment and willingness to lose his life for others. The passion predictions (8:31; 9:31; 10:33–34) reveal Jesus' willingness to die for others. The assertion that the Son of Humanity came "to give his whole life as a ransom" (10:45), very vividly underpins Jesus' great service to all humans. Jesus' service of losing his whole life for others reached its peak when he was crucified and breathed his last on the cross (15:24–25, 37). This death was the consequence of his commitment to do God's will. Mark's hearers may have viewed Jesus not only as the one who wants others to serve but also as the one who serves all. They may have been inspired to follow his example and become slaves in order to serve everyone. However, with respect to the enslavement associated with the war, the call to become slave of all may have been very bitter.

Willingness to Lose One's Life in Serving Others

As we have already noted elsewhere, while travelling to Jerusalem with his disciples, Jesus predicted three times about his suffering, death, and resurrection (8:31; 9:31; 10:33–34), and called people to deny themselves, to carry their cross, and to follow him (8:34). In his teaching on the proper use of power, he identified himself as the Son of Humanity who "came not to be served but to serve, and to give his whole life as a ransom" (10:45). These expressions provide a clear picture of Jesus' greatest service to everyone. Both the predictions and the teachings demonstrate Jesus' willingness to suffer and to lose his life on behalf of others.

In serving others, Jesus gives his whole life as a "ransom" for others (10:45b). The word ransom connotes liberation by purchase of "a prisoner of war, a slave or a forfeited life."[87] The term stood for "the price required to redeem captives or purchase freedom for indenture servants."[88] It implies servitude or an imprisonment from which a human being cannot free himself. On this ground, the service of Jesus' whole life can be understood "as the price for liberation of many."[89] Such serve underlines Jesus' role of being

---

87. Lane, *Mark*, 383. Cf. Wilhelm, *Preaching Mark*, 185, who notes that the "term 'ransom' refers to purchasing a slave or prisoner in order to grant him or her freedom and redemption."

88. Dowd and Malbon, "Significance of Jesus' Death," 281.

89. Santos, *Slave of All*, 208. See also Kaminouchi, *Not So among You*, 154, who proposes that the Greek term for "ransom" (*lystron*) "can be interpreted as liberation

a slave of everyone—giving his own life so that others may live. The key is Jesus' willingness to serve, even when it meant crucifixion. In Mark, Jesus' death ransoms Barabbas from humans who wield power. While Barabbas, "son of the father" is freed, Jesus, the "beloved son" of "Abba" is led away to be crucified (15:15). In addition, Jesus' death ransoms the many whom he frees from oppressive illnesses and demonic powers (cf. 3:20–30). The idea that Mark's Jesus gave his whole life as a ransom for others may have transformed Mark's hearers to the extent that they would be inspired to be willing to give their own lives for others. Jesus' call of his disciples to lose their life for his sake and for the sake of the good news (8:35) may have been understood in this light. They may have considered surrender of their life for others as an expression of their commitment to the good news.

It is intriguing to note that Jesus' willingness to give life for others has a close parallel to an event of the war. In a speech in which he urges the Jews to surrender to Titus in order to achieve their own salvation and to prevent Jerusalem and the temple from destruction, Josephus claims that he is prepared to lose his own life for the salvation of the Jews. He refers to himself as having told the Jews: "take my blood as the price of your own salvation! I too am prepared to die, if my death will lead to your learning wisdom" (J.W. 4:419).[90] These words suggest Josephus's willingness to shed his blood as a price for the salvation of the Jews.

The parallel between Josephus's words and those of Jesus in relation to the issue of willingness to lose one's own life for the benefit of many is clear. The contrasts between the two statements, however, need to be highlighted. On his part, Josephus wants to die in the context of war where force and

---

from the ideologies and relationships of power in which the world, including its rulers, is entrapped"; Mark illustrates this entrapment in his portrayal of Herod (6:14–29) and Pilate (15:1–15), who though powerful leaders, are "unable to do their will" (196); Dowd and Malbon, "Signficance of Jesus' Death," 280.

90. Another incident from Josephus in relation to giving life for the benefit of others is expressed outside the context of the war. I note it here only to highlight the insight it provides for our study. The incident relates to Petronius, who is depicted to have shown willingness to surrender his own life on behalf of the lives of many Jews (J.W. 2:201). The incident took place in 40 CE when Emperor Gaius ordered his statues to be installed in the temple in Jerusalem. The Jews resisted the installation of Caesar's statues based on the law and the customs of their ancestors. Being willing to die rather than to disobey the law, the Jews refused even to plant crops. Such a situation forced Petronius, Caesar's agent, to concede, thereby showing his willingness to risk his own life before Caesar for the benefit of the Jews (J.W. 2:184–203). According to Josephus, Petronius told the Jews, "It is better that I should take the risk. Either, God aiding me, I shall prevail with Caesar and have the satisfaction of saving myself as well as you, or, if his indignation is roused, I am ready on behalf of the lives of so many to surrender my own" (J.W. 2:201–202).

violence are involved. He plays an active role in the war, and his willingness to give his life on behalf of others is not founded on commitment to the good news, but rather on the loyalty to the Roman imperial power. In contrast, Jesus does not advocate war, neither does he use force to confront oppression (14:43–50). Jesus' willingness to give his life for others is grounded on his commitment to the proclamation of the good news of God's empire. His arrest, trial, and death by crucifixion were occasions for giving witness and preaching the good news of God.[91] Mark's reference to Jesus as having given his whole life as a ransom for others may have evoked memories of Josephus's speech referred to above. The hearers, however, may have recognized that Jesus' willingness to give life was a sharp contrast to Josephus's claim for the same. Mark's hearers may have chosen to identify with Jesus because he embodied the values of God's empire, and not Josephus, who exercises the values of the Roman Empire.

Scholars have different views about the proper meaning of the death of Jesus as a ransom for others (10:45). Some have interpreted the statement as a death for the forgiveness of sins.[92] Fiorenza strongly objects to this idea because the "text does not speak about liberation from sin but of making free citizens of many."[93] A close reading of Mark's story of Jesus supports Fiorenza's position in that the pardon of sins takes place without death. In Mark, Jesus forgives the sins of the paralytic before his death (2:5), suggesting that Jesus doe not die in order to forgive sins.[94] Jesus' death comes as a consequence of his commitment and faithfulness to doing God's will. His "faithfulness in the face of execution liberates others from the grip of self-preservation so that they too might live for others, even in the face of loss and persecution."[95] The faithfulness of Jesus in death and his resurrection liberates people from fear of death and empowers them to live courageously and faithfully for the advantage of others. The message not only may have brought new hope to Mark's hearers, it may also have empowered them to have courage to proclaim the good news regardless of their failures and ongoing persecutions so that others may benefit from the blessings of God's empire.

91 Schüssler Fiorenza, *In Memory of Her*, 317.

92 Cf. Wilhelm, *Reading Mark*, 186. She understands Jesus' death as "a ransom for many" in terms of Isaiah's vision of the Suffering Servant, who bears the sins of others and "poured out of himself to death" (Isa 53:12); Dowd and Malbon, "Significance of Jesus' Death," 271, 280.

93 Schüssler Fiorenza, *In Memory of Her*, 318.

94 Cf. Dowd and Malbon, "Significance of Jesus' Death," 285n40, who rightly argue that in Mark forgiveness is not connected with the death of Jesus.

95 Rhoads, *Reading Mark*, 59.

Mark's hearers may have interpreted the message about Jesus' death as a word of empowerment. Rhoads has underscored this idea when he emphasizes that:

> Mark empowers people to take risk for the good news in spite of the threat of opposition and persecution. Mark's audience lived just after the Roman-Jewish War of 66–70 CE at which time followers of Jesus were threatened by authorities on both sides. They were persecuted by the Judeans, who thought of them as traitors because they had refused to fight in the war, and they were persecuted by the Roman authorities, who thought of them revolutionaries because, after all, their leader had been executed as a messianic pretender.[96]

Jesus' example of giving his whole life as a ransom may have empowered Mark's hearers to be willing to risk their lives for the good news. In the face of threats of persecution and death, they may have been encouraged to willingly proclaim the good news to all nations (13:9–13) in order that others might receive the blessings available in God's empire. They may have viewed Jesus' call to risk life for others as a call to proclaim the good news to the point of facing death so that others may live. Mark's Jesus wished that those who followed him should serve as liberators of others from "their great ones who are tyrants over them" and "their rulers (who) lord it over them" (10:42). The key here is service to others, especially the undervalued, the marginalized, the powerless, and the oppressed in society "even if such service provokes a response from the powerful that leads to suffering and/or death."[97] Jesus' followers are called to liberate the many from the tyranny of the elite by bearing the good news of God's empire.

Conclusion

The purpose of this chapter was to examine the contrasts between the values of the Roman Empire and the values of God's empire in Mark's Gospel as portrayed in Jesus' teachings while he journeys with his disciples to Jerusalem. The focus was centered on the values related to wealth, status, and power. I have shown that in the Roman Empire, the authorities and their retainers were self-oriented in that they wished to "acquire the whole world" and to accumulate wealth for themselves; that they desired to be "great" and to be "first" among other humans; and that they used power to control

---

96 Rhoads, "Diversity in the New Testament," 354.
97 Dowd and Malbon, "Significance of Jesus' Death," 281–82.

others. Moreover, I have shown that because of their self-aggrandizement and fear of losing their positions of power and honor, the authorities representing the Roman imperial power in Judea wished to secure and to save their own lives by destroying others.

By contrast, Mark's Jesus who represents the values of God's empire taught his followers not to imitate the values of the Roman Empire. Instead of being self-oriented, he taught them to be God-centered; instead of the desire to accumulate wealth, he taught them to give up wealth by sharing their possessions with the poor. Moreover, I have shown that Mark's Jesus taught that whoever wishes to be great and to have high social status must become least and slave of all in the service of everyone. Instead of killing others to save one's own life, Jesus taught to be willing to lose one's own life for the sake of the good news and for the sake of serving others. Jesus demonstrated this teaching in his own death in which he gave his whole life as ransom to liberate others. Furthermore, instead of using power to lord over and to tyrannize others, Jesus urged his followers to exercise power from God to serve people. In this way, the contrasts between the values of the Roman Empire and those of God's empire are evident. Given their social location, Mark's hearers very likely received Jesus' teachings on the values of God's empire as truly good news.

7

Conclusion

THE GOAL OF THIS book was to read Mark's story of Jesus in the light of the Roman-Jewish War of 66–70 CE, seeking to determine how Mark's hearers with fresh memories of the war would have responded to Mark's story of Jesus. The following paragraphs highlight some major issues discussed in this book. In chapter 2, I addressed the question of date and place of origin of Mark. Based on Mark's internal evidence, supported with archaeological finds, I have ruled out the date prior to the temple destruction in favor of a date shortly after the fall of the temple that took place in 70 CE. In this case, I argued that Mark wrote the Gospel with the knowledge of the destruction of both the temple and the city of Jerusalem. As for the place of origin, I have argued in favor of Galilee and/or southern Syria. This location takes into account Mark's special interests on a rural area particularly Galilee and the war situation expressed in Mark 13.

In chapter 3, I paid attention to Josephus and his works. Here I argued that despite Josephus's biases, inconsistencies, exaggerations, and inventions in his stories, he is generally credible and deserves to be used as a source. Josephus's works provide useful information about the dynamics, causes, course, and events of the Roman-Jewish War of 66–70 CE. These works were used in this book to reconstruct the context of Mark's Gospel crucial for clarifying the hearers' possible response to Mark's story of Jesus.

In chapter 4, I evaluated Mark's opening as an onset of God's empire in the light of the onset of Vespasian's imperial rule seeking to understand the meaning of the "good news" concept, the divine agent of the empire, and the entrances of the divine agent. The investigation has revealed that Vespasian and Jesus are the divine agents and the focus of the good news related to the Roman Empire and God's empire respectively. Vespasian's military achievements, his rise to the imperial throne, and entrances in cities were celebrated as good news. Such good news associated with Vespasian involved military forces that brought destruction of life. In contrast, the good news associated with the onset of God's empire is nonviolent. Instead of employing military forces, it is based on the proclamation, teachings, and redemptive deeds of Jesus. In regard to the divine nature, I have shown that Vespasian's claim to divinity was primarily a propaganda tool to legitimatize his imperial power. Since he was declared Emperor while on the Judean soil, he claimed to be the fulfillment of the Jewish oracle that expected a world ruler to come from Judea, implying that he became ruler by the approval of the God of the Jews. In a way, Vespasian claimed to be God's messiah. By contrast, the divinity of Mark's Jesus is legitimatized by God who proclaimed him to be his Beloved Son, and hence the Messiah. Jesus' faithfulness and commitment to God's will, as affirmed by Mark, may have convinced hearers that Jesus, not Vespasian, was truly the Messiah and Son of God.

Another contrast between the onset of Vespasian's imperial rule and that of God's empire proclaimed by Jesus, relates to entrances of the divine agents. Vespasian's entrances focused primarily in cities; receptions were by kings and city elites; and usually marked with pomp, in that they involved military convoys and extravagant feasts. By contrast, Jesus' advent was without splendor. He was preceded by John, a desert man, who prepared the way and proclaimed his coming. Jesus came alone from Nazareth, an insignificant place in the empire, to the wilderness where God's empire begins. After his baptism, the Holy Spirit led him into the wilderness where, by the power of the Holy Spirit, he successfully encountered Satan, signaling victories in the entire life-giving campaign presented in Mark's Gospel.

In chapter 5, I examined Jesus' campaign in Galilee in the light of Vespasian's military campaign in the same area, seeking to show the contrasts between the two campaigns. Several contrasts have been observed. First, Vespasian, the general from Rome, the centre of the Roman Empire, led a military campaign, seeking to conquer Judea, and to subject the Jews under the Roman imperial control, and thereby consolidating the Roman Empire. By contrast, Mark's Jesus emerged from Nazareth of Galilee, the margin of the empire, with the twelve disciples as his assistants. Jesus' campaign was nonviolent and focused on spreading God's empire through proclamation. Next, while Vespasian's campaign focused primarily on fortified cities where the general was received and hosted by kings and powerful men, Jesus' campaign was based in villages and towns in the countryside. While the authorities and the powerful men rejected Jesus and challenged his campaign, Jesus welcomed the poor and oppressed, the outcasts, and the untouchables in society, and provided them with the blessings of God's empire.

Moreover, Vespasian's campaign was destructive. It brought about a huge loss of human life, enslavement, displacement, starvation, and destruction of property. Despite the destructions his campaign caused, Vespasian was hailed by the populous as savior and benefactor. By contrast, Jesus' campaign was life-giving. It involved the removal of demonic powers, health improvement, elimination of hunger, bringing the dead back to life, and the calming of life-threatening sea storms. It is ironic that even though Mark's Jesus showed mercy and compassion to people through his redemptive actions, he was never addressed as savior or benefactor. Furthermore, since Vespasian was proclaimed emperor on the Jewish soil, he claimed to have been the fulfillment of prophecy that hoped for a world ruler, and used it as a propaganda tool to legitimatize his imperial rule. By contrast, when Jesus was declared by Peter at Caesarea Philippi as the Messiah, he never publicized his divinity. Instead, he ordered his disciples not to publicize about his identity as Messiah. Given this contrasts, I argued that Mark's hearers may have rejected Vespasian in favor of Jesus as the true God's Messiah, hence their identification with the later.

In chapter 6, I analyzed the contrasts between the values of the Roman Empire and those of God's empire as portrayed in Mark's Gospel in the context of Jesus' travel to Jerusalem. Special focus was centered on the values related to wealth, status, and power. In this chapter, I have shown that the Roman authorities and the Jewish ruling elite embodied the values of the Roman Empire. Besides being self-oriented, they had desire to acquire the world and to accumulate wealth for themselves, desire to be great and to be first (to occupy high positions of power), desire to destroy the life of others in order to save their own, and desire to use power to tyrannize and to lord over others. I have indicated that while the Jewish revolutionaries opposed the Roman imperial values, they however, employed violent means to deal with the Roman imperial domination, and oppression by the Jewish ruling elite.

By contrast, Mark's Jesus embodied the values of God's empire. He taught his followers to abandon the Roman imperial values in favor of the values of God's empire. Jesus encouraged his followers to be God-oriented; to give up everything for the sake of the good news; to share their possessions with the poor; to be least, and to become slave in serving everyone; to be willing to lose one's life in order to save the life of others; and to use power and authority from God for serving others, instead of using power to lord over and to tyrannize others. In contrast to using violent means to deal with domination and oppression, Jesus favored the use of nonviolent means as he demonstrated in his own life and death.

Overall, in this book, I have demonstrated that Mark's audience with fresh memories of the events of the recent war may have evaluated Mark's story of Jesus in terms of the war events. I have indicated that Mark's hearers may have evaluated God's empire proclaimed by Jesus as a contrasts to the Roman Empire under Vespasian; Jesus' Galilean redemptive campaign as a contrast to Vespasian's military and destructive campaign in Galilee; and the values of God's empire that Jesus advocates while on the way to Jerusalem with his disciples, as a contrast to the Roman imperial values which were the source of the war. I have argued that Mark's hearers may have understood Jesus' teachings on the values of God's empire as a call to avoid any attempt to dominate others, or to use violent means to end imperialism, domination, and oppression because those things lead to destruction.

Bibliography

Aberbach, Moshe, and David Aberbach. *Roman-Jewish Wars and Hebrew Cultural Nationalism.* New York: St. Martin's, 2000.
Achtemeier, Paul J. *Invitation to Mark: A Commentary on the Gospel of Mark with Complete Text from the Jerusalem Bible.* Garden City, NY: Image, 1978.
———. *Mark.* Proclamation Commentaries. 1986. Reprint, Eugene, OR: Wipf & Stock, 2004.
Agosto, Efrain. *Servant Leadership: Jesus & Paul.* St. Louis: Chalice, 2005.
Alon, Gedalia. "The Burning of the Temple." In *Jews, Judaism, and the Classical World: Studies in Jewish History in the Times of the Second Temple and Talmud,* 252–68. Translated by Israel Abrahams. Jerusalem: Magnes, 1977.
Anderson, Janice C., and Stephen D. Moore, eds. *Mark & Method: New Approaches in Biblical Studies.* 2nd ed. Minneapolis: Fortress, 2008.
Applebaum, Shimon. "Economic Life in Palestine." In *The Jewish People in the First Century,* edited by Shemuel Safrai and Menahem Stern, 2:631–700. 2 vols. Philadelphia: Fortress, 1976.
Aristotle. *Politics.* Translated by Harris Rackham. LCL. Cambridge: Harvard University Press, 1950.
Atwill, Joseph. *Caesar's Messiah: The Roman Conspiracy to Invent Jesus.* Berkeley: Ulysses. Distributed in the United States by Publishers Group West, 2005.
Aubert, J. J. "Threatened Wombs: Aspects of Ancient Uterine Magic." *GRBS* 30 (1989) 421–29.
Aus, Roger David. *My Name Is "Legion": Palestinian Traditions in Mark 5:1–20 and Other Gospel Texts.* Studies in Judaism. Lanham, MD: University Press of America, 2003.
Avi-Yonah, Michael. *The Holy Land from the Persian to the Arab Conquests.* Grand Rapids: Baker, 1966.
Bacon, Benjamin W. *Is Mark a Roman Gospel?* Harvard Theological Studies 7. Cambridge: Harvard University Press, 1919.
Baird, Mary M. "The Gadarene Demoniac." *ExpTim* 31 (1920) 189.
Balanski, Vicky. *Eschatology in the Making: Mark, Matthew and the Didache.* Cambridge: Cambridge University Press, 1997.
Barton, John. "Thinking about Reader-Response Criticism." *ExpTim* 113 (2002) 147–51.
Beardslee, William A. "Saving One's Life by Losing It." *JAAR* 47 (1979) 57–72.
Ben-Dov, Meir. *In the Shadow of the Temple: The Discovery of Ancient Jerusalem.* Translated by Ina Friedman. New York: Harper & Row, 1985.
Bilde, Per. "The Causes of the Jewish War according to Josephus." *JSJ* 10 (1979) 179–202.

Benjamin, Isaac. "Judea after AD 70." *JJS* 35 (1984) 44–50.
Bird, Michael F. "Tearing the Heavens and Shaking the Heavenliness: Mark's Cosmology in Its Apocalyptic Context." In *Cosmology and New Testament Theology*, edited by Jonathan T. Pennington and Sean M. McDonough, 45–49. LNTS 355. London: T. & T. Clark, 2008.
Black, C. Clifton. *Mark: Images of an Apostolic Interpreter*. Studies on Personalities of the New Testament. 1994. Reprint, Minneapolis: Fortress, 2001.
Blenkinsopp, Joseph. "Prophecy and Priesthood in Josephus." *JJS* 25 (1974) 239–62.
Bligh, P. H. "A Note on *Huios Theou* in Mark 15:39." *ExpTim* 80 (1968–69) 51–53.
Blount, Brian K. *Go Preach! Mark's Kingdom Message and the Black Church Today*. Bible & Liberation Series. Maryknoll, NY: Orbis, 1998.
Boers, Hendrikus. *Who Was Jesus? The Historical Jesus and the Synoptic Gospels*. San Francisco: Harper & Row, 1989.
Bohrmann, Monette. *Flavius Josephus, the Zealots and Yavne: Towards a Reading of "The War of the Jews."* Translated by Janet Lloyd. Bern: Lang, 1994.
Bolt, Peter G. "Life, Death, and the Afterlife in the Greco-Roman World." In *Life in the Face of Death: The Resurrection Message of the New Testament*, edited by Richard N. Longenecker, 51–79. McMaster New Testament Studies. Grand Rapids: Eerdmans, 1998.
Borg, Marcus J. *Conflict, Holiness, and Politics in the Teachings of Jesus*. Harrisburg, PA: Trinity, 1998.
———. *Jesus: A New Vision; Spirit, Culture, and the Life of Discipleship*. New York: Harper, 1987.
Boring, M. Eugene. *Mark: A Commentary*. NTL. Louisville: Westminster John Knox, 2006.
———. "Mark 1:1–15 and the Beginning of the Gospel." *Semeia* 52 (1991) 43–81.
Botha, Pieter J. J. "The Historical Setting of Mark's Gospel: Problems and Possibilities." *JSNT* 51 (1993) 27–55.
Brandon, S. G. F. *The Fall of Jerusalem and the Christian Church: A Study of the Effects of the Jewish Overthrow of A.D. 70 on Christianity*. 1951. Reprint, Eugene, OR: Wipf & Stock, 2010.
———. *The Fall of Jerusalem and the Christian Church: A Study of the Effects of the Jewish Overthrow of A.D. 70 on Christianity*. 1951. 2nd ed. Eugene, OR: Wipf & Stock, 2010.
———. *Jesus and the Zealots: A Study of the Political Factor in the Primitive Christianity*. New York: Scribner, 1967.
———. *The Trial of Jesus of Nazareth*. London: Batsford, 1968.
Bratcher, Robert G., and Eugene A. Nida. *A Handbook on the Gospel of Mark*. UBS Handbook Series. Helps for Translators 2. New York: UBS, 1961.
Brent, Allen. *The Imperial Cult and the Development of Church Order: Concepts and Images of Authority in Paganism and Early Christianity before the Age of Cyprian*. Supplements to Vigiliae Christianae 45. Leiden: Brill, 1999.
Brighton, Mark A. *The Sicarii in Josephus' Judean War: Rhetorical Analysis and Historical Observations*. Early Judaism and Its Literature 27. Atlanta: SBL, 2009.
Broshi, Magen. "The Credibility of Josephus." *JJS* 33 (1982) 379–84.
———. "The Population of Western Palestine in the Roman-Byzantine Period." *BASOR* 236 (1979) 1–10.

Brown, John P. "Techniques of Imperial Control: The Background of the Gospel Event." In *The Bible and Liberation: Political and Social Hermeneutics*, edited by Norman Gottwald, 357–77. Rev. ed. Maryknoll, NY: Orbis, 1993.

Brown, Raymond E. *An Introduction to the New Testament*. ABRL. New York: Doubleday, 1997.

Brown, Schuyler. "Reader Response: Demythologizing the Text." *NTS* 14 (1988) 232–37.

Brownmiller, Susan. *Against Our Will: Men, Women, and Rape*. Harmondsworth, UK: Penguin, 1976.

Buchanan, George Wesley. "An Additional Note to 'Mark 11:15–19: Brigands in the Temple.'" *HUCA* 31 (1960) 103–5.

———. "Mark 11:15–19: Brigands in the Temple." *HUCA* 30 (1959) 169–77.

Byatt, Antony. "Josephus and Population Numbers in First Century Palestine." *PEQ* 105 (1973) 51–60.

Camery-Hoggatt, Jerry. *Irony in Mark's Gospel: Text and Subtext*. SNTSMS 72. Cambridge: Cambridge University Press, 1992.

Carcopino, Jerome. *Daily Life in Ancient Rome: The People and the City at the Height of Empire*. Translated by E. O. Lorimer. London: Routledge, 1941.

Carter, Warren. *Pontius Pilate: Portraits of a Roman Governor*. Interfaces. Collegeville, MN: Liturgical, 2003.

———. "Proclaiming (in/against) Empire Then and Now." *WW* 25 (2005) 149–58.

———. *The Roman Empire and the New Testament: An Essential Guide*. Abingdon Essential Guides. Nashville: Abingdon, 2006.

Catchpole, David R. "The 'Triumphal' Entry." In *Jesus and the Politics of His Day*, edited by Ernst Bammel and C. F. D. Moule, 319–34. Cambridge: Cambridge University Press, 1984.

Chapman, Dean E. "Locating the Gospel of Mark: A Model of Agrarian Biography." *BTB* 25 (1995) 24–36.

Chávez, Emilio G. *The Theological Significance of Jesus' Temple Action in Mark's Gospel*. TST 87. Lewiston, NY: Mellen, 2002.

Chilton, Bruce. "Jesus *ben David*: Reflections on the *Davidssohnfrage*." *JSNT* 14 (1982) 88–112.

Chow, John K. "Patronage in Roman Corinth." In *Paul and Empire: Religion and Power in Roman Imperial Society*, edited by Richard A. Horsley, 104–25. Harrisburg, PA: Trinity, 1997.

Cline, Eric H. *Jerusalem Besieged: From Ancient Canaan to Modern Israel*. Ann Arbor: University of Michigan Press, 2004.

Cohen, Shaye J. D. *Josephus in Galilee and Rome: His Vita and Development as a Historian*. Columbia Studies in the Classical Tradition 8. Leiden: Brill, 2002.

———. "Masada: Literary Tradition, Archaeological Remains, and the Credibility of Josephus." *JJS* 33 (1982) 385–405.

Collins, Adela Yarbro. "The Apocalyptic Rhetoric of Mark 13 in Historical Context." *BR* 41 (1996) 5–36.

———. *The Beginning of the Gospel: Probings of Mark in Context*. Minneapolis: Fortress, 1992.

———. "The Eschatological Discourse of Mark 13." In *The Four Gospels, 1992: Festschrift Frans Neirynck*, edited by F. van Segbroeck et al. 2:1125–40. 3 vols. BETL 100. Leuven: Leuven University Press, 1992.

———. *Mark: A Commentary*. Hermeneia. Minneapolis: Fortress, 2007.

———. "Mark and His Readers: The Son of God among Greeks and Romans." *HTR* 93 (2000) 85–100.

———. "The Messiah as Son of God in the Synoptic Gospels." In *The Messiah: In Early Judaism and Christianity*, edited by Magnus Zetternholm, 21–32. Minneapolis: Fortress, 2007.

———. "Rulers, Divine Men, and Walking on the Water (Mark 6:45–52)." In *Religious Propaganda and Missionary Competition in the New Testament World: Essays Honoring Dieter Georgi*, edited by Lucas Bormann et al., 207–27. NovTSup 74. Leiden: Brill, 1994.

———. "The Signification of Mark 10:45 among Gentile Christians." *HTR* 90 (1997) 371–82.

Collins, John J. "Pre-Christian Jewish Messianism: An Overview." In *The Messiah in Early Judaism and Christianity*, edited by Magnus Zetternholm, 1–20. Minneapolis: Fortress, 2007.

Combs, Jason R. "A Ghost on Water? Understanding an Absurdity in Mark 6:49–50." *JBL* 127 (2008) 345–58.

Cotter, Wendy J. "Cosmology and the Jesus Miracles." In *Whose Historical Jesus?*, edited by William E. Arnal and Michel Desjardin, 118–31. Studies in Christianity and Judaism 7. Waterloo, ON: Wilfrid Laurier University Press, 1997.

Cousar, Charles B. "Eschatology and Mark's *Theologia Crusis*: A Critical Analysis of Mark 13." *Int* 24 (1970) 321–35.

Cranfield, C. E. B. *The Gospel according to Saint Mark*. CGTC. Cambridge: Cambridge University Press, 1963.

———. "St. Mark 13." *SJT* 6 (1953) 189–96, 287–303.

Crossan, John D. *The Historical Jesus: The Life of a Mediterranean Jewish Peasant*. San Francisco: HarperSanFrancisco, 1992.

———. *Jesus: A Revolutionary Biography*. San Francisco: HarperSanFrancisco, 1994.

Crossan, John Dominic, and Jonathan L. Reed. *In Search of Paul: How Jesus's Apostle Opposed Rome's Empire with God's Kingdom; A New Vision of Paul's Word & World*. New York: HarperSanFrancisco, 2004.

Crossley, James G. *The Date of Mark's Gospel: Insight from the Law in Earliest Christianity*. JSNTSup 266. London: T. & T. Clark, 2004.

Cunningham, Phillip J. *Mark: The Good News Preached to the Romans*. New York: Paulist, 1995.

Davies, Stevan L. *Jesus the Healer: Possession, Trance, and the Origins of Christianity*. New York: Continuum, 1995.

———. "The Quest for the Community of Mark's Gospel." In *The Four Gospels, 1992: Festschrift Frans Neirynck*, edited by F. van Segbroeck et al., 2:817–38. 3 vols. BETL 100. Leuven: Leuven University Press, 1992.

Deissmann, Adolph. *Light from the Ancient East: The New Testament Illustrated by Recently Discovered Texts of the Graeco-Roman World*. Translated by Lionel R. M. Strachan. London: Hodder & Stoughton, 1927.

De Mingo Kaminouchi, Alberto. *"But It Is not so among You": Echoes of Power in Mark 10:32–45*. JSNTSup 249. London: T. & T. Clark, 2003.

Derrett, J. Duncan M. "Contributions to the Study of the Gerasene Demoniac." *JSNT* 3 (1979) 2–17.

Dewey, Joanna. "The Gospel of Mark: A Galilean Provenance?" Paper Presented at the Jesus Seminar on Christian Origins. Spring 2008.

———. "'Let Them Renounce Themselves and Take Up Their Cross': A Feminist Reading of Mark 8:34 in Mark's Social and Narrative World." In *A Feminist Companion to Mark*, edited by Amy-Jill Levine and Marianne Blickenstaff, 23–36. Cleveland: Pilgrim, 2004.

———. "The Survival of Mark's Gospel: A Good Story?" *JBL* 123 (2004) 495–507.

"Distance between Tiberias and Capernaum." https://www.distancefromto.net/between/Tiberias/Capernaum/.

Dittenberger, Wilhelmus, ed. *Orientis Graeci inscriptiones selectae: Supplementum Sylloges Inscriptionum Graecarum*. Hildesheim: Olms, 1960.

Donahue, John R. "Windows and Mirrors: The Setting of Mark's Gospel." *CBQ* 57 (1995) 1–26.

Donahue, John R., and Daniel J. Harrington. *The Gospel of Mark*. SP 2. Collegeville, Minnesota: Liturgical, 2002.

Dormandy, Richard. "The Expulsion of Legion: A Political Reading of Mark 5:1–20." *ExpTim* 111 (2000) 335–37.

Dowd, Sharyn, and Elizabeth Struthers Malbon. "The Significance of Jesus' Death in Mark: Narrative Context and Authorial Audience." *JBL* 125 (2006) 271–97.

Duff, Paul B. "The March of the Divine Warrior and the Advent of the Greco-Roman King: Mark's Account of Jesus' Entry into Jerusalem." *JBL* 111 (1992) 55–71.

Dyer, Keith D. *The Prophecy on the Mount: Mark 13 and the Gathering of the New Community*. International Theological Studies 2. Bern: Lang, 1998.

Edwards, Douglas R. "Religion, Power and Politics: Jewish Defeats by the Romans and Iconography and Josephus." In *Diaspora Jews and Judaism*, edited by J. Andrew Overman and Robert S. MacLennan, 293–310. South Florida Studies in the History of Judaism 41. Atlanta: Scholars, 1992.

Eisenman, Robert. *James, the Brother of Jesus: The Key to Unlocking the Secrets of Early Christianity and the Dead Sea Scrolls*. New York: Viking, 1997.

Ellingworth, Paul. "'To Save Life or to Kill?' (Mark 3:4)." *BT* 52 (2001) 234–46.

Ellis, E. Earle. "The Date and Providence of Mark's Gospel." In *The Four Gospels, 1992: Festschrift Frans Neirynck*, edited by F. van Segbroeck et al., 2:801–16. 3 vols. BETL 100. Leuven: Leuven University Press, 1992.

Eusebius. *The Ecclesiastical History*. Translated by Kirsopp Lake and J. E. L. Oulton. 2 vols. LCL. Cambridge: Harvard University Press, 1926–1932.

Ehrenberg, Victor, and A. H. M. Jones, eds. *Documents Illustrating the Reigns of Augustus and Tiberius*. 2nd ed. Oxford: Clarendon, 1955.

Evans, Craig A. "The Beginning of the Good News and the Fulfillment of Scripture in Mark's Gospel." In *Hearing the Old Testament in the New Testament*, edited by Stanley E. Porter, 83–108. McMaster New Testament Studies. Grand Rapids: Eerdmans, 2006.

———. "From 'House of Prayer' to 'Cave of Robbers': Jesus' Prophetic Criticism of the Temple's Establishment." In *The Quest for Context and Meaning: Studies in Biblical Intertextuality in Honor of James A. Sanders*, edited by Craig A. Evans and Shemaryahu Talmon, 417–42. BibIntSer 28. Leiden: Brill, 1997.

———. "Jesus and the 'Cave of Robbers': Toward a Jewish Context for the Temple Action." *BBR* 3 (1993) 93–110.

———. *Mark 8:27—16:20*. WBC 34B. Nashville: Nelson, 2001.

———. "Mark's Incipit and the Priene Calendar Inscription: From Jewish Gospel to Greco-Roman Gospel." *JGRCJ* 1 (2000) 67–81.
Faulkner, Neil. *Apocalypse: The Great Jewish Revolt against Rome AD 66–73*. Stroud, UK: Tempus, 2004.
Fears, J. R. "The Theology of Victory at Rome: Approaches and Problems." In *ANRW* II.17.2 (1981) 736–826.
Feldaman, Emmanuel. *Biblical and Post-Biblical Defilement and Mourning: Law as Theology*. The Library of Jewish Law and Ethics. New York: Yeshiva University Press, 1977.
Feldman, Louis H. "Josephus (Person)." In *ABD* 3:981–98.
———. "Josephus' Portrait of David." *HUCA* 60 (1989) 129–74.
Ferguson, John. "Ruler-Worship." In *The Roman World*, edited by John Wacher, 2:766–84. 2 vols. London: Routledge, 1990.
Fish, Stanley. *Is There a Text in This Class? The Authority of Interpretive Communities*. Cambridge: Harvard University Press, 1980.
Forster, George M. "Peasant Society and the Image of Limited Good." *American Anthropologist* 67 (1965) 293–315.
Fowler, Robert M. *Let the Reader Understand: Reader-Response Criticism and the Gospel of Mark*. Harrisburg, PA: Trinity, 2008.
———. *Loaves and Fishes: The Function of the Feeding Stories in the Gospel of Mark*. SBLDS 54. Chico, CA: Scholars, 1981.
———. "Reader-Response Criticism: Figuring Mark's Reader." In *Mark & Method: New Approaches in Biblical Studies*, edited by Janice C. Anderson and Stephen D. Moore, 59–93. 2nd ed. Minneapolis: Fortress, 2008.
———. "The Rhetoric of Direction and Indirection in the Gospel of Mark." *Semeia* 48 (1989) 115–35.
———. "Who Is 'The Reader' in Reader-Response Criticism?" *Semeia* 31 (1985) 5–23.
France, R. T. *The Gospel of Mark: A Commentary on the Greek Text*. NIGCT. Grand Rapids: Eerdmans, 2002.
Fredriksen, Paula. "Jesus and the Temple, Mark and the War." *SBL Seminar Papers* (1990) 293–310.
Freedman, David Noel, ed. *Anchor Bible Dictionary*. 6 vols. New York: Doubleday, 1992.
Freyne, Seán. "Galilee, Sea of (Place)." In *ABD* 2:899–901.
Friedrich, Gerhard. "*euangelion*." In *TDNT*. Abridged in 1 vol. by Geoffrey W. Bromiley, 267—73. Grand Rapids: Eerdmans, 1985.
Fuller, Reginald H. "The Son of Man Came to Serve, not to Be Served." In *Ministering in a Servant Church*, edited by Eigio A. Francis, 45–72. Proceedings of the Theology Institute of Villanova University. Villanova, PA: Villanova University Press, 1978.
Gager, John G. ed. *Curse Tablets and Binding Spells from the Ancient World*. Oxford: Oxford University Press, 1992.
Garnsey, Peter, and Richard Saller. *The Roman Empire: Economy, Society and Culture*. Berkeley: University of California Press, 1987.
Garroway, Joshua. "The Invasion of a Mustard Seed: A Reading of Mark 5:1–20." *JSNT* 32 (2009) 57–75.
Garrett, Susan R. *The Temptations of Jesus in Mark's Gospel*. Grand Rapids: Eerdmans, 1998.
Geva, Hillel. "The Camp of the Tenth Legion in Jerusalem: An Archaeological Reconsideration." *IEJ* 34 (1984) 239–54.

———. "Searching for Roman Jerusalem." *BAR* 23 (1997) 34–45.
Gibson, Jeffrey B. "Jesus' Wilderness Temptation according to Mark." *JSNT* 16 (1994) 3–34.
Goodman, Martin. "A Bad Joke in Josephus." *JJS* 36 (1985) 195–99.
———. "The First Jewish Revolt: Social Conflict and the Problem of Debt." *JJS* 33 (1982) 417–27.
———. *Rome and Jerusalem: The Clash of Ancient Civilizations.* New York: Penguin, 2008.
———. *The Ruling Class of Judaea: The Origins of the Jewish Revolt against Rome A.D. 66–70.* Cambridge: Cambridge University Press, 1987.
Grabbe, Lester L. *Judaism from Cyrus to Hadrian.* 2 vols. Minneapolis: Fortress, 1992.
Grant, Frederick C., ed. *Ancient Roman Religion.* Library of Religion 8. New York: Liberal Arts, 1957.
Gray, Timothy C. *The Temple in the Gospel of Mark: A Study in Its Narrative Role.* WUNT 242. Tübingen: Mohr/Siebeck, 2008.
Greenleaf, Robert K. *The Servant as Leader.* Indianapolis: Robert K. Greenleaf Center, 1991.
Guelich, Robert A. *Mark 1—8:26.* WBC 34A. Dallas: World, 1989.
Guijaro, Santiago. "Why Does the Gospel of Mark Begin as It Does?" *BTB* 33 (2003) 28–38.
Gundry, Robert H. *Mark: A Commentary on His Apology for the Cross.* Grand Rapids: Eerdmans, 1993.
Hanson, K. C., and Douglas E. Oakman. *Palestine in the Time of Jesus: Social Structures and Social Conflicts.* 2nd ed. Minneapolis: Fortress, 2008.
Harrington, Daniel J. *What Are They Saying about Mark?* What Are They Saying About. New York: Paulist, 2004.
Harter, William H. "The Causes and Course of the Jewish Revolt against Rome, 66–74 C.E. in Recent Scholarship." Union Theological Seminary, 1982.
Hatina, Thomas R. "The Focus of Mark 13:24–27: The Parousia, or the Destruction of the Temple?" *BBR* 6 (1996) 43–66.
Hay, Lewis S. "The Son-of-God Christology in Mark." *JBR* 32 (1964) 106–14.
Head, Ivan. "Mark as a Roman Document from the Year 69: Testing Martin Hengel's Thesis." *JRH* 28 (2004) 240–59.
Heil, John P. *The Gospel of Mark as a Model of Action: A Reader-Response Commentary.* 1992. Reprint, Eugene, OR: Wipf & Stock, 2001.
———. *Jesus Walking on the Sea: Meaning and Gospel Functions of Matthew 14:22–23, Mark 6:45–52 and John 6:15b–21.* AnBib 87. Rome: Biblical Institute, 1981.
Hengel, Martin. *Crucifixion in the Ancient World and the Folly of the Message of the Cross.* Philadelphia: Fortress, 1977.
———. *Studies in the Gospel of Mark.* 1985. Reprint, Eugene, OR: Wipf & Stock, 2003.
———. *The Zealots: Investigations into the Jewish Freedom Movement in the Period from Herod I until 70 A.D.* Edinburgh: T. & T. Clark, 1989.
Herst, Roger E. "The Treachery of Josephus Flavius." *CCARJ* 19 (1972) 82–88.
Herzog, William R., II. *Jesus, Justice, and the Reign of God: A Ministry of Liberation.* Louisville: Westminster John Knox, 2000.
———. *Parables as Subversive Speech: Jesus as Pedagogue of the Oppressed.* Louisville: Westminster John Knox, 1994.

Higginson, Richard. *Transforming Leadership: A Christian Approach to Management.* London Lectures in Contemporary Christianity 1994. London: SPCK, 1996.

Hollenbach, Paul W. "Jesus, Demoniacs, and Public Authorities: A Socio-Historical Study." *JAAR* 49 (1981) 567–88.

Hooker, Morna D. *The Gospel according to Saint Mark.* BNTC. Peabody, MA: Hendrickson, 1991.

Horsley, Richard A. *Hearing the Whole Story: The Politics of Plot in Mark's Gospel.* Louisville: Westminster John Knox, 2001.

———, ed. *In the Shadow of Empire: Reclaiming the Bible as a History of Faithful Resistance.* Louisville: Westminster John Knox, 2008.

———. "Jesus and Empire." In *In the Shadow of Empire: Reclaiming the Bible as a History of Faithful Resistance,* edited by Richard A. Horsley, 75–97. Louisville: Westminster John Knox, 2008.

———. *Jesus and Empire: The Kingdom of God and the New World Disorder.* Minneapolis: Fortress, 2003.

———. *Jesus and the Spiral of Violence: Popular Jewish Resistance in Roman Palestine.* Minneapolis: Fortress, 1993.

———. "Menahem in Jerusalem: A Brief Messianic Episode among the Sicarii—Not 'Zealot Messianism.'" *NovT* 27 (1985) 334–48.

———. "Power Vacuum and Power Struggle in 66–70 C.E." In *The First Jewish Revolt: Archaeology, History, and Ideology,* edited by Andrea M. Berlin and J. Andrew Overman, 87–109. London: Routledge, 2002.

Horsley, Richard A., and John S. Hanson. *Bandits, Prophets & Messiahs: Popular Movements in the Time of Jesus.* Harrisburg, PA: Trinity, 1999.

"How Far Is It from Tiberias to Capernaum?" http://www.trueknowledge.com/g/how_how_far_is_it_from_tiberias_to_capernaum/.

Hull, John M. *Hellenistic Magic and the Synoptic Tradition.* SBT 2/28. London: SCM, 1974.

Human Rights Watch. "Democratic Republic of Congo: Ending Impunity for Sexual Violence." June 10, 2014. https://www.hrw.org/news/2014/06/10/democratic-republic-congo-ending-impunity-sexual-violence/.

Hurtado, Larry W. "The Gospel of Mark: Evolutionary or Revolutionary Document?" *JSNT* 13/40 (1990) 15–32.

Hutchison, John C. "Servanthood: Jesus' Countercultural Call to Christian Leaders." *BSac* 166 (2009) 53–69.

Iersel, B. M. F. van. "Failed Followers in Mark: Mark 13:12 as a Key for the Identification of the Intended Readers." *CBQ* 58 (1996) 244–63.

———. *Mark: A Reader-Response Commentary.* JSNTSup 164. Sheffield: Sheffield Academic, 1998.

———. "The Sun, Moon, and Stars of Mark 13:24–25 in a Greco-Roman Reading." *Bib* 77 (1996) 84–92.

Ilan, Tal. *Jewish Women in Greco-Roman Palestine.* Peabody, MA: Hendrickson, 1996.

Incigneri, Brian J. *The Gospel to the Romans: The Setting and Rhetoric of Mark's Gospel.* BibIntSer 65. Leiden: Brill, 2003.

Isaac, Benjamin. "Judaea after AD 70." *JJS* 35 (1984) 44–50.

Iser, Wolfgang. *The Act of Reading: A Theory of Aesthetic Response.* Baltimore: Johns Hopkins University Press, 1978.

———. *The Implied Reader: Patterns of Communication in Prose Fiction from Bunyan to Beckett*. Baltimore: Johns Hopkins University Press, 1974.

Iverson, Kelly R. *Gentiles in the Gospel of Mark: 'Even the Dogs under the Tables Eat the Children's Crumbs.'* LNTS 339. London: T. & T. Clark, 2007.

Jeffers, James S. *The Greco-Roman World of the New Testament Era: Exploring the Background of Early Christianity*. Downers Grove, IL: InterVarsity, 1999.

Johnson, Luke Timothy. *The Writings of the New Testament: An Interpretation*. With the assistance of Todd C. Penner. Rev. ed. Minneapolis: Fortress, 1999.

Jones, Brien W. "Titus (Emperor)." In *ABD* 6:581–82.

Josephus. *Works*. Translated by H. St. J. Thackeray et. al. 10 vols. LCL. Cambridge: Harvard University Press, 1926–1965.

Joyce, Paul. "First among Equals? The Historical Criticism Approach in the Marketplace of Methods." In *Crossing the Boundaries: Essays in Biblical Interpretation in Honour of Michael D. Goulder*, edited by Stanley E. Porter et al., 17–27. BibIntSer 8. Leiden: Brill, 1994.

Juel, Donald H. *Mark*. Augsburg Commentary on the New Testament. Minneapolis: Augsburg, 1990.

———. *A Master of Surprise: Mark Interpreted*. 1994. Reprint, Mifflintown, PA: Sigler, 2002.

———. *Messiah and the Temple: The Trial of Jesus in the Gospel of Mark*. SBLDS 31. Missoula, MT: Scholars, 1977.

Juvenal. *Satire*. Translated by G. G. Ramsay. LCL. Cambridge: Harvard University Press, 1950.

Kaminouchi, Alberto de Mingo. *'But It Is Not So Among You': Echoes of Power in Mark 10.32–45*. JSNTSup 249. New York: T & T Clark International, 2003.

Kautsky, John H. *The Politics of Aristocratic Empires*. With a new introduction by the author. New Brunswick, NJ: Transaction, 1997.

Kazen, Thomas. *Jesus and Purity Halakhah: Was Jesus Indifferent to Purity?* Coniectanea biblica: New Testament Series 38. Stockholm: Almqvist & Wiksell, 2002.

Kealy, Sean P. *Mark's Gospel, A History of Its Interpretation: From the Beginning until 1979*. New York: Paulist, 1982.

Keck, Leander E. "The Introduction to Mark's Gospel." *NTS* 12 (1966) 352–70.

Kee, Howard C. *Community of the New Age: Studies in Mark's Gospel*. Philadelphia: Westminster, 1977.

———. *Medicine, Miracle, and Magic in New Testament Times*. SNTSMS 55. Cambridge: Cambridge University Press, 1986.

Kelber, Werner H. *The Kingdom in Mark; A New Place and a New Time*. Philadelphia: Fortress, 1974.

———. *Mark's Story of Jesus*. Philadelphia: Fortress, 1979.

Kennard, J. Spencer. "Judas of Galilee and His Clan." *JQR* 36 (1945–46) 281–86.

Kennedy, David. "Roman Army." In *ABD* 5:789–90.

Kimeme, Joseph A. *Reporting a Scientific Study in Flying Colors: A Quick and Practical Guide to Content and Research Process*. Dar es Salaam: Niim Computers and Graphics, 2012.

Kinukawa, Hisako. *Women and Jesus in Mark: A Japanese Feminist Perspective*. Bible & Liberation Series. Maryknoll, NY: Orbis, 1994.

Kim, Tae Hun. "The Anarthrous υἱὸς θεοῦ in Mark 15:39 and the Roman Imperial Cult." *Bib* 79 (1998) 221–41.

Kimondo, Stephen S. "Milking a Starving Cow?: An Investigation of the Attitude of Jesus towards Taxes in First Century Palestine and Its Implications for the Evangelical Lutheran Church in Tanzania (ELCT)—Konde Diocese." MTh Thesis, University of Natal, Pietermaritzburg, 1999.

Kingdon, H. Paul. "Who Were the Zealots and Their Leaders in A.D. 66?" *NTS* 17 (1970) 68–72.

Kingsbury, Jack Dean. *The Christology of Mark's Gospel*. Philadelphia: Fortress, 1983.

———. "The Significance of the Cross within Mark's Story." *Int* 47 (1993) 370–79.

Kloppenborg, John S. "*Evocatio Deorum* and the Date of Mark." *JBL* 124 (2005) 419–50.

Koester, Helmut. "Jesus the Victim." *JBL* 111 (1992) 3–15.

———. "Imperial Ideology and Paul's Eschatology in 1 Thessalonians." In *Paul and Empire: Religion and Power in Roman Imperial Society*, edited by Richard A. Horsley, 158–83. Harrisburg, PA: Trinity, 1997.

Kombo, Donald K., and Delno L. A. Tromp. *Proposal and Thesis Writing: An Introduction*. Nairobi: Paulines, 2006.

Krentz, Edgar J. "Paul, Games, and the Military." In *Paul in the Greco-Roman World: A Handbook*, edited by J. Paul Sampley, 344–383. Harrisburg, PA: Trinity, 2003.

———. "The Starting Point of the Gospel: The Year of Mark." *CurTM* 23 (1996) 405–15.

Kyle, Donald G. *Spectacles of Death in Ancient Rome*. London: Routledge, 2001.

Lagrange, Marie-Joseph. *Evangile selon Saint Marc*. 4th ed. EBib. Paris: Gabalda, 1947.

Lane, William L. *The Gospel according to Mark*. NICNT. Grand Rapids: Eerdmans, 1974.

Larsen, Kevin W. "The Structure of Mark's Gospel: Current Proposals." *CurBR* 3 (2004) 140–60.

LaVerdiere, Eugene. "Hosanna in the Highest! Mark Chapter 11:1–11." *Emm* 99 (1993) 322–29.

———. "Jesus' Entry into Jerusalem: Mark 11:1—13:37." *Emm* 99 (1993) 270–76.

Lawrence, Paul. *The IVP Atlas of Bible History*. Edited by Alan Millard et al. Downers Grove, IL: IVP Academic, 2006.

Lee-Pollard, Dorothy A. "Powerlessness as Power: A Key Emphasis in the Gospel of Mark." *SJT* 40 (1987) 173–88.

Lenski, Gerhard E. *Power and Privilege: A Theory of Social Stratification*. 2nd ed. Chapel Hill: University of North Carolina Press, 1984.

Leoni, Tommaso. "'Against Caesar's Wishes': Flavius Josephus as a Source for the Burning of the Temple." *JJS* 58 (2007) 39–51.

Levine, Lee I. "Jewish War (66–73 C.E.)." In *ABD* 3:840–45.

LiDonnici, Lynn R. *The Epidaurian Miracle Inscriptions: Text, Translation and Commentary*. SBLTT 36. Graeco-Roman Religion Series. Atlanta: Scholars, 1995.

Liew, Tat-Siong Benny. "Tyranny, Boundary and Might: Colonial Mimicry in Mark's Gospel." *JSNT* 73 (1999) 7–31.

Maier, Paul L. "The Episode of the Golden Roman Shield at Jerusalem." *HTR* 62 (1969) 109–21.

Malbon, Elizabeth Struthers "Galilee and Jerusalem: History and Literature in Marcan Interpretation." In *The Interpretation of Mark*, edited by W. R. Telford, 253–68. 2nd ed. Edinburgh: T. & T. Clark, 1995.

———. "The Jewish Leaders in the Gospel of Mark: A Literary Study of Marcan Characterization." *JBL* 108 (1989) 259–81.

———. *Mark's Jesus: Characterization as Narrative Christology*. Waco: Baylor University Press, 2009.

Malina, Bruce J., and Richard L. Rohrbaugh. *Social-Science Commentary on the Synoptic Gospels*. 2nd ed. Minneapolis: Fortress, 2003.
Marcus, Joel. "The Jewish War and the *Sitz im Leben* of Mark." *JBL* 111 (1992) 441–62.
———. *Mark 1–8*. AB 27. New York: Doubleday, 2000.
———. *Mark 8–16*. Anchor Yale Bible 27A. New Haven: Yale University Press, 2009.
———. "Mark 14:61: Are You the Messiah-Son-of-God?" *NovT* 31 (1989) 125–41.
———. *The Way of the Lord: Christological Exegesis of the Old Testament in the Gospel of Mark*. Louisville: Westminster John Knox, 1992.
Mason, Steve. "Figured Speech and Irony in T. Flavius Josephus." In *Flavius Josephus and Flavian Rome*, edited by Jonathan Edmondson et al., 243–88. Oxford: Oxford University Press, 2005.
———. *Josephus and the New Testament*. 2nd ed Peabody, MA: Hendrickson, 2003.
Matera, Frank J. "The Prologue as the Interpretive Key to Mark's Gospel." *JSNT* 11/34 (1988) 3–20.
———. *New Testament Christology*. Louisville: Westminster John Knox, 1999.
———. *New Testament Theology: Exploring Diversity and Unity*. Louisville: Westminster John Knox, 2007.
———. *What Are They Saying about Mark?* What Are They Saying About. New York: Paulist, 1987.
Mattingly, Harold. *Coins of the Roman Empire in the British Museum*. Vol. 1, *Augustus to Vitellius*. London: British Museum, 1965.
McLaren, James S. *Power and Politics in Palestine: The Jews and the Governing of Their Land 100 BC—AD 70*. JSNTSup 63. Sheffield: JSOT Press, 1991.
———. *Turbulent Times? Josephus and Scholarship on Judaea in the First Century CE*. JSPSup 29. Sheffield: Sheffield Academic, 1998.
Mendels, Doron. *The Rise and Fall of Jewish Nationalism: Jewish and Christian Ethnicity in Ancient Palestine*. ABRL. New York: Doubleday, 1992.
Meyers, Eric M. "Roman Sepphoris in Light of New Archaeological Evidence and Recent Research." In *The Galilee in Late Antiquity*, edited by Lee I. Levine, 321–38. New York: Jewish Theological Seminary of America, 1992.
Michaelis, Wilhelm. "Lépra." In *TDNT* 4:233–34.
———. "Prōtos." In *TDNT* 865–82.
Milns, R. D. "Vespasian (Emperor)." In *ABD* 6:851–53.
Moloney, Francis J. *The Gospel of Mark: A Commentary*. Peabody, MA: Hendrickson, 2002.
Moore, Stephen D. *Empire and Apocalypse: Postcolonialism and the New Testament*. Bible in the Modern World 12. Sheffield: Sheffield Phoenix, 2006.
———. "Mark and Empire: 'Zealot' and 'Postcolonial' Readings." In *Postcolonial Theologies: Divinity and Empire*, edited by Catherine Keller et al., 134–48. St. Louis: Chalice, 2004.
Moss, Candida R. "A Man with the Flow of Power: Porous Bodies in Mark 5:25–34." *JBL* 129 (2010) 507–19.
Moulder, W. J. "The Old Testament Background and the Interpretation of Mark X.45." *NTS* 24 (1977) 120–27.
Moxnes, Halvor. *The Economy of the Kingdom: Social Conflict and Economic Relations in Luke's Gospel*. 1988. Reprint, Eugene, OR: Wipf & Stock, 2004.
Myers, Ched. *Binding the Strong Man: A Political Reading of Mark's Story of Jesus*. Maryknoll, NY: Orbis, 1988.

———. "'The Ideology and Social Strategy of Mark's Community.'" In *The Bible and Liberation: Political and Social Hermeneutics*, edited by Norman K. Gottwald and Richard A. Horsley, 429–52. Rev. ed. Bible & Liberation Series. Maryknoll, NY: Orbis, 1993.

Nardoni, Enrique. *Rise Up, O Judge: A Study of Justice in the Biblical World*. Translated by Seán Charles Martin. Peabody, MA: Hendrickson, 2004.

Neusner, Jacob. *The History of the Jews in the First Century of the Common Era*. History of Judaism 6. New York: Garland, 1990.

Newheart, Michael Willett. *"My Name Is Legion": The Story and Soul of the Gerasene Demoniac*. Interfaces. Collegeville, MN: Liturgical, 2004.

Neyrey, Jerome H. "John 18–19: Honor and Shame and the Passion Narrative." *Semeia* 68 (1996) 113–37.

———. *Render to God: New Testament Understandings of the Divine*. Minneapolis: Fortress, 2004.

Nikiprowetsky, Valentin. "Josephus and the Revolutionary Parties." In *Josephus, the Bible, and History*, edited by Louis H. Feldman and Gohel Hata, 216–36. Leiden: Brill, 1989.

Notley, R. Steven. "The Sea of Galilee: Development of an Early Christian Toponym." *JBL* 128 (2009) 183–88.

Oakman, Douglas E. "The Countryside in Luke-Acts." In *The Social World of Luke-Acts: Models for Interpretation*, edited by Jerome H. Neyrey, 151–79. Peabody, MA: Hendrickson, 1991.

O'Collins, Gerald G. "Crucifixion." In *ABD* 1:1207–10.

Peterson, Dwight N. *The Origins of Mark: The Markan Community in Current Debate*. BibIntSer 48. Leiden: Brill, 2000.

Petronius. *Satyricon*. Translated by Michael Heseltine. LCL. Cambridge: Harvard University Press, 1951.

Philo. *Against Flaccus*. Translated by F. H. Colson. LCL. Cambridge: Harvard University Press, 1926.

———. *Embassy to Gaius*. Translated by F. H. Colson. LCL. Cambridge: Harvard University Press, 1954.

Pilch, John J. *Healing in the New Testament: Insights from Medical and Mediterranean Anthropology*. Minneapolis: Fortress, 2000.

———. "Sickness and Healing in Luke-Acts." In *The Social World of Luke-Acts*, edited by Jerome H. Neyrey, 181–209. Peabody, MA: Hendrickson, 1991.

Pixley, George V. "God's Kingdom in First-Century Palestine: The Strategy of Jesus." In *The Bible and Liberation: Political and Social Hermeneutics*, edited by Norman K. Gottwald and Richard A. Horsley, 378–97. Maryknoll, NY: Orbis, 1983.

Pliny the Elder. *Natural History*. Translated by H. Rackham. LCL. Cambridge: Harvard University Press, 1955.

Plutarch. *Plutarch's Moralia*. 15 vols. Translated by Frank C. Babbitt. LCL. Cambridge: Harvard University Press, 1957.

———. *Plutarch's Lives*. 11 vols. Translated by Bernadotte Perrin. LCL. Cambridge: Harvard University Press, 1955.

Polybius. *The Histories*. 6 vols. Translated by W. R. Paton. LCL. New York: Putnam, 1925.

Powell, Mark Allan. *What Is Narrative Criticism?* GBS. Minneapolis: Fortress, 1990.

Preisker, Herbert "λεγιών." In *TDNT* 4:68–69.

The Preterist Archive. "Vespasian's Galilean Campaign 67." *The Preterist Archive.* http://www.preteristarchive.com/JewishWars/gs-siege.html/.

Price, Jonathan J. *Jerusalem under Siege: The Collapse of the Jewish State 66-70 C.E.* Brill's Series in Jewish Studies 3. Leiden: Brill, 1992.

Price, S. R. F. *Rituals and Power: The Roman Imperial Cult in Asia Minor.* New York: Cambridge University Press, 1984.

Queller, Kurt. "'Stretch Out Your Hand!' Echo and Metalepsis in Mark's Sabbath Healing Controversy." *JBL* 129 (2010) 737–58.

Radcliffe, Timothy. "'The Coming of the Son of Man': Mark's Gospel and Subversion of the Apocalyptic Imagination." In *Language, Meaning and God: Essays in Honour of Herbert McCabe OP*, edited by Brian Davies, 176–89. London: Chapman, 1987.

Rajak, Tessa. *Josephus: The Historian and His Society.* Philadelphia: Fortress, 1984.

Reiser, William. *Jesus in Solidarity with His People: A Theologian Looks at Mark.* Collegeville, MN: Liturgical, 2000.

Reed, Jonathan L. *Archaeology and the Galilean Jesus: A Re-examination of the Evidence.* Harrisburg, PA: Trinity, 2000.

Resseguie, James L. "Reader-Response Criticism and the Synoptic Gospels." *JAAR* 52 (1984) 307–24.

Reynolds, Barrie. *Magic, Divination and Witchcraft among the Barotse of Northern Rhodesia.* Robins Series 3. Berkeley: University of California Press, 1963.

Rhoads, David M. "Diversity in the New Testament." *CurTM* 35 (2008) 354–62.

———. *Israel in Revolution 6–74 C.E.: A Political History Based on the Writings of Josephus.* Philadelphia: Fortress, 1976.

———. "Narrative Criticism: Practices and Prospects." In *Characterization in the Gospels: Reconceiving Narrative Criticism*, edited by David Rhoads and Kari Syreeni, 264–85. JSNTSup 184. London: T. & T. Clark, 2004.

———. "Political Jesus: Can There Be Any Other?" Lecture Notes, Lutheran School of Theology at Chicago. Unpublished, 2007.

———. *Reading Mark: Engaging the Gospel.* Minneapolis: Fortress, 2004.

———. "Social Criticism: Crossing Boundaries." In *Mark & Method: New Approaches in Biblical Studies*, edited by Janice Capel Anderson and Stephen D. Moore, 135–61. Minneapolis: Fortress, 1992.

———. "Zealots." In *ABD* 6:1043–54.

Rhoads, David M., et al. *Mark as Story: An Introduction to the Narrative of a Gospel.* 2nd ed. Minneapolis: Fortress, 1999.

Rives, James. "Flavian Religious Policy and the Destruction of the Jerusalem Temple." In *Flavius Josephus and Flavian Rome*, edited by Jonathan Edmondson et al., 145–66. Oxford: Oxford University Press, 2005.

Robbins, Vernon K. *Jesus the Teacher: A Socio-Rhetorical Interpretation of Mark.* With a new introduction. Minneapolis: Fortress, 1992.

Roberto, John Rocco. "Flavius Josephus and the Jewish Wars: The Question of Flavius Josephus' Validity as a Source or Whether His Work Should Be Considered at All." http://www.historyvortex.org/Josephus.html/.

Roetzel, Calvin J. *The World That Shaped the New Testament.* Rev. ed. Louisville: Westminster John Knox, 2002.

Rohrbaugh, Richard L. "The Social Location of the Markan Audience." *Int* 47 (1993) 380–95.

Roskam, H. N., ed. *The Purpose of the Gospel of Mark in Its Historical and Social Context.* NovTSup 114. Leiden: Brill, 2004.

Roth, Cecil. "The Pharisees in the Jewish Revolution of 66–73." *JSS* 7 (1962) 63–80.

Rudolph, David J. "Jesus and the Food Laws: A Reassessment of Mark 7:19b." *EvQ* 74 (2002) 291–312.

Sabin, Marie Noonan. *Reopening the Word: Reading Mark as Theology in the Context of Early Judaism.* New York: Oxford University Press, 2002.

Safrai, Zeev. "The Description of the Land of Israel in Josephus' Works." In *Josephus, the Bible, and History*, edited by Louis H. Feldman and Gohel Hata, 295–324. Leiden: Brill, 1989.

Saldarini, Anthony J. *Pharisees, Scribes and Sadducees in Palestinian Society: A Sociological Approach.* Grand Rapids: Eerdmans, 2001.

Samuel, Simon. *A Postcolonial Reading of Mark's Story of Jesus.* LNTS 340. T. & T. Clark Library of Biblical Studies. London: T. & T. Clark, 2007.

Sanders, E. P. *Jesus and Judaism.* London: SCM, 1985.

Sanders, E. P., and Margaret Davies. *Studying the Synoptic Gospels.* London: SCM, 1989.

Santos, Narry F. *Slave of All: The Paradox of Authority and Servanthood in the Gospel of Mark.* JSNTSup 237. Sheffield: Sheffield Academic, 2003.

Schäfer, Peter. *The History of the Jews in Antiquity: The Jews of Palestine from Alexander the Great to the Arab Conquest.* Luxembourg: Harwood Academic, 1995.

Schmidt, Sergio A. "The Jewish War in the Time of the Second Temple." Term Paper supervised by David Rhoads, Lutheran School of Theology at Chicago, 2008.

Schmidt, Thomas E. "Jesus' Triumphal March to Crucifixion: The Sacred Way as Roman Triumphal Procession." *BRev* 13 (1997) 30–37.

———. "Mark 15:16–32: The Crucifixion Narrative and the Roman Triumphal Procession." *NTS* 41 (1995) 1–18.

Schürer, Emil. *A History of the Jewish People in the Time of Jesus.* Edited and introduced by Nahum N. Glatzer. New York: Schocken, 1961.

Schüssler Fiorenza, Elisabeth. *In Memory of Her: A Feminist Theological Reconstruction of Christian Origins.* 10th ann. ed. New York: Crossroad, 1994.

———. *The Power of the Word: Scripture and the Rhetoric of Empire.* Minneapolis: Fortress, 2007.

Schwartz, Daniel R. "Wilderness and Temple: On Religion and State in Judea in the Second Temple Period" (in Hebrew). In *Priesthood and Kingship* (in Hebrew), edited by Isaiah M. Gafni and Gabriel Gideon Motzkin, 61–78. Jerusalem: Zalman Shazar Center, 1987.

Scott, Kenneth. *The Imperial Cult under the Flavians.* Ancient Religion and Mythology. New York: Arno, 1975.

Seeley, David. "Jesus' Temple Act." *CBQ* 55 (1993) 263–83.

———. "Jesus' Temple Act Revisited: A Response to P. M. Casey." *CBQ* 62 (2000) 55–63.

———. "Rulership and Service in Mark 10:41–45." *NovT* 35 (1993) 234–50.

Seneca. *Apocolocyntosis.* Translated by W. H. D. Rouse. LCL. Cambridge: Harvard University Press, 1951.

———. *Moral Epistles.* 3 vols. Translated by Richard M. Gummere. LCL. New York: Putnam, 1925.

———. *Moral Essays.* Vol. 3. Translated by John W. Basore. LCL. New York: Putnam, 1928.

Senior, Donald. "The Gospel of Mark in Context." *TBT* 34 (1996) 215-21.

———. "'With Swords and Clubs . . .'—The Setting of Mark's Community and His Critique of Abusive Power." *BTB* 17 (1987) 10-20.

Smallwood, E. Mary. "High Priests and Politics in Roman Palestine." *JTS* 13 (1962) 14-34.

———. "Jews and Romans in the Early Empire, Part I." *HT* 15 (1965) 235-39.

———. "Jews and Romans in the Early Empire, Part II." *HT* 15 (1965) 313-19

Smith, Morton. "Zealots and Sicarii: Their Origins and Relations." *HTR* 64 (1971) 1-19.

Smith, Stephen H. "The Function of the Son of David Tradition in Mark's Gospel." *NTS* 42 (1996) 523-39.

———. "The Literary Structure of Mark 11:1—12:40." *NovT* 31 (1989) 104-24.

Smith-Christopher, Daniel L. "Listening to Cries from Babylon: On the Exegesis of Suffering in Ezekiel and Lamentations." In *A Biblical Theology of Exile*, 75-104. OBT. Minneapolis: Fortress, 2002.

Spilsbury, Paul. "Josephus on the Burning of the Temple, the Flavian Triumph, and the Providence of God." *SBL Seminar Papers* 41 (2002) 306-27.

Spitaler, Peter. "Welcoming a Child as a Metaphor for Welcoming God's Kingdom: A Close Reading of Mark 10:13-16." *JSNT* 31 (2009) 423-46.

Spivey, Robert A., and D. Moody Smith. *Anatomy of the New Testament: A Guide to Its Structure and Meaning*. 5th ed. Englewood Cliffs, NJ: Prentice Hall, 1995.

Staley, Jeffrey L. "'Clothed and in Her Right Mind': Mark 5:1-20 and Postcolonial Discourse." In *Voices from the Margin: Interpreting the Bible in the Third World*, edited by R. S. Sugirtharajah, 319-27. Maryknoll, NY: Orbis 1991.

Stegner, W. Richard. "Jesus' Walking on the Water: Mark 6:45-52." In *The Gospels and the Scriptures of Israel*, edited by Craig A. Evans and W. Richard Stegner, 212-34. JSNTSup 104. Studies in Scripture in Early Judaism and Christianity 3. Sheffield: Sheffield Academic, 1994.

Stern, Menahem. "Aspects of Jewish Society: The Priesthood and Other Classes." In *The Jewish People in the First Century*. 2 vols. Edited by S. Safrai and M. Stern. Philadelphia: Fortress, 1976.

Stern, Menahem, and Shemuel Safrai, eds. The Priesthood and Other Classes. The Jewish People in the First Century 2. Philadelphia: Fortress, 1976.

Storkey, Alan. *Jesus and Politics: Confronting the Powers*. Grand Rapids: Baker Academic, 2005.

Strabo. *The Geography of Strabo*. 8 vols. Translated by Horace L. Jones, based in part upon the unfinished version of John H. S. Sterrett. LCL. New York: Putnam, 1957.

Strange, James F. "Sepphoris, (Place)." In *ABD* 5:1090-93.

———. "Tiberias, (Place)." In *ABD* 6:547-49.

Strecker, Georg. *Theology of the New Testament*. Edited and completed by Friedrich Wilhelm Horn. Translated by M. Eugene Boring. Louisville: Westminster John Knox, 2000.

Strelan, Rick. "A Greater Than Caesar: Storm Stories in Lucan and Mark." *ZNW* 91 (2000) 166-79.

Such, W. A. *The Abomination of Desolation in the Gospel of Mark: Its Historical Reference in Mark 13:14 and Its Impact in the Gospel*. Lanham, MD: University Press of America, 1999.

Suetonius. *The Lives of the Caesars*. Translated by J. C. Rolfe. 2 vols. LCL. Cambridge: Harvard University Press, 1913-14.

Tacitus. *Dialogus, Agricola, Germania*. Translated by W. Peterson and M. Hutton. LCL. Cambridge: Harvard University Press, 1944.

———. *The Histories and the Annals*. Translated by C. H. Moore and J. Jackson. 4 vols. LCL. Cambridge: Harvard University Press, 1925–1937.

Talbert, Charles H., and John H. Hayes. "A Theology of Sea Storms in Luke-Acts." *SBL Seminar Papers* 34 (1995) 321–36.

Tate, W. Randolph. *Reading Mark from the Outside: Eco and Iser Leave Their Marks*. San Francisco: International Scholars, 1994.

Tatum, W. Barnes. "Jesus' So-Called Triumphal Entry: On Making an Ass of the Romans." *Forum* 1 (1998) 129–43.

Taylor, Lily Ross. *The Divinity of the Roman Emperor*. Philological Monographs 1. Middletown, CT: American Philological Association, 1931.

Telford, W. R. *The Barren Temple and the Withered Tree: A Redaction Critical Analysis of the Cursing of the Fig-Tree Pericope in Mark's Gospel and Its Relation to the Cleansing of the Temple Tradition*. JSNTSup 1. Sheffield: JSOT Press, 1980.

———. "Introduction: The Interpretation of Mark—A History of Development and Issues." In *The Interpretation of Mark*, edited by William R. Telford, 1–61. 2nd ed. Studies in New Testament Interpretation. Edinburgh: T. & T. Clark, 1995.

———. *Mark*. New Testament Guides. Sheffield: Sheffield Academic, 1995.

———. *The Theology of the Gospel of Mark*. New Testament Theology. Cambridge: Cambridge University Press, 1999.

Theissen, Gerd. *The Gospels in Context: Social and Political History in the Synoptic Tradition*. Translated by Linda M. Maloney. Minneapolis: Fortress, 1991.

———. *The Miracle Stories of the Early Christian Tradition*. Edited by John Riches. Translated by Francis McDonagh. Philadelphia: Fortress, 1983.

Theron, Daniel Johannes. *Evidence of Tradition: Selected Source Material for the Study of the History of the Early Church Introduction and Canon of the New Testament*. London: Bowes & Bowes, 1957.

Thurston, Bonnie B. *Preaching Mark*. Fortress Resources for Preaching. Minneapolis: Fortress, 2002.

Tolbert, Mary Ann. "Is It Lawful on the Sabbath to Do Good or to Do Harm? Mark's Ethics of Religious Practice." *PRSt* 23 (1996) 199–214.

———. *Sowing the Gospel: St. Mark's World in Literary-Historical Perspective*. Minneapolis: Augsburg Fortress, 1996.

Tomasino, Antony J. "Oracles of Insurrection: The Prophetic Catalyst of the Great Revolt." *JJS* 59 (2008) 86–111.

Udoh, Fabian E. *To Caesar What Is Caesar's: Tribute, Taxes, and Imperial Administration in Early Roman Palestine 63 B.C.E.—70 C.E.* BJS 343. Providence, RI: BJS, 2005.

Ulansey, David. "The Heavenly Veil Torn: Mark's Cosmic *Inclusio*." *JBL* 110 (1991) 123–25.

Virgil. *Eclogues, Geogics, Aeneid*. 2 vols. Translated by H. Rushton Fairclough. LCL. Cambridge: Harvard University Press, 1953.

Von Wahlde, Urban C. "Mark 9:33–50: Discipleship; The Authority That Serves." *BZ* 29 (1985) 49–67.

Waetjen, Herman C. *A Reordering of Power: A Sociopolitical Reading of Mark's Gospel*. 1989. Reprint, Eugene, OR: Wipf & Stock, 2014.

Watson, David F. "The *Life of Aesop* and the Gospel of Mark: Two Ancient Approaches to Elite Values." *JBL* 129 (2010) 699–716.

Weinfield, Moshe. "The King as the Servant of the People: The Source of the Idea." *JJS* 33 (1982) 189–94.

Wiedemann, Thomas. *Adults and Children in the Roman Empire*. London: Routledge, 1989.

Wilde, James A. "Social Description of the Community Reflected in the Gospel of Mark." PhD diss., Drew University, 1974.

———. "The Social World of Mark's Gospel: A Word about Method." *SBL Seminar Papers* 2 (1978) 47–70.

Wilhelm, Dawn Ottoni. *Preaching the Gospel of Mark: Proclaiming the Power of God*. Louisville: Westminster John Knox, 2008.

Willette, Dorothy. "The Enduring Symbolism of Doves: From Ancient Icon to Biblical Mainstay." March 2, 2018. *Bible History Daily*. Biblical Archaeology Society. https://www.biblicalarchaeology.org/daily/ancient-cultures/daily-life-and-practice/the-enduring-symbolism-of-doves/.

Williams, Joel F. "Mission in Mark." In *Mission in the New Testament: An Evangelical Approach*, edited by William J. Larkin Jr. and Joel F. Williams, 137–51. American Society of Missiology Series 27. Maryknoll, NY: Orbis, 1998.

Winn, Adam. *The Purpose of Mark's Gospel: An Early Christian Response to Roman Imperial Propaganda*. WUNT 2/245. Tübingen: Mohr/Siebeck, 2008.

Witherington, Ben, III. *The Gospel of Mark: A Socio-Rhetorical Commentary*. Grand Rapids: Eerdmans, 2001.

Yavetz, Zvi. "Reflections on Titus and Josephus." *GRBS* 16 (1975) 411–32.

www.ingramcontent.com/pod-product-compliance
Lightning Source LLC
Chambersburg PA
CBHW051518230426
43668CB00012B/1653